Jacob Hoke

Reminiscences of the War

Or, Incidents which Transpired in and about Chambersburg....

Jacob Hoke

Reminiscences of the War
Or, Incidents which Transpired in and about Chambersburg....

ISBN/EAN: 9783337209582

Printed in Europe, USA, Canada, Australia, Japan

Cover: Foto ©ninafisch / pixelio.de

More available books at **www.hansebooks.com**

HISTORICAL.

REMINISCENCES

OF

HE WAR;

OR INCIDENTS WHICH TRANSPIRED

IN AND ABOUT CHAMBERSBURG,

DURING THE WAR OF THE REBELLION.

BY J. HOKE.

CHAMBERSBURG, PA:
M. A. FOLTZ, PRINTER AND PUBLISHER.
1884.

"REMINISCENCES OF THE WAR,"
Written expressly for PUBLIC OPINION, by J. Hoke, Esq., appeared in that journal from week to week until completed, commencing with the issue of January 12, 1884. The chapters are thus gathered and given in book form for greater convenience and permanency, and the work may be had of the Publisher, M. A. FOLTZ.

Copyrighted by
M. A. FOLTZ,
1884.

INTRODUCTION.

No town in the Northern States is more inseparably interwoven with the thrilling events of the late war, than Chambersburg. Gettysburg was made more widely memorable by the great and decisive battle fought there, but Chambersburg was the great centre of great events on our Southern border, from the advent of General Patterson's army early in 1861, until the vandal horde of McCausland left the town in ashes, in 1864. The insurgents had possession of Chambersburg in Stuart's raid in 1862; in Lee's occupation in 1863, when on his march to the death-blow to the Confederacy at Gettysburg, and in McCausland's raid in 1864, when Southern vengeance was glutted by the destruction of the most important and valuable portions of the town. Lee held his councils of war in the grove on the eastern outskirts of Chambersburg, for several days, and finally decided to cross the South Mountain and accept the shock of battle on the direct line for Baltimore and the National Capital. And not only did the first trump of war sound in Chambersburg when the three months' troops crossed the Potomac, under Patterson in the Spring of 1861, but each year thereafter, until peace came at Appomattox in 1865, the columns of "emergency men" and of militia called out after each invasion, made Chambersburg their objective point and liberally enjoyed the proffered or enforced hospitality of the people of the "Green Spot."

It was in Chambersburg that John Brown, then known only as "Dr. Smith," the prospector of Maryland ores, planned his mad raid on Harper's Ferry and fought the first skirmish of the war two years before the divided sections could realize that war was upon them, and the blackened walls and broken columns and withered shades which told of Chambersburg's desolation in 1864, were measurably the sequel of the innocent hospitality given to the unknown John Brown five years before. There is, therefore, much of the thrilling romance of the war's history that centres in and about Chambersburg, and it is unfortunate that it has not been preserved by some competent historian. The unwritten chapters of the war which relate to Chambersburg, would make a volume of surpassing interest, and add much to the as yet imperfect history of the greatest war of modern times. With the exception of a few unpretentious scraps of history about the Lee invasion and the burning of Chambersburg, there has been nothing written in any way calculated to preserve in history the trials and sacrifices of the faithful border people.

I am glad to preface the effort of Mr. Hoke to record some of the most important episodes of the eventful four years of civil war in Chambersburg. He was one of the most loyal of loyal citizens, and he witnessed every invasion of the town by the enemy. A close observer, a methodical recorder of events as they transpired, and possessing uncommon clearness of memory as to details, he is peculiarly fitted to recall into permanent history the interesting records which merit preservation. His chapters cover much unknown history pertaining to two of the great battles of the war— Antietam and Gettysburg—and preserve occurrences which are of absorbing interest to the descendents of the now rapidly lapsing actors in the dark days of the rebellion. All this work has been performed by Mr. Hoke with less pretension as a historical writer than as a conscientious delineator of the truth of history, and it will not only greatly entertain and instruct the people of the Cumberland Valley, but it will preserve for the future historian of the war, many links in the chain of the greatest conflict of man for man.

A. K. M.

NOTE BY THE AUTHOR.

When entering upon the preparation of these REMINISCENCES OF THE WAR, I was unacquainted with the fact that the files of the *Valley Spirit* and *Franklin Repository*, which have been kindly placed in my hands by the editors and proprietors of those papers, contained such full and accurate statements of the events which transpired during the eventful period of the great War of the Rebellion. To one unacquainted with those events from personal observation, the accounts therein given would be but fragmentary; but to one who saw them and passed through them, they afford ample data for a truthful and consecutive history.

Then I supposed, too, that my own record, written at the time the events narrated occurred, had been destroyed in the burning of our town in July, 1864. That record has been found carefully stored away with other books and papers, and it has proven of incalculable advantage to me.

I am also indebted to others for valuable papers, narrating events known in their details only to themselves. The papers furnished by T. M. Mahon, Esq., John A. Seiders, Esq., and J. W. Douglass, Esq., are notable examples. Mr. Douglass is one of the few living persons who saw and read General Early's order for the ransom of our town, and in default of its ransom, its destruction. The importance of placing such facts upon permanent record for the use of after generations and historians cannot be over-estimated.

To Col. A. K. McClure for a copy of ANNALS OF THE WAR, I am also under obligations. In the statements written by General Longstreet and other participants in the great struggle at Gettysburg, and in the dates and facts they have given in relation to the previous movements and purposes of their respective commands, I have derived valuable assistance.

I have been particularly careful to give exact and correct dates to the events narrated, and I can with the utmost confidence assure the reader of their correctness. In the main the data furnished me by so many persons, and gathered from so many sources, when carefully compared, entirely harmonized, except in one case alone, and upon that fact I have the most indubitable evidence in favor of the date I have given.

Chambersburg, Jan. 22d, 1884.   J. HOKE.

REMINISCENCES OF THE WAR.

CHAPTER I.

COMMENCEMENT OF THE WAR, AND MARCHING OF TROOPS FROM CHAMBERSBURG.

In the preparation of these reminiscences of events which occurred in and about Chambersburg during the four years of the war of the rebellion, I am confronted by several difficulties, which may be stated as follows: In the destruction of our town by the torch of the invaders, July 30th, 1864, nearly all the records kept by our citizens were destroyed. My cash books of those days in which I noted principal events, were all, as I supposed, destroyed. Recently, however, I found among some books and papers boxed up and stored away, one of those books, containing dates of important events. This book begins with May, 1862, and prior to that date 1 am dependant for information furnished by others, as well as to files of the *Valley Spirit* and *Franklin Repository*, kindly placed at my disposal by the editors and proprietors of those papers, for which I hereby express my thanks. The files of these papers, however, were all burnt in the great calamity of July 30th, 1864, and in the replacement of the same from their subscribers, they were unable to procure every number. Important links, therefore, are here and there wanting. Then, for convenience of narration, and to give authenticity to the facts stated, I write under my own signature, and as an eye witness of many of the incidents which I shall relate. This, I am aware, exposes me to the charge of egotism or a desire for notoriety. While disclaiming this, I shall in a series of articles, place upon record a simple statement of facts, many of which have hitherto never been published. This I do as a modest contribution to the annals of that eventful period when the destiny of our government seemed to hang in the balance, and when our valley was the theatre of the most stirring events which are likely ever to occur in the life of a generation.

In the early morning of April 12th, 1861, the telegraph announced that Fort Sumpter had been fired upon and the war commenced. The rebel batteries opened fire precisely at 27 minutes past 4 o'clock. Despatch after despatch was placed upon the bulletin board and printed in extras by our papers. These despatches read thus: "The War Commenced; Fort Sumpter Fired on." "Fort Sumpter Makes a Vigorous Reply." "Fort Sumpter in flames." "The Fire Still Raging, and the Surrender of the Fort Inevitable." On the following day the announcement was made that Maj. Anderson, after a gallant resistance, had surrendered, and the rebel flag waved over the Fort. On the following day, April the 14th, President Lincoln issued his proclamation calling for 75,000 troops to serve for three months.

With the announcement of the commencement of hostilities, intense excitement seized upon all classes of people. The stars and stripes were run up upon the public buildings, bank, hotels, and many private dwellings. A great demand set in for material to make flags, and red, white and blue flannels, delaines and muslins could scarcely be supplied in sufficient amount to meet the demand. Badges, shields and other devices containing the national colors, met with ready sale, and almost every person bore upon him some token of love for the Union. Volunteering for the defense of the government, in response to the call of the President, went on vigorously and many enrolled themselve for service.

On the evening of Wednesday, April 17th, a public meeting was held in the Court House to take into consideration such matters as might be necessary to meet the exigencies of the times. Hon. Wilson Reilly was called to the chair, and Mr. B. B. Henshey was appointed Secretary. Mr. Reilly on taking the chair, made an eloquent and patriotic speech, in which he declared his readiness to support the Government by every means in his power, and his willingness to shoulder a musket if needs be to save the flag of his country from dishonor. Mr. Reilly was followed by brilliant and thrilling addresses by Messrs. Brewer, Sharpe, Douglas, Rowe, McCauley, Stewart and Cook. The following committees were then appointed to prepare for the departure of the soldiers who were soon to march from our midst.

On General Regulations: D. W. Rowe, Samuel Shryock and W. C. Eyster.

Committee on Contributions: J. Allison Eyster, J. W. Douglas and James Nill.

Committee to supply Pocket Bibles to the soldiers: Ex-Sheriff Brown, I. H. McCauley and A. N. Rankin.

In response to the call of this Committee on Contributions several thousand dollars were pledged by our citizens for the support of the families of the departing soldiers, if needed.

On Thursday, April 18th, but five days after the fall of Fort Sumpter, a pole 120 feet high was raised in the centre of the Diamond. As soon as the pole was raised, the stars and stripes were run up upon it, when a number of ladies standing upon the balcony in front of the Franklin hotel, which stood where the Central Presbyterian church now stands, sang with thrilling effect the Star Spangled Banner. After this followed patriotic speeches by Messrs. Reilly, Stumbaugh, McClure, Brewer, Everett, Stenger and Welsh. When the flag of our country was run up to the top of the pole, a citizen of the town, James H. Bratton, now dead, standing by my side, was so overcome by his patriotic feelings, as to burst into tears. That same evening I remarked to a number of persons, that if Virginia adopted the ordinance of secession, the seat of war would be right along our border; and being in the great Cumberland Valley, which extended away down through Maryland and Virginia into Tennessee, armies of both the two contending parties would doubtless pass through our town, and one of the possibilities was that the rebel flag might some day float from that pole. My remark was considered wild and impossible, but although no hated secession flag ever floated from that pole, sixty thousand rebel troops, with many banners, passed under its shadow, and it was at last cut down by Gen. Imboden's Cavalry, which constituted the rear of Lee's army, and were the last to pass through the town on the way to Gettysburg. The only rebel flag that was raised in town, was the regimental flag of a Mississippi regiment, which was hung out from the cupola of the Court House, the Colonel of that regiment being made Provost Marshal with headquarters in the Court House.

On the evening of the day of the pole raising, a public meeting was held in the Court House for the purpose of doing honor to the Chambers Artillery, which was to leave the next morning for Harrisburg. Hon. George Chambers was made president, and Hon. James Nill and D. K. Wunderlick, vice presidents. The venerable president, on taking the chair, delivered an address of nearly an hour's length replete with interesting personal reminiscences of the past. He told of the exciting scenes of the "Whiskey Insurrection" of 1794—of his having seen General Washington in our town, when on his way to take command of the army sent to suppress the insurrection. He told also of the perils of the Indian Wars a few years later, and also of the war of 1812. He then spoke at length of the causes of the then present difficulties, paid a high tribute to Capt. Housum and the noble body of men he was about to lead forth in the defense of the Union, and in thrilling language besought Capt. Housum and his command to fight valiantly for the glorious old flag, and die if they must on the field of battle with their faces toward the foe. After the adoption of some resolutions offered by Isaac McCauley, Esq., the soldiers repaired to Franklin Hall, where they partook of a farewell supper furnished by the citizens. After the supper a sword was presented to Lieut. John Doebler through Mr. Brewer, and accepted upon the part of Doebler by Mr. Sharpe.

The day following these interesting occurrences—Friday, April 19th,—was one of thrilling events, not only in our own town, but elsewhere. In the morning train the Chambers Artillery embarked for Harrisburg. This company was composed of about 150 men—several persons uniting with it immediately upon the call for troops. Its officers were: P. B. Housem, Capt., John Doebler, 1st Lieut., Matthew Gillan, 2d Lieut., George Miles, 3d Lieut. Col. F. S. Stumbaugh, long associated with military organizations here, accompanied this company to Harrisburg with the understanding that he was to command the Regiment as soon as formed.

The departure of these men, was one of the most affecting and impressive scenes that had ever up to that time been witnessed in our town. The fathers, mothers, wives, children, brothers and sisters, of the volunteers, together with almost the entire population of the town, were collected at the depot to bid farewell to the gallant band. Almost every eye was bathed in tears. This was a new scene to our citizens, but they witnessed others like it during the war.

About one o'clock in the afternoon of the same day, five or six wagons drawn by two horses each, appeared upon the brow of the hill opposite the Reformed church. They were driven hurriedly down through the town to the depot. They were filled with U. S. troops under command of Lieut. Jones, and had been quartered at Harper's Ferry. Upon the approach of the Virginia troops to seize the arsenal and workshops there, Lieut. Jones, unable with his small command to defend the place, set fire thereto and fled with his men to this place and thence by rail to the barracks at Carlisle. Before applying the torch, Lieut. Jones blew up the arsenals and shops, destroying about 15,000 stand of arms. That part of the machinery remaining uninjured, was taken by the rebels down South and used to manufacture arms to destroy the Union. The arrival of these troops increased the excitement in the town, and we were made to feel that the seat of war was coming uncomfortably near.

Upon the evening of this day, word was received by telegraph of the riot in Baltimore and the massacre of the Massachusetts soldiers. Soon came the news of the destruction of the bridges along the Northern Central and Philadelphia, Wilmington and Baltimore railroads, and the stoppage of travel by those routes. Hundreds of Northern people sojourning in the South, and Southern people in the North, unable to pass to their respective destinations, availed themselves of the Franklin and Cumberland Valley railroads, and for a time travel was exceedingly brisk along this line. Among the distinguished persons who passed through our town at that time, was Hon. Caleb Cushing, of Massachusetts. He was in Washington, and had no other way to return home. One of our citizens, Mr. H. E. Hoke, having occasion to take a sewing machine to Greencastle to deliver to a person who had purchased it, rode in the baggage car one of those days. In this car were two men whose features were distinctively Southern. They each carried a Sharpe's rifle and had in charge several large chests which they stood by and guarded with great care. Whether these chests contained money or, what the South needed then more than money, percussion caps, he did not know. There were no military regulations then made to see after such things.

About that time Capt. Charles Campbell received a commission from the Governor to recruit an Artillery company. He quartered his men in Franklin Hall, and had his cannon in front of it, within a short distance of our store, where he drilled his men.

A rifle company, under command of Capt. John S. Eyster, was about this time rapidly recruited. Also a large German company was organized and tendered their services to the Governor. A company of Home Guards was also organized, and their services tendered to the Governor to march if needed. On Sabbath, April 23d, a fine body of men, some sixty in number, under command of Capt. Walker, from Fannettsburg, arrived in town and were quartered in the Court House. While passing through Strasburg, a number of persons joined them, and others from the Valley were yet expected to swell their number. In a few days thereafter the following companies were encamped upon the Fair Grounds upon the hill along the Pittsburg pike, west of town. This encampment was called "Camp Irvin." Capt. Walker's company from Fannettsburg, Capt. Dixon's company from St. Thomas, Capt. Eyster's company from Chambersburg, two companies from Fulton county, and Capt. Campbell's company of Artillery. The companies of Captains Dixon and Eyster afterwards became incorporated into the Pennsylvania Reserves. Capt. Campbell's Artillery also went into active service. As to what was done with the company of Capt. Walker and the two Fulton county companies, I am unable to say. The Fair Grounds after this became the rendezvous for various companies of recruits. It is said that one time during the war a company of recruits was encamped there. The officer in command had drilled the men up to that point where they learned the significance of "the Long Roll." And in order to test the promptness of his command in responding to this alarm and preparing for battle, he directed it to be sounded one night at midnight. The whole command upon awaking out of sleep and hearing this signal for battle, and supposing that the rebels were upon them, fled in every direction and the majority never returned.

CHAPTER II.

The Roll of Honor; or the Names of Those Who First Flew to the Rescue of Their Imperilled Country from Franklin County.

The Chambers Artillery, after arriving at Camp Curtin, near Harrisburg, was divided into two companies, Lieut. Doebler taking command of the second company formed. These two companies, with one other, composed mostly of men from Greencastle and St. Thomas and under command of J. G. Elder, were attached to the Second Regiment Pennsylvania Volunteers. F. S. Stumbaugh, Esq., of our town, was made Colouel of this regiment; —— Irwin, of ——, Lieut. Colonel; Jas. S. Given, of West Chester, Major; Isaac S. Waterburry, of Harrisburg, Ad'jt. General; D. Watson Rowe, Serg't. Major; Isadore A. Stumbaugh, Quarter Master Serg't; John A. King, M. D., Acting Asst. Surgeon.

The names and residences of the persons composing these three companies, are as follows:

LIST OF CO. A, 2ND REGT. PENNA. VOLUNTEERS.

Capt., Peter B. Housum, Chambersburg.
1st. Lieut., George Stitzell, "
2nd Lieut., K. Shannon Taylor, "
1st Sergt. Thomas G, Cochran, "
2nd Sergt., Sam'l McDowell, "
3d Sergt. Adam Smith, "
4th Sergt., Bruce Lambert, "
1st Corporal, Allison McDowell, "
2nd " Thomas Myers, "
3d " John F. Snyder, "
4th " Jno. F. Pensinger, "

PRIVATES—*Chambersb'g.*
Justina McGuigan,
Josephus Senseny,
Alexander Flack,
John F. Metz,
George S. Houser,
James C. Sample,
R. B. Fisher,
Jacob W. Miles,
John C. Gerbic,
Thomas W. Merklein,
Robert F. McCurdy,
Frederick Shinefield,
Richard Hardin,
John W. Jones,
John C. Hullinger,
John King,
Geo. J. Ludwig,
Jacob Lutz,
Geo, S. Eyster,
Abraham A. Huber,
David W. Newman,
Peter Danner,
James Shuman,
Lewis Monath,
Fancis Donovan,
Ephraim Finefrock,
George Goetman,
Peter Myers,
Edmund Ferry,
Thomas Durborow,
Wm. Harmony,
Ernest Causler,
Allison Whitstone,
Edgar D. Washabaugh
Janus E. Cook,
Franklin Yeager,
John A. Stiders,
Samuel A. Stouffer,
James Aughinbaugh,
Frank Fortescue,
Harry Fortescue,
Lewis Fisher,
Edward Kline,
Frederick Batner,
John F. Peiffer,

Greenvillage.
John Gaff,
Franklin D. Ditzlear,
Daniel Shatzler,
David Wallace.

New Franklin.
Henry Hannagan.

Waynesboro'.
John E. Walker,
John N. Hullinger.

Fayetteville.
Sylvester Weldy,
Walter B. Crawford,
Jeremiah Burkholder.

Caledonia Iron Works.
Alexander J. Stevens.

Newville.
Wm. B. Over,
John B. Johnston,
Wm. D. Cobaugh,
John P. Wagner.

James C. Eckenrode.
Jonas B. Huntsberger.

McConnellsburg.
David Hoke,
Ed. E. Fairweather,
John H. Neely.

LIST OF CO. B, 2ND REGT. PENNA. VOLUNTEERS.

Captain, John Doebler, Chambersburg.
1st Lieut., George Miles, "
2nd " Geo. W. Welsh, "
1st Sergt., Benjamin Rhodes, "
2nd " Peter Ackerman, "
3d " Joseph Thomas, "
4th " George Cook, "
1st Corpl., Henry Melvin, "
2nd " Alexander C. Landis, "
3d " Henry McCauley, Shippensburg.
4th " Porter J. Brown, Chambersburg.

PRIVATES—*Chambersb'g.*
Hamilton Spence,
Theophilus Stratton,
James Ridgley,
Jeremiah Smith,
Peter Dorty,
John Elser,
Samuel K. Snively,
Franklin Gipe,
Michael Harmony,
Edward Monath,
Wm. Fentiman,
Emanuel H. Forney,
Samuel Uglow,
James Borland,
Isaac S. Noel,
(Honorably discharged)
Charles Jones,
I. A. Stumbaugh,
(Transferred to Col's. Staff,)
John Hicks,
John H. Frederick,
Hugh Brotherton,
Dennis Riley,
John J. Hersbberger,
Jacob Jones,
Wm. Henneberger,
Robert Smith,
Wm. Eaker,
John King,
Charles Shancbrook,
Frank Kline,
Geo. W. Baker,
Robert W. Moore,
Jacob W. Smith,
James McGeehan,
John Fisher,
P. A. J. Snider,
Harrison Hutton,
Adolphus McGuigan,
John S. White,
Wm. T. Smith,
Peter Snider,
John Stoner,

Quincy,
Harrison Seabrooks,

John W. Bryson,
Wm. H. Pence,
John Pence,
Geo. Seabrooks.

Newville.
Samuel Hardy,
Isaac Hardy.

Scotland.
Lanson Coleman.

Greenwood.
Jeremiah Perri.

Fayetteville.
Wm. T, Hazlett.

Mercersburg.
Martin Louman,
George W. Daley,
David L. Hoffman.

Loudon.
Alexander McCurdy.

McConnellsburg.
Alexander Prosser,
Samuel Shoemaker.

Strasburg.
Walker Shearer.

Springville Lancaster co
J. H. Martin.

Fairview township, York county.
Peter Corden,
Edgar Wolf,
(Honorably discharged)

Alexandria, Huntingdon county.
Edgar G. McLaughlin.

New York.
Julius C. Ludd.

Poland.
John Swuninski.

Reminiscences of the War.

LIST OF CO. C, 2ND REGT. PENNA. VOLUNTEERS.

Captain, J. G. Elder, St. Thomas.
1st Lieut., J. B. Strickler, Greencastle.
2nd   "   Jacob West, St. Thomas.
Q. M. Sergt., T. J. Reilly, Greencastle.
1st   "   W. B. Shirk,   "
2nd   "   G. H. Miller,   "
3d   "   Jacob Snyder, Loudon.
4th   "   G. A. Pool, Greencastle.
1st Corpl., T. J. Koonse.
2nd   "   Christian Burkholder, Loudon.
3d   "   Thomas Hill, St. Thomas.
4th   "   David C. Shaffer, Greencastle.

PRIVATES—*Greencastle.*
Edwin P. Byers.
Geo. Rence.
Charles Byers.
Cor. Barnhisel.
John D. Byers.
Wm. Byers.
Geo. Bush.
James B. Comins.
Emanuel Carpenter.
James Gaff.
David Hess.
John F. Koonse.
John H. Logue.
Geo. F. Missavey.
John A. Marshal.
Jessie K. Norris.
Miller H. Pensinger.
Samuel H. Prather.
John E. Pool.
John G. Rowe.
Abraham H. Shealy.
Emanuel F. Shatzer.
Wm. Shorts.
David Tracy.
Jacob Watson.
Joseph Wildern.
Wm. A. Weyant.
Wm. A. Wildern.
Leander B. Zook.

Waynesboro'.
Joel Huffly.
Jacob H. Funk.
Cyrus Gossert.
Henry Grabill.
John Mickle.
David Morehead.

St. Thomas.
Samuel Antrim.

Jacob Detrich.
John Ferry.
Wm. A. Hosler.
Jeremiah Martin.
Samuel Rennecker.
Geo. Sulavan.
Alexander Speer.
Wm. H. Snow.
George Vorler.

Marion.
George Butts.
John H. Stickel.

Upton.
Thomas Dayley.
John Doubleman.
Joseph Stoner.

Mercersburg.
David E. Hays.
John S. King.
John Shatzer.

Chambersburg.
Christian Miller.

Cashtown.
Simon Rupert.

Loudon.
John H. Unger.
James McElrea.
Henry M. Spidle.

Gettysburg.
Wm. G. Little.
Geo. Little.

Leitersburg, Md.
Martin Morgan.
Wm. A. Cassatt.

These lists are all certified to by the respective captains. It will be seen that in this first rush to arms, Franklin county furnished in these three companies alone, including regimental officers, 205 men. Of these, 112 were from Chambersburg. It will be recollected, too, that several other companies in process of forming, and numbering about 60 men each, offered their services to the Governor, and could not at that time be accepted. Many of these men, when their three months' enlistment expired, re-entered the service: and several of them sealed their devotion to their country by laying down their lives upon the field of battle. Prominent among those who fell is Col. Peter B. Housum. One of our excellent citizens and business men, he was loved and respected by all. Upon the bloody field of Stone River he poured out his life blood that the government he loved so well

might live. Let his memory ever be held in grateful remembrance by the people. Then there were others among those who first flew to the rescue of their country in her hour of peril, and died upon the field, or in the hospital, besides Col. Housum, who deserve to be gratefully remembered, but I cannot recall them, nor tell of their deeds of noble daring and heroism. Nor is our gratitude due to those only who fell in battle or hospital. Some were wounded and maimed for life. Others contracted diseases which rendered their after-life unpleasant and painful. The cases of Col. Elder and Sergeant Thomas G. Cochran are familiar to all.

It will be recollected that at a meeting of citizens of Chambersburg, held in the Court House, on the evening of April 17th, to take into consideration the preparations necessary for the comfort and welfare of our departing volunteers, a committee was appointed to supply each soldier with a copy of the Scriptures. This committee taking no action in this matter, the Managers of the Franklin County Bible Society directed the writer, as their Treasurer and Librarian, to send to these men a copy each of the New Testament. Rev. W. B. Raber, then a resident pastor at York, near which these men were encamped, and who was personally known by nearly all of the Franklin county men, was selected to present these Testaments. The following is a copy of the proceedings in connection with these presentations. The originals, with every other vestige connected with this affair, were destroyed with the Society's library and records in the great calamity of July 30th, 1864. For this record I am indebted to the *Valley Spirit*, in whose issue of May 15th, 1861, it is printed.

CAMP SCOTT,
Headquarters 2d Regt., Penna. Vols.,
YORK, PA., May 2d, 1861.

On Thursday morning, May 2d, 1861, the volunteers of Franklin county, quartered at Camp Scott, after morning drill, were assembled together in companies at the request of Col. F. S. Stumbaugh, for the purpose of making some suitable acknowledgement of their appreciation of the care and generosity of the Franklin County Bible Society, in presenting each one of the soldiers from Franklin county with a copy of the New Testament.

Companies A, B and C were formed in a triangle, the officers in the centre. Col. F. S. Stumbaugh stated the object of the meeting in some appropriate remarks. Capt. J. G. Elder, of company C, was elected President, and Capt. P. B. Housum, of company A, and D. Watson Rowe, were chosen Secretaries.

The following resolutions were offered by Mr. Rowe, and were unanimously adopted:

WHEREAS, The Franklin County Bible Society has presented each one of the Volunteers of Franklin county with a copy of the New Testament; and

WHEREAS, We acknowledge the word of God contained therein as the only will to direct us how we may honor and serve our Maker, and fulfil our whole duty as soldiers, citizens and men ; and find in its teachings the preparation for death as well as the rule of life, and therefore hold it precious above all things : Therefore,

Resolved, That we return our warmest thanks to the Franklin County Bible Society for their tender care of our spiritual welfare and comfort; and that as our best return to the Society, we will regularly and studiously ponder the words of life and wisdom which they have placed in our hands.

Resolved, That a copy of these resolutions be furnished by the Col. of our Regiment to the Franklin County Bible Society, with the request that they be published in all the County Papers.

JAMES G. ELDER,
P. B. HOUSUM, *President.*
D. W. ROWE,
Secretaries.

In accordance with the request contained in this last resolution, Col. Stumbaugh transmitted a copy of the action taken, with the following letter:

To *J. Hoke and others, Committee of the Franklin County Bible Society :*

RESPECTED SIRS : The package containing 300 copies of the New Testament reached Camp Scott on Tuesday evening of last week, and on Wednesday morning, I proceeded, in pursuance with the promise previously made, to distribute them among the members of the companies from Franklin county, under my command, in 2d Regiment Penn'a Volunteers, viz : Companies A, B and C. I wish you could have been present to see how every countenance beamed with joy on the reception of the precious book.

I herewith enclose you a list of the recipients of your generosity, and also a Preamble and Resolutions expressive of the thanks of the companies, which were unanimously adopted. It affords me pleasure to add that I notice the men in clusters, whenever they have a leisure moment, either reading or listening to the blessed Scriptures being read by some one of their number.

I have no doubt it will exert a powerful influence for good over the conduct of the men, and make them feel ever grateful for the kindness of the Franklin County Bible Society. Allow me to tender to you, and through you to the members of the Franklin County Bible Society, my earnest, heartfelt thanks, well knowing that the precious gift that you have bestowed, will not only teach men to render to God the things that are God's, but also stimulate them to sustain their country's honor and glory. In conclusion, let me ask the prayers of the members of your Society for myself and command at all times and under all circumstances.

I am, Dear Sirs, your ob't servant,

F. S. STUMBAUGH.

CHAPTER III.

CAMP SLIFER.

A glance at the map of the United States will demonstrate that in a conflict between the Northern and Southern States of the Union, the great valley extending from the Susquehanna through the States of Maryland and Virginia, and into the State of Tennessee, would be the great thoroughfare of the contending armies. That such was the case during the war of the rebellion, and that it was the theatre of important events, are well known to all familiar with that eventful period.

From the time of the destruction of the arsenals and workshops at Harper's Ferry, April 19th, to some time in June following, that place was occupied by about four thousand Virginia troops. The presence of this formidable force there, and the fact that large bodies of soldiers from all parts of the South were hurrying northward into Virginia, the ultimate destination of whom was not known, made the concentration of a considerable force somewhere in this valley, and near the Potomac, a necessity. The presence of a force here would also be necessary in order to be prepared for an aggressive movement south of the Potomac, if such a movement should be determined on. Chambersburg, because of its location in the valley, and because of its excellent railroad facilities and the loyalty of its people, was naturally chosen as the place for this gathering. Accordingly some time near the close of April—probably the 25th or 26th—two regiments, the 7th Penna. Volunteers, under Col. William H. Irwin, and the 8th, under Col. A. H. Emley, came to our place. These troops were the first to reach our town, and they constituted the nucleus of Gen. Patterson's Army. These regiments came by the Cumberland Valley railroad, and reached town about 10 o'clock at night. They marched from the depot up Second street to Market, down Market through the Diamond, and out to the old Fair Ground on the hill west of town. This was the first time many of our citizens had seen so large a body of soldiers, and their arrival created great excitement and great interest.

A day or two after the arrival of these two regiments, they were removed from the Fair Ground to a field east of the town belonging to Mr. Eberly. This place was much better adapted for the purpose of an encampment than the one they first occupied. Water of the best kind and in abundance was near at hand. This camp was called "Camp Slifer," after the then Secretary of the Commonwealth. Wooden buildings were hastily erected for the accommodation of the soldiers, but tents were needed for the quarters of the officers. The Government was unable for a while to furnish these because of its unpreparedness for the sudden and unexpected emergency. A dispatch was received by the writer from Col. A. K. McClure, at Harrisburg, by direction of Gov. Curtin, requesting me to ascertain how many Camp Meeting tents I could procure, and report the result to Gen. Williams in command of Camp Slifer. I reported to the General that I could get some eight or ten, but some were without covers. General Williams directed me to have covers made, and the tents put up in the camp at such places as his officers should direct. Covers were made and the tents put up and used; and when the camp was broken up and the advance towards Virginia made, they were taken along by the troops. It was several years and after much difficulty that I succeeded in getting them paid for, so as to compensate their owners.

On Thursday evening, about 9 o'clock, May 2d, the 10th Regiment, commanded by Col. S. A. Meredith, reached town and were marched out to Camp Slifer. On the following night, Friday, May 3d, snow four or five inches in depth fell. This newly arrived regiment was without adequate shelter, and on Saturday morning Capt. D. W. Patterson, in command of the Lancaster City Guards, brought his company into town, and they took shelter in the lower corridor of the Court House, where provisions were taken by some of our citizens and these hungry men fed.

From the 2d day of May until the 28th, a period of nearly four weeks, these three regiments—the 7th, 8th and 10th Penna. Volunteers—were the only troops in actual service quartered here.

To meet the exigencies arising from the presence of so large a number of men in our community, many of whom had left their business and comfortable homes to contract disease from exposure and hardships, our citizens, male and female, did all in their power to provide for the comfort and welfare of the gallant strangers in their midst. Houses, hearts and tables were open to them. People from the surrounding country came in crowds to visit the camp, and many brought evidences of their regard in the way of bread, cakes and delicacies.

Some of the arrangements made by our citizens for the comfort of the soldiers, especially for the sick, are worthy of notice and permanent record. I shall detail a few here. On Sunday, May 12th, announcements were made in the churches of this place, that on the following day the ladies of the various denominations would meet in the Presbyterian Lecture Room, to organize an association to supply regularly the delicacies needed by the sick soldiers in the hospital. The hospital was then in one of the large rooms of what was known as the Mansion House. It was then occupied and owned by the Reformed Church as their printing establishment. The meeting was held and committees appointed—one for each day in the week. It fell to the lot of the writer to go to the hospital each morning and receive from the Surgeon in charge—Dr. B. H. Throop, of Scranton, Pa.—a paper in which he stated the number of patients for whom he needed food. These he would divide into classes, according to the degree of their illness or convalescence, so that the proper provison might be made. This paper I would deliver to the President of the Committee for that day, who, with the assistance of her associates, would prepare what was wanted and send it to the hospital. In this way delicacies for the weak and suffering, and stronger food for the convalescent, were furnished in abundance. The ladies also set to work to prepare bandages, scrape lint, and gather old linen for bandaging wounds, all of which they delivered to the Surgeon and his assistants. The sending of food and delicacies was kept up until a General Hospital was established in Franklin Hall, when, to some extent, the wants of the soldiers were met then by the better organization which there prevailed. Many, however, visited the hospitals daily throughout the war, and carried to the sick and wounded such things as they needed, and could not otherwise procure. Later on in the war the ladies worked vigorously in collecting money, lint, and bandages for the Christian and Sanitary Commissions. It would be a deserved tribute to the humanity and patriotism of these noble women to place their names upon permanent record here, but I would not do injustice to the many, both dead and living, whose names have escaped my memory, by recording the few I can recollect.

During the months of May and June a considerable number of soldiers took sick, and several died. A disease called the "Spotted Fever," induced by exposure and laying upon the damp ground, broke out in Camp Slifer. The blood seemed to have left the veins and come out in dark blotches or spots upon the surface of the body under the skin. In most cases death ensued, and few survived two or three days after having been stricken with it. One of the nurses in the hospital in Franklin Hall was an Englishman, and had been a nurse in the Enlish Army in the Crimean war. He said they had a great many cases of this terrible disease there, and his services in caring for such patients was in great demand in Franklin Hall. One of the persons who died after a short illness from this terrible scourge in Franklin Hall, was a soldier in Capt. Patterson's command from Lancaster City. His name, I think, was Pastor. His wife came on to see her husband, and we gave her a home as our house adjoined the hospital. Capt. Patterson, the dying soldier's wife, one of the nurses, and the writer, stood by his mattress upon the floor, and witnessed his dying struggles. His heartbroken wife was led away from the sad scene and passed a sleepless night until the next day, when Capt. Patterson, leading the bereaved widow, and surrounded by a military guard from his own company, bore the dead body of the soldier to the depot, when it was taken to Lancaster and interred. Capt. Patterson was a noble man. He loved his men, and they loved and respected him. His profession, I think, was that of a lawyer. He lived in Lancaster. The scenes of suffering and agony that occurred in Franklin Hall Hospital and other hospitals afterwards established here, and the touching circumstances connected with some cases, can never be told. I may detail a few cases further on in these reminiscenses in their appropriate places.

Through the organization of the Franklin County Bible Society, money was collected to defray the expenses of coffins and shrouds for some soldiers who had died, and whose friends desired to take their bodies home for burial, but had not the means. Through the same organization tracts were distributed in the camps, the jail and camps visited, and preaching each Sabbath by one of the resident ministers of the town, provided for.

But the presence of the soldiers among us had its bright side as well as its sombre aspect. There were many very clever persons among them who became favorites of our people. And as in almost any assemblage of persons there is one who is the acknowledged genius for fun-making, so it was with these soldiers. The universal genius of Camp Slifer was a little, wiry, and glib-tongued fellow who was called "Old Abe." Wherever Old Abe appeared there was fun and laughter. He loved to tell of his bravery, and what terrible havoc he would make if ever he got into battle with the rebels. It was said that his after-conduct did not correspond with his high pretensions.

An officer attended service one Sabbath in the German Reformed church, and while the pastor, Rev. B. Bausman, was preaching, he suddenly, and somewhat angrily, disturbed the Reverend gentleman and his listening congregation by the words: "Attention men! attention!! Shoulder arms." It was said that he was the drill master of the "Awkward Squad," and having fallen asleep he imagined he was going through the provoking duty of drilling raw recruits. It is needless to say that the solemnity of the occasion was somewhat broken, and many were excited to laughter, amidst which the mortified officer quietly withdrew.

Occasionally one of the regiments from the camp would favor the town by a parade through its streets; and on one occasion the three regiments marched through the Diamond and two or three miles out into the country. On May 15th, the 7th and 8th Regiments were drawn up into several lines in the Diamond, when a handsome flag was presented to the 7th Regiment, as a mark of regard from the ladies of Chambersburg. The flag was presented by W. S. Stenger, Esq., on behalf of the ladies, in a neat and able address. Lieut. Col. Rippey responded on the part of the Regiment in a speech of great beauty and force. The affair was witnessed by a large concourse of citizens, and was an occasion of great interest.

On the same day of this flag presentation. Gov. Curtin visited the town to review the troops. He and his suite arrived in the 11 o'clock train, and were received at the depot by the 7th Regiment and conducted to the Franklin Hotel. In the afternoon the Governor reviewed the troops. They were stationed along Main street The 7th, 8th and 10th Regiments were present; also five companies from "Camp McAllen," on the Fair Grounds. The Governor returned to Harrisburg in a special train the same evening.

Among the companies encamped on the Fair Grounds at this time awaiting acceptance by the Governor, was the "McClure Rifles," under command of Capt. Wilson Reilly, This company was named after Hon. A. K. McClure. When the Government refused to accept any more troops for a short term, part of this company refused to enter the service under these terms and returned to their homes, and subsequently the balance were dismissed. Capt. Campbell's company of Artillery also divided upon this condition, and part of the command returned home.

CHAPTER IV.

GENERAL PATTERSON'S CAMPAIGN.

On the morning of Tuesday, May 28th, about seven o'clock, our town was thrown into a state of excitement by the announcement that the 2nd and 3d Regiments from Camp Scott, near York, were at the depot. In a short time a large part of the population of the place gathered there to receive them. Companies A and B were nearly all from this place, and Co. C. from Greencastle, St. Thomas, and other parts of the county. A hearty reception was given these defenders of their country by friends and relatives here, as well as a generous welcome to all who composed that splendid body of men. These troops had left Camp Scott at 9 o'clock on the previous evening. The secret of their coming had been known to the Railroad employees only. They were well equipped in everything necessary for the march, the camp, and the battlefield. After having formed into line, the column, led by Colonel Stumbaugh, marched up Second Street to Market, and down Market and up to the Fair Grounds. Shortly after reaching this encampment, furloughs were granted to many of the soldiers from this and neighboring places, and they hurried to their respective homes.

On Thursday following the day of the arrival of the 2nd and 3d Regiments—May 30th—the 6th Regiment commanded by Col. James Nagle and the 23d, commanded by Col. Charles P. Dare, arrived by trains from Perrysville Camp, opposite Havre de Grace. During the afternoon of the same day, the 21st Regiment, Col. John F. Ballier, and the 24th, Col. Joshua T. Owens, both from Philadelphia, also arrived. On Friday morning the "Scott Legion," Col. Gray, numbering about one thousand men, arrived from Philadelphia. The whole number of troops which had arrived up to this time was about eight thousand. These men were quartered in the following places: The 2nd and 3d upon the Fair Grounds, which they called "Camp Givens," named after Maj. James S. Givens, of the 2nd Regiment. These two Regiments were subsequently for a short time quartered in the Court House, churches and other public buildings. The 6th, 21st and 23d, at Camp Carbon, on the grounds of Col. McClure, north of the town. The Scott Legion and the 24th, encamped about three miles south of the town on the farm of Mr. Christian Bitner—the 2nd and 3d Regiments being removed to this encampment. Changes were made in some of these encampments afterwards as better locations were found.

On Saturday morning, June 21st, a large number of U. S. Baggage Wagons arrived; also a brigade of cavalry, numbering about five hundred. The cavalry encamped in the grove north of the town, near where the Gate House then stood.

In the afternoon of Saturday, June 1st, the horrible tragedy of the killing of the colored man, Frank Jones, occurred.— Jones, it was said, kept a disorderly house in that part of the town known as "Wolfstown." His place was the frequent resort of soldiers, and for some cause on that afternoon they attacked his place, forcing open the doors, breaking in the windows, upsetting the stove and beating Jones and his wife. In the confusion Jones discharged his gun, the contents of which wounded two soldiers in the legs. The cry was then raised, "kill the nigger, kill the nigger." Jones fled from his house, going out of the back door and crossing the lots in the direction of West Market Street.—When his flight was discovered, a Lieutenant of one of the Pittsburg companies, attached to the Seventh Regiment, who had just arrived on the ground, called out for the men to pursue Jones, he following in the pursuit. Jones succeeded in reaching the house standing upon what is known as Federal Hill, now occupied by Mr. Boyer, but then the residence of George Eyster, Esq. Upon the arrival of the soldiers, Jones was found in one of the chimnies, from which he was dragged against the protests of Mrs. Eyster, led out into the front of the house and brutally killed, the Lieutenant himself firing five shots from his pistol into the body of Jones. He was also beaten over the head with a club, and several bayonets and swords were thrust into him. The body of Jones was subsequently taken into the jail yard, where an inquest and *post-mortem* examination were held. He bore upon his body twenty wounds, six being bullet wounds and the balance incised and contused wounds. Warrants were issued for the arrest of the persons implicated in this foul tragedy, but owing to the excitement of the war, nothing was done in the case. Some years after this occurrence, the Lieutenant implicated in this murder voluntarily came to Chambersburg and gave himself up for trial, but he was acquitted for want of sufficient evidence.

On Sunday afternoon about five o'clock, General Patterson, attended by Capt. McMullen's company of Independent Rangers from Philadelphia, came to town by a special train. Up to this time the sanctity of the Sabbath had been but seldom disturbed by the military in our midst, but on this day the first great street parade on the Sabbath occurred. A large body of soldiers were drawn up in line on North Main street. When the train arrived, Gen. Patterson, and some of his staff, in a carriage, specially prepared for him, took his place in the line, and the imposing procession marched up Main street, which was filled with a sea of glittering bayonets from the Presbyterian church to the German Reformed. After parading about town to the delight of many, but the regret of others because of the violation of the Sabbath, the General with his military family took up his headquarters in the large stone building which stood in the vacant ground opposite the Montgomery hotel, formerly used as a Female seminary.

It is a significant fact that many of the great battles of history were fought upon the Sabbath, and in almost every instance the attacking party was defeated. This fact alone, if not the higher consideration of the divine prohibition, should have deterred those in command of the armies of a Christian Nation from all unnecessary military movements upon that day. In this case there was no necessity for selecting the Sabbath to come to this place, much less for the uncalled for display attending it. The contrast between the arrival of Gen. Patterson in our town and his passing through it on his return, some few weeks afterwards, was decided and humiliating. When he returned he rode in a regular train, in an ordinary car with others, and with but a few persons to look at him. He may not have deserved the reproach our people heaped upon him, but his case is another illustration of the propriety of the Scriptural injunction, "Let not him that girdeth on his harness boast himself as he that putteth it off."

During the night of Sunday, June 1st, the 1st Regiment of Pennsylvania Volunteers, commanded by Col. Samuel Yohe, arrived; and early on Tuesday morning, June 3d, the 14th, commanded by Colonel John W. Johnston, and the 15th, Colonel Richard A. Oakford, also made their appearance. Between this date and the 8th inst., two more Regiments arrived, viz: the 9th Pennsylvania, Col. H. C. Longenecker and the 13th, Col. Thomas A. Rowley. Following these in close succession came the 1st Rhode Island, Colonel Burnside, about eleven hundred men and a field battery of six pieces with horses, wagons and equipments; the 4th Connecticut, Col. Levi Woodhouse, one thousand strong, the 1st Wisconsin, Colonel Starkweather, the 11th Pennsylvania, Colonel Jarrett, and the 16th Pennsylvania, Col. Thomas A. Zeigle. On Saturday, the 8th, there arrived a Company of Regulars from Fort Leavenworth, Kansas, and five more companies from Washington on Sunday. Almost every day and night trains of cars arrived freighted with horses, baggage wagons, amunition and provisions, and every indication pointed to a speedy movement upon the foe.

The troops after arriving here were organized as follows:

FIRST DIVISION.

Brevet Major General George Cadwallader commanding, consisting of First, Third and Fourth Brigades.

1st Brigade—Col. George H. Thomas. 2d U. S. Cavalry, commanding, consisting of

4 companies U. S. Cavalry, and 1st Philadelphia City Troop, Capt James.

Battalion of Artillery and Infantry, Capt. Doubleday.

1st Rhode Island Regt. and Battery, Col. Burnside.

6th Penna. Regt., Colonel Nagle.
21st   "   "   Col. Ballier.
23d   "   "   Col. Dare.

3d Brigade—Brig. Gen. E. C. Williams commanding, consisting of
7th Regt. Penna. Volunteers, Col. Irwin.
8th   "   "   "   Col. Emly.
10th "   "   "   Col. Meredith.
20th "   Scott Legion, Col. Gray.

4th Brigade—Col. D. S. Miles, U. S. Infantry, commanding, consisting of
2d and 3d U. S. Infantry, Maj. Sheppard.
9th Penna., Col. Longenecker.
13th   "   Col. Rowley.
16th   "   Col. Zeigle.

SECOND DIVISION.

Major General Wm. H. Keim, commanding, consisting of the Second and Fifth Brigades.

2d Brigade—Brig. Gen. G. C. Wyncoop, commanding, consisting of
1st Penna., Col. Yohe.
2d   "   Col. Stumbaugh
3d   "   Col. Minier.
24th "   Col. Owens.

5th Brigade—Brig. Gen. J. S. Negley, commanding, consisting of
1st Wisconsin, Col. Starkwenther.
4th Connecticut, Col. Woodhouse.
11th Penna., Col. Jarrett.
14th   "   Col. Johnson.
15th   "   Col. Oakford.

Gen. Patterson's command, as will be seen from the foregoing, consisted of about twenty thousand strong. These forces were well armed and equipped, and judging from the record which many of them afterwards made during the war, they were fully competent to perform the duty entrusted to them. Gen. Johnston, commander of the rebel forces in the Valley of Virginia, had evacuated Harper's Ferry and fallen back to Winchester, where he had collected a considerable force. To Gen. Patterson was entrusted the duty to either attack and defeat this force, or to hold it there while another force under Gen. McDowell marched from Washington to attack Beauregard at Manassas. That either or both these objects was not accomplished was not the fault of the men. I am aware that Gen. Patterson, a few years before his death, felt at liberty to make public some facts which seemed to place the responsibility of the failure of his expedition upon others. Impartial history will attach that responsibility where it justly belongs.

On Friday morning, June 7th, the advance towards Virginia commenced. The troops encamped upon the grounds of Col. McClure, north of the town, marched up Main street, amidst the intense enthusiasm of the people. Some of the regiments, with some of the artillery belonging to Gen. Cadwallader's division, had already gone southward by railroad.

As these troops passed up our street, that familiar and eccentric character, Aleck Orbison, known to the older persons in this place, stood upon the pavement in front of Gen. Patterson's headquarters. He was dressed in a suit of old regimentals which some one had given him. As the officers rode by he greeted them with a salute and bow, gracefully touching his old high crowned and plumed Revolutionary hat. Supposing him to be some one connected with headquarters and high in rank, some of the officers, failing to take in the situation until the laughter of the people led them to see it, returned his salute, to the great amusement of all who witnessed it.

On Saturday morning the troops from Camp Slifer, under Gen. Williams, left their encampment and followed Gen. Cadwallader southward. These were followed day after day by others, until all were gone. The 2d and 3d Regiments, to which the two companies from this place belonged, left their encampment upon Mr. Bitner's farm on Saturday, the 15th.

It is not our purpose to follow this grand army in its marchings and counter marchings, its crossing and recrossing the Potomac, its victory over the enemy at Falling Waters and triumphant march to Bunker Hill, within striking distance of the enemy, and its inglorious turning aside and falling back to Charlestown and Harper's Ferry, leaving Johnston to flee to Manassas and snatch from the Union forces the wreath of victorious battle already won. Somebody either blundered, or was incompetent for the trust confided to him.

Immediately after the departure of the troops from this place, all the inmates of the hospitals, who were well enough, were sent to their respective companies. Others, not sufficiently recovered, were sent to their homes or to other hospitals. There were quite a number, however, who were too weak and ill to be sent away. These our citizens agreed to care for, without compensation, and they were distributed among families in the town. One was taken in charge by Mr. Samuel Myers, one by Mr. Henry Embich, one by Mrs. Wolfkill, one by Daniel Trostle, two by A. H. McCulloh, three by Charles Eyster, one by Hon. George Chambers, one by Frederick Deitrich, and one by the writer. Dr. A. H. Senseny was put in charge of them. Within a week the three in the families of Mr. Embich, Mrs. Wolfkill and Frederick Deitrich died. The soldier assigned to us was named Summerfield. He came from Pittsburg. He was slowly recovering from a long and severe attack of typhoid fever. His mind was weak and he seemed like a child. He imagined that he had captured Jeff. Davis with five hundred thousand dollars in gold and two horses. He would every day look out of the window to see if the bank, in which he imagined his money was stored, was still there, and would then go down to the stable at the lower end of our lot, in which Sheriff Brandt had two horses, which he claimed as those he captured, to see if they were yet on hand. Dr. A. H. Senseny called every day to see him and inquired if he still had old Jeff, and his money and horses ? After he became stronger and better he would smile when this question was asked him. When able to travel we sent him to his home in Pittsburg. In about two months afterwards we received a letter from him from Washington. He had again enlisted and was then in service. The case of the soldier who died at the residence of Mr. Deitrich is peculiarly interesting. One day, about a week or ten days before the departure of the troops, I visited, as was my frequent custom, the hospital in the Hall. Seated beside the cot of a youthful soldier, sorely afflicted with typhoid fever, was a middle aged German woman. She resided in Allegheny City, and was the mother of the young soldier, and having heard of his illness had come on to see after him. Her dress and scanty bundle indicated poverty, and inability to pay lodging, and she could not be entertained in the hospital. Mr. Frederick Deitrich and his good old wife kindly consented to give her a home. After showing her to her room the first night she lodged with them, she was overheard in earnest prayer for her poor sick boy, and for the kind family who had opened its door and taken her in. Mr. Deitrich and his wife were pious people, and from that time became greatly attached to their guest. This woman's son, the soldier boy already referred to, was the last one in the hospital. All the others had been removed and provided for. A stretcher was procured and he was borne to Mr. Deitrich's residence. Going up to see him late in the afternoon, I found him dead. As soon as he was comfortably fixed in bed after his removal, his mother, joined by Mr. and Mrs. Deitrich, knelt by his bed and prayed repeatedly for him and pointed him to the dying soldier's Friend. They had the satisfaction to see him die in peace and hope. A coffin and shroud were procured, and the next morning, followed by the family of Mr. Deitrich and a few others, his body was borne to the depot and taken by his mother, the railroad officials granting free transportation, to Allegheny City, where it was received and buried by the military. As the train bearing the mother and her dead son moved around the curve at Grier's warehouse, the woman waved her hand out of the car window and then pointed upwards, as if to say: "Farewell; we will meet up there." Mr. Deitrich and his good old wife are long dead. They have doubtless met both mother and son where wars are unknown, and where death and tears are forever ended.

CHAPTER V.

Organization of the 126th Regiment; Fugitives From Slavery.

It is not my purpose to enter into the details of all the military movements which occurred in and about our town during the war. Large armies of both Union and Confederates, several times congregated about the place, and Regiments, Companies and detachments were almost constantly passing to and from the seat of hostilities. Recruiting was going on all the time, and there was scarcely a period in those four eventful years, when military encampments were not located about the place. Chambersburg and Franklin County furnished their full share of recruits, and to give the names of all these, and the times of the leaving and their destination, would swell these articles beyond the limits I have prescribed. I shall therefore confine myself to some of the leading occurrences, and detail events not generally known.

On Monday, July 22d, our town was in a state of intense excitement, occasioned by the news of a great victory gained over the rebels by the army of Gen. McDowell at Manassas on the day previous. But in the evening our rejoicing was turned into disappointment and alarm, by the later received news that, owing to General Johnston's arrival upon the field from Winchester with a large part of his army, and after the victory had already been won, defeat had ensued. Execrations upon Gen. Patterson for failing to prevent this junction were many and bitter. It was too looked upon as an addition of another to the multitudes of other cases of disastrous results to the attacking party upon the Sabbath. Then the National Capitol was in danger, and the indefinite prolongation of the war, with the threatening condition along our borders, excited universal alarm.

On Sunday afternoon following this defeat, July 28th, the town was again excited by the arrival of the Franklin County companies belonging to the 22nd Regiment. The period of their enlistment had expired, and they were discharged. The companies were marched from the depot, followed by a vast concourse of people, to the Public Square, where they were dismissed.

During the summer of 1862, indeed throughout nearly the whole period of the war, a great many sick and wounded soldiers almost daily passed through the town. Owing to the crowded state of the hotels, and sometimes to the diseases under which some of them were suffering, it was determined by our citizens to procure a suitable lodging place for them, where they could remain over night, or longer if necessary. Accordingly a public meeting was held in the Court House for the purpose stated, and a committee appointed to have charge of this matter. The committee consisted of Captain J. M. Brown, J. S. Brown, B. F. Nead, John Mull and Jacob Hoke. The lower part of the Masonic Hall was procured and fitted up with beds, and other things necessary for the comfort of the soldiers. Arrangements were also made with one of the hotel keepers to furnish their meals. The expenses of this worthy enterprise were willingly borne by our citizens. The propriety of this arrangement was afterwards seen in the number of soldiers who there found a comfortable resting place and entertainment free of charge.

About this time the ladies of the town organized themselves into an association called the Ladies' Aid Society for the purpose of collecting money to purchase material for clothing, and other comforts for the sick and wounded soldiers. Lint and bandages for dressing wounds were also prepared. Mrs. B. S. Schneck was President of this Society, and its head quarters were in the Associate Reformed Church, on Second Street, where the residence of Mr. John Lortz now stands, and which was burned by the rebels, July 30th, 1864. On Sunday, August 31st, after the disastrous battles of Centreville, Manassas and Chantilly, a despatch was received from Governor Curtin, requesting all our physicians to proceed to Washington to assist in caring for the large number of wounded from those battles. Our people at once flocked to the church, and assisted the ladies in packing the articles which they had prepared. These were taken in charge by the physicians, who left that night in a special train. The physicians who responded to this call were, Drs. A. H. Sensen y, J. C. Richards, Jas. Hamilton, Wm. H. Boyle, J. Montgomery, and H. Langhein. They were however sent back by the authorities at Washington.

On the 17th of July the President was authorized to accept the services of one hundred thousand volunteers for nine months. Three weeks after this call, the 126th Regiment was organized and ready for service. Franklin County furnished eight companies for this Regiment, except part of one company, which was furnished by Fulton County. Three of these companies were composed mostly of young men from Chambersburg. Greencastle, Mercersburg, Waynesboro', St. Thomas, and Path Valley, contributed the other five companies. Juniata County furnished the remaining two companies to complete the Regiment. Captain James G. Elder was elected Colonel; D. Watson Rowe, now Judge of this district, Lieut. Colonel; James C. Austin, Major; John Stewart, now a Senator of the State, Adjutant; T. J. Nill, Quarter Master; Washington G. Nugent, Surgeon; Franklin Grube, Ass't. Surgeon, Rev. Samuel J. Niccolls, Pastor of the Falling Spring Presbyterian Church of this place, Chaplain. Major Austin was afterwards succeeded by Capt. Robert S. Brownson, and Rev. Mr. Niccolls by Rev. John Ault. Captain John Dœbler, of Company A, Captain John H. Reed, of Company D, and Capt. George L. Miles, of Company G, were from Chambersburg; Capt. William H. Davidson, of Company B, and Capt. Andrew R. Davidson, of Company K, were from Greencastle; Captain and afterwards Major Robert S. Brownson, was from Mercersburg; Capt. W. W. Walker, of Company E, from Waynesboro', and Capt. John H. Walker, of Company H, from Path Valley; Capt. John F. Wharton, of Company F, and Capt. Amos H. Martin, of Company I, were from Juniata County. It would be a matter of interest to record here the names of the remaining officers and privates of this Regiment, but our space forbids.—They were the flower and pride of the county, and among the survivors in our own town are many of our leading business and professional men. Never before, nor afterwards, in the history of the war, did one single town of the size of Chambersburg, send forth to the field of strife so many of her best and most honored young men. The only motive which could have prompted them to break away from the fond hearts and homes in which they were the life and light, was pure patriotism.

Their imperilled country needed their services, and they readily responded to her call.

When the three companies from this place, which formed part of the 126th Regiment, embarked upon the cars for Harrisburg, the touching scenes of April 19th, 1861, when the Chambers Artillery left, were re-enacted. Great crowds gathered at the depot. Tears were shed, farewells were spoken, and hearts were made desolate. To some of these noble ones it was the last greeting from home and friends. Some sleep in honored graves in distant places, and others were brought here to be followed in solemn and mournful procession to our beautiful cemetery, where upon each return of the day set apart specially to do honor to their memories, their graves, with those of others who laid down their lives upon their country's altar, are strewn with flowers. Honored men! Let their names and deeds be ever kept in grateful remembrance.

The men which Chambersburg contributed to the 126th Regiment, left this place for Harrisburg enrolled as members of the "Chambers Artillery." This was the name of the company which left under Capt. Housum at the outbreak of the war. Like that company it was also divided, and in this case three companies were made out of it. It proved to be *the first company* which arrived at Harrisburg under the call for additional troops.

Arriving at Harrisburg the men were quartered at Camp Curtin, where the organization of the Regiment was made, immediately after which it was sent to the front. At Fredericksburg and Chancellorsville the Regiment demeaned itself so well that the expectations of its friends were more than realized.

About the time the call of the Government was made, in response to which the 126th Regiment was formed, an order was issued for the first draft of the war. D. K. Wunderlich, Esq., was appointed Marshal of Franklin county, and William G. Reed, Esq., Deputy Marshal. Mr. Reed appointed his deputies in all the districts of the county, and they proceeded to enrol the names of all male persons between the ages of 18 and 45. Notices were then served on each person thus enrolled, requiring them to appear before a Commissioner to hear and decide upon all claims for exemption. Dr. A. H. Senseny was the Commissioner for Chambersburg and vicinity. He held his examinations in one of the jury rooms of the Court House. Never before in the history of the county were there so many invalids gathered in and about the Court House. The Doctor, however, possessed the happy faculty of detecting the cases which were simulated. In the several drafts which were afterwards made, the drafted persons alone were required to appear for examination.

The foregoing brings us to the first week in August, 1862. I shall now go back and narrate some exciting events which occurred along the border and in and about our town, May 26th, and the week or two succeeding. These events could not be narrated in their proper sequence without interfering with the statement of events of a like order which occurred during this period.

Early on Monday morning, May 26th, our town was thrown into a state of great excitement by the announcement that Gen. Banks, who had succeeded to the command of the Union forces in the Valley of the Virginia, had been surprised and driven back from Strasburg to Winchester, and from thence to Martinsburg, and to the north side of the Potomac, by a large rebel force under Generals Ewell and Johnson. Extras were issued from the printing offices detailing the situation, and circulating the orders issued by the Governor calling out the militia and volunteers for the protection of our border from a threatened raid. Drums were beaten, the people collected in large numbers about the Diamond, and many enrolled themselves to meet the emergency. During the afternoon a body of men, about sixty in number, arrived from St. Thomas under the command of Captain Elder. Towards evening and during the next day a considerable number of stragglers from Gen. Banks' command, and large numbers of colored persons, came streaming through our streets. The colored persons were fugitives from slavery, and they fled northward with the Union forces. They consisted of men, women and children. Many of them carried large bundles upon their heads, and articles of furniture and clothing in their hands. The most of them went on down the valley towards Harrisburg, while a considerable number tarried about Chambersburg. About four hundred in all composed that band of homeless fugitives. After Gen. Banks again went up the Valley, the most of these contrabands returned to Virginia. My attention was called one day to the fact that about thirty or forty of these poor people were collected in and about a shed attached to the warehouse belonging to Messrs. Oaks and Caufman, but now to Messrs. Linn and Coyle. I went down to see them, and found some old and gray-headed veterans, men and women, who had given the whole of their lives to unrequited toil. There were some able bodied men and also children. Some half dozen were sick with the measles, and they were lying on straw under the shed. They were strangers in a strange land, and were without food or friends. After conversing awhile and learning their condition, I proposed that if they would all consent to obey the orders of "Uncle Ned," an old patriarch among them, I would furnish them with something to eat, which would be placed in his care, and he was to deal it out to them as it was needed. To this they readily consented, and Uncle Ned sent two stout young men with me. I procured a basket and purchased twenty or thirty loaves of bread which they carried down. When they returned with the basket I filled a large crock with molasses and they carried it down also. For about ten days or two weeks they were furnished with a like number of loaves of bread each day, and occasionally a crock of molasses and a large flitch, or side of bacon, boiled. I was assisted to pay for these things by contributions which I had only to ask for to receive. I had, however, to exercise discretion in knowing who to ask and who to avoid. I was told by persons residing in the lower end of the town that prior to the provision made for them, these people would frequently ask for work, but would never beg. And while they were taken care of, the able bodied men would often go out into the country seeking employment. In a few weeks they went away—some to places which they had secured and where work could be had, and some back into Virginia.

A very deeply interesting event occurred at the time of the foregoing. Some few years before the war a colored family, by the name of Robinson, came to this place and purchased a property on West King street. The house stands on the hill next to where the Baltimore and Cumberland Valley Railroad passes King street. Robinson was an industrious shoemaker and carried on his trade after his settlement here. His wife aided to support the family by taking in washing. The wife of Robinson, when he married her, was a slave, and they resided in Fauquier county, Virginia. After being married about ten years, Robinson, by his industry and economy, was enabled to purchase the freedom of his wife. Prior to her purchase two children were born to them, who, according to the laws of Virginia, were slaves. One day when Mrs. Robinson was out in the fields of her master gathering berries, her daughter Mary, then eight years old, was sold. For over thirty years these parents never heard a word concerning this little one. Mrs. Robinson was a devout Christian, and often prayed that if her child were living she might yet be restored to her. Among the fugitives who came to our town at the time of Gen. Banks' retreat, was a colored man from the neighborhood of Winchester. Falling into the company of Robinson, and hearing his story about his daughter, this man imparted to him the thrilling information that he knew Mary, that she had lived near Winchester, had been married, that her husband was dead, leaving her with three children, and that she had accompanied him in his flight as far as the Virginia side of the Potomac, nearly opposite Williamsport, where, unable to proceed further, she with her three children had taken refuge in a deserted school house. Early the next morning Robinson started after his long-lost child with a wagon. Arriving at the school house he found it filled with fugitive slaves, who, like his daughter, could proceed no further. After a little while he succeeded in finding among the number his own lost one. Some of the neighbors who resided near the residence of the Robinsons here, and respected them for their industry, having heard of the probability of the father's return with the daughter, had gathered in the evening in and about the house to witness the scene. At length after dark the sound of approaching wheels was heard. The wagon stopped in front of their residence, and Mrs. Robinson, followed by a grown up daughter and other children born after little Mary's departure, rushed to the wagon and received and embraced the long-lost one. The scene was intensely affecting, and all present wept with the family. The next morning I visited the residence of Robinson and saw Mary and her children. A few days ago I visited the place again to verify the foregoing. I found Mrs. Robinson in the same house, surrounded by her children and grand children. Her husband died about ten years ago. Mary, the long-lost one, is alive, and is now living with Mrs. William McLellan, on East Market street. Thank God, the accursed system of iniquity which produces such results as those narrated has perished forever from our country. It took a million brave hearts, hundreds of thousands of noble lives, a martyred President, and three thousand millions of dollars to overthrow it, but it has perished, and there is none so mean now to shed a tear over its loathsome carcass. May its like, wherever found upon the face of the earth, share a similar fate.

CHAPTER VI.

CHAMBERSBURG UNDER MARTIAL LAW; VISIT TO THE BATTLEFIELD OF SOUTH MOUNTAIN; BATTLE OF ANTIETAM.

Immediately after the disastrous battles of August 27th, 28th and 29th, usually known as the second battle of Bull Run, and the retreat of the Union Army to the defenses about Washington, the Confederate Army under Gen. Lee crossed the Potomac at Edward's Ferry, and moved westwardly through Frederick towards the borders of our State. The advance of this army reached Hagerstown, and their picket line extended to State Line, some sixteen miles from this place. As the information of the approach of these forces was received, intense excitement prevailed throughout the entire country. Business was practically suspended in our town, and the work of secreting or sending away merchandize and other valuables was at once commenced. On Monday, Sept. 8th, we packed and sent away to Philadelphia, for storage, the most valuable part of our stock of merchandize, and on Wednesday sent off another lot. It will give some idea of the difficulties under which business was transacted here and along the border during the war, when I state that on a large part of our stock we paid transportation to and from Philadelphia from three to five times. In addition to this were the expenses of secreting in the country, and in houses on the outskirts of the town. During Lee's invasion we had nearly all our stock secreted in a fire proof beer vault under Dr. Langhein's back building, adjoining our store; and in this same vault we had a considerable amount stored when the town was burnt in July, 1864.

On Wednesday, Sept. 10th, our town was placed under Martial Law. Hon. F. M. Kimmell, formerly President Judge of this Judicial District, was made Provost Martial, with headquarters in his law office in the Hall. Martial law prevailed in the town for about three weeks. Judge Kimmell proved to be an excellent man for this position. His authority was respected not only within the town, but for many miles around it. The writer, in company with three others, on returning at a late hour of the night from the battlefield of Antietam on Friday, 19th, was stopped by a sentinel below Marion. Upon presenting a pass from Judge Kimmell we were permitted to pass through the lines to town.

On Friday, Sept. 12th, the excitement increasing, many of the citizens of the town left for more safe and quiet quarters. It had been arranged that if the rebels would advance, notice was to be given by ringing the Court House bell. One evening near sundown, despatches were received from Greencastle that the enemy were advancing. Immediately the signal was given, and a scene of excitement ensued which no language of mine can fully describe. An Artillery Company, with four pieces, were encamped in the field across from the Foundry of Messrs. T. B. Wood & Sons. These came galloping up into the Diamond, and added no little to the consternation. There were too few troops here to justify any formidable opposition outside of the town, and it was decided to make the Diamond the line of defense. One piece of artillery was placed between Mr. Nixon's drug store and the grocery of Messrs. Lortz & Wolfinger, pointing south; another was placed at the corner of Main and King streets, pointing west, and covering the approach by West King street; another was placed in front of the residence of Mr. T. B. Kennedy, pointing east; and the fourth piece was planted a short distance below the Diamond in Market street, pointing west. Under the authority of Marshal Kimmell, a number of citizens were taken to a vacant field near the depot to fill bags with earth for a breastwork. These bags were furnished by the Battery. In this work of digging and shoveling, Judge Kimmell set a creditable example by taking off his coat and assisting. These bags of earth were hauled up and placed across Market street, about in range with the rear end of the Central church. A gap was left for the cannon. This was the only defensive work, or fortification, ever thrown up here during the war. Sharp shooters were also placed in several houses at eligible places. Had the rebels come that night, the Diamond would have been the scene of a fearful slaughter, for the few hundred troops there were entirely inadequate to meet the force that was usually sent in advance. Before ten o'clock we received word that the enemy had again fallen back to State Line, and our people retired to rest. In the morning we found the soldiers lying around the

Diamond upon the pavements. Some were cooking their breakfasts. During the forenoon they were withdrawn and taken back to their former encampment. Under the authority of the Marshal all our able-bodied citizens were ordered to report for duty, and many shouldered the musket and performed picket and guard service. The writer, on going to Sabbath School, was picked up on the street with a number of others, and compelled to assist in unpacking boxes filled with harness and putting the same together. It was his first attempt in the saddlery business, and it commenced and ended on the Sabbath. The place of business was in the alley back of Mr. D. Trostle's stable, and although we had neither advertised our business, nor hung out a sign, we had an abundance of customers in the persons of a lot of boys who gave us the preference over the Sabbath Schools.

A call had been issued by the Government for volunteers to meet the emergency, and companies and regiments came in from all directions. Major Gen. J. F. Reynolds was here in command of these emergency men and had his headquarters in the house now occupied by Mr. W. H. Hiteshew on North Second street.— Among the troops who were sent here at that time were many of the leading citizens of the country—ministers, lawyers and other professional and business men. And it was not an unusual sight to see a man worth his tens of thousands of dollars standing guard, musket in hand, over a huge stack of hay and other government property. Some of the companies from abroad had aged persons among them armed with their own tried rifles. In order to provide for the immediate wants of some of these newly arrived men, provisions were gathered throughout the town and county and stored in one of the rooms of our house back of the store. When companies came who had no provision made for them, they were taken into our yard and house and fed. Anything other than bread, as coffee, butter, apple-butter and molasses, we provided gratuitously. A word here in relation to my duties during this period: I was exempted from military service, but was actively engaged in the hospitals and camps throughout the entire war. I yet preserve as a relic my exemption paper, signed by Dr. A. H. Seuseny and his clerk, Mr. W. V. Davis, and Provost Marshal Kimmell's pass permitting me to go in and out of all these places at my pleasure.

Among the troops gathered here at that time, none rendered greater service, nor endeared themselves more to our people, than several companies of the 29th Pennsylvania Volunteers. These men had seen considerable service, and were considered as veterans. The usual accompaniments of nearly all the first soldiers who came to our midst during the earlier period of the war, as an unnecessary amount of clothing, and the luxuries of home life, were not found with them. They were stripped for fight, and seemed always about as ready to do service as to partake of the hospitalities of our people, which were freely offered them. In connection with our Home Guards—companies composed of our citizens—these veterans did picket duty out on the Greencastle and Waynesboro roads. The chief post was on South Main street, opposite the Taylor Works. From this post the guards were relieved. Many adventures occurred while our Home Guards were on picket duty during the night, which tried their courage. In every case they were equal to the occasion.

On Sunday, the 14th, word was received that the pickets had been withdrawn from the State line. This indicated a backward movement, and enabled the community to breathe easier. The reason for this withdrawal was afterwards found to be the approach of the Army of the Potomac, under Gen. McClellan, who had again been put in command. On this same day —Sabbath, Sept. 14th—Gen. Lee took up a strong position upon the top of South Mountain, to the right and left of the pike, to prevent the Union Army from crossing. After a desperate battle, in which large numbers on both sides were killed and wounded, the rebels were outflanked and driven from the mountain. Gen. Lee took up another strong position near Sharpsburg, and calling in his troops, who were encamped all along the road to Hagerstown, prepared for the great battle of the Wednesday following.

On Monday, the 15th, another great excitement was caused by the unexpected arrival of a company of Cavalry having in charge some fifty or sixty rebel prisoners and a long train of wagons. This train with its guard was captured that morning between Williamsport and Hagerstown by about 1,500 Union Cavalry, who had cut their way through General Jackson's lines around Harper's Ferry. Seeing defeat inevitable, these brave men by permission of the officer in command, made their escape. Harper's Ferry with its defenders and a large amount of military stores fell into the enemy's possession two days afterwards. The train proved to be part of General Longstreet's amunition train, and the contents of the wagons were stored in the warehouse of Messrs. Wunderlich & Nead where, on Oct. 11th, it was destroyed under Gen. Stuart's raid. Among the prisoners was Cleggett Fitzhugh, a citizen of our county and a nephew of Hon. Gerritt Smith, the able and fearless opponent of slavery. In connection with Daniel Logan, he captured Captain Cook in his flight from Harper's Ferry, after the failure of the John Brown raid, and returned him to Virginia, where he paid the penalty of his life upon the scaffold for his fool hardy attempt to free the slaves. Fitzhugh had left Hughes' Furnace (Alto Dale) but a few days before for Hagerstown where he joined the rebel army. The feeling against him when he was marched through our streets along with the other prisoners, was intense. He was followed by an excited crowd, who yelled and shouted. "Hang him," "Shoot him," "Kill the villain." Under a strong escort these men were guarded to the jail and turned into the yard. Shortly after these men had been lodged in the enclosure behind the jail, I was directed by the Provost Marshal to select a number of men and take a sufficient amount of bread from the store in our room and feed them. The men were lying upon the ground under the shadow of the high stone wall, and Fitzhugh among them lying upon his face. He would neither eat, speak, nor permit any one to see his face. He evidently felt that he was in bad company, and that his short military career had come to a hasty and ignoble conclusion.

On the day following the capture of Gen. Longstreet's ammunition train, word was received of the withdrawal of the rebels from Hagerstown, and their falling back towards Sharpsburg. A train for Hagerstown was announced, and about one hundred of our citizens, the writer among the number, took passage upon it. Our destination was the battle field of South Mountain. Arriving at Hagerstown I obtained passage to Boonsboro' in a spring wagon, my fellow passengers being Col. A. K. McClure, Wm. McLellan, Esq., an editor of one of the Harrisburg papers, and Mr. Lewis Wampler. Few others from Chambersburg were fortunate enough to obtain conveyances, and the large majority had to walk —the distance being about ten miles. Here and there below Hagerstown the fences were down, and the usual evidences of recent encampments were seen. When approaching Boonsboro' we saw some of the results of the Cavalry engagement there a day or two previously. Limbs were shot off of the trees by the roadside, and a few dead rebels lay along the fences. A party of citizens were engaged in burying them when we passed. This was our first sight of real war. It was as but a drop before a shower to what we saw when we reached the field of strife. Ar

riving at Boonsboro', we found all astir. People were coming in from all directions. Army wagons seemed to be everywhere. The fields south of the town were white with them, and an almost continuous stream, heavily loaded, came down from the mountain and turned south towards Sharpsburg, while an equal number, unloaded and empty, returned by the same route. Straggling and foot-sore soldiers were also slowly making their way towards the encampments south of the town.

After a short stay in Boonsboro', Mr. Wampler and myself started for the battle field—about two miles distant. The other occupants of the wagon engaged the driver to take them to Gen. McClelland's headquarters. As soon as we reached the top of the mountain the evidences of the contest were visible. Knapsacks, haversacks, articles of clothing, old hats, caps and shoes, paper, envelopes, &c., were scattered everywhere. I picked up an envelope with a Zouave grasping the flag upon it. It also bore the inscription, "The 51st New York; always ready when wanted." That relic was esteemed of great interest by a friend in New York, to whom I afterwards gave it. We turned south on the old Sharpsburg road, which runs parallel with the mountain, along its eastern slope and near the summit. When we came near where this road crosses to the western side of the mountain, we saw the first dead man. He was a rebel —the Union dead having been all buried. He had fallen with his head down hill, and pools of blood which had run from his body, had collected in the hollow places, and were swarming with flies. His face was black, eyes open and glaring, tongue protruding, and his whole body swollen. The stench was horrible and I became sick. I ran from the place, but all around me were similar loathsome objects. In a short time I became used to it, and in company with Mr. William Heyser, Sr., whom I met at this juncture, we took in the awful situation. In an undergrowth of laurel bushes we saw dozens upon dozens of men, who had apparently taken refuge there after being wounded, and had there died. Some were youthful, and doubtless the light and joy of many a mother's heart and Southern home. We passed thence to a yard in front of a cabin by the road side. In the cabin and all around it were collected the wounded who could not be taken to distant hospitals. A youthful soldier lay by the doorstep upon the grass. He was apparently near his end. In his delusion he gasped "Ida, Ida." Mr. Heyser and I thought he was calling some loved one. Leaving Mr. Heyser and his son William

—our fellow townman—standing by this youthful soldier, I went into the garden attached to the cabin. The vegetables had been pulled up, and upon blankets laid upon the ground were about fifty badly wounded rebels. The only protection they had from the sun and threatened rain, were branches of trees stuck in the ground. Upon the outer edge of this row of suffering men lay a tall, fine looking man. His black slouched hat was partly drawn down over his face. Kneeling by his side I endeavored to engage him in conversation. At first he seemed somewhat disinclined to converse with me, but I soon overcame his reluctance by expressions of sympathy, and at length to my inquiry as to whether I could do anything for him, he replied, "Yes, I want you to send for my wife. I promised her that if I would get wounded or sick that I would send for her." "Where does she live?" I asked. "In South Carolina." I then told him how far he was from his home, and that there were no mail communications with that section, and that it was impossible that his wife could come on to see him. I then said to him that if he had any message which he wished to send his wife, that I would take it down in writing, and that as soon as I could reach her by a letter I would write to her. To this he assented, and taking out my pocket memorandum and pencil, I said, "Now tell me your name." "William J. Cotton." His company and regiment were also noted down. "What is your wife's name?" "Mary J. Cotton." "Where does she live?" The precise address I cannot give. It was at some Cross Roads—either Fairfax Cross Roads, or in Fairfax county, South Carolina. "When and where were you wounded?" "Shot through the thigh on Sunday afternoon." "Do you expect to recover?" "Well, I have a good constitution, and if I could be taken somewhere where I could be sheltered from the sun and rain, I think I might get well. But the doctors are kind; they are doing all for me they can, but if it rains to-night, as I think it will, I suppose I will have to die." "Well, my friend," I said, "suppose you were to die, are you prepared for death?" After a pause and with deep emotion and heaving chest, and almost choking voice, he replied, "Well, I want you to tell Mary that I could never forget the promise I made her when I left home—O my poor wife, perhaps she is dead now, for she was sick and in bed when I left,—tell her I have kept it every day." "What was that promise?" "She made me promise that I would pray every day, and I could never forget that promise, and I have tried to pray, and somehow I feel that if I

never see my wife again on earth I will meet her in heaven." By this time I was in deep sympathy with him, and tried to commend him to the only Friend who could help him in the terrible condition he was in. He then further said, "Tell Mary that she must do the best she can."
While engaged with this man, other wounded men were calling me, thus, "say Mister, will you write me a letter to my mother?" "Will you write to my father?" Said one, "O, Mister, the doctor wants to cut my leg off; shall I let him do it?" He was shot through the knee. Another said, "Mister, you have a pair of scissors in your pocket; will you please throw them to me." When I threw him my scissors he struggled to sit up, leaning upon one elbow long enough to cut away his pantaloons, which were somewhat twisted around under his limb and pressed too tightly upon his wound. About that time Mr. Jacob S. Brand, another of our townsmen, came upon the scene, when I said, "Now, Jacob, if you have seen enough of the horrors of this scene, come and help me take down the messages for these men. Mr. Brand remained a short time and then left, leaving me alone with the men, but I continued until it became too dark to write. I had the messages of but four of them, and the case of the first which I have related is the only one I can recollect. When Gen. Lee's army was in our town, on its way to Gettysburg, I wrote letters to the addresses given me, and after showing the letters to one or two of our citizens, to see that I was not communicating improper information to the enemy, I gave the letters, unsealed, to an officer on Gen. Ewell's Staff, who said he would put them in their mail and send them to their destination. My memorandum, containing these records, was destroyed in the burning of our town in 1864, and I have never heard whether my letters were received. If this record should ever come under the notice of any of the persons referred to, it would afford me inexpressible pleasure to hear of the fact.

After leaving these wounded ones, but comparatively few of whose messages were taken, I crossed over to a narrow lane which intersected the Sharpsburg road. A worm fence, built upon a continuous heap of stone, ran along this lane, and for some distance along the Sharpsburg road northwardly. This stone wall, or heap, had evidently been used as a breast work, for it commanded the ravine up which the Union forces were expected to come. I was informed that the rebels were there outflanked and shot down in great numbers. This was evident from the great numbers of dead laying all along the lane, as far as I could see. Standing in one position, I touched with my cane nine dead bodies. While looking upon this terrible scene, an officer, who had been detailed to superintend the burial of the dead, came up the lane from the woods eastwardly, and said to me, "This is nothing; if you want to see dead rebels, just go over there to the brow of the hill; there they are lying in heaps." An old dry well, I was told by some of our party who had seen it, was filled almost to the top with dead and then covered over with earth. A dead rebel lay in a brick smoke house near by with a bullet hole in his forehead. He had evidently been a sharp shooter, and had used a hole where a brick had been left out for air and light, as a loop hole. The displacement of the dust in the hole showed this. Some sharp shooter on the other side had detected him, and watching his chance had planted a ball in his brain as he was looking out. This, be it remembered, was but a very small part of the field of the previous Sunday's battle, which extended North and South of the turnpike for a mile or more. Similar scenes of horror, no doubt, could have been seen along that line, as well as on the eastern slope of the mountain, up which the Union forces pressed their way and strewed the ground with their dead and wounded.

Looking about me as I stood amidst this scene of horrors, I saw that all my company had gone but Mr. Wampler. It was getting dark. The katydids were already lending their solemn dirge to the mournful scene, and an occasional shot from the batteries of the two great armies, which were manœuvring for positions for the great battle of the ensuing day, came booming up from the plain below, warning us that it was time for us to hasten away and seek shelter for the night. Coming down the mountain we met a minister, a friend of mine, who had fled before the approach of the rebels, and had been with me the day before, and was now returning to his charge. I inquired of him where we could find lodging in Boonsboro in case the hotels were filled. He told me to go to Mr. Lewis Watson and tell him who I was and he would keep us. Finding no place in the hotel, we went to Mr. Watson, and he kindly lodged Mr. Heyser and his son, Mr. Wampler and myself. In the morning, with the first appearance of daylight, the great battle of Antietam began. We were within about two miles of the scene of conflict in the rear of the Union line. The sound of the artillery was fearful. It resembled a succession of terrific discharges of thunder—scarcely a perceptible interval between them, and sometimes a half dozen or more at once. Mr. Watson told us that we should remain for breakfast, and when it was ready he called us into his parlor and handed me the Bible to lead in their family devotions. I motioned to him to give it to Mr. Heyser. Taking the Bible, Mr. Heyser read the 46th Psalm. Let the reader turn to that Psalm and read it and see how appropriate it was to the occasion. Amidst the terrific roar of two hundred pieces of artillery, which almost drowned his voice, he slowly, reverently, and with subdued tone, read the awfully significant words, *"The heathen raged; the kingdoms were moved; he uttered his voice; the earth melted. The Lord of hosts is with us; the God of Jacob is our refuge. Come, behold the works of the Lord, what desolations he hath made in the earth. He maketh wars to cease unto the end of the earth; he breaketh the bow, and cutteth the spear in sunder; he burneth the chariot in the fire. Be still and know that I am God."* His prayer, which followed, was about as appropriate as the scripture he read.

During part of the forenoon, while the great battle was in progress, I sat upon an eminence with a reporter of a New York paper. The field of battle was about two miles below us. It was about four miles long. The circular flight of the shells, as they flew hither and thither, and the dashing to and fro of the cavalry, were distinctly seen. With the aid of a glass some of the movements of the infantry were also visible. The whole valley below us was like a seething caldron of fire, and smoke rose up and hung like a dark pall, as if heaven were shutting out the terrible scene. It seemed hard to realize that upon that bloody field nearly 200,000 men —the flower and chivalry of the North and South—were engaged with the most approved weapons of destruction which modern science had invented to destroy each other, and that each hour of that day six hundred human beings were sent into an awful eternity, and twice that number were crippled and maimed for life. And what was all this for? Simply that a small part of our Nation might live upon the unrequitted labor of their fellow men, and upon the part of the heroes of the Union, that "the government of the people, by the people, and for the people, should not perish from the earth." The destiny of our government hung upon the issue of the struggle, and heaven gave the victory to the right.

During the progress of the battle many wounded soldiers came from the bloody field. Some were bleeding from ghastly wounds and begrimed with powder. They all told of the fearful whipping which the rebels were getting, and some told of the charging and counter-charging back and forth through the historic corn field, and about the Dunkard church. Occasionally a wounded officer would be brought from the field in an ambulance, and would be taken eastward over the mountain, toward Frederick. In a field south of the town, and guarded by Union soldiers, were two or three hundred rebel prisoners. In conversation with a particular friend, Rev. W. R. Coursey, then a resident of Boonsboro, while the battle was in progress, I asked him how he felt as to the probable issue of the conflict? We both knew that if the Union army was defeated, Baltimore and Washington would most likely be taken, and the whole Southern border of our State, as well as Maryland, be overrun and robbed by the victorious foe. Smilingly, he said, "I have no fear of the result. I saw both armies as they marched through here on Sunday and Monday, and the Boys in Blue are able to pick the rebels up one by one and smack them." He also related the following incident as word came from the field of the death of Gen. Mansfield: "As Gen. Mansfield rode by my house on Monday, at the head of his column, he said to Mrs. Coursey, as she stood at the door, 'Madam, would you have the kindness to make me a few biscuits for my supper?'" "Certainly, General, I will do so with pleasure." An Orderly was directed to remain for the biscuits which, in a short time, were ready for him. Two days afterward that veteran soldier sealed his devotion to his country by pouring out his life blood upon the field of battle.

About four o'clock a number of paroled officers from Harper's Ferry came to Boonsboro, and with them I rode in a wagon, which we hired, to Hagerstown. There all was excitement. The artillery fire seemed almost as distinct as at Boonsboro, and it ceased only at dark. About nine or ten o'clock, the same night, I crept into one of the cars of a long train which had brought a regiment of volunteers from Philadelphia, and had a free ride to Chambersburg. Two days after I in company with several others visited the field of Antietam, and saw there similar scenes to those witnessed at South Mountain. At the outskirts of Keedysville we were stopped by the guard, and the officer in command said to another, who reported that he with about ten thousand volunteers were encamped about Hagerstown, "Why don't you come on here, and we will end this cursed war at once?" At that time, unknown to those in command of the Union forces, the rebels were crossing the Potomac. If a Grant, a Sherman, or Sheridan had been in command, the after bloody battles with the army of Northern Virginia would have never occurred. The Potomac would have been its grave and winding sheet.

Immediately after the battle of Antietam many of the wounded who could bear transportion, were taken to the Hospitals at Washington, Baltimore, Frederick, Hagerstown and this place. About four hundred were brought here, and quartered in Franklin Hall, the large school house adjoining the jail, and the Academy. A number of persons connected with the Christian Commission came to this place to look after the wounded. The ladies of the town, through their Aid Society, rendered invaluable services in distributing towels, handkerchiefs and delicacies. In this benevolent work they were aided by ladies from the country, and adjoining towns. Fayetteville had a Ladies' Aid Society which greatly assisted in caring for these wounded men, sending many delicacies. The Steward of the School House Hospital, on King street, Mr. George Bayne, made weekly acknowledgments, through the town papers, of articles of food, &c. Among the names of the donors thus acknowledged are Mrs. Schofield, Mrs. Ebert, Mrs. Thompson, Mrs. Newman, Mrs. Nead, Mrs. Brewer, Mrs. Jordan, Mrs. Reeves, Mrs. Dr. Fisher, Mrs. Chambers, Mrs. Radebaugh, Mrs. Hutton, Mrs. Britton, Mrs. Hoke, Mrs. Trostle, Mrs. Sprecher, Mrs. Linn, Mrs. Long, Mrs. E. D. Reed, Mrs. Charles Eyster, Mrs. Wood, Mrs. Ritner, Lizzie Lester, Mrs. Banker, Mrs. Fry, Mrs. Lindsay, Mrs. W. Chambers, Mrs. Benj. Chambers, Miss Sarah Reynolds, Miss Sally Ann Chambers, Miss Susan B. Chambers, Mrs. Funk, Mrs. Emblek, Mrs. Miller, Mrs. Grier, Mrs. Auld, Miss Lizzie Flack, Mrs. Hull, Mrs. Grove, Mrs. Montgomery, Mrs. Stumbaugh, Mrs. Wunderlich, Mrs. Beatty, Mrs. Eckart, Mrs. Stine, Mrs. Gellespie, Mrs. Nill, Mrs. McGrath, Mrs. Dechart, Mrs. Huber, Mrs. Spangler, Mrs. Sewell, Mrs. Fahnestock and Mrs. Perry. The foregoing names I have copied from the Steward's acknowledgments in the *Valley Spirit.* If any have been omitted, the fault is not mine. This, it will be recollected, is a list of donors to that one hospital alone. The other two fared equally as well. Affecting scenes were frequently seen when persons would visit these hospitals in search of friends and relatives. Fathers from a distance would find a son with arm or limb amputated, or otherwise wounded. Devoted wives would find their husbands maimed and suffering. A woman from Philadelphia came here to see after her husband. He was shot through the lung, and she found him in Franklin Hall Hospital. Situated next to the Hall we gave her a home. When her husband was able to be moved he was carried into our house, where his devoted wife cared for him. In a few weeks he was able to travel and his wife took him home. Some time after this my wife and I, while walking in Philadelphia, were somewhat surprised and confused by a woman rushing up and embracing and kissing us. She was that soldier's wife. We visited their home and saw her husband. He was able to work at his trade—book binding, but had a cough. His physician said he thought his lung was affected, and he was going into consumption. We never heard of him afterwards. The scenes of suffering which occurred in these hospitals, and the tears which were shed over wounded, sick, dying and dead soldiers, can never be told. They are parts of the price paid for the perpetuity of the government. It was a fearful price, but the government is worth all it cost.

A gentleman came into our store shortly after the bringing of these wounded here. He was on his way to the battle field. He requested me to go to each of the hospitals here and take down the names of all the Massachusetts soldiers, with the nature of their wounds, and send the list to the *Boston Journal.* Soon after its publication papers, letters, &c., came to me for some of these soldiers. About eight years after the war I was introduced to the President of the Young Men's Christian Association in Dayton, Ohio. He said he had been in Chambersburg once, but under such circumstances that he knew but little of the place. He said he was a member of a Massachusetts regiment, and had been wounded at the battle of Antietam and brought here. I referred to the circumstance of my visit, when he said he recollected it. Our acquaintance formed under such peculiar circumstances, was kept up for many years. He was afterwards transferred to Baltimore to take charge of the Association there. About two years ago failing health compelled him to resign his position, after which he went back to Massachusetts.

Many occurrences of an interesting and touching character might be related, where scenes of suffering and death, amid the agonies and tears and prayers of newly arrived friends, took place in families throughout the town where wounded soldiers were taken and cared for. I have been present on such occasions, and have knelt around dying beds where departing heroes were ebbing away their life, while fathers, mothers and brothers wept and sobbed, and then, wrapped in the folds of the flag they loved so well, and for which they gave their lives, their lifeless bodies were borne back to desolated homes. Space however forbids these details.

NOTE.—Since the publication of the foregoing, some persons have said that the alarm which occasioned the ringing of the Court House bell, and the planting of the cannon in and about the Diamond, occurred at a later period, probably sometime before the Invasion, or at the time of Early's raid across the Potomac. I have had written records by which to fix the dates of all the events referred to except this one circumstance, and I may have erred in placing it. If I have not fixed the precise time upon which it occurred, then it must have been prior to Lee's invasion.

I should have stated in this chapter that during the period of excitement prior to the battle of Antietam, certain persons were empowered to press horses for the use of the military, and many horses were taken from the farmers and others, some of which were never returned nor paid for.

CHAPTER VII.

STUART'S RAID.

In consequence of the defeat of the rebels at the battles of South Mountain and Antietam, and their retreat to the south bank of the Potomac, all fears for the safety of the border for that time subsided, and our town settled down to its usual quiet. By the first of October the military called here to defend the State from invasion had all returned to their homes, and the only visible evidences of the recent exciting scenes through which we had passed, was the presence among us of about four hundred sick and wounded soldiers in the three hospitals named in the previous chapter. These were carefully attended by the surgeons and stewards left in charge, as well as by our own people and those in the country and neighboring towns. The Ladies Aid Society, comprising many of the persons named in the previous chapter, was unremitting in its attentions to these sick and wounded patriots. The ladies composing this organization visited the hospitals daily, and supplied freely such delicacies as were needed, and not furnished by the regular service. Once in a while one of these soldiers died, and his body was either taken away by friends, or buried with military honors in our beautiful cemetery. Between us and the defeated hosts of rebellion stood the grand army of the Potomac, constituting, as we supposed, an impassible barrier through, or around which, no one dreamed of the foe passing. Those of our citizens who had gone to distant places upon the approach of the foe, had returned. Merchandize and other valuables which had been sent away, or secreted, had been brought back. Our stores, shops, and other places of business had been reopened, and freshly stocked to meet the demands of customers. All was quiet, not only along the Potomac, but along the Conococheague. But another danger was about to burst upon us, and we knew it not. It came unheralded, and as a sudden clap of thunder out of a cloudless sky. Its very unexpectedness added to the alarm which it occasioned.

On Friday, Oct. 10th, rain fell all day. Business as a consequence was dull, and I took advantage of the dullness to re-arrange some things which I had just brought back from the places where they had been sent upon the approach of the foe. A gentleman from Mercersburg had been in the store during the afternoon, and was telling of the fright which had been occasioned a few days previously by some mischievous ones by getting up a story of the rebels coming. He laughed heartily over the ludicrousness of the affair; but his laughter was turned into consternation when he fell into the hands of the raiders on his way home.

About half past four o'clock in the afternoon, a soldier rode up to the front of our store, and hitching his horse came in. He was a splendid specimen of a man. Tall—about six feet, well shaped and muscular, he looked the very ideal of a soldier. He had on a blue overcoat, but the balance of his clothing was decidedly butternut. A saber dangled at his side, and pistols were in his holsters, and probably about his person. He walked up to the counter and asked for a pair of socks. While selecting a pair, seemingly in no hurry, he took in the whole store. I said to him, "Are you from the Army of the Potomac?" "No sir," said he, "I'm from Virginia; just from the sod." When he handed me a piece of silver in payment for his purchase, my suspicions were confirmed.— After another survey of the contents of the store, he went out, mounted his horse and rode away. That he was a rebel, and a scout from the approaching foe, there can be no question. After gathering the information of the defenceless condition of the town, he doubtless carried the information to his commanding officer.— That others may have visited other parts of the town is altogether probable.

I think it can be shown, as it will be in their appropriate places in these reminiscences, that before every appearance of the rebels in force across our borders, they were preceded by scouts. One of these visited one of the camps south of the town previous to Jenkin's Raid, in June 1863. And it will be recollected by some of our older citizens, that in the fall of 1864, after the destruction of the town by fire, Gen. Couch, then in command of the Department of the Susquehanna, with headquarters in this place, called a public meeting of the citizens in the basement of the M. E. Church—the Court House and other public buildings having been burnt, and there informed us that the rebels were about to make another raid; that the usual indications of such an intention were evident, and that we should not only arm and organize for their reception, but put our merchandize and valuables in places of safety. The indications which pointed to this intended raid, were the arrest of several suspicious persons travelling along the railroad from Hagerstown to Harrisburg.

During the afternoon of the day in question—the day of Stuart's raid—some five or six soldiers rode up to the front of Mr. Bratton's hotel, four miles west of town. After some consultation with Mr. Bratton, one of them said, "Are you for the Union, or the rebels?" Mr. Bratton supposing them to be Union soldiers, said, "Well boys, get off and come in, and if you will keep old Jackson away, I will treat." "Are you afraid of old Jackson?" said one. "No, I'm not afraid, but the women are." "Well," said another, after they had taken a drink, "We are rebels." And to convince the old gentleman they unbuttoned their blue overcoats and displayed the rebel gray.

At about 6 o'clock in the evening, Mr. Samuel Etter came in the store and said, "Well, the rebels are coming now for certain." Mr. Anthony Hollar, then in our employ, said, "No sir, that's all played out; you can't come that over us." "Well, if you don't believe it, go over to Judge Kimmell's office and see for yourselves. There's two men there from St. Thomas who saw the rebels, and were chased by them half ways to town." Fearing that I would be laughed at were I to appear to credit this story, and yet half believing it, I went out the back door and went around to the Judge's office, and there saw Mr. David A. Fohl and Daniel Stitzel, of St. Thomas, who assured us of the fact of the rebels coming. Mr. Fohl, who is employed in the office of Mr. McKinley, of the Montgomery Hotel in this place, gives me the following statement of this occurrence.— Information of the coming of the rebels was sent to St. Thomas from near Loudon by Mr. John Mullen. Immediately upon the reception of this news, the church bells were rung, and the Home Guards—about twenty-five men, turned out. Mr. Fohl rode to the hill at the lower end of the town, and from it saw the pike from the bridge where Mr. Campbell lived, as far back as he could see, crowded with rebel soldiers. He at once rode back to town, made some hurried preparations, and, joined by Mr. Stitzel, rode rapidly for Chambersburg, pursued for several miles by some of the foe.

Assured of the fact of the approach of the rebels, I hastily returned to our store and closed it, and went up stairs to one of the front windows to see the coming invaders.

About this time the Court House bell was rung as the signal for the gathering of our Home Guards. A supply of muskets was procured from one of the warehouses, where a number had been stored, and the command—about fifty or seventy-five in number—under Captain John Jeffries, started across the Diamond and down Market Street. As the head of the column reached the bridge, they met a squad of probably twenty-five cavalry, the one in advance having a stick with a white handkerchief attached to it. A bugler riding by his side sent out the first notes from rebel lips yet heard in our town. "Halt," cried Captain Jeffries, "Who are you, and by what authority do you come here?" "By the authority of the Confederate Army and Gen. Hampton. He wants to see the authorities of the town." "There are no authorities here sir, they are all left." About this time Captain John Eyster, who had been in actual service, said, "Capt Jeffries, these men have a flag of truce, and it must be respected.— Take them to Judge Kimmell's office." Mr. Jeffries informed me that he saw a dirty white rag on the end of a stick, but he didn't know what the thunder that was for. About this time the Home Guards, seeing their inability to defend the place, scattered to their homes and secreted their arms. Coming up through the Diamond, the flag was hastily lowered and carried away by Mr. George Snyder, and the rope cut so that the hated rebel rag should not wave from that pole. Men usually like to be complimented by some title, as Esquire, or Colonel, or Captain, but the captain of the Home Guard on that occasion thought that it would not be healthy to be called by that title in the presence of the enemy, and when some one addressed him as "Captain Jeffries," that worthy officer exclaimed, "For gracious sake, men, don't call me captain here." He worthily wears that title now, and, I suppose, ever shall while he lives.

As the rebel squad rode into the Diamond, the bugle sounded out its shrill notes, announcing to our people that the foe was truly in our midst. They rode over to the front of Judge Kimmell's office, and one or two dismounted and went in. When in the Judge's office these men assured those present, Col. A. K. McClure, Mr. T. B. Kennedy, and a few others, that Gen. Wade Hampton, with a force of about twenty-eight hundred men, with four pieces of artillery, were on the hill west of the town and demanded its surrender. The Judge said, "Well, we don't like to surrender without knowing the truth of what you say." The officer in command then said, "Well, gentlemen, a number of you accompany us to the west end of the town, and you will see for yourselves." That officer's name, Judge Kimmell thinks, was "Snodgrass." Judge Kimmell, Col. McClure and Mr. T. B. Kennedy procured horses and accompanied the guard out west Market Street to the brow of the hill this side of the Western Hotel, and were there introduced to Gens. Wade Hampton and J. E. B. Stuart.— This was the first intimation they had that General Stuart was along with the invaders—his name not having been previously mentioned. After the formalities of the introduction, Judge Kimmell inquired: "Well General, What is it that you want?" "The unconditional surrender of the place." "But what about unarmed citizens and women and children?" "You know that we do not wage war against such." "How about private property?" "That will be respected."— At this juncture Col. McClure said, "Well General, we are without protection, and of course can offer no resistance, and your terms must be accepted." Judge Kimmell then proposed that they would return to the centre of the town, and disperse whatever persons might be collected and might make trouble. To this the Gen. assented, but immediately put the column in motion and its head entered the Diamond as soon as they did. The whole command—said to be about 2800, with four pieces of artillery, filed through the Diamond, some remaining there, and others going out to picket all the roads leading to the town.

Simultaneously almost with the entrance of these troops, the telegraph wires were cut, and the bakeries and warehouses where flour was stored visited and cleaned out of their contents. The knowledge which they possessed of the location of these places, and the full acquaintance they evinced of the by-roads by which they came and departed, indicated the presence among them of one or more persons entirely familiar with our town and county. We have heard the name of a person, then a citizen of the county, used in that infamous connection, but fearing to do him injustice in the absence of positive knowledge, his name is withheld.—His previous record would strengthen the conviction of his guilt. Officers were also detailed to parole the sick and wounded in the hospitals. Some of the soldiers immediately put on their best clothing, saying that if any was taken it should be their old. In Franklin Hall were a number of colored men, who, a short time previous, had escaped from the rebel army. These were terribly alarmed and hid themselves up under the roof in the attic. A number of officers also visited the bank and demanded the money in its vault. Mr. Messersmith, the cashier, unlocked the door and led them into the vault and showed them a few pennies—all it contained. The specie had, upon the approach of the enemy a month or two previously, been stored in Philadelphia; and between the time when the news of the approach of the foe was received, and their entrance into the town, Mr. Messersmith had wisely carried away and secreted all the money in the vault, excepting some small change. When the officers saw this change, one of them said that such a poor bank had better be helped than any thing taken from it. With the exceptions of the bakeries, warehouses, and a few shops entered without the knowledge of the officers, the terms of surrender were respected and private property unmolested.

As one of the amusing evidences of the unexpectedness of this raid, the following occurrence, communicated by Mr. P. D. Frey, one of the participants, is given. A political meeting was announced to be held at Marion, and the Chambersburg Band was sent there to furnish music for the occasion. But owing to the inclemency of the weather (the rain) or some other cause unknown to the gentlemen composing the Band, not a single speaker put in an appearance, and but few spectators were present. After treating the slim audience to a few pieces of excellent music, and no one appearing to address the meeting, the party started for home. There were present on that occasion, Messrs. H. B. Hatnick, D. M. Eiker, J. W. Leedy, P. D. Frey, George Gruce, Godfrey Snyder, and a musician from Cumberland, Md. The hack in which they rode and the two fine animals by which it was drawn, were owned by Mr. Samuel F. Greenawalt, who also drove for them. When about three miles from Chambersburg, they met Mr. Frederick Walk, who told them that the rebels were in town, and that according to the terms of surrender private property was to be respected, but horses and all public property were liable to seizure. A council was held, and the musicians decided to walk to town and Mr. Greenawalt should not enter but take his team to a place of safety. This Mr. G. refused to do, and drove on towards town. When they reached the school house on the hill on the Slaughenhaup farm, about a half mile from the edge of the town, they were commanded to halt by a rebel vidette. After ascertaining who the party were and where they were going, they were allowed to pass on. After proceeding a short distance they were again halted. At this point the road and adjoining fields were filled with men and horses and several pieces of artillery. Gen. Hampton in command then was called, and after satisfying himself that the story told by the men was true, he allowed them to proceed and ordered the road to be cleared for them—himself riding by the side of the carriage. Upon reaching the Diamond the names of the party were taken and they were paroled to appear at Gen. Stuart's headquarters at 6 o'clock in the morning. Mr. Greenawalt was about to drive his team into the alley leading to his livery, when an officer ordered him to drive over to the old depot where Gen. Stuart was at that time. Arriving there the rebels were about to appropriate his horses, but Mr. Greenawalt pleaded to be permitted to take them to his stable and give them one more "good, last supper." He was allowed to do so under promise that he would turn them over in the morning. No sooner, however, had he driven under his carriage shed, than the harness was stripped off and the animals were taken up an alley as far as German street, and then turning east he went out what is called "long lane." Fortunately there were no pickets to intercept him in that lane, and he succeeded in saving his valuable horses. It is needless to say that the gentlemen composing the Band failed to put in their appearance to Gen. Stuart the next morning, for had they done so, they might have been held for the delivery of the horses.

Gen. Stuart and other officers lodged that night at the Franklin Hotel. Among the guests was an officer—a Colonel or Lieut. Colonel—whose term of service had expired, and he had with him his papers certifying to that fact. His papers were respected, Gen. Stuart observing that he was gratified that his papers were all right, otherwise their relations would be different. Encouraged by his treatment, the officer told the General that he would like to have some conversation with him, and in the presence of J. W. Douglass, Esq., in a side room of the hotel, he put in a plea for the return of his horse—a very valuable animal—which had been taken. To this Gen. Stuart replied, "We are not horse thieves, nevertheless we do want horses, and shall have to retain yours." The General, Mr. Douglass says, was in excellent humor and very lively.

This body of Cavalry, under that dashing leader, who had made a successful raid around Gen. McClellan's army upon the Peninsula near Richmond, was upon a similar movement around the same army and under the same commander. It crossed the Potomac above Williamsport at Cherry Run Ford, and made a rapid march through Mercersburg, thence by Bridgeport to the Pittsburg pike, which it entered a short distance west of the gate house beyond St. Thomas, and from that point to Chambersburg. Previous to reaching this place the rebels, for some cause unknown, captured Perry A. Rice, Esq., Daniel Shaffer, C. Louderbaugh, John McDowell, George G. Rupley and George Steiger, of Mercersburg; Joseph Wingert, Post Master at Clay Lick Hall, and William Conner, of St. Thomas. Steiger escaped at Bridgeport. McDowell, Rupley, Louderbaugh and Wingert were either released or made their escape here, and Rice, Shaffer and Conner were taken to Richmond and incarcerated in Libby prison. Shaffer and Conner were afterwards exchanged and returned home. Rice died in imprisonment. Mr. Rice lodged the night the rebels were here in the Franklin Hotel, and was importuned by some of our citizens to make his escape but he did not. The last we saw of him he was seated upon a caisson in front of the Mansion House. He formerly studied law in Chambersburg, and was esteemed by all who knew him. In passing through Fairfield, Adams county, one or two citizens of that place were also captured, but in the excitement of crossing the Potomac into Virginia, they escaped. The reason why none of our citizens were taken was probably because the terms of the surrender of the town exempted citizens from molestation. It was said, however, that pressing inquiries were made for the post master here, but that official was prudently absent.

On the following morning—Saturday—the raiders took their departure eastward across the South Mountain. Before leaving a guard was detached to burn the Depot House, the Machine Shops, and the Warehouse of Messrs Wunderlich & Nead. The latter was burnt because it contained the ammunition taken from Gen. Longstreet. In this warehouse and in some cars upon the siding, were a considerable amount of government stores, consisting of clothing, hats, boots, pistols, &c. As much of these as the guard could carry were taken with them. Some soldiers had on as many as three hats. After the guard departed some of our citizens endeavored to save the burning buildings, and adjoining property, but they were much annoyed by the exploding shells. These did not go off at once as some feared, but gradually as the fire reached them. Fearing for the safety of the sick and wounded in the lower end of the town, in case the whole of the ammunition in the burning warehouse would explode at once, many of the ladies who had been ministering to their necessities went to their assistance, and at the usual hour at noon these good Samaritans had dinner prepared for these men.

Upon the reception of the information at army headquarters of this raid, a strong cavalry force was despatched from the army of the Potomac near Sharpsburg to the fords of the Potomac at Williamsport and Cherry Run. And when it was ascertained that the raiders had gone east, another force was sent in that direction to intercept them, but they came up only in time to see the last of the raiding force cross the river below Frederick. A regiment of Vermont soldiers, with a battery of four field pieces, also came here on Sunday. They took their position in Shetter's woods, along the Baltimore pike, east of the town. The artillery was planted on the hill a little beyond their encampment. On Monday about noon a report reached town that the rebels had been intercepted east of the mountain and were coming back. The bank, stores and shops were closed, and many of our citizens armed themselves and joined the soldiers upon the outskirts of the town. Horseman after horseman came dashing in from towards Fayetteville, announcing the approach of the enemy. No one, however, saw them, but had their information from some one else. At length the scare subsided, the people returned to town and resumed business, and as soon as it was ascertained that the raiders had crossed back into Virginia, the soldiers were recalled. One of the men of this Vermont regiment, a year or two ago, visited our town as a minister of the gospel, and went out to Shetter's woods—then Messersmith's—and viewed the place where he was encamped.

Gen. Stuart took with him, as was supposed, about 1,000 horses from Franklin county.

On Tuesday afternoon, Oct. 18th, the town was again thrown into a state of excitement by the report that another rebel raid was about bursting upon us. The information was that a strong rebel force was seen near Loudon, and was advancing towards Chambersburg. This report was soon backed up by another statement that one of our citizens had been up the pike and had been turned back by them. The last person named said he did not see the rebels, but had been advised by some one to turn back as it was *reported* that the rebels were up the road. The Public Square by this time was pretty well filled with people, discussing the probabilities of the truth of the rumor, and casting anxious glances in a westward direction. A number of farmers living west of the town, came in, bringing their horses with them and passing on to a place of safety. The soldiers encamped on the Fair Grounds west of the town, being without arms and ammunition, were ordered to strike their tents and leave. They passed through town and down below Scotland. Courier after courier was despatched in the direction of the rumored approaching foe, but they returned with the story that they did not see the rebels, but some one told them that some one else had told him that a man up the road had heard that they were coming. At last it was ascertained that the whole affair originated in several children having said that they saw some cavalrymen up in the neighborhood of Loudon. They were Union cavalry engaged in purchasing horses for the use of the Government.

The last raid of the season, and before the excitements of the summer and fall had given way to the quiet of winter, was by a single person, and that person a woman. On Friday, Nov. 21st, a somewhat singular looking woman made her appearance in town. She came by the Western turnpike, mounted on a venerable looking gray horse. Her dress and general appearance indicated that she was a stranger in this section of the country. On alighting and securing her horse to an awning post on Main street, she proceeded to several of our drug stores and made extensive purchases of quinine, morphine, opium, &c. Suspicion being excited that she was purchasing these articles for purposes unallowable during war, she was arrested by order of Capt. Ashmead, A. Q. M., then on duty here, and searched, when several hundred dollars worth of these drugs were found concealed in secret recesses of her dress. This woman had spent the night previous at the hotel of Mr. Josiah Allen, three miles west of the town, where she stated that she was in search of several horses which had been taken by the rebels from her father in Virginia, and having heard that a number had been turned loose by Stuart's cavalry in this section, she thought that she might possibly find her father's among them. She had in her possession a pass from Gen. Banks, dated about a year previous. This woman was ascertained to be a Mrs. Sloan, and that her residence was near Winchester, Virginia. She was sent to jail for a while and was subsequently discharged.

The people of Chambersburg have often been found fault with for not rising up and repelling this raid of Gen. Stuart. Those that thus blame us fail to remember that a large part of our able bodied men were away from home in their country's service, and that at most we could not have raised more than a few hundred persons. These, without organization, arms and discipline, would have been of but little account against twenty-eight hundred armed, disciplined and experienced soldiers, backed by four pieces of artillery. And had resistance by citizens been undertaken, it would not only have been injudicious and fool-hardy, but would have subjected them, our whole population of women and children and their homes and property, to destruction and plunder.

CHAPTER VIII.

JENKINS' RAID.

Throughout the winter of 1862-3, quiet prevailed in Chambersburg and along the border, interrupted only by the usual recruiting and the presence of considerable number of soldiers in our midst, the disheartening influence of the repulse of our army at Fredericksburg, and the occasional bringing to this place of some one of its fallen sons for interment. One of these fallen ones was John S. Oaks, son of our former fellow townsman, David Oaks, Esq. John S. Oaks was a member of Captain Doebler's company from this place, and connected with the 126th Regiment of Pennsylvania Volunteers.— He was wounded at the battle of Fredericksburg, Virginia, and taken to one of the Hospitals in Washington, where on Thursday, Dec. 25th, in the presence of his sorrowing father and mother, who had hastened to his bedside upon the reception of the news of his presence there, he died. His body was subsequently brought to this place, and on the afternoon of the Sabbath following, Dec. 28th, followed by a large concourse of citizens and soldiers, he was interred in Cedar Grove Cemetery.

Immediately after the battle of Chancellorsville, and the falling back of the Union Army to the north bank of the Rappahannock, the authorities at Washington were convinced from the aggressive movements of the enemy, and from papers captured from General Stuart's command, that another invasion north of the Potomac was contemplated. Early in the month of June this aggressive movement was begun, and the rebel hordes again passed into the Shenandoah Valley, and marched northward.

On Saturday, June 13th, the divisions of Rhodes and Early of Ewell's Corps, leading the advance of Lee's army on its way to the invasion of the State, reached Winchester, Va., and after a series of battles lasting two days, defeated Gen. Milroy, who with a force of 8,000 or 10,000 men occupied that place. Milroy's army was driven in confusion from Winchester and about 2,000 infantry and cavalry succeeded in crossing the Potomac and reaching Bloody Run in Bedford Co., Pennsylvania. The General with several hundred men and a considerable train of wagons reached Harper's Ferry. The wagons were sent by way of Hagerstown and Chambersburg down to Harrisburg to prevent them from falling into the hands of the pursuing rebels.— This remnant of Milroy's army were reorganized at Bloody Run, and, joined by recruits from the Pennsylvania militia, they stood guard over the upper fords of the Potomac.

On Sunday evening, June 14th, information was received of the disaster to our forces in the Valley, and the approach of the enemy. Immediately, as upon former occasions, when news of rebel approaches were received, great confusion and excitement prevailed. The usual work of sending away and secreting merchandise and other valuables was begun. We opened our store and packed and sent away some of our goods; and during the next day we stored the balance of our stock in a beer vault, under the back building of the residence of Dr. Langheim, adjoining our store. The railroad men here were also prompt to prepare for the emergency, and by noon of Monday had all their portable property ready for shipment at their pleasure.

On this day, Monday, 15th, we witnessed the greatest excitement which had occurred up to that time during all the history of the war. Large numbers of colored persons, as at the time of Gen. Bank's retreat, men, women and children, came streaming through the town, bearing with them articles of clothing, furniture, &c. Horses, wagons, and cattle crowded every avenue of escape northward. About ten o'clock in the morning, the advance of General Milroy's retreating wagon train came dashing down Main Street, attended by a few cavalry and affrighted wagon-masters, all of whom declared that the rebels were in close pursuit; that a large part of the train had been captured, and that the enemy were about to enter Chambersburg. This startling information, coming from men who had fought valiantly until the enemy had got nearly within sight of them, naturally gave a fresh impetus to our citizens, and the rush from town assumed immense proportions. As these wagons, drawn by tired and jaded horses, came dashing down Main Street, the drivers alternately lashing their teams and looking back to see if the foe was within sight, the scene of terror and confusion was perfectly terrific. Said one whose courage never failed during all the excitements of the war, up to that event, and afterwards to its close, "Of all the exciting events which have taken place since the beginning of the war, this is the worst, and I hope I may never witness such an awful scene again." Near the corner of Main and Queen streets, a horse dropped dead; and when opposite our store one of the teamsters stopped, and in order to lighten his load that he might go faster, took from his wagon and set upon the side walk a large box, with the remark, "Take care of that." It proved to be the regimental chest of a New York Regiment, and contained some parts of a uniform, blanks for company reports, books on military tactics, &c. In a communication to the *New York Tribune*, after the falling back of Gen. Jenkins, giving a detailed statement of his operations while here, I noticed this chest and gave the regiment it belonged to. The only application my article brought was from an officer to ascertain whether it contained a photograph, with instructions where to send it. It was not in the chest. The chest was finally turned over to Provost Marshall Eyster.

At length, and when the panic was at its height, Lieut. Palmer, then on Provost duty here, advanced from the front of the Franklin Hotel, pistol in hand, and ordered the teamsters to halt. This determined act of a cool and brave officer brought the whole column of panic stricken soldiers and teamsters to a halt, after which they were permitted to proceed slowly down the valley towards Harrisburg. This stampede, it was said, occurred near the Potomac, and broken wagons and dead or exhausted horses were strewn all along the way to this place. The rebels however were not within twenty miles of them, for at 10½ A. M., near the time this train reached our town, Gen. Jenkins entered and passed through Hagerstown.

At an early hour in the evening of this day, information of the approach of Jenkins' cavalry was received, and about 11 o'clock at night they had reached the southern end of the town. Some few were sent forward to reconnoiter, and two of them were unhorsed and captured in the Diamond, as will be related in its proper place. About two hundred more were detailed to make a rapid charge into the town after those scouts, and these were immediately followed by the balance of the command—about 2,000 in all.

Seated at an open window in the second story of our house over our store room, and overlooking the Diamond, I heard the clatter of horses' feet coming rapidly down Main Street. When opposite the residence of Mr. H. M. White the report of a gun was heard. Some eight or ten cavalrymen rode into the Diamond and passed through it on down Main Street, except about four or five. In the darkness—the gas in front of the bank only being lighted, they became separated, and one of them, evidently the officer in command, who was over near the bank, called out in a peculiarly Southern tone, which is about half negro—"Hawkins! Hawkins!! Whar the D—l are you, Hawkins?" If *Lieut. Smith*—for such was the gentleman's name, as will appear hereafter, had called upon John Selders and Thad. Mahon instead of his Satanic majesty, they *might* have given him the information he so earnestly desired, but they were about that time having a little matter of business transacted with "Hawkins" over on the Court House pavement. But the Lieutenant's anxiety concerning his friend was soon relieved, for on his going across the Diamond to ascertain what had become of him, he fell into the hands of Seiders, and soon thereafter joined the object of his anxiety, both of them however horseless and without arms.

Following this call for his absent comrade, the officer again called out, "Whar's the Mayau of this town? Whar's the Mayau of this town? If the Mayau does not come here in five minutes we will burn the town." In a short time the two hundred detailed to follow these scouts came thundering down Main street, followed by the balance of the command. The larger part passed on through the town and out to the grounds of Col. McClure, along the Philadelphia pike, where they picketed their horses in the Colonel's clover field. Gen. Jenkins and his staff did the Colonel the honor to lodge with him over night at his fine mansion, after first partaking of a bountiful supper prepared for them—the honors of the table being royally done by his accomplished wife, in the absence of the Colonel, who had discretely placed himself beyond the possibility of capture and sojourn in a Southern clime. Leaving Jenkins and his staff so comfortably quartered for the night, we will go back to relate some incidents which occurred in and about the Diamond.

As the scouts came galloping down Main street, with carbines levelled and cocked, the darkness prevented them from seeing some piles of stones, lime and sand in front of Mr. H. M. White's residence, then being built, and one of the horses stumbled and threw his rider into a mortar bed. This fall caused his carbine to go off, and he, as well as the cavalry with him, supposed that a citizen had fired on them. Simultaneously with the report of this carbine Mr. Jacob S. Brand, then living where Mr. Isaac Stine's grocery now is, threw open the shutters of a second story window to see what was transpiring. Some cavalry then opposite this window, hearing the opening of these shutters, cried out that the shot came from that place, and a number of them went to the door seeking admittance, and declaring that they would hang the man who fired the shot. Mrs. Brand became greatly alarmed and urged her husband to go up into the attic and hide himself. At length to gratify her he complied, but finding his hiding place so very warm, and concluding that if the house was searched and he found secreted, their suspicions would be confirmed, he came forth from the attic. But as the soldiers were yet at his door clamoring for entrance, and threatening to break in, he at the urgent solicitation of his wife crept into a bake oven in his yard, and drew to the iron door. But if the attic was too *warm* for him the oven was too *hot*, for that same day it had been used to bake bread. After shifting himself from one hand and knee to the other until he could endure it no longer, he once more came forth to brave the foe. In the early morning a member of Mr. John Jeffries' family, a few doors adjacent, came over and inquired the occasion of the wrath of the rebels, saying that they were overheard to declare that as soon as it was daylight they were going to search the house and hang the men they might find. These ladies then hit upon the expedient of disguising Mr. Brand and having him leave the house. Accordingly he was arrayed in one of Mrs. Brand's dresses, and a large, flowing sun bonnet was put upon his head to hide his beard. In this disguise he went out the back door, passed up the lot in the presence of the foe, many of whom were in the alley, and crossed over to the residence of Mr. Jeffries where he was disrobed, and where he was undisturbed. Like Jeff. Davis Mr. Brand found his last ditch in a woman's clothes; but, unlike that arch traitor, he passed undetected. Whether his better luck was owing to his more elaborate toilet, or to the fact that he had unsuspecting Southern rebels to deal with rather than shrewd, inquisitive Northern Yankees, or to his huge sun bonnet I am unable to say. I rather think that it was the sun bonnet that did the business. The situation of Mr. Brand was an alarming one, and he availed himself of the only method of escape which presented itself; and for this he is indebted to the ingenuity of women. Mr. Brand says that while it will look "a little rough" to see this circumstance in print, he yet consents that it may be so used as an historical fact, and as going to show some of the dangers to which our people were exposed in those perilous times. Shortly after the entrance of the advanced pickets into the Diamond, and while some of them were yet back at the door of Mr. Brand, threatening vengeance upon him, a cavalryman rode up to Mr. John A. Seiders and T. M. Mahon, Esq., as they stood upon the Court House pavement, and, supposing them to belong to their party, inquired in what direction the balance of the squad had gone. These two men had just returned home from the service, and they concluded to try their hands on that fellow. Neither of them were armed, but Mahon, using a plastering lath which he held in his hand as a sword, grabbed one rein of the bridle and Seiders the other and quietly demanded his surrender. He at once dismounted, and his sabre, pistol,—the other taken by Seiders—and spurs, were at once taken by Mahon, who quickly mounted the horse and rode rapidly out Market street to Third, up Third to Queen, and down Queen to the Market House into which he rode. While there a party of cavalry rode down Second street towards Market, and Mahon, as soon as they passed, started at a rapid gait out Queen. At the junction of Queen and Washington streets he encountered a squad, who called upon him to halt, but he flew on out towards Fayetteville. At Downey's he turned from the pike and proceeded to Scotland. There on the next day he gave the horse into the care of another, and after watching the destruction of the railroad bridge at that place, he eluded the pickets and entered Chambersburg, and reported to the railroad officials the burning of the bridge. Finding that the rebels were on the hunt for him, he, after a short time hid in the house of his law preceptor, William McClellan, Esq., left and found refuge in safer quarters. Mr. Mahon desires me to present his compliments to *Mr. George Hawkins*, if he is yet alive and this should come to his notice, and to assure him that the saddle, sabre, carbine and case of medicines, borrowed of him under such pressing circumstances, are all safely kept, and he will be happy to return them to him now that "this cruel war is over." Immediately after the departure of Mahon with his prize—the rebel having been handed over to Mr. Henry Peiffer and George Welsh, who started with him towards the jail but released him when they found that they were likely to be caught—another cavalryman, Lieut. Smith, rode up to where Mr. Seiders was standing and inquired what had become of his comrade. Seiders now being armed with one of the pistols taken from Hawkins, presented it and demanded his surrender. To this demand he at once complied and dismounted. Seiders disarmed him, taking his sabre, pistols and spurs, and mounting his horse rode rapidly out east Market street. At Market and Second streets he encountered the head of the column which passed the Market House while Mahon was in it. To their command to halt he paid no attention but put his horse upon his speed and galloped out towards Fayetteville. Arriving at Fayetteville he took an inventory of his capture, and it was found to be as follows: A valuable horse, saddle, four blankets rolled up and fastened behind the saddle, two fine pistols, sabre and belt, and a pair of saddle bags, containing a dress coat, two shirts, a Testament, a pack of cards, a package of love letters, some smoking tobacco, and several other articles. Mr. Seiders desires me to present his compliments to Lieut. Smith, and say to him that in case he is yet living, and this article should fall under his notice, that he will be happy to return to him whatever of these articles he has preserved. From Fayetteville Mr. Seiders proceeded to Cumberland county, and throughout the whole period of the invasion he made good use of his captured horse in the way of scouting service, some of which will be detailed in a chapter on "Scouting," yet to follow.

I return now from this extended but interesting digression to our main narrative. After spending the night under the hospitable roof of Col. McClure, Gen. Jenkins and staff came early in the morning of Tuesday, 16th, into town and established his headquarters at the Montgomery hotel. One of the first acts of the rebel chieftain, after arriving in town, was to issue an order requiring all arms in possession of our citizens, whether public or private, to be brought to the front of the Court House within two hours; and in case of disobedience, houses were to be searched, and all in which arms were found concealed were to be lawful objects of plunder. Many of our citizens complied with this humiliating order, and a committee of our people was appointed to take down the names of all who brought in arms. Some, of course, did not comply, but enough did so to avoid a general search and probable sacking of the town. Capt. Fitzhugh, Jenkin's chief of staff--the same officer who took so prominent a part in the burning of the town a year afterwards—assorted the guns as they were brought in, retaining those that could be used by his men, and twisting and breaking such as were unfit for this service. This he did by striking them over the stone steps in front of the Court House, or twisting them out of shape in the ornamental attachments of the iron gas posts. When Dr. W. H. Boyle brought in a beautiful silver mounted Sharp's rifle, Capt. Fitzhugh appropriated it to his own use.

The next thing which demanded the attention of Gen. Jenkins, was to summon the Town Council and demand of them the return of the two horses and their accoutrements captured by Mahon and Seiders, or the payment of their value; and in default of either he threatened the destruction of the town. His plea for this extreme resort was, as he said, the firing upon his soldiers by our citizens. As the captured property was beyond the reach of the Council, the matter was finally adjusted by the payment of $900. Doubtless Jenkins expected this amount in United States currency, but as he had flooded the town with Confederate scrip, pronouncing it better than Greenbacks, the city fathers evidently took him at his word, and paid him in his own money. This money was bought up of our citizens, who had received it for articles sold to Jenkins' men, at a few cents on the dollar. A few days after this transaction, and when Jenkins' force had fallen back beyond Greencastle, Mr. Seiders returned to town as the pilot of Gen. Knipe, who, with parts of two New York regiments, was sent to this place. Of these men I will have more to say hereafter. While here the Town Council seized Mr. Seiders' horse, but desiring to retain him for scouting purposes during the invasion, promising to make the matter right afterwards, he was permitted to do so upon the presentation of a petition signed by a number of our citizens, they also pledging themselves responsible for the return of the horse. And now, to show some of the inconveniences which the possession of this horse and the wearing of the captured rebel's coat brought upon Mr. Seiders, and the routine through which he had to pass in order to retain his property, I will yet digress from my main subject to put upon record the following interesting facts: When carrying important information of the movements of the rebels to the authorities at Harrisburg, Seiders was captured near Bridgeport and taken into Harrisburg, where he was looked upon as a rebel spy and came near being mobbed. His horse and equipments were taken from him, and to all his protestations of his true character, the Provost Marshall, before whom he was taken, turned a deaf ear. At length Mr. D. W. Deal, then Postmaster at this place, but in Harrisburg for prudential reasons, made affidavit to his knowledge of Mr. Seiders, and to the circumstances under which he became possessed of the horse and rebel outfit, and also to the action of the Town Council in loaning the same to Seiders, for which he (Deal) was one of the bondsmen. Col. A. K. McClure, William McClellen, Esq., and Mr. J. M, Cooper then followed in an affidavit vouching for Mr. Deal and the truth of his statement, after which Mr. Seiders was released from custody, but his horse and equipments were not returned to him—the Provost Marshall, John Kay Clement, saying that they were beyond his reach. In company with Mr. McClure Mr. Seiders called upon Gen. Couch, Commander of the Department of the Susquehanna, to whom he was personally known, who issued a peremptory order for the return of the horse and equipments, and gave him a paper which saved him from further annoyance. Upon the presentation of this order from Gen. Couch, the Marshall wrote an order for the delivery of the property on the back of Gen. Couch's paper which reads thus :

"WILLIAM W. CALDER : Sir : You will please deliver the gray mare to John Seiders, Esq.; it is in the stable of *private horses*, and is the one I gave to your charge this morning. Please hand over the accoutrements.

Yours, &c.,
ED. WILSON,
Capt. and Quartermaster."

After the retreat of the rebels from Gettysburg, Mr. Seiders sold the horse for $175, and the saddle for $85. Deducting from this the claim of the Town Council —$75—he had $185 left. The original papers relating to this whole transaction are now before me, but they are too voluminous to give in full here.

On Wednesday morning, Gen. Jenkins ordered that the stores, shops and business places should all be opened from 8 to 10 o'clock A. M., and that his men should be permitted to buy such articles as they personally needed, but must in all cases pay for what they got. Business for about an hour was very brisk, and to avoid giving offense they patronized all. Fortunately for us and many others, stocks of goods were generally sent away or hid, but what little we had was bought up and paid for in Confederate scrip and shin plasters issued by the City of Richmond and other Southern corporations. While this traffic was in progress a rebel soldier seized a number of remnants of ladies' dress goods, which we did not think worth hiding, and putting them under his arm walked out and down past Jenkins' headquarters. Jenkins came quickly out and caught the fellow and pushed him back on the double quick into the store, and said: "Did this man get these things here, and did he pay for them?" Upon being told that he took them without paying for them, he drew his sword and flourishing it above the man's head and swearing terribly, he declared that he had a mind to cut his head off. Turning to us he said, "Sell my men all the goods they want, but if anyone attempts to take anything without paying for it, report to me at my headquarters. We are not thieves." Some of the rebel officers visited the drug stores of Messrs. Miller, Spangler, Nixon and Heyser, and purchased liberally, telling them to make out their bills, or if they could not do that, to guess at the amount and it would be paid.

About nine o'clock, while we were all doing a lively business, an officer came galloping up Main Street to headquarters and told Jenkins that the Yankees were advancing. Jenkins came out in haste and mounting his horse he, in a voice of great power, ordered the men to the field. A rush was made down Main street and out to what is known as Gelsinger's hill, a few miles below the town, on the Harrisburg pike, where a line of battle was formed. In a short time a number of men returned leading the horses, the soldiers dismounting and preparing to fight as infantry. They were all armed with carbines as well as pistols and sabres. After an hour or two they fell back through the town and out where their horses were taken and rode back beyond Greencastle. A few daring scouts coming from the direction of Shippensburg, caused this alarm, and supposing that they were too far in advance of the infantry, they retreated to the Southern part of the county, where for nearly a week they plundered the people. As Jenkins and his staff rode up street, after the dismounted men had all passed, a number of our citizens were standing upon the Court House pavement. Supposing that they were armed and might fire upon them, these officers drew their revolvers and rode towards the citizens. A stampede of course resulted. As the last of these soldiers were leaving the lower end of the town, they set fire to the warehouse of Messrs. Oaks & Linn, but it was speedily extinguished. This firing and the destruction of the Scotland bridge were the only acts of real destruction attempted. Many incidents of interest which occurred during the stay of Jenkins' command, might be given, but I have space for but a few. The large brick building which then stood back of the railroad, opposite the present depot, and which had been erected by the Franklin Railroad Company for an engine house, was at the time of this raid used for the packing of hay. A large stack of hay was also near this building. Mr. T. B. Wood and other property holders in that neighborhood got Rev. Dr. B. S. Schneck to go to Gen. Jenkins and ask him not to burn this hay, but if it was his intention to burn it, they would move it away so that it would not endanger their property. To this request Jenkins replied that he had no intention to burn that hay, for Lee and his whole army were coming and would want the hay. Many of the soldiers were engaged during Tuesday and Wednesday morning in scouring the fields around the town for negroes. Many were caught and some, free and slave, were bound and sent under guard South. Some escaped, and some were captured from their guard by citizens of Greencastle. Among their captures was that well and favorably known colored man, Esque Hall. A rebel rode past our store with this poor frightened man on behind him. I went immediately for Dr. Schneck, who went to Jenkins' headquarters, and after assuring Jenkins that Hall was long a resident of this place, and not a fugitive slave, he was released. Dr. Schneck told me that one of Jenkins' staff officers recognized him, having heard him preach once in Virginia, and his intercession helped to save poor Hall. They also caught Henry Deitrick and Samuel Claudy, who were repair hands upon the railroad, and were coming up from the direction of Scotland upon a hand car. Again Dr. Schneck's services were called for and these men were released. Some years ago a citizen of this place was traveling in Virginia, down where the Natural Bridge is, and after riding some ten miles with a man who resided there, he was asked where he was from. When he replied, Chambersburg, the man said, "Do you know Dr. Schneck? I've got his card. I was with Gen. Jenkins in Chambersburg, and some of our men caught a negro and would have taken him South, but Dr. Schneck interceded for him and he was released."

Gen. Jenkins, fearing an attack by the emergency men then congregating at Harrisburg, fell back, as already stated, below Greencastle and near to Hagerstown, there to await the arrival of Gen. Lee's infantry. From this retreat he sent out marauding parties to various places in search of additional plunder. One detachment proceeded by way of Mercersburg over the Cove mountain into Fulton county, where they were rather roughly handled, as the following account will show. There were stationed in and about McConnellsburg, the county seat of that county, parts of three companies of the First New York Cavalry under Capt. Jones, numbering about sixty men. These cavalrymen were noted for their fearlessness, amounting in some cases to daring rashness. Some thirty-six of these men with their intrepid leader were in the town when the scouts came dashing in from the Mercersburg road, and reported the approach of the foe. It happened that there was also a company of volunteer cavalry from the neighborhood of Orbisonia then in the town, and Capt Jones proposed to the commander of this company that if he would place his men in a cross street, so that the rebels could not see them, until he with his small company had passed them in pursuit of the foe, and then only to show themselves and so impress the rebels with their numbers, that he would do all the fighting. To this the officer consented, and stationed his men accordingly. The New Yorkers formed in a column and rode slowly down street as about sixty-two of the rebels appeared at the brow of the hill at the upper end of the town. At length, when they had drawn the enemy almost down to the cross street where the volunteers were placed, they suddenly wheeled about and, with a terrific yell, dashed for the foe, firing and yelling as they rode. The volunteers failed most ingloriously to perform their part, but fled up the valley in great confusion, and the last heard of them they were still running. The rebels, however, notwithstanding their superiority in numbers, turned and fled by the way they came, and a short distance from where the roads leading to Chambersburg and Mercersburg diverge, two of them were killed and one badly wounded. The citizens afterwards went out and buried them by the way side, and while thus engaged the defeated force, reinforced largely, returned to renew the conflict, but the New Yorkers were as cunning as brave, for suspecting that a large force would return, prudently withdrew to the hills west of the town, the rebels, fearing to pursue them, having a wholesome fear of Milroy's force, which they knew was not far away. I may err in saying that this exciting skirmish occurred with this detachment of Jenkin's force, but after making all due inquiry I am at a loss to place it elsewhere.

It was this reinforced body of cavalry. if I mistake not, who captured a drove of cattle from our former towsman, ex-Sheriff Taylor, valued at about $7,000, which he unwittingly drove within their thieving reach. We shall have occasion to refer to these brave New Yorkers on two subsequent occasions, which will be given in their appropriate places.

One other detatchment from Jenkin's force was sent east, and after plundering the rich country about Waynesboro', crossed over the Southeastern flanks of the South Mountain, where, at the Monterey pass, on Sunday, 21st, the Philadelphia City Troop and Bell's cavalry from Gettysburg, encountered their pickets. In the evening of the same day about 120 of them entered Fairfield, and returned again by the Furnace road, taking with them all the good horses they could find.

The whole Southern portion of our county was plundered by these men, Welsh Run especially receiving a thorough scouring. The plunder thus taken by Jenkins was sent south of the Potomac, and delivered over to Lee's approaching army. It would be difficult to estimate the value of the property taken by this raid, but it certainly amounted to not less than one hundred thousand dollars. Then its coming in the season of the year when the farming interests required the use of horses, added immensely to its inconvenience and loss. Many croppers who had little else than their stock, were bankrupted. The effect of this raid, however, was to arouse the people of Pennsylvania and the adjacent states, and volunteers for the defense of the border hurried to Harrisburg.

The various detachments of Jenkin's command had all joined the main body by Monday morning, at or near Hagerstown, where he awaited the arrival of Rhode's division of infantry preparatory to another advance into our State. For the present we will leave him there and take a look at Harrisburg and see what preparations were being made for the reception of the foe.

As soon as it was definitely known that the invasion of Pennsylvania was imminent, our State authorities were notified of the fact, and they were assured that the aspect of the war at that time rendered it unwise to divide the army of the Potomac, and that Pennsylvania must furnish her own men for her defense. Accordingly Maj. Gen. D. N. Couch was made, by an order of the War Department. Commander of the Department of the Susquehanna, with headquarters at Harrisburg, and Maj. Gen. W. T. H. Brooks was assigned to the Department of the Monongahela, with headquarters at Pittsburg. On the day following the establishment of these Departments, Friday, June 12th, Governor Curtin issued a proclamation, addressed to the people of Pennsylvania, telling them of the danger which threatened them, and calling for volunteers to meet the emergency. On the same day Gen. Couch, on assuming command of the Department, also issued an address to the people, reiterating what Governor Curtin had said, and calling for a general and speedy enlistment for the defense of the State, and if possible to drive back the foe before he should touch our soil. Soon after the issuing of these addresses—on June 15th—the construction of breastworks and the digging of rifle pits along the river front, and on the opposite bank of the river, was commenced, and carried forward from day to day. In response to the call of the Governor and Gen. Couch, the militia of Pennsylvania and New York hastened to Harrisburg, and on Monday, 22nd, they were organized by Gen. Couch into two divisions, one under General Smith and the other under General Dana. On Saturday previous, 20th, General Knipe was sent from Harrisburg with parts of two regiments of New York militia, numbering about 800 men—the first to reach Harrisburg after the Governor's call. Their destination was first to assist in rebuilding the railroad bridge at Scotland, destroyed by Jenkins a few days previously, and then to occupy and defend Chambersburg. These troops marched from Scotland on Sunday, 21st, and reached this place sometime in the afternoon. The Colonel commanding these men made an excellent speech from the Court House steps, in which he assured us that they had come here to assist in repelling the rebel invaders. After resting awhile in the diamond and partaking of the hospitalities of our people, these troops marched out to the strip of woods then upon the farm known as the Oyler property, but then belonging to Mr. G. R. Messersmith. The men comprising these regiments were mostly young gentlemen connected with business establishments in the city of New York, and evidently had not been accustomed to the hardships which usually attend a soldier's life. They brought with them two beautiful brass howitzers which, with their caissons, were drawn by hand. These howitzers were placed in position and masked with branches from the trees on the hill overlooking and commanding the Greencastle road, where the school house now stands. On the morning following, Monday, 22nd, the two companies of Home Guards raised in this place went out and joined this regiment. During the day these New Yorkers did a considerable amount of drilling with their artillery, and not a little boasting of what they would do in case the rebels came within reach of their guns. About 3 o'clock in the afternoon a person supposed to be a woman came into the camp. She, or he, was disguised in a woman's attire of deep mourning, with her face almost entirely hid in a black bonnet. She went through the camp pretending to be silly, and inquiring where a certain farmer lived, whom no one knew. Some of our Home Guards felt assured that the person was a man disguised, and that he should be arrested. The Colonel in command of these troops, when told of these suspicions, said that she was only some silly woman, and that she should not be disturbed. At length she left the camp and the last seen of her she was making quick time out the Railroad towards Greencastle. It will be recollected that this occurred but one day preceding the reappearance of Gen. Jenkins, and that previous to his first approach two strange men came to Greencastle and remained at a hotel until Jenkin's command entered, when they threw off their disguise by uniting with the rebels and telling the landlord to charge their bill to the Southern Confederacy. That this pretended woman was one of Gen. Jenkin's scouts, sent in advance to ascertain what preparations were made for their reception, there can be no doubt.

Leaving these gallant strangers in their camp, about a half mile from the Southern border of the town, with their two beautiful howitzers planted so as to command the approaches by the Greencastle road, and our Home Guards thrown out in advance as pickets, we will turn our attention to events further South, promising the reader that he will hear from these men further on in this narrative.

References have been frequently made in these chapters to our Home Guards. It is but justice to our citizens to state that in addition to the hundreds who went from our town into active service, where many of them were distinguished for their bravery and good conduct, and many fell, nearly all who were not away in service were enrolled in companies, under competent officers, for home service. In the emergency under consideration the old men of the town organized a company, headed by the venerable Judge Chambers, for the defense of the place. None were admitted to this company under forty-five years of age. Upon all occasions, when their services were needed, these Home Guards were on duty, and on this day, Monday, June 22ud, every man capable of bearing arms had his gun and was in some organization to resist the rebels.

CHAPTER IX.

THE INVASION OF PENNSYLVANIA.

Before proceeding to narrate the events connected with the invasion of our border by the Army of Northern Virginia, and its retreat from the disastrous field of Gettysburg, I will place upon record certain facts concerning the previous movements of that army and its designs and purposes in the invasion, which will greatly aid the reader in understanding the movements and counter-movements of the two great contending armies upon the great chessboard of war. These facts may be stated thus:

1. *The number of forces on each side in this campaign.*

(1) The Confederate force.

Hon. Edward Everett, in his address at the dedication of the Soldier's National Cemetery at Gettysburg, Nov. 19th, 1863, estimates the Confederate force at 90,000 infantry, upwards of 10,000 cavalry, and 4,000 or 5,000 artillery, making a total of 105,000 of all arms.

Gen. Longstreet in one of his contributions to the *Annals of the War*, page 621, gives the rebel force upon the authority of Gen. Lee, in a confidential communication made to him, as but a little over 70,000.

Col. W. H. Taylor, one of Lee's staff officers, in an article contributed to the same book, (page 318), gives the strength of the army as 67,000 of all arms—fifty-three thousand five hundred infantry, nine thousand cavalry, and four thousand five hundred artillery.

In the *Franklin Repository* of July 8, '63 while the matter was fresh in the the minds of our people, many of whom had made by actual count pretty correct estimates of the strength of the Confederate army, it is stated that the two Corps, Ewell's and Hill's, amounted to 47,000 men and 192 guns. Add to these Early's Division of Ewell's Corps, which did not pass through this place, and Longstreet's Corps, which was not included in this computation and which it may be supposed was equal to either Hill's or Ewell's, and it will be seen that Mr. Everett's estimate is entirely too high. In all the estimates made by our citizens, as these troops passed through here none, so far as I have heard, placed the number above 70,000.

(2.) *The Union force.*

Gen. Mende in his evidence taken before a committee of Congress on the conduct of the War, (page 337), gives the strength of his army as follows: "My strength was a little under one hundred thousand—probably ninety-five thousand men." This, of course, is decisive, and it establishes the fact that the Union army was considerably larger than the Confederate. This superiority in numbers was in part offset by the prestige of the victories gained at Fredericksburg and Chancellorsville. That this success had its effect upon the confederates is proven by the following extract from a report of the battle of Gettysburg, made by Col. Freemantle of the British army, who with one or two other British officers passed through here with the rebels, and was with Gen. Lee's staff when the battle was fought, and doubtless strongly sympathized with them: "The staff officers spoke of the coming battle as a certainty, and the universal feeling was one of contempt for an enemy whom they had beaten so constantly, and under so many disadvantages." (Annals of the War page 206.)

Gen. Fitzhugh Lee, a son of the Commander of the Confederate Army, says that his father was controlled too far by the great confidence he had in the fighting qualities of his troops, who begged only to be *turned loose* upon the Federals. This feeling of confidence was equally shared by the officers high in command. (*Annals of the War*, pages 421, 422.)

The rebels as they passed through Greencastle and this place were confident and boastful, and seemed to think that their success was assured.

2. *The plan and object of Gen. Lee.*

Hon. Edward Everett, whose information was drawn from the archives of the War Department, which were placed at disposal for the preparation of his address at Gettysburg, states Lee's purposes as follows:

(1.) By rapid movements northward, and by manoeuvring with a portion of his army on the East side of the Blue Ridge, to tempt Gen. Hooker from his base of operations and thus uncover the approaches to Washington, and throw it open to a raid by Stuart's cavalry, and also to enable Lee himself to cross the Potomac at Poolsville and fall upon the Capitol. This design of the rebel General was promptly discovered by Gen. Hooker, and, moving with great rapidity from Fredericksburg, he preserved unbroken the inner line, and stationed the various corps of his army at all the points protecting the approaches to Washington, from Centreville up to Leesburg. In the meantime, by the vigorous operations of Pleasanton's cavalry, the cavalry of Gen. Stuart, though superior in numbers, was so crippled as to be disabled from performing the part assigned it in the campaign. In this manner, Gen. Lee's first object, the defeat of Hooker's army on the South of the Potomac and a direct march on Washington, was baffled.

(2.) The second part of the Confederate plan, which is supposed to have been undertaken in opposition to the views of Gens. Lee and Longstreet, was to turn the demonstration northward into a real invasion of Maryland and Pennsylvania, in the hope, that, in his way, Gen. Hooker would be drawn to a distance from the capitol, and that some opportunity would occur of taking him at a disadvantage, and after defeating his army, of making a descent upon Baltimore and Washington. This was substantially the repetition of the plan of 1862, and as the latter was defeated at Antietam, so was the former at Gettysburg.

(3.) One other plan was a movement upon Harrisburg. Whether this place was Lee's objective point when he crossed the Potomac and marched his forces into our valley is not known; but that he had planned an attack upon the capitol of our State, and that he held to that plan up to the night of June 29th, when Gen. Longstreet's scout brought information to him at his headquarters near this place, of the movements of the army of the Potomac, which information caused him to change his plan and march eastwardly across the South Mountain, will clearly appear in the following taken from Longstreet's account in the *Annals of the War*, (pages 418 and 419.)

This statement is as follows: "While at Culpepper, I sent a trusty scout (who had been sent to me by Secretary Seddens, while I was in Suffolk,) with instructions to go into the Federal lines, discover his policy, and bring me all the information he could possibly pick up. When this scout asked me, very significantly, where he should report, I replied, 'Find me, wherever I am, when you have the desired information.' I did this because I feared to trust him with a knowledge of our future movements. I supplied him with all the gold he needed, and instructed him to spare neither pains nor money to obtain full and accurate information. The information gathered by this scout led to the most tremendous results, as will be seen * * *. I reached Chambersburg on the evening of the 27th (Saturday.) At this point, on the night of the 29th (Monday), information was received by which the whole plan of the campaign was changed. We had not heard from the enemy for several days, and Gen. Lee was in doubt as to where he was; indeed, we did not know that he had yet left Virginia. At about ten o'clock that night, Col. Sorrell, my chief of staff, was waked by an orderly, who reported that a suspicious person had just been arrested by the provost marshal. Upon investigation, Sorrell discovered that the suspicious person was the scout Harrison that I had sent out at Culpepper. He was dirt-stained, travel-worn, and very much broken down. After questioning him sufficiently to find that he brought very important information, Col. Sorrell brought him to my headquarters and awoke me. He gave the information that the enemy had crossed the Potomac, marched northwest, and that the head of his column was at Frederick City on our right. I felt that this information was exceedingly important, and might involve a change in the direction of our march. Gen. Lee had already issued orders that we were to advance toward Harrisburg. I at once sent the scout to Gen. Lee's headquarters, and followed him myself early in the morning. I found Gen. Lee up, and asked him if the information brought by the scout might not involve a change of direction of the head of our column to the right. He immediately acquiesed in the suggestion, possibly saying that he had already given orders to that effect. The movement toward the enemy was begun at once."

Gen. Lee himself in his report, says:— "Preparation had been made to advance upon Harrisburg; but, on the night of the 29th, information was received from a scout that the enemy had crossed the Potomac, was advancing northward, and the head of his column had already reached South Mountain. As our communications with the Potomac were thus menaced, it was resolved to prevent its further progress in that direction by concentrating our army on the east side of the mountain." (*Annals of the War*, 420.)

General Longstreet in a second article contributed to the *Annals of the War*, page 632, says that he erred in his first article in stating that this scout reported to him on the night of the 29th, and that it should be on the night of Sunday, 28th. That he was right in his first statement will clearly appear in the following considerations:

(1.) According to his own statement, as well as the official declaration of Gen. Lee, the order countermanding the attack upon Harrisburg and a rapid concentration towards Gettysburg, was issued immediately upon the receipt of the information brought by this scout. If the scout reported on the evening of Sunday, 28th, then the concentration must have taken place on Monday, whereas it is placed beyond all question that it occurred on Tuesday. This will clearly appear in the statements yet to follow.

(2.) Gen. Longstreet says that early in the morning after the arrival of this scout, he rode with Gen. Lee from his headquarters near Chambersburg to Greenwood, where they remained over night, and the next day, after riding together three or four miles towards Gettysburg, they heard the sound of artillery, at which Gen. Lee rode forward to ascertain what occasioned it. This was the cannonading of the first day's engagement, as he himself admits, which occurred on Wednesday, July 1st. This fact alone fixes Tuesday morning as the time they left Chambersburg for Greenwood, and, as a consequence, Monday night the 29th, as the time of the scout's arrival.

(3.) Gen. Lee officially declares that it was on the night of the 29th, when the scout reported to him. This official declaration is of more importance than Gen. Longstreet's memory, upon which, it is evident, he relies.

There is another way of harmonizing this discrepancy, which is that the scout reported on the evening of Sunday, 28th, and the orders for the concentration were immediately issued and sent to their respective destinations on Monday, but the concentration did not commence until Tuesday, 30th. This seems to be inferred from an account of this affair given by Dr. Cullen, Medical Director of Longstreet's Corps in the *Annals of the War*, page 439. Dr. Cullen says:—"I distinctly remember the appearance in our headquarters of the scout who brought from Frederick the first account that Gen. Lee had of the definite whereabouts of the enemy; of the excitement at Gen. Lee's headquarters among couriers, quartermasters, commissaries, etc., all betokening some early movement of the commands dependent upon the news brought by the scout. That afternoon Gen. Lee was walking with some of us in the road in front of his headquarters, and said, 'Gentlemen, we will not move to Harrisburg as we expected, but will go over to Gettysburg and see what Gen. Meade is after.' Orders had then been issued to the corps to move at sunrise on the morning of the next day, and promptly at the time the corps was put on the road."

The chief difficulty to this last explanation is, how could that scout report to Gen. Lee *on Sunday evening* that Gen. Meade was in command of the Army of the Potomac, when he had only been placed in that position the afternoon of the same day in Frederick, some forty miles away?

The reader may accept either explanation, but he will see by closely following the movements I shall detail that the concentration commenced on *Tuesday morning* the 30th.

3. *What was the plan of the commander of the Army of the Potomac?*

After a period of three weeks—from June 3d—when Gen. Lee broke up his encampment at Fredericksburg, to the 24th, when the main body of his army crossed the Potomac into Maryland, Lee manoeuvred his army so as to outwit and entrap Gen. Hooker, but in every case he utterly failed. And so successfully did Hooker handle his army that he compelled Lee to cross the Potomac at Shepherstown and Williamsport, west of the Blue Ridge, instead of the east, as intended, thus materially damaging his entire plan of campaign north of the river as he had defeated it south. It was probably this forced march up through the valley west of the mountain, instead of the east, that made Harrisburg Lee's objective. And then owing to the severe handling which Gen. Pleasanton administered to Stuart at Beverly Ford, Aldie and Upperville, in connection with Hooker's strategy, that chieftain was forced away from his proper connection with Lee's army, compelling him to make the entire circuit of the Union forces and only reaching the rebel lines on the evening of July 2nd. Gen. Stuart's proper course, and the one he would have taken had he not been forced to do otherwise, after Lee's forced route west of the mountain, would have been along the eastern side, guarding its passes, masking Lee's movements, protecting his line of communication, reporting information of the Union forces, and harassing whatever of those forces he might come in contact with. All these advantages were lost to Lee by the course Stuart was compelled to take. Of this loss not only Gen. Lee, but several of his officers in reports subsequently published, greatly complained. Gen Lee says:

"No report had been received (on the 27th) that the enemy had crossed the Potomac, and the absence of the Cavalry rendered it impossible to obtain accurate information." Gen. Longstreet said, "The army moved forward as a man might walk over strange ground with his eyes shut."

Upon Thursday, June 25th, the day after Lee's army crossed the Potomac, Gen. Hooker crossed at Edward's Ferry, and by Sunday, 28th, the Union Army lay between Harper's Ferry and Frederick City, in a position either to protect Washington and Baltimore, fall upon Lee's communications, or march to any point where the enemy might show himself. The strategy of Gen. Hooker seems to have been as faultless as it proved to be successful.

On Sunday, June 28th, General Joseph Hooker was removed from the command of the army, and General George G. Meade was placed in that responsible position. The cause of Gen. Hooker's removal was some disagreement between him and Gen. Halleck, then General in Chief of the Army. There were 10,000 men at Harper's Ferry under Gen. French, which Halleck desired to remain there to protect that place and threaten Lee's communications with Virginia. These troops Hooker wanted, and because his request was refused, complications ensued which resulted in his tendering his resignation. Immediately after receiving the order placing him in command, Gen. Meade sought an interview with Hooker, and used every effort to obtain of him his plans an purposes, as also the strength and position of the different Corps of the army, but Hooker left the camp in a short time and gave him no information whatever. It is said that Meade summoned Gen. Reynolds to his presence, and together they agreed upon a plan of campaign. (*Annals of the War, page 62.*) Placed unexpectedly in a position of immense responsibility, and involving results of momentous importance, even the life of a great Nation, it certainly reflects the highest credit upon Gen. Meade, that he was able at once to meet the emergency; and also reflects the highest honor upon the whole army that the change made in the chief command of so large a force on the eve of a general battle,—the various Corps necessarily moving on lines somewhat divergent, and yet not an hour's hesitation should ensue in the advance of any portion thereof. Can history produce anything that exceeds it?

Gen. Meade at once directed his left wing, under Gen. Reynolds, upon Emmittsburg, and his right upon New Windsor, leaving Gen. French with 10,000 men to protect the Baltimore and Ohio railroad, and convey the public property from Harper's Ferry to Washington. Buford's cavalry was on that day at Gettysburg, and Kilpatrick's at Hanover, where he defeated the rear of Stuart's cavalry, who was roving about the country in search of the main army of Lee. I have thus given the strength and purposes of the two armies, with the position of Lee on the 24th (Wednesday) and of Meade on the 28th (Sunday) and shall now lift the curtain and give the reader a view of the movements and occurrences in and about this place, while the Southern hosts were passing through to their terrible discomfiture. And that these important occurrences may be given in their proper connection, and in comparison with other events transpiring elsewhere within the lines of the two great opposing armies, I will detail the events of each day in the following daily summary. Let the reader follow me through these details, mark well each movement, with Harrisburg as Lee's objective up to the night of Monday 29th, and after that night, some position east of the South Mountain, and he will be amazed at the skill and genius displayed in the mind of the one man planning, directing and controlling the whole. I will also detail the corresponding movements of the Army of the Potomac, that the equal skill of its commander may be seen. I will commence with

SATURDAY, JUNE 20TH.

I have been unable to learn the precise day when the divisions of Generals Rhodes and Early crossed the Potomac into Maryland. They had defeated Milroy at Winchester on the 13th and 14th, and crossed the Potomac either on Saturday, the 20th, or Sunday, 21st. From all the information I have been able to gather this crossing occurred on Saturday, and probably on Sunday also. At Hagerstown on Monday, 22d, these two Divisions connected with Jenkins and proceeded down the valley by different roads.

Gen. Knipe was sent from Harrisburg with parts of two New York regiments to Chambersburg.

SUNDAY, 21ST.

Gen. Lee this day issued his first General Order (No. 72, given hereafter) relating to the conduct of his army and the regulations to be observed in procuring supplies.

The New York Militia this day entered and passed through town.

MUNDAY, 22D.

The remaining division—Johnson's—of Ewell's Corps crossed the Potomac, part at Shepherdstown and the balance at Williamsport, and formed a junction at Hagerstown. At that place Early's division deflected to the east and passed on down the valley by Waynesboro' and Funkstown, coming out into the pike leading from this place to Gettysburg at Greenwood. It then crossed the South Mountain reaching Gettysburg on Friday, the 26th, and York on Sunday, 28th. The advance of this force was commanded by Gen. Gordon. After entering this latter place a detachment was sent forward to Wrightsville on the western bank of the Susquehanna, with the probable intention to seize the bridge crossing the river there and probably to plunder Columbia on the eastern bank. After a skirmish with the rebels, Col. Frick, in command of the Union forces, set fire to the bridge and thus prevented any further advance in that direction. It was by General Early's order that the iron works of Hon. Thaddeus Stevens, situated at the foot of the South Mountain on the Gettysburg pike, were destroyed while passing that way towards Gettysburg. This will be noticed more fully hereafter.

Another detachment from Ewell's corps, under Gen. Stuart, turned to the west and crossed the Cove Mountain into Fulton county, taking possession of McConnellsburg to watch that part of Milroy's command which had escaped from Winchester to Bloody Run. Gen. Imboden, previous to Lee's crossing the Potomac, was sent with his cavalry, numbering about 3,300 men, to Cumberland, Md., with instructions to sweep eastwardly down the Baltimore & Ohio railroad and the Chesapeake and Ohio Canal, and destroy all the bridges, depots and canal boats and locks as far as Martinsburg. After the execution of this order he crossed the river at Hancock and penetrated the valley west of the Cove Mountain to McConnellsburg, where for the present we will leave him. He, however, will appear in important connections further on in this narrative.

On this day Gen. Ewell issued his Order (No. 49, given hereafter) in relation to the behavior of his troops during the invasion.

During this day the advance under Jenkins and Rhodes reached Greencastle. Gen. Jenkins sent forward a reconnoitering party as far as Marion, at which place they captured Mr. D. K. Appenzellar, who had just returned from service with the 126th Regiment Penna. Volunteers, and was on his way to this place, mounted upon an excellent horse, to join some military organization here. After his capture, Mr. Appenzellar was closely questioned as to the number of troops then in Chambersburg. Having been in the latter place a day or two previously, and having heard a rumor that Gen. Couch was coming up from Harrisburg with a force of twenty thousand men, he repeated this story to them. They at once fell back to the main body, and in the hearing of Mr. Appenzellar communicated this intelligence to those in command. About this time the bold, dashing New York cavalrymen from Fulton county, under their intrepid leader, put in an appearance, and at once a scene of great excitement ensued. The audacity with which these cavalrymen dashed towards the rebels led them to suppose that they were the advand guard of a large body, and naturally they supposed that body was Gen. Couch's twenty thousand men. A line of battle was at once hastily formed. Fences were torn down to the right and left of the Greencastle road, and Rhodes' infantry took a position upon the high ground of Mr. John Kissecker's farm, about a half mile this side of Greencastle. Jenkins threw his cavalry forward and formed a skirmish line upon the land of Mr. Wm. Flemming, about a quarter of a mile from the infantry. Gen. Jenkins established his headquarters in Mr. Flemming's house. As soon as the Union cavalry came within range of their guns, fire was opened upon them, and for a time the noise and clatter were lively. A sister of Mr. Flemming, going to the window to look out, barely escaped a ball which came crashing in the glass right beside her head. As soon as the dash and curiosity of these bold riders were satisfied they withdrew out of range, and the rebels fearing it to be a Yankee trick to draw them into an ambuscade, did not pursue. Mr. Appenzellar says that of all the bold and fearless soldiers he ever saw—and he saw many and had large experience during the war—these New York cavalrymen exceeded any in these qualities. And had they gone but a very short distance further they would have come into a cross fire which would have swept them all away. Their foresight and understanding, however, were equal to their courage, and they knew when to stop.

This skirmish has been claimed by some to have been the first battle of the war upon Pennsylvania soil. If the affair which occurred in McConnellsburg between this same body of cavalry and a detachment of rebels, supposed to have been from Jenkins' force, took place at the time stated, of which I am not positively certain, then it was the second battle. If the rebel force engaged at McConnellsburg was not a detachment from Jenkins' command, but from some other later on in the invasion, then the affair near Greencastle was the first of the war upon our soil. The result of this battle—if it can properly be called such—was one man killed and one wounded. The killed was Corporal Rife. He was shot through the upper lip, the ball passing through his head. His blood bespattered the paling fence near Mr. Flemming's dwelling. The wounded was Lieut. Cafferty. He was shot through the leg. No casualties were known on the rebel side. These brave New Yorkers will be again introduced to our readers in a subsequent chapter, in a scene enacted near this same historic place, but under widely different circumstances.

We return now to the camp of the New York soldiers near Chambersburg. About 5 o'clock in the afternoon of this same day a great commotion was observed all over the camp. The officers were running around, and in an excited manner giving commands. The soldiers at the guns hastily abandoned them, and the whole command hurriedly left and marched to town and embarked upon a train in readiness for them, leaving guns, caissons, tents, &c., standing. Word had been brought, probably by some of the cavalrymen already spoken of, of the proximity of the rebel infantry and cavalry. Our home guard, by direction of Col. McClure, then in line with other of our citizens, hauled the guns and caissons to town and placed them upon the train with the panic-stricken soldiers. Two of these soldiers were taken with nervous spasms, and one of them, unable to proceed with his comrades, was taken to the residence of Mr. Emanuel Kuhn on East Market street, where he remained concealed during all the period of the invasion and until after the retreat of the rebels after the battle of Gettysburg. The authorities, under whose command this regiment was acting, were aware of the situation, and gave them timely notice to leave, but there was no occasion for their hasty flight, for the next morning before Jenkins' cavalry appeared some of our citizens went out and brought in their tents and camp equipage. Among these were boxes of sardines and other delicacies, more suitable for a picnic than for the stern realities of the camp.

Some of these New Yorkers went home and complained of the bad treatment which they had received. Some years after the close of the war I heard one of them tell to a number of admiring listners in a store in New York of their treatment, and saying that our citizens charged them for the water they drank. It did not take me long to take the romance out of his story. It is not pleasant to supplement the statement of the heroism of the gallant cavalrymen from this same State with this delineation of cowardice and misrepresentation, for doubtless many of these men were moved by the highest considerations of patriotism to rush to our border for our defense, but the statement I have given is one link in the chain of history of that exciting period which I dare not omit, and for the truth of which several of our most reliable citizens, who were eye-witnesses of it, stand ready to corroborate if called upon.

TUESDAY, 23D.

On Tuesday morning, at about nine or ten o'clock, Gen. Jenkins again entered our town. Unlike his former entrance, which was in the night and under evident alarm, and were made with a wild rush down our streets, he this time came in slowly and confidently. A part of his force proceeded on down towards Shippensburg and others remained in the town. Shortly after his arrival he issued an order for a large amount of provisions for his command, all of which was to be brought to the Court House pavement in a short time. Of course we had to respond to this order and like the citizens of Greencastle, who in response to a similar demand, were all of one mind and brought onions, so we all seemed to have been moved by one idea and that was that this was a good time to get rid of old bacon, and sides and jowls, with a sprinkling of bread were brought in sufficient quantities to meet the occasion. This requisition, like his former one for firearms, was accompanied with the threat that all who did not comply would have their houses searched; and as flitch after flitch and jowl after jowl was deposited upon the greasy pile, the name of the unwilling contributor to the stomach of the Southern Confederacy was taken down. It would be an interesting item of news to see that list, and ascertain who all were in the bacon business that day, but as I have not a copy of it I am compelled to deny my readers that gratification.

About one or two hours after the entrance of Gen. Jenkins, the sound of music was heard up Main street. Rhode's division of infantry, preceded by a band of musicians playing "Dixie," made its appearance, coming over the brow of the hill by the Reformed church. This was the first rebel infantry that had ever penetrated a free State.

As to the precise day when the first infantry entered our town, there is some difference of opinion; and upon this fact I have experienced the only difficulty in harmonizing the several accounts before me. Some few of our citizens, and one record made at the time, fix upon Wednesday, 24th, the day after Jenkins' entrance, as the day. The evidence, however, in favor of Tuesday, 23d, is so overwhelming that I am constrained to decide upon that day. That evidence is as follows:

1. The recollections of some our citizens.
2. The editorial of Col. McClure in the *Franklin Repository* of July 15th, 1863. Col. McClure says: "On the 23d, a portion of his (Ewell's) command reached this place, and on the 24th, Gen. Ewell himself arrived.
3. The statement of Professor Jacobs in his *Battle of Gettysburg*. On page 12, Professor Jacobs says: "During the forenoon of this day (Tuesday, 23d) Gen. Rhodes' Division entered and occupied Chambersburg.
4. On this day—Tuesday—the head of Early's division, which marched parallel with Rhodes, but by the road through Waynesboro' and Funkstown, reached Greenwood. It is not to be supposed that it would be a day in advance of its supporting division.
5. The advance of Rhodes' division reached Carlisle on Thursday, 25th.

This they could not have done in one day from Chambersburg.

Throughout the remaining part of this day—Tuesday, 23d—our street was at no time clear of soldiers. Regiment after regiment and brigade after brigade, with immense trains of artillery and wagons, were continually passing, until, according to one account handed me, 10,300 men—infantry, artillery and cavalry—passed through and on down the valley towards Harrisburg.

During the afternoon of this day, a raid of a most shameful and yet ludicrous character occurred in the neighborhood of where the new depot now stands. Upon the site of this depot stood a large frame building, once used as a forwarding or railroad freight warehouse. In this building were stored a large amount of government stores, such as crackers, beans, bacon, &c. The rebels had not yet found these stores, and some of our people—mostly those who resided in the eastern part of the town, and had no scruples against taking anything from Uncle Sam they could, rather than have the rebels take them—made a raid upon these stores and in a short time cleaned out the whole stock. Men, women and children came running in crowds, and a general scramble took place, and upon every street and alley leading from the warehouse persons were seen carrying bacon and rolling barrels of crackers and beans. In the general melee some came in contact with others, and scolding, kicking and fighting ensued. One woman in rolling away a barrel of crackers came in contact with another rolling away a similar prize, and, crowding her too much, she turned around and kicked at the other, but not being acquainted with the laws of gravitation and momentum, missed her aim and went sprawling backward over her own barrel. By the time she had gathered herself up some one had rolled away her prize, at which a general fight set in. A reliable witness to whom I am indebted for this description of this shameful and ludicrous occurrence, assures me of its correctness, and says that he saw one man roll away four barrels and put them in his cellar.

WEDNESDAY, 24th.

Throughout this day long columns of infantry and artillery, with the usual accompaniments of immense trains of wagons and cattle, streamed through our streets, following those of the preceding day down the Harrisburg pike. About ten o'clock a carriage drawn by two horses came down street and stopped in front of the Franklin hotel, then kept by Mr. Daniel Trostle. One of the occupants of this carriage was a thin, sallow-faced man with strongly marked Southern features and a head and physiognomy which clearly indicated culture, refinement and genius. When he came out of his carriage it was discovered that he had an artificial limb and used a crutch. After making his way into the hotel, he was at once surrounded by some six or eight gentlemanly looking persons who constituted his staff, and in the front room of this hotel he established his headquarters. This intellectual, but crippled soldier, was Lieutenant General R. S. Ewell, the commander of the second corps of the army of Northern Virginia.

Gen. Ewell was a graduate of West Point, and was for some time a civil engineer on the Columbia Railroad in this State. He had been at one time stationed at Carlisle in charge of the U. S. Barracks there. Soon after the commencement of the rebellion he joined the rebel cause, and rapidly rose to the position of Lieut. General. He lost a leg at the second battle of Bull Run and, it was said, when he rode on horseback that he was always strapped to his horse. After the death of Stonewall Jackson, he became the commander of that corps, and was at the time I am writing of in Chambersburg in command of the advance corps of the Army of Northern Virginia on its way to its Waterloo.

But Gen. Ewell was a man of business, and among his first acts was to seize the large public school house on King street, adjoining the jail, for a hospital. This was followed by a requisition upon some of the hotels for a number of beds, which were taken to this building and the sick of his corps was placed thereon. A Provost Marshall was appointed, with headquarters in the Court House, and from the cupalo hung a rebel flag. This was the only hated symbol of the Confederacy which was put up anywhere in the town. A summons was also sent for the business men to convene in the parlor of the bank, and the few who had not fled upon the approach of the foe repaired there. After assembling, three of Ewell's staff officers joined us and opened up their business. By the authority of Gen. Ewell the following requisitions were laid before us:

To the Authorities of Chambersburg, Pa.

HEADQUARTERS 2ND ARMY CORPS, }
June 24th, 1863. }

By direction of Lieut. Gen. R. S. Ewell, I require the following articles:
5,000 Suits of Clothing, including Hats, Boots and Shoes.
100 good Saddles.
100 good Bridles.
5,000 Bushels of Grain (corn or oats.)
10,000 lbs. Sole Leather.
10,000 lbs. Horse Shoes.
400 lbs. Horse Shoe Nails.

Also, the use of printing office and two printers to report at once. All articles, except grain, will be delivered at the Court House Square, at 3 o'clock, P. M. to-day, and grain by 6 o'clock, P. M. to-day.

J. A. HARMON,
Maj. and C. Q. M. 2nd Corps D. Arm.

HEADQUARTERS 2ND ARMY CORPS, }
June 24th, 1863. }

By the command of Lieut. Gen. R. S. Ewell, the citizens of Chambersburg will furnish the following articles by 3 o'clock this afternoon:
6,000 lbs. Lead.
10,000 lbs. Harness Leather.
50 Boxes of Tin.
1,000 Curry Combs and Brushes.
2,000 lbs. Picket Rope.
400 Pistols.
All the Caps and Powder in town.
Also, all the Neat's Foot Oil.

WM. ALLEN, *M. and C.*

HEADQUARTERS 2ND ARMY CORPS, }
June 24th, 1863. }

By direction of Lieut. Gen. R. S. Ewell, the following are demanded:
50,000 lbs. Bread.
100 Sacks Salt.
30 Barrels Molasses.
500 Barrels Flour.
25 Barrels Vinegar.
25 Barrels Beans.
25 Barrels Dried Fruit.
25 Barrels Saurkraut.
25 Barrels Potatoes.
11,000 lbs. Coffee.
10,000 lbs. Sugar.
100,000 lbs. Hard Bread.

This last requisition is without signature; it was probably omitted in copying it for the press. It was, however, presented by Maj. Hawke's Quartermaster General of Ewell's Corps, who was present and presented it in person. These requisitions, as well as the General Orders issued by Lee and Ewell, which will be introduced further on in this narrative, I have taken from the *Franklin Repository* of July 8th and 15th, 1863. Col. M'Clure was editor and proprietor of the *Repository* at that time, and being intimate with the late G. R. Messersmith, in whose hands these requisitions were left, he copied them into his journal either from the originals or copies furnished by Mr. Messersmith. As to Lee's and Ewell's orders, they had been liberally distributed throughout the town, and at the time of their republication in the *Repository*, they could have been easily obtained. It is a fortunate circumstance that these important papers have been thus preserved, for their scarceity now, if not their entire disappearance from the possession of any, may be inferred from the fact that notwithstanding I advertised through PUBLIC OPINION for them, I had but one response, and that was one of the originals of Ewell's General Order in the possession of Miss M. E. Heilleman of this place. My recollections of these papers are such that I am positive in the statement that they are correct and faithful copies of the originals.

After an introduction to the three officers, and the reading of the papers, there was a period of silence. Here was a chance for business on a magnificent scale, but the terms did not seem to be satisfactory. Then, too, it was a little out of season for saurkraut, but our Southern visitors seemed to think that as they were among "the Pennsylvania Dutch," that luxury could be had the whole year round. They did not know that like their "Hog and Hominy" saurkraut was specially a home dish, and never set before strangers. Judge Kimmell, who had acted as Provost Marshal the year previous, and had been appointed by Gov. Curtin to superintend affairs here during the war, was, by common consent, permitted to act as spokesman, and taking up the papers and scanning them for a while threw them down upon the table, saying: "Why, gentlemen, you must suppose that we are made of these things—*ten—thousand—pounds—of Sole Leather—ten—thousand—pounds—of—Harness Leather—one—hundred—thousand—pounds—of—bread—twenty-five—barrels—of—saurkraut*—It is utterly out of our power to furnish these things, and now, if you are going to burn us out you will only have to do it. That's all I have to say about it." Whether the Judge's anger was excited by the disproportion between the amount of saurkraut and the bread, or whether he feared this demand would exhaust the market of his favorite dish, I am not able to say. The officers, however, did not become in the least excited, and replied, "Why, gentlemen, we are no vandals; we have not come here to burn and plunder, but to wage an honorable warfare. We have studied the Census Reports, and know the resources of your county, and now if the town cannot furnish these things, send out throughout the county and bring them in." "How can we send out," replied the Judge; "we have no horses, and all that have not been sent away have been taken by your men." "Well," said one of the officers, "it will not do for you to say that you cannot furnish these articles; Gen. Ewell will not receive such a reply. You must say just what you can do, and now we will give you time to consult together, and let those who deal in the same articles get together and make out a written report of what they can furnish, and we will meet here again in two hours to receive these reports."

At this we scattered, and the business of stock-taking was at once begun. I went at once to consult the other merchants in town in relation to the groceries demanded, for at that time and up to the burning of the town, the dry goods merchants all dealt in groceries; but I could not find one of them. Most of them had gone off upon the approach of the rebels. I then sat down and wrote out my report about thus: "Gentlemen, There are in our cellar the following articles. (Then followed the number of hogsheads and barrels, tapped and untapped, of syrup and molasses,— the amount of sugar, &c.) I have gone around town and tried to see other dealers in these articles, but have failed to find one of them. I now submit the question to you whether it would be right to take all our stock to meet your requisition, or let the burden fall equally upon all." Signing our firm name to this paper, I went over to the bank and handed it to Judge Kimmell, telling him of its contents. At the time appointed the citizens again convened with the officers in the parlor of the bank, but another requisition was laid upon the table from the Chief of the Signal Corps, calling for a first-class field glass, adapted for night service. Among the reports handed in was one from that well-remembered dealer in made up clothing, Mr. Marks Fellheimer. He had called to his assistance Rev. J. Dickson to write out his report, and proposed to furnish as his quota about five vests, two pairs of pants and three jackets, saying, "*indeed,* Mr. Dickson, that's all I've got." When the officers came Judge Kimmell handed them the papers, calling special attention to the one handed in by me. We were directed to remain until Gen. Ewell had time to examine the reports. In about half an hour one of the officers returned, saying that Gen. Ewell directed that every one of us should go at once to his place of business, and he would send a guard to examine for themselves. Standing in front of our store, key in hand, ready to unlock the door when called upon, Maj. Hawkes riding by, stopped and said, "You are Mr. Hoke, are you not?" Gen. Ewell says that you have made the only satisfactory report, and your groceries will not be disturbed. It may be necessary for us to have a barrel or two of that New Orleans molasses, but otherwise you shall not be disturbed." A short time after this squads of six or eight men, under command of an officer, were seen going here and there throughout the town examining the contents of stores, shops and cellars. When one of these squads came to our store, and the officer in command ordered me to unlock the door, I told him what Maj. Hawkes had told me. He replied, "That's all right; I have my orders; open your door." When the door was opened he gave an order, when a soldier was placed at each side of the door, and crossing their bayonets, no one was permitted to enter but the officer. He went back to the rear end of the store, and without attempting to examine any place, came out and told me to lock the door, saying, "All right now; you will not be disturbed." He did not enter the cellar at all. After these squads had reported at headquarters, Grocery, Drug, Hardware, Book and Stationary, Clothing, Boot and Shoe, and other stores, were relieved of a considerable part of their contents. In some cases payment was made in confederate scrip. In this work of plunder, Major Todd, a brother of the wife of our honored President, Lincoln, seemed to be the leading spirit. During this day he came near losing his life, for while attempting to force an entrance into the cellar of Dr. Richards, his daughter flourished an axe over his head, and threatened to split it open if he persevered, when the miserable miscreant ingloriously fled.

It is out of my power to give any estimate of the amount of property taken from our citizens on that day, and on other days during the invasion. This much can be said, that many persons who had toiled and economized for years and years together to gain an honorable support for themselves and families, were ruined financially, and although the most of them started again in a smaller way, they never recovered from the losses of that day, and some of them, after meeting other losses were finally burned out a year later, and died in poverty. I am aware that the appropriation of this property for the use of the army was in accordance with the rules of war, but why it is that the government, which reimburses loyal men in the South —and it is feared in many cases rebels also —for losses sustained, refuses as much to our loyal people here, seems a problem hard to solve.

On the day following this plunder of our town, Maj. Hawkes rode up to me and told me that he was under the necessity of having two barrels of our New Orleans molasses. These he took, paying me in confederate scrip. After this our cellar was undisturbed until the following Sunday, when it was cleaned out, as shall be related in its proper place. In paying me for this molasses, Maj. Hawkes told me that he was born, I think, in New York, but for a number of years had been engaged in the manufacture of carriages in Charlestown, West Virginia. Dr. Haycock, of this place, tells me that he was intimately acquainted with him; that he was an excellent man, and that during the occupancy of Manassas Junction by the confederate forces in the winter of 1861-2, he visited that camp and saw him there. When here he had his son—a boy of probably 12 to 14 years of age—with him. He asked me to give this boy a pair of pants, and seeing that he needed them badly, I purchased a second-hand pair for him. This boy, too, when he came for the pants, seeing my wife baking bread, asked for a loaf, saying that flour was issued to them, and they had to bake for themselves, and he was tired of fresh cakes.

As nearly as I can recollect it was to Major Hawkes that I gave the letters containing the messages of the wounded rebels on South Mountain, referred to in chapter 6.

Among the things demanded of our town in the requisitions made, as will have been seen, was "the use of a Printing office and two printers" to do some printing for the invading army. And as no response was made to this demand, the printing fraternity were dealt with as the merchants and shopkeepers. A guard in charge of an officer was sent out to take possession of some one of our printing establishments, and the office of the *Reformed Messenger*—the printing establishment of that church, then located in the building known as the Mansion House, and standing where the cigar store of Mr. H. B. Hatnick and the dry goods establishment of Messrs. Hollar & Appenzellar now stands—was chosen. The officer in charge of this guard called at the residence of Mr. Samuel Etter, on East Market street, in which Mr. M. A. Foltz, the editor and proprietor of PUBLIC OPINION, and at that time employed as foreman in this office, resided, and informed him of the object of his visit. He proposed to Mr. Foltz to superintend the execution of the work they wished to have done, assuring him that if he complied with this request a guard would be placed to protect the property, and that nothing would be taken from it; otherwise forcible possession would be taken and no guarantee would be given as to the contents of the building. At that time paper and printing material were very high, and the office having a large stock of expensive paper on hand for an edition of a book they were publishing, Mr. Foltz at once saw the propriety of accepting the proposition, and without waiting for the consent of Dr. S. R. Fisher, the editor of the *Messenger* and Business Manager of the establishment, he proceeded to the office, calling to his assistance Mr. Henry Richter, another compositor of the house. The task required of them was the printing of a large number of General Orders issued by Generals Lee and Ewell, several thousand parole papers intended for the parolement of the prisoners they expected to take, and a large amount of other blank work for the use of the army. The execution of this work took several days, and when it was completed war prices were charged and the bill paid in Confederate scrip. Dr. Fisher, whose financial ability was unsurpassed by no other person in the community, succeeded in some way of disposing of this worthless paper at twenty-five cents on the dollar. This was the best conducted business transaction with the Confederates that occurred here during the invasion, and it was only surpassed by one other, which occurred in the Valley of Virginia —and by a preacher, too, about this same time—which will be related further on in this narrative.

Among the first papers that were printed at that time, and profusely scattered throughout the town and army, were some General Orders issued by Generals Lee and Ewell. Some of these had been written before the army reached this place, but were only printed and circulated here. The first of these orders was one by General Lee, and bore date of June 21st. This was on the preceding Sabbath, and before that part of the army which Gen. Lee was with had crossed the Potomac. Its object was, as will be seen by its perusal, to define the general plan of the operations of his army while in our State in procuring supplies. This plan, to the credit of Gen. Lee be it said, was designed to confine the demands of his army, and the methods to be employed in securing them, within the limits of civilized warfare. The execution of these demands, however, would bear heavily upon the people where his army would march, but would and did prevent entering private houses, and the indiscriminate plundering of private property. This order was as follows:

HEADQUARTERS ARMY OF NORTHERN)
VIRGINIA.
June 21st, 1863.

General Orders No. 72.—While in the enemy's country, the following regulations for procuring supplies will be strictly observed, and any violation of them promptly and vigorously punished:

1. No private property shall be injured or destroyed by any person belonging to or connected with the army, or taken, except by the officer hereinafter designated.

II. The chiefs of the Commissary, Quartermaster, Ordnance and Medical departments of the army will make requisitions upon the local authorities or inhabitants for the necessary supplies for their respective departments, designating the places and times of delivery. All persons complying with such requisitions shall be paid the market price for the articles furnished, if they so desire, and the officer making such payment shall make duplicate receipts for the same, specifying the name of the person paid, and the quantity, kind, and price of the property, one of which receipts shall be at once forwarded to the chief of the department to which such officer is attached.

III. Should the authorities or inhabitants neglect or refuse to comply with such requisition, the supplies required shall be taken from the nearest inhabitants so refusing, by the orders and under the directions of the respective chiefs of the departments named.

IV. When any command is detached from the main body, the chiefs of the several departments of such command will procure supplies for the same, and such other stores as they may be ordered to provide, in the manner and subject to the provisions herein prescribed, reporting their action to the heads of their respective departments, to which they will forward duplicates of all vouchers given or received.

V. All persons who shall decline to receive payment for property furnished on requisitions, and all from whom it shall be necessary to take stores or supplies, shall be furnished by the officers receiving or taking the same with a receipt specifying the kind and the quantity of the property received or taken, as the case may be, the name of the person from whom it was received or taken, the command for the use of which it is intended, and the market price. A duplicate of said receipt shall be at once forwarded to the chief of the department to which the officer by whom it is executed is attached.

VI. If any person shall remove or conceal property necessary for the use of the army, or attempt to do so, the officers hereinbefore mentioned will cause such property and all other property belonging to such persons that may be required by the army, to be seized, and the officer seizing the same will forthwith report to the chief of his department the kind, quantity and market price of the property so seized, and the name of the owner.

By command of Gen. R. E. Lee.

R. H. CHILTON, *A. A. and I. G.*

On the day following this Order by Gen. Lee, Gen. Ewell, the remainder of whose Corps crossed the Potomac on this day and led the advance into our State, issued the following general order:

HEADQUARTERS 2D CORPS,)
Army of Northern Virginia, June 22d, 1863.

General Orders, No. 49.—In moving in the enemy's country the utmost circumspection and vigilance are necessary for the safety of the army and the success of the great object it has to accomplish depends upon the observance of the most rigid discipline. The Lieut General commanding, therefore, most earnestly appeals to the officers and men of his command, who have attested their bravery and devotion to the cause of their country on so many battle fields, to yield a ready acquiescence in the rules required by the exigencies of the case.

All straggling and marauding from the ranks, and all marauding and plundering by individuals are prohibited, upon pain of the severest penalties known to the service.

What is required for the use of the army will be taken under regulations to be established by the Commanding General, according to the rules of civilized warfare.

Citizens of the country through which the army may pass, who are not in the military service, are admonished to abstain from all acts of hostility, upon the penalty of being dealt with in a summary manner. A ready acquiescence to the demands of the military authorities will serve greatly to lessen the rigors of war.

By command of
Lieut. Gen. R. S. EWELL.
A. L. PENDLETON, *A. A. Gen.*

This order was evidently issued by Gen. Ewell in ignorance of Lee's order to the same effect. This is accounted for in the fact that Ewell was not with Lee, but in the advance with his troops.

On Wednesday, 24th, shortly after Ewell's arrival here, and two days after issuing the Order just given, he issued an Order, which, it will be seen, was designed to prevent his men from seizing upon the liquors here and becoming intoxicated. It is to be regretted that this Order was not made permanent in our place for all time to come. The following is that Order:

HEADQUARTERS 2D CORPS,)
Army of Northern Virginia,
CHAMBERSBURG, June 24th, 1863.

General Orders.—1. The sale of intoxicating liquors to this command, without written permission from a Major General, is strictly prohibited.

II. Persons having liquor in their possession are required to report the fact to the Provost Marshal, or the nearest general officer, stating the amount and kind, that a guard may be placed over it, and the men prevented from getting it.

III. Any violation of Part I of these orders, or failure to comply with Part II, will be punished by the immediate confiscation of all liquors in the possession of the offending parties, beside rendering their other property liable to seizure.

IV. Citizens of the country through which the army may pass, who are not in the military service, are admonished to abstain from all acts of hostility, upon the penalty of being dealt with in a summary manner. A ready acquiescence to the demands of the military authorities will serve to lessen the rigors of war.

By command of
Lieut. Gen. R. S. EWELL.
A. S. PENDLETON, *A. A. General*.

I am not aware to what extent those having liquor in their possession responded to this requisition and reported the same at headquarters, but very soon after Ewell's entrance guards were stationed at all places where it was kept. If there were any cases of drunkenness among the whole of the Southern army, I did not see a single instance. One of our citizens now residing here—Mr. John F. Croft—at the time of this invasion, kept a wholesale liquor store in one of the rooms of Franklin Hall. The guard stationed over his liquors were always on hand and kept strict vigilance. Officers would sometimes call for a gallon or two for *hospital purposes*. Mr. Croft says that not only during the day were these calls made, but frequently during the night. Either the old and worn out plea of "a little for the stomach's sake" was employed as a pretext, or else high living and Conococheague water did not agree with them. Still there was no drunkenness that we could see; but that there was at least one case, will be seen in the proceedings of the Court Martial of an officer hereinafter given.

It will be seen from these Orders of Lee and Ewell, that private property was to be respected, and in no case taken except when needed by the army, and then only by officers specially charged for this duty and under the regulations prescribed. Candor compels me to state that, except in the plundering of our citizens by Longstreet's Corps, and some few robberies committed by stragglers while away from their commands, these humane regulations were observed. The taking of groceries, provisions, stationery, hardware, hats, boots and shoes, drugs, horses, cattle, corn, oats, hay, etc., was clearly within the rules of civilized warfare, and nothing more than our own army did in the enemy's country. And having been recognized by the Government as beligerents in the exchange of prisoners, and in other ways, the Confederate army had the right while in the enemy's country, to the usages accorded to beligerents. This to their credit, be it said, they exacted of us without many acts of wanton and useless plunder. Longstreet's Corps while here, as I shall relate hereafter, made no formal demands but helped themselves to whatever they wanted and could find. I will add what truth and candor compels me to state, however distasteful it may be to some, that from all the conceptions I had formed from history of the desolations produced by an invading army—in a civil warfare especially, which is usually attended with more rancor and bitterness than one between opposing Nations, this invasion of our State widely differed. Except in some instances private houses were not entered with hostile intent, and then only by stragglers from the main columns. But one person—Mr. Strite—was killed. He resided some distance from the road over which the army passed, some three miles south of town, and while standing in his yard three stragglers from Hill's Corps came up to him and demanded his money, which he immediately gave them. Soon afterward two more stragglers came and demanded money, and having no more, they killed and buried his body under a pile of manure. Hats, boots, watches and pocket books were taken, but never in the presence of an officer. Rev. Dr. B. S. Schneck was caught on the outskirts of the town, and his pocket book containing about fifty dollars and a valuable gold watch were taken from him. The watch had been presented to him by a friend while in Europe a few years previously. Rev. Father Cullom of the Catholic church was also robbed of his boots and pocket book. It is said that when he returned to town he used some language neither complimentary to the rebels nor in harmony with the sanctity of his profession. Other similar robberies were reported, but they were always by stragglers and marauders. The rebels, however, had a way of confiscating hats, even in the presence of officers, which is worthy of mention. And as a specimen of the way it was usually done, I will relate the following case: On Saturday evening, the 24th, while the Louisiana Tigers, as they were called, were marching past our store, Dr. Langbein and I sat upon our door step. Many of these soldiers had their miserable old slouched hats under their arms, and walked along bare-headed. This was by mutual understanding and for a purpose as will shortly appear. Some of these men had no hat at all, and it was for the purpose of capturing one that this ruse was resorted to. As we sat thus upon the door step, the rebels leaving the street because it was badly cut up and muddy and marching upon the pavements, one of them grabbed the doctor's fine, sleek drab slouch hat and thrusting it under his arm and crushing it all out of shape, marched on as if nothing had occurred. The doctor sprang to his feet and ran after him, when the officer in command, who was riding along in the street near where it occurred, rode up and said, "Show me the man who has taken your hat and I will see to it." But the men marched on in silence, the streaming column dare not be interrupted, and unable to recognize either the man or his hat, he gave up the pursuit in disgust. There was considerable profanity and a mixture of English and Dutch when the doctor returned.

Generals Hill's and Longstreet's corps this day crossed the Potomac, the former at Shepherdstown and the latter at Williamsport, and united at Hagerstown—Hill in advance.

With the purpose to preserve another important paper, although not directly connected with the operations of the Confederates in this place, and to present the meanness and inhumanity of Gen. Early, one of Lee's Division Commanders, in contrast with the humanity of Lee himself, I introduce here the order, or address, of the former to the citizens of York during its occupancy by his troops. Be it remembered that this address was issued after Early had exacted of the people of York $28,000 for the ransom of that place :

To the citizens of York :—I have abstained from burning the railroad buildings and car shops in your town, because, after examination, I am satisfied the safety of the town would be endangered ; and, acting in the spirit of humanity, which has ever characterized my Government and its military authorities, I do not design to involve the innocent in the same punishment with the guilty. Had I applied the torch without regard to consequences, I would have pursued a course that would have been vindicated as an act of retaliation for the many authorized acts of barbarity perpetrated by your own army upon our soil. But we do not war upon women and children, and I trust the treatment you have met with at the hands of my soldiers will open your eyes to the monstrous iniquity of the war waged by your government upon the people of the Confederate states, and that you will make an effort to shake off the revolting tyranny under which it is apparent to you all you are yourselves undergoing.

J. A. EARLY, Maj. Gen. C. S. A.

This Gen. Early seems to have an instinct for burning the property of our people, which only needed an opportunity to manifest itself. It was he who issued the order to McCausland to burn Chambersburg, and it was the same dastardly villain who burned the Caledonia Iron Works belonging to Hon. Thaddeus Stevens, as previously referred to. These works were situated at the base of the South Mountain, about ten miles from this place, on the road leading to Gettysburg. They consisted of a large Charcoal Furnace, Forge, Rolling Mill, Coal House, Shops, Stables, &c. Hon. John Sweney, at that time Mr. Stevens' business manager, gives me the following account of their destruction : On Tuesday, 16th, while Jenkins occupied Chambersburg, one of the marauding parties which went all about the county after horses and other plunder, visited these Iron Works, and after promising that they should not be destroyed if all the horses and mules were given up, left with about forty valuable animals with gears, &c. Mr. Sweney says they came near capturing Mr. Stevens himself, who was then on a visit, and had been taken hurriedly away, against his protests, to Shippensburg. On Tuesday, 23d, the same day that Rhodes' division of Ewell's corps entered this place, the advance of Early's division of the same corps reached Caledonia Iron Works, on its way to Gettysburg and York. Mr. Sweney had a conversation with Early as he sat on his horse on the bridge there, and endeavored to dissuade him from carrying out his threat to destroy the works. He told him that so far as Mr. Stevens was concerned, he would have been better off if his works had been destroyed ten years before, but for the sake of the many poor people who would be thrown out of employment, he should spare the works. Early replied : "That is not the way Yankees do business." He also said that Mr. Stevens was "an enemy of the South, in favor of confiscating their property and arming their negroes, and the property must be destroyed." He then placed a guard around it and gave special instructions that it should not be destroyed until he gave the order. Early then returned to Greenwood, where he had his headquarters, but returned the next day and personally detailed Col. French to apply the torch. The work of destruction was thoroughly done, and soon all the works were in ashes. Mr. Stevens' loss was estimated at about $50,000.

Chambersburg, has never, so far as I know, been dishonored by the presence of Gen. Early. I have never seen him, and do not particularly desire ever to do so. But if the choice of one of the rebel leaders to fall into the hands of Phil. Sheridan, had been left to me, next to Jeff Davis himself, I would have selected Jubal A. Early as the right man for the right place. Long live Phil Sheridan for the repeated thrashings he gave to this ill-natured rebel and traitor.

THURSDAY, 25TH.

On this, as on the day previous, infantry, artillery and long trains of wagons passed through town and on down towards Harrisburg. As already stated the corps of Hill and Longstreet crossed the Potomac on the day previous—Wednesday, 24th. It will thus be seen that the army which was moving into our State extended from the Potomac to Shippensburg, a distance of forty miles. I have no hesitation in saying that if Early's Division, Stuart's and Imboden's cavalry, and other detachments from the army which passed through here, had all been called in and added to the line, it would have extended nearly all the way from this place to Harrisburg. This may seem incredible, but its truthfulness will appear when I state that I shall have occasion hereafter to tell of one single wagon train which extended from *seventeen to twenty-five miles*, and another *fourteen miles*. No idea can be formed of the *immenseness* of an army such as Lee's, with its appendages, by any description which can be given. Actual observation alone can give an adequate idea of its magnitude. Pemit me here to digress from the order I have chosen, to give the following observations which may assist the reader in forming some conceptions of this immense host.

First, as is usually the case with armies on the march, came a brigade of cavalry, and after an interval, the different regiments and brigades composing a division. There were here and there along the line bands of excellent music. "Dixie" and "My Maryland" were the favorite pieces played. These were followed by a train of artillery composed of cannon, caissons and forges; then a long train of heavily loaded wagons, filled with shot, shells and other ammunition. These wagons were each drawn by four or six horses or mules, and in passing through our streets they made that grinding noise which indicated immense weight of freightage. The wagon train was usually followed by another train of reserve artillery, and from fifty to one hundred cattle for the use of the division. Following this division, after a short interval, came another, and another, in the same order, until an entire corps had passed. The passage of a corps usually occupied about a day and a half, and so closely was one succeeded by another that it would be impossible to fix upon the precise time when one departed and another came. Many of the wagons, horses, mules, and cannon bore the inscription "U. S.," and were evidently captured or stolen from the government. The rear of the army, like its advance, was a large force of cavalry. Each regiment and brigade had its flag, but there seemed to be no two entirely alike. Some bore the ensignia of the State from which it came, and others some other device, and but few the Stars and Bars of the Confederacy. This diversity of flags was typical of the cause for which they fought—for a government composed of a number of independent sovreignties, while the grand army of the Union carried but one flag—the glorious Stars and Stripes, representing a sovereign head with many members.

The rebel infantry, as they marched through our streets, presented a solid front. They came in close marching order, the different brigades, divisions and corps, all within supporting distance. Their dress consisted of nearly every imaginable style and color, the butternut largely predominating. Some had blue blouses, which they had captured, or stripped from the Union dead. Hats, or the skeletons of what were once hats, surmounted their partly covered heads. Many were ragged, dirty and shoeless, affording unmistakable evidence that they sadly stood in need of having their wardrobes replenished. They were all, however, well armed and under perfect discipline. They seemed to move as one vast machine, and laughing, talking, singing or cheering, was not indulged in. Straggling was scarcely seen, but when any did wander away from the lines, and find any of our citizens in retired places while they occupied the town, they did not hesitate to appropriate to themslves hats, boots, watches and pocket books. This proves that their good behavior when under the eyes of their officers was due to discipline rather than innate honesty or good breeding.

There was a perceptible difference between the character of the cavalry and the infantry. The former, as a class, were superior in all respects. This may be accounted for in the fact that the cavalry was composed mostly of the well to do, the educated, the slave holders,—those belonging to "the first families," while the rank and file of the infantry were the lower classes, the uneducated, the non-slave holding, "the poor white trash" of Southern society, the most of whom were conscripted into the service. These had no intelligent understanding of what they were fighting for, and when interrogated would say that they were fighting for "our rights." What rights any of them ever possessed, except to bow obsequiously to the aristocratic classes, to lounge in idleness, to eat clay, curse the abolitionists, hate niggers and denounce "nigger equality," would be hard to tell. That the majority of them ever owned a home of their own, or could read and write, or had any adequate conceptions of the value and greatness of the government they were trying to overthrow, no one who conversed with them could believe. There was a marked difference in these men, which seemed a peculiarity of all from the same State. Those from Mississippi and Texas were more vicious and defiant than those from other parts of the South. Usually the dissatisfied and those seeking opportunities to escape, were from North Carolina. Some said that they at first were for the preservation of the Union, but having been forced into the army, they only desired that their side should win. Here and there were some geniuses, and lovers of fun. They supposed that being among the "Pennsylvania Dutch," the German language, was mostly spoken here. The following laughable incident will illustrate this fact. Judge Kimmell relates that remembering one day that Mrs. McClure was alone, and probably would be glad to see some one from town—the Colonel being prudently absent—concluded he would go out to see her. At the place on the Harrisburg pike where the gate house then stood, he encountered a sentinel who, after learning his mission, permitted him to pass. While with Mrs. McClure, Hood's division was passing, and the Judge and Mrs. McClure went down to the front of the yard to see them. As the Judge's round, plump, Teutonic form and face beamed out from the foliage of the Colonel's magnificent grounds, a soldier looking toward him said to his companion, "I'll bet that old fellow drinks lots of beer." "No, no," said the Judge, "I never drink beer." At this the soldier cried out, trying to imitate Pennsylvania Dutch, "Och, Mine Gott! Mine Gott!! My Countree! My Countree!!" Another time a soldier stopped the Judge on the street, and thus accosted him : "Can you tell where a fellow can get a little whiskey?" "I can't tell you," said the Judge," "I never drink whiskey." Looking him squarely in the face, and estimating the truthfulness of the reply by the flush of his countenance, the soldier significantly replied, "Oh, I guess not."

The officers in command of the infantry like the men composing the cavalry, were of the higher and better class. Many of them with whom we had business transactions seemed to be perfect gentlemen, and while compelled to appropriate to the use of their army our property, to be paid for in worthless scrip, they did it in an apologizing way. Some of them were overheard to express their fears that they had run into a trap by coming over into our State, but the usual remark was, "Uncle Robert has brought us here, and he will see us out all right." In looking upon the large number of persons who gathered into the town on Sunday to see them, some of the rebels inquired if they were not soldiers in disguise. When answered that they were not, and the population and resources of the North were not yet scarcely touched, they seemed greatly astonished. A case of this kind occurred one morning in front of the residence of Mr. H. E. Hoke, on East Market street. Imboden's cavalry had came in the evening previous and some of the officers were sitting on the steps of Mr. Hoke's residence, their horses being hitched to the shade trees. Upon Mr. Hoke's appearance one of the officers, apparently one of considerable rank, thus addressed him, "How long is this war going to last?" He replied, "You can answer that question better than I can." "What do you mean by that?" inquired the officer. "I mean that this war will last as long as you in the South are able to fight. If you can stand it twenty years more, then the war will last twenty years yet." The officer was evidently impressed, which emboldened Mr. Hoke to say further : "You must have seen for yourselves since you have come North that there are any number of able-bodied men yet to draw on, and the people of the North have scarcely awakened to the fact that there is a war on their hands, but this invasion will stir them up, and if it were possible for you to annihilate the whole of our armies now in the field, that would only bring out another to take you some morning for breakfast." They all listened in silence, and seemed to be thunderstruck, when one, who was lying on the cellar door, said with an oath, "There is more truth than fun in what he says." This remark led to a considerable discussion among themselves about the large number of men they had seen since they had entered Pennsylvania.

It was a subject of frequent remark by the rebels about the magnificent country and large and flourishing towns they had seen since coming north. The dwelling houses of the farmers and the large and excellent barns also excited their admiration and astonishment. Letters written while here to be sent to their friends in the South, but lost from their pockets, were picked up on the streets. In some of these their expressions of astonishment at the rich and beautiful country, the excellent farming and fine large houses and barns, were profuse and decided. One young officer connected with Ewell's Corps placed in my hands a number of letters stamped with the government postage stamp, asking me to put them in our mail when communications were again opened. I did not like to tell I could not do so, but received and held their letters until after the invasion, when I concluded to dispose of them. They were directed to young ladies in Baltimore, and among other things said in them were expressions of surprise and admiration for our rich and beautiful country and excellent farming.

During the time we were under rebel rule, we were without information of what was going on, only as an occasional paper was brought through the lines by some of our scouts. The first information of the first day's battle at Gettysburg and the death of Gen. Reynolds, was received from a copy of the Philadelphia *Inquirer* brought from Harrisburg by Mr. Benjamin S. Huber. The rebels had their regular mails from Richmond, and an occasional Richmond paper would be received, in which it was told how successfully the Confederate cause was going on elsewhere. One edition of one of the Richmond papers received here announced that Gen. Johnston had defeated Gen. Grant and raised the siege of Vicksburg. It was said that the lying account was read to the army when on parade and the men cheered themselves hoarse over their imaginary triumph. One of their mails from Richmond was captured in Greencastle, in which were found important papers from the Confederate authorities at Richmond. These were as soon as possible delivered to the commander of the army of the Potomac. From two statements prepared by residents of Greencastle, who were witnesses of the heroic acts I am about to describe, I condense the following account. After the main body of Lee's army had passed through the town to Gettysburg, the communications with Virginia were kept open by detachments of rebel cavalry, which frequently passed through. Ignorant of Lee's destination, and discouraged by the mighty host of defiant and boastful rebels, with their immense trains of artillery, which had passed down the valley, the surprise and joy of the people knew no bounds when, on Thursday, July 2d, a company of Union cavalry dashed into the town. These men were under command of Capt. Dahlgreen, the same who afterwards became a Colonel, and was killed in front of Richmond. Says one of my informants: "If a band of angels had come down, they would not have been more unexpected. I may probably add, not so welcome. It required only a few minutes to apprise the town of their presence, and all Greencastle seemed to be on the street. Hats flew into the air. Cheer followed cheer. Even the old and most staid ministers, everybody was ready to bid them welcome, and some wept for joy. Their leader, the gallant Dahlgreen, though a mere youth, had the entire confidence of his men and handled them with ease and skill." Dahlgreen ordered everyone off the streets, and after hiding his men behind the recesses of the public square, went up into the steeple of the Reformed church, from which, with his glass, he could scan the country for miles around. Perceiving a company of cavalry coming, and ascertaining their number, he rapidly descended, determined to give battle, notwithstanding their number was double his own. He hastily placed his men so that the advancing enemy could not see them until they would reach the Diamond, he placed himself at their head, pistol in hand, and leaning down upon the neck of his horse, with every nerve strained with eagerness to meet the foe, he waited until they were within a few hundred yards, when the word was given and with a wild yell and the bang, bang of their carbines, these brave defenders of the Union dashed after the astonished and panic-stricken foe. Although from the superior numbers of the enemy it was feared that these brave scouts would be annihilated, yet 17 of the rebels were captured, three of whom were officers. A mail bag intended for Gen. Lee was also taken, which was deemed so important that Dahlgreen hastily left with it. Galloping out the Waynesboro' road, he detailed a detachment to barricade the road on the hill east of the town, near John Ruthrauff's house. This they did by piling wagons, hay ladders and other things across the road. The guard, after erecting this barricade, remained there to meet any foe who might attempt pursuit, and at length left and went after their companions. This mail containing important documents from the Confederate Government to Gen. Lee, was, with the prisoners captured, delivered to Gen. Meade across the mountain.

Captain Dahlgreen returned again on Saturday morning and on that day captured 17 infantry and 7 cavalry. In the engagement of that day a number of rebels were wounded, but the Union force escaped in every one of these engagements without injury or loss.

Occasionally when rebel soldiers inquired for such articles as kid gloves, which we had sent away or secreted, they would say, "All right, we can get them when we get to Philadelphia or Baltimore or Washington." One day Judge Kimmell came to me and said an officer told him he wanted a web of bleached muslin and some other things for the use of his own family and that he was willing to pay a good price for in gold. I told the Judge that I had the things wanted stored away in a beer vault, but if we were to furnish them it would show that our stock of goods was not sent away but only hid and the probability was that the whole thing was a trick to find out this fact. The Judge replied that this was probably so, and that he did not think of it or he would not have made the proposition to me.

The rebels all seemed especially to hate President Lincoln. They had been made to believe that he was responsible for the war and that he was brutal and barbarous and drunk nearly all the time. A report was circulated among them that he had fled from Washington to Boston, and that the army of the Potomac was still in Virginia and that they would have Pennsylvania militia only to overcome and then Harrisburg, Philadelphia, Baltimore and Washington would fall into their hands. Seeing the statue of Dr. Franklin on the cupola of the Court House, one of them declared that it was intended to represent "Old Pete Lincorn." Passing by our store one day, one of the men looked up to our sign and mistaking the inscription of J. Hoke & Co. cried out—"Hurrah for old Joe Hooker! Here he is, and he is the very fellow we are after."

I will state here that in speaking of a division encampment at a certain place, it is not to be supposed that it all occupied one encampment. Usually it divided and the several brigades occupied such positions as were assigned them, all, however, within supporting distance of each other. From these various encampments marauding parties, mostly of cavalry, would go out in all directions after horses, cattle, corn, oats, and such other articles as were needed. In this way the whole country for many miles beyond these encampments was visited. The only instance in which armed resistance was attempted by the people, or would have been at all practicable, was by the citizens of Horse Valley. This Valley is very narrow and of considerable length, and being surrounded by mountains which are passable only at a few places, it was made the hiding place for a large number of horses from all parts of the county. Mr. Stephen Keefer, a resident of that valley, has kindly furnished me with the following statement of the preparations made for defense against raiding parties. The horses belonging to residents of the valley, as well as all those taken there from other parts, were hidden in the upper—the *southern*—end of the valley. The road from Loudon into this end of the valley is very narrow, precipitous and winding, and could be easily barricaded against cavalry. Mr. Keefer was Supervisor of the township, and he summoned his neighbors to his assistance and cut down a number of trees across this road, effectually closing it against all intruders. On the top of the mountain covering the approach by the Strasburg road, breastworks of logs and bushes were erected, and about thirty of the hardy mountaineers with their tried rifles stood guard there for several days. This guard having been withdrawn one day, about thirty Confederate cavalry entered the valley by that gap, and passed on across it into Path Valley and up into Amberson's Valley. They then turned about and retraced their steps by the same route, taking with them but six horses from this valley. Had the mountaineers been at their posts a battle would most certainly have taken place and some of those rebels would have fallen by the sure aim of these expert marksmen. Or had they gone on up the valley some eight miles, two or three hundred valuable horses might have been taken. The reader may inquire, how did these men, unacquainted with these mountain roads, find their way into and out of these remote places? They were guided no doubt by some sympathizer, for Mr. Keefer says that while passing through Fannettsburg, a man rode with them with his face covered with a handkerchief. The traitorous guide, notwithstanding his disguise, was recognized by some, but fearing that they might be mistaken and do an innocent person injustice, his name has not been given.

As portions of Lee's army passed through Fulton, Franklin, Cumberland, Adams and York counties, these plundering parties visited almost every nook and corner, and a vast amount of plunder was taken. Many of the farmers in this and adjoining counties took their horses down below Harrisburg for safety, and in this way saved them from being stolen.

One day a horseman rode up in front of the bank and after hitching his horse stood upon the pavement. He was decidedly clerical in appearance. Some officers passing by saluted him as "Doctor." He replied, "Well, we are back again in the Union." He was Rev. Dr. Pryer, father of Gen. Roger A. Pryer, at one time a member of Congress. I felt like telling him that many of them were destined never again to go out of the Union, but would find a permanent lodgment somewhere in northern soil. I had some respect for the poor ignorant privates who had been conscripted into the army, and also for the officers who were only acting out the legitimate results of their States Rights teachings, but for such clerical rascals who professed to be the servants of the Most High, and acting under His guidance, I had and have no respect whatever. The different regiments had each their chaplain, and I have been told that when in camp they had their regular religious services, and prayer meetings were often held by the men.

The ladies of the town did not conceal their sentiments from the rebels. Many of them wore small Union flags pinned to their breasts. They did not imitate the chivalry of the ladies of the South, by spitting in the faces of the soldiers, and otherwise insulting them. In some cases they gave their dresses to such as desired to desert, and arrayed in women's clothes furnished by some of our ladies, several were enabled to escape. I stood one evening in front of a house where a number of ladies were congregated and singing patriotic songs. Some five or six rebels were upon the pavement, near the window listening to the music. At the conclusion of the Star Spangled Banner, one of the soldiers said, "It is the prettiest flag the world ever saw."

As descriptive of one of the ways by which some of our citizens assisted disaffected soldiers to escape, I relate the following: On the evening of July 1st a rebel soldier called at the residence of Mr. H. E. Hoke and declared to Mr. Hoke his desire to escape from the army and remain in the North. After satisfying himself that the man was sincere and not endeavoring to get him into a difficulty, Mr. Hoke arranged to meet him with a suit of citizen's clothes in the first wood out along the Cumberland Valley railroad. On the morning of the following day, according to agreement, he met the soldier there and gave him the clothing in which he escaped, leaving Mr. Hoke his musket and accoutrements. Before leaving the soldier told Mr. Hoke that many of the army were disheartened because that while the South had put its entire force in the field, they beheld any number of able bodied men here yet, and but few of their army had any hope of success. Upon bidding Mr. Hoke farewell, the soldier put his hand upon the top of the fence and sprang over, saying, "Farewell to Jeff. Davis and the Southern Confederacy."

Some of our citizens in looking at the vast army passing through the town became faint-hearted, and one said to me, "In five days this government will be overthrown." I give it as my opinion that all the unorganized, undisciplined and inexperienced militia of the State could not have vanquished that mighty host. It required an army equal in numbers, arms, organization, discipline and experience to accomplish this. Thanks be to God—ten thousand thanks—that the grand army of the Potomac was equal to the occasion, and it was found at the right place at the right time, and under the right commanders, and that it did its work well and effectually. And thanks, too, that God planted Round Top and Cemetery Hill and Culp's Hill just where He did. My father said that when he was a boy and lived in Gettysburg, he often hunted rabbits on these hills, and sometimes wondered why they were put there, but after the battle of Gettysburg he understood why God put them there. Rev. Dr. Stockton, in his eloquent prayer at the dedication of the Soldiers' National Cemetery in Nov. 1863, at that place, caught the proper idea when he called those hills the "Altar of Sacrifice," the "Field of Deliverance," the "Mount of Salvation," and the "Munitions of Rocks."

On the morning of this day, General Ewell removed his headquarters from Mr. Trostle's hotel in town to the Mennonite church one mile north on the pike leading to Harrisburg. At that place there was held on that day a Court Martial to try a number of persons for breaches of discipline. At the time it was reported that a soldier was condemned to death and shot, but such was not the fact, as the following official order will show:

HEADQUARERS 2ND CORPS,
Army Northern Virginia, June 25th, '63.

General Order, No. 51.—I. Before the military court, convened at the headquarters of the Army Corps of Lieut. Gen. R. S. Ewell, and of which court Col. B. H. Lee is presiding Judge, were arraigned and tried. (The specifications in the various cases being lengthy and minute, are omitted.)

1st. Lieutenant J. B. Countiss, Georgia Regiment.

Charge I. Drunkenness on duty.

Charge II. Conduct to the prejudice of good order and discipline.

Finding: Of the specifications of 1st charge, Guilty.

Of the 1st charge, Guilty.

Of the specifications of the 2nd charge, Guilty.

Of the 2nd charge, Guilty.

Sentence: And the Court do therefore sentence the said Lieutenant J. B. Countiss, 21st Georgia Regiment, to be cashiered.

2nd. Private Charles Smith, Co. C, 45th N. C. Regiment.

Charge: Desertion.

Finding: Of the specification, Guilty.

Of the charge, not Guilty, but

Of absence without leave, Guilty.

Sentence: And the Court do therefore sentence the said Private Charles Smith, Co. C, 45th N. C. Regiment, to forfeit three months pay, and to be branded on the left hip with the letter S, two inches in length, in the presence of his Regiment.

3d. Private Louis M. Waynock, Co. B, 45th Regiment.

Charge: Desertion.

Finding: Of the specification, Guilty.

Of the charge—not Guilty, but

Of absence without leave, Guilty.

Sentence: And the Court do therefore sentence the said Louis M. Waynock, Co. B, 45th N. C. Regiment, to forfeit three month's pay, and to be branded on the left hip with the letter S, two inches in length, in the presence of his Regiment.

4th. Private Patrick Herne, Co. C, 5th Alabama Regiment.

Charge: Violation of 9th Article of War.

Finding: Of the specification, Guilty. Of the charge, Guilty.

Sentence: And the Court do therefore sentence the said Patrick Herne, Co. C, 5th Alabama Regiment, to forfeit his pay for three months, to perform extra police and fatigue duty for two months, and to be bucked two hours each day, for seven days.

11. The proceedings, findings and sentence in the case of Lieutenant J. B. Countiss, 21st Georgia Regiment, are approved, and the sentence will be carried into effect; and Lieutenant J. B. Countiss ceases, from this date, to be an officer of the Confederate States Army. He will be enrolled and conscripted by his Brigade commander, and will be allowed to join any company in his present Brigade that he may select.

The proceedings, findings and sentence in the cases of Private Charles Smith, Co. C, 45th N. C. Regiment, and Louis M. Waynock, Co. B, 45th N. C. Regiment, are approved, and the sentences will be carried into effect, except so much of them as inflict the punishment of branding, which is hereby remitted.

The proceedings, findings and sentence in the case of Private Patrick Herne, Co. C., 5th Alabama Regiment, are approved, and the sentence will be carried into effect.

By command of Lieutenant General R. S. EWELL.

A. S. PENDLETON, A. A. General.

The superior discipline of the Southern army will be seen in this, that officers in command were promptly cashiered for drunkenness, and not permitted to remain in positions which would endanger others. And when cashiered they were not permitted to resign their commissions, or leave the army and return to civil life, but were reduced to the ranks and compelled to do service in that humble position. If that kind of discipline had prevailed in the Union army, there would have been fewer disasters from the use of intoxicating liquors. The penalty inflicted upon others for the violations of the rules of war, as stated in the charges and specifications given, requiring the forfeiture of three months pay, did not amount to much, for the pay of a private soldier in Confederate scrip it was worth only the value of the paper it was printed on. For the benefit of those who do not know what "Bucking" is, I will state that it consisted in tying a person's hands together and closing his arms around his knees and passing a stick through to keep him in that helpless and ludicrous condition.

Some time during the day, two young men—officers connected with the artillery —came with a requisition for all the flannels and other woolen goods we had, suitable for making cartridges for cannon. Having removed everything of value out of the store, they found only a few remnants which we did not think worth secreting. These they had me to measure for them, one of them noting down the lengths. When asked the price I told him I should have a dollar a yard, counting upon Confederate scrip as the pay. He inquired what we sold them at, saying they would not allow me more for them than our usual price, for their money was as good as ours, and if it was not they intended to make it so before leaving the State. After striking an average price he wrote and gave me a paper of which the following is a correct copy—the original I yet have in possession:

I hereby certify that I have received of J. Hoke & Co., merchants, Chambersburg, Pa., this 25th day of June, 1863, and in accordance with General Order, No. 72, Headquarters, and have furnished duplicate vouchers, 9 (nine yards) flannel at 63¼ cents per yard, $5.90.

JOHN M. GREGORY, JR.,
1st Lieut. and Ord. officer Art'y 2nd Corps.

I was directed to present this voucher to the Pay Master and get my money, but counting their scrip of no value, and not believing their threat to make it as good as U. S. Greenbacks likely to be fulfilled, I never presented it. It is now held as a relic of those troublous days.

Not long after the departure of these ordinance officers, two more from the Medical department came, demanding all the tea we had for their hospitals. Like the flannel, they got only what we did not think of sufficient value to hide away. During the day other officers also came for such articles as Castile soap, etc., for their own use. We had unlocked our fire proof safe and left the door stand open, thinking that if locked they would suppose it contained valuables and break it open. This we did at Jenkin's raid and during the invasion. In not a single instance did an officer approach it, or attempt to look in it, but nearly every private soldier that got into the store made straight for the safe and examined it.

Jenkin's cavalry in advance of Rhode's Division this day reached Carlisle. On this and the succeeding day the Union Army crossed the Potomac into Maryland at Edward's Ferry, and took a position between Harper's Ferry and Frederick city, to be ready either to protect Washington, or march to meet Lee wherever he might offer battle.

FRIDAY, 26th.

This day was fraught with great events, and stands as an era in the history of Chambersburg. In the morning Heth's division of Hill's corps entered the town, and turning east in the Diamond proceeded out on the road leading to Gettysburg, and encamped in the evening near Fayetteville. About 9½ o'clock I was in the Diamond looking at Gen. Hill, the commander of this corps. He had his horse hitched in front of the residence and hotel of Mr. John Noel, where the large building now stands, in which the *Valley Spirit* is printed. Hill was standing out near the middle of the Diamond as if watching for some one to come from South Main street. Mr. Henry Bishop, the Photographer, informs me that on the occasion referred to he had a conversation with Gen. Hill. The General inquired of him concerning a number of persons who had resided in Carlisle, with whom he was acquainted while at the barracks there. Mr. Bishop gave him whatever information he could concerning the person inquired about, and then asked him when Gen. Lee was expected? Hill replied that he was expecting Lee every moment, and casting his eyes up Main street, said, "There he is now." Mr. Bishop hurried to his photograph gallery, which was in the building about where he now resides, and having everything in readiness to take a picture of the General and his staff, pushed the shutters of his window open and run the end of his camera out, at which some teamsters and soldiers, sitting along the curbstones, rose to their feet to see what was going on. At the same instant Lee and his staff left the Diamond and the picture was not taken. It is to be regretted that Mr. Bishop did not succeed in taking a picture of the historic scene. It would afford an occasion worthy the genius of the best artist.

Gen. Hill seemed to me to be a man of splendid physical make. He was entirely unlike Ewell, who was angular and thin in feature, and of sallow complexion, but eminently intellectual. He was killed in the final struggle about Petersburg, Virginia, in April, 1865. After satisfying my curiosity concerning General Hill, I went up into the front room of the second story of my dwelling, right over the store, on the north-east corner of the Diamond. This room was the usual resort of the ministers of the town, for from its windows an uninterrupted view could be had of Main street, the street the Confederates came through, from the Reformed church to the lower end of the town, some six squares. There were in that room, as near as I can recollect, the Rev. Dr. B. S. Schneck, Rev. B. Bausman, Rev. J. Dickson, the writer and a few others whom I cannot now recollect. Observing a group of about twenty or thirty finely mounted officers coming over the brow of the hill opposite the Reformed church, I called the attention of the persons present to them. Mr. Bausman exclaimed, "That's Lee and his staff." Snatching his hat he made rapid strides down stairs and out into the Diamond, followed by all in the room. Taking a position in the Diamond in front of the Mansion House, then the printing establishment of the Reformed church, and where the building now stands in which Hatnick's segar store and Messrs. Hollar & Appenzellar's dry goods store are located, I watched the entrance of these men into the Diamond and the memorable events which then and there transpired. Lee and his staff stopped immediately in front of where I stood. General Hill mounted his horse and rode slowly towards Lee, holding his hat gracefully above his head. Lee and Hill then rode a short distance apart, and held a short whispered consultation. In an article written for the Philadelphia *Times*, some few months ago, upon this same subject, I stated that Lee and Hill *dismounted* and held this consultation while standing. Mr. J. N. Snider and J. W. Douglass, who, with many others, were present and witnessed this event, tell me that in this I am mistaken, and that they did not dismount, but held their consultation on horseback. Mr. Snider also tells me that in locating the place in the Diamond where that consultation was held, as about where the bronze soldier stands within the enclosure of the Soldier's Memorial Fountain, I am also mistaken, that it was some fifteen or twenty feet from the soldier in the direction of the bank. A large part of Heth's division of Hill's corps had already passed through town and not following the two divisions of Ewell's corps down the valley towards Harrisburg, but turning east on the pike leading by way of Gettysburg to Baltimore, I concluded that if Lee followed in the same direction, Baltimore and Washington were his destination. In this opinion others shared, as will be shown in a chapter on "Scouts," yet to follow. With this impression upon my mind, I watched with intense interest the result of the council then taking place, and observing Mr. Benjamin S. Huber, now a resident of Letterkenny township, Franklin county, standing by my side, and remembering that he had been sent a few days previously with a message to the authorities at Harrisburg, I thus addressed him: "There, Ben, is perhaps the most important council in the history of this war, and the fate of the government may depend upon it. If Lee goes on down the valley, then Harrisburg and Philadelphia are threatened; if he turn east, Baltimore and Washington are in danger, and the government ought to know which way he goes as soon as possible." Said Huber: "Well, I have just got back from Harrisburg and I am tired, but as soon as Lee starts so that I see which way he goes, I will be off again for Harrisburg." In a short time the council between the two Generals ended, and Hill pointing eastwardly to the road leading to Gettysburg, fell back, allowing Lee to go in advance. Reaching nearly the middle of the Diamond he turned his hore's head eastward and was followed by his staff. Looking around for Huber I saw him making his way through the crowd for the mountains to convey this important information to Harrisburg. I will detail the account of his trip to the Capital in my chapter on Scouts.

There were with the Confederates at this time two officers of the British army, and one of the Prussian. These officers were no doubt with that brilliant cortege and expected and desired to see the downfall of the Republic. That such were the feelings of at least one of them—Col. Freemantle—one of the British officers, is clearly demonstrated in an article contributed by him to *Blackwood's Magazine*, in which he narrates the events of the Pennsylvania campaign. His abuse of the people of the border, and of the ladies of Chambersburg, whom he calls "Viragos," his congratulating Gen. Longstreet upon the apparent success of Pickett's great charge on the third day of the battle, and his regret at their repulse and annihilation, clearly show his hatred of our country and her institutions, and his sympathy with the rebels. We heard of those officers when passing through here, but did not distinguish them from others.

Gen. Lee, as he sat upon his horse in the public square of our town, looked every inch a soldier. He was at that time about fifty-two years of age, stout built, of medium height, hair strongly mixed with gray, and a rough gray beard. He wore the Confederate gray, with some ornamentation about the collar of his coat which designated his rank. His hat was a soft black without ornament other than the cord around the crown. Any one who had ever seen his picture would have no difficulty in singling him out in a crowd. He seemed to have not only the most profound respect of his men—officers and privates—but their admiration and love. The men composing his staff were a splendid looking body. Finely mounted, neatly dressed, and excellent in horsemanship, they presented an appearance which those who witnessed it will be likely ever to remember. In that group were comprised the brains of the vast, moving host which came swarming into our borders, and while we felt to admire the genius of these men, we yet looked upon them as the enemies of our country, and could only hope and pray that they would meet the terrible overthrow which they deserved. In precisely one week from the day of this imposing pageant, our hope and prayer was realized, and the defeated and decimated hosts of treason and rebellion, were thrown back from the heights around Gettysburg, and with their crushing defeat commenced the downfall of the accursed cause for which they fought.

General Lee selected for his headquarters a grove which then stood along the pike leading to Gettysburg, near the eastern edge of the town. It was once known as "Shetter's Woods," but afterwards as "Messersmith's Woods," after the late George R. Messersmith, Esq., who at the time referred to owned it. It was for many years the place were picnics and Fourth of July celebrations were held. The Centennial Anniversary of American Independence, on July 4th, 1876, was held there. The grove has recently been cut down, and the place is now a cultivated field. It was a beautiful location, and from Friday, June 26th, to Tuesday morning, 30th, General Lee and his staff tarried there. There he held his councils of war, there he received reports from the various parts of his vast army, and there he planned and ordered an attack on the Capital of our State, and there on the night of Monday, 29th, when Longstreet's scout brought information of the whereabouts of the Army of the Potomac, he recalled that order and decided to cross the South Mountain and fight a battle upon the direct line to Baltimore and Washington. Other acts of importance which transpired upon this historic spot during those memorable four days of General Lee's residence there, will be given in their appropriate places.

As previously stated, on this day Heth's division of Hill's corps passed through town and on out east to Fayetteville, where it encamped. This division was followed on the day following, Saturday, 27th, by Pender's and Anderson's divisions—Pender in advance. On Sunday, 28th, according to Professor Jacobs in his *Battle of Gettysburg*, page 19, the camp fires of the advance of Heth's division were seen on the eastern slope of the mountain, about a mile above Cashtown. On the following day, Monday, 29th, according to the same reliable authority, by the aid of a field glass, it was seen that the rebel encampments about Cashtown had been considerably enlarged, the whole of Heth's division having crossed the mountain and encamped there (page 21). On the next day, Tuesday, 30th, the remaining two divisions of Hill's corps left their encampments about Fayetteville and Greenwood and marched for Cashtown—Pender in advance. On this same day, 30th, about

9½ A. M., a portion of Heth's division under Gen. Petigrew, advanced from Cashtown, as far as the crest of Seminary Hill, one-half mile north-west of Gettysburg, throwing about two dozen infantry pickets as far down as Mr. Shead's house. Several officers on horseback were seen reconnoitering with their field glasses, and engaged in conversation with the people residing near the road on the hill, eliciting, no doubt, as much information as they could obtain. They had with them fifteen wagons, probably with the intention of going into the town for such provisions and merchandize as they might be able to obtain. They were also accompanied with artillery, and thus were prepared for any resistance which they might encounter. This movement was doubtless a reconnoisance in force, probably for the purpose of taking possession of Gettysburg, or for the purpose of ascertaining the condition of things there. There were several thousand men in that advance, for their line extended at least a mile and a-half. At 10½ A. M., they again withdrew towards Cashtown, probably having heard of the approach of General Buford's cavalry, which arrived about one hour afterwards. (Battle of Gettysburg, pages 21, 22.)

On the succeeding day, Wednesday, July 1st, Heth's and Pender's divisions advanced from Cashtown and participated in the first day's engagement. Anderson's division halted too long at Cashtown to take part in this first day's engagement, but reached the scene of conflict in the evening after the close of the battle.

On the evening of this day, Friday, 26th, Early's division of Ewell's Corps, Gordon's brigade in advance, entered Gettysburg.

SATURDAY, 27TH.

On this day, as above stated, Pender's and Anderson's divisions of Hill's Corps passed through town out to Fayetteville and Greenwood, encamping within supporting distance of the main body of Heth's division, which on the following day threw out an advance to near Cashtown east of the mountain.

On this day the following General Order was written and issued by General Lee:

HEADQUARTERS, ARMY NORTHERN
VIRGINIA,
Chambersburg, Pa., June 27th, 1863.

General Orders, No. 73.—The Commanding General has observed with marked satisfaction the conduct of the troops on the march, and confidently anticipates results commensurate with the high spirit they have manifested.

No troops could have displayed greater fortitude, or better performed their arduous marches of the past ten days.

Their conduct in other respects has, with few exceptions, been in keeping with their character as soldiers, and entitles them to approbation and praise.

There have, however, been instances of forgetfulness on the part of some, that they have in keeping the yet unsullied reputation of this army, and that the duties exacted of us by civilization and christianity are not less obligatory in the country of the enemy than in our own.

The Commanding General considers that no greater disgrace could befall the army, and through it, our whole people, than the perpetuation of the barbarous outrages upon the unarmed and defenseless, and the wanton destruction of private property, that have marked the course of the enemy in our own country.

Such proceedings not only degrade the perpetrators and all connected with them, but are subversive of the discipline and efficiency of the army, and destructive of the ends of our present movement.

It must be remembered that we make war only upon armed men, and that we cannot take vengeance for the wrongs our people have suffered without lowering ourselves in the eyes of all whose abhorrence has been excited by the atrocities of our enemies, and offending against Him to whom vengeance belongeth, without whose favor and support our efforts must all prove in vain.

The Commanding General, therefore, earnestly exhorts the troops to abstain, with most scrupulous care, from unnecessary or wanton injury to private property, and he enjoins upon all officers to arrest and bring to summary punishment all who shall in any way offend against orders on this subject.

R. E. LEE, *General*.

This order, unlike the former one from General Lee, it will be seen, was written by the General himself and not by his Adjutant. And now as evidence that the humane policy of the Commander in Chief was not entirely respected by his subordinates, the conduct of Longstreet's plunderers fully attests. In further proof, however, I introduce two extracts from a report of the Pennsylvania campaign written by one of the British officers who was with General Lee, and published in *Blackwood's Magazine*, of Sept., 1863. The writer says that so completely was the country through which the Confederate army passed robbed and plundered that all the cattle and farm horses having been been seized by General Ewell, farm labor had come to a complete standstill." In another place the same writer says that "Lee's retreat was encumbered by Ewell's immense train of plunder." Why it was that General Ewell's Corps gained this distinction over the other two for its plundering propensities, may probably be accounted for in the fact that as it always went in advance, it left but little for the others to take.

In the evening of this day Longstreet'

Corps approached the town. Hood's division passed on through and encamped north of the town along the Harrisburg pike. McLaws' and Pickett's divisions encamped about two or three miles south of the town. These three divisions remained in their camps on the Sabbath, excepting the detachments which entered and plundered our town on Sunday as will shortly be related.

During this day Ewell's infantry passed through Carlisle towards Harrisburg; and on the same day two despatch bearers, sent by Gen. Ewell, then at Shippensburg, to Gen. Early, were captured in the streets of Gettysburg by three Union scouts from the advance cavalry near Emmittsburg. The purport of their distpatches was, that Gen. Early should not advance his division too rapidly, as that might be attended with some danger in an enemy's country. (Battle of Gettysburg, page 19).

Some time in the evening of this day something of such importance occurred that it was deemed necessary to send information of it to Harrisburg at the earliest possible moment. About 10 o'clock that night, after a consultation with Judge Kimmell, who informed me that Mr. Kinney, a teacher in the Academy, was willing to carry a dispatch but did not know the road, I went to the residence of Mr. Christian Fuller on Second street, where Mr. Anthony Hollar, then a salesman in our store, resided. Mr. Hollar was well acquainted with the roads, but deemed it unsafe to start in the night. He, however, consented to start early next morning and pilot Mr. Kinney to Roxbury at the base of the North Mountain. On Sabbath morning they started with this information, Mr. Kinney reaching Harrisburg on Monday morning and delivered his message. Of this I shall have more to say in my chapter on Scouts. What the movements of that day were which we considered so important I cannot now tell. It may have been the fact that the two remaining divisions of Hill's Corps had followed Lee and his staff and Heth's division of the same Corps eastwardly towards Gettysburg.

SUNDAY, 28th.

There were but few movements of troops through our streets this day. The last of Hill's forces had passed through the day previous and encamped about Fayetteville and Greenwood. Longstreet's corps was encamped South and North of town. Plundering parties from the latter, however, visited the town and cleaned out our stores of what the preceding troops had left. After returning from church in the forenoon, and while at dinner, the sound of an axe chopping somewhere about our house was heard. In a little time we discovered that a party of soldiers, under an officer, had chopped away the doors leading into our cellar, and had taken possession. The officer in command had a blank book, and with a pencil noted down the contents of the cellar, after which he placed a guard there to watch over the same. This guard of some three or four soldiers remained in the cellar until towards evening, ransacking our private cellar, back of the store cellar, and carrying off cans of fruit and other things. About four o'clock in the evening a number of teams were brought into town, and distributed around at the various places of business and the contents of every store and cellar were taken and put in these wagons. The dry goods stores at that time dealt in groceries, and all suffered greatly by the loss of their entire stock. I saw the contents of some places of business on that day cleaned out, from the loss of which the owners never recovered. We had in our cellar a considerable amount of molasses, syrup, sugar, &c. About thirty soldiers took hold of the ropes and drew the large hogsheads of syrup from the cellar, and after all was up in front of the store, an officer with a book and pencil took down the number of gallons in each, the number of pounds of sugar, &c. In doing this he seemed particularly desirous to get the exact amounts and called me to see each guage and entry. Before he gave the order to load them in his wagons, his heart seemed to relent, and he told me to select whichever hogshead I desired to retain, which he had his men to put back into the cellar. That was the largest sale of groceries we had ever made at one time, and that on the Sabbath, too. Our loss on that day was heavy, but so was it with every other establishment in the town. A greater calamity, however, was yet in store for us a year later. Throughout the afternoon of this day a young man employed in Mr. William Wallace's store—Thomas Lindsay, now residing in Pittsburg—was compelled by the rebels to remain in Mr. Wallace's cellar filling their canteens with molasses. While engaged in the patience provoking process of running this thick stuff into their narrow necked canteens, the soldiers would reciprocate his kindness by pouring some of it over his head. Mr. Lindsay says he was the *stickiest* and best preserved boy in town that day.

This wholesale robbery was entirely against Gen. Lee's order. There was no requisition made so far as I have been able to ascertain. Colonel Freemantle, of the British Army, in his article in *Blackwood's Magazine*, as already referred to, says of this day's transactions in our town :

"Major Moses tells me that his orders are to open the stores in Chambersburg by force, and seize all that is wanted for the army in a regular and official manner, giving in return its value in Confederate money or a receipt. The storekeepers have, doubtless, sent away their most valuable goods on the approach of the Confederate army. Much also has been already seized by Ewell, who passed through nearly a week ago. But Moses was much elated at having already discovered a large supply of excellent felt hats hidden away in a cellar, which he 'annexed' at once." These hats were taken from Mr. Jacob Dechert, whose place of business was then where J. N. Dyson & Co's. hat and shoe store now is, and the value of the lot captured was about two thousand dollars.

Colonel Freemantle continues:—"Moses proceeded into town at 11 A. M. with an official requisition (from Gen. Longstreet), for three day's rations for the whole army in this neighborhood. These rations he is to seize by force, if not voluntarily supplied. * * Neither the Mayor nor the Corporation were to be found anywhere, nor were the keys of the principal stores forthcoming until Moses began to apply the axe. * * I returned to the camp at 6 P. M. Major Moses did not get back till very late, much depressed at the ill-success of his mission. He had searched all day most indefatigably, and had endured much contumely from the Union ladies, who called him 'a thievish, little rebel scoundrel,' and other opprobious epithets. But this did not annoy him so much as the manner in which everything he wanted had been sent away or hidden in private houses, which he is not allowed by Gen. Lee's order to search. He has only managed to secure a quantity of molasses, sugar and whiskey." The molasses and some of the sugar he took from our cellar and the whiskey from Mr. John F. Croft.

The following day Major Moses, Commissary General of Longstreet's corps, rode around to each place plundered, and paid for the things taken. When he came to settle with me, he drew from his pocket a book in which the articles were carefully noted down. Taking his seat at my desk he wrote in a hurried and business-like manner an itemized bill. He then asked me the price we sold each article at, which he scrutinized for awhile and then sat down what he thought was right. Footing the whole up he paid me in Confederate scrip. While writing so hurriedly I said to him, "Why, Major, you write just like a Philadelphia lawyer." "That's just what I am," he replied. "I studied law on Walnut street, Philadelphia, but some years ago I removed South, where I resided ever since." After receiving my pay in his worthless scrip, I said to him, "Now, Major, tell me what to do with this *money!*" Straightening himself up and listening to what I said, he replied, "Well, now, that is an important question, and deserves the best answer I can give. My advice to you is to invest this money in Confederate Bonds. They are at least as good as the money, and if our cause succeeds, as we expect it will, the bonds will be paid. If we fail, then of course our bonds will be worthless, but so will yours, for your government will be bankrupt by that time." The reader may, perhaps, be curious to know whether I took the Major's advice, or what I did with my "money." It will be recollected that when telling of the shrewdness of Rev. Dr. Fisher in disposing of the scrip given him for printing done for the rebels, I stated that the Doctor made the best with his dealings with the rebels of any transaction I knew, with one exception, and that was a preacher also. The present is about the time to introduce that incident. Shortly after the retreat of the Confederates from our State, an elderly gentleman came into our store and after purchasing a few things, took me aside and proposed to leave a deposit with me of a considerable sum of Greenbacks, for the purpose of buying up all the Confederate scrip I could get. He did not inform me what he wanted it for, nor where he lived, but I found these out afterwards. He instructed me to pay from four to five cents on the dollar, and because of my consenting to rid our county of this worthless trash, with which it was flooded and counted of no value at all, he allowed me *six cents* on the dollar for mine. Major Moses allowed us fifty cents per gallon for molasses and syrup. Six cents on the dollar for our scrip netted us just *three cents per gallon* for what we could not long after that have gotten one dollar per gallon for. The reader can have some idea of the profit or loss of that day's transaction, when in addition to our whole stock of sugar and other groceries, eight hundred gallons of molasses and syrup were taken.

I have often felt anxious to know what the rebels did with our molasses. Perhaps the solution of this question is given by Gen. Imboden in an article contributed by him to the *Galaxy* of November, 1871. Speaking of Gen. Lee's great simplicity, and sharing the lot of his soldiers, Gen. Imboden says:—"On one occasion some molasses was obtained and sent to the field. One of General Lee's staff who was caterer that week—that is, he drew the rations for the headquarters mess—set a small pitcher of molasses before the General at dinner, who was delighted to eat it with his hot corn bread. Seeing his satisfaction, the catering Colonel remarked, 'General, I secured five gallons for headquarters.' 'Was there so much for every mess the size of ours?" Oh, no. The supply won't last a week." Then I direct, Colonel, that you immediately return every drop you have, and send an order that no molasses shall be issued to officers or men except the sick in hospital.'"

In a week or two my strange friend called again and taking what scrip I had procured, left another deposit. This he continued until he had gotten about all that could be had. One day I heard of an accident befalling the family of a poor man residing on the outskirts of the town. His son—a lad of about fourteen years of age—had the misfortune to get his leg crushed. I called to see the family and inquiring as to their necessities, was told that for the present they needed nothing, but the trouble that most perplexed them was how to raise money to pay the doctor for his services in amputating the limb. The man then told me that his boy had picked up, here and there, a whole bundle of rebel money and said if he could make anything out of it it might help him through. Counting it I found he had about five hundred dollars, and I gave him enough for it to pay the doctor and something over. But who was the strange man who was dealing in Confederate money? The following was his history as I afterwards learned it. He was a Presbyterian minister and resided somewhere in the Valley of Virginia, and being such an inveterate Union man he thundered the terrors of the law upon the heads of his rebel congregation until they locked the church against him. When the rebels advanced near where he lived he would flee North across the Potomac, and when the Union forces would secure the territory he would return, and, surrounded by a guard of Union soldiers, would open his church and preach again. Three of his rebel neighbors desiring to sell their farms and move further down in rebeldom, he bought their farms, payable in *currency*, and would thus follow the wake of the confederate army and buy up their scrip and pay it over for the farms. He was a sharp financier, and what became of him and how he made out with his purchases, I never heard.

While this scene of plunder was taking place in our town, the following interesting incidents occurred at General Lee's headquarters. As the key to what is to follow is so interesting, I will allow the principal actor therein to relate her own story. The person referred to is Mrs. Ellen McLellan, widow of our former townsman, William McLellan, Esq.

MR. J. HOKE, *Dear Sir:*—I take pleasure in complying with your request, and will give you a brief account of my interview with General Lee, as nearly as I can recollect it now. The mills, provisions and stores throughout the town and surrounding country were all in the hands of the enemy, and in many families supplies were running short. On the Sunday before the battle of Gettysburg, (June 28th), matters had become so serious that it became necessary for some one to seek an interview with the enemy, and obtain flour. I sent for one of the body guards, and a captain came in response. From him I learned that I could see General Lee by going to his headquarters in Messersmith's woods. This captain offered me an escort, but assured me that I could go alone with perfect safety, showing me a copy of Gen. Lee's order that any one who would insult a woman by word, look, or act, would be instantly shot. I then decided to decline an escort, and taking my young daughter, I set out for the camp. I found the rules were stringently enforced, but had no difficulty in passing through the ranks. Everything was in most perfect order; even the horses were picketed so as to do no injury to the trees in the grove where their tents were pitched. Reaching headquarters I found the General seated with his officers at the table. A subordinate met me and learning my errand placed two camp stools, and in a short time I found myself seated by Gen. Lee himself. I stated to him our need, and told him starvation would soon be at hand upon many families, unless he gave us aid. He seemed startled by this announcement, and said that such destitution seemed impossible in such a rich and beautiful grain growing country, pointing to the rich fields of grain all around his camp. I reminded him that this growing grain was useless to us now, and that many of our people had no means to lay in supplies ahead. He then assured me that he had turned over the supplies of food he found to his men to keep them from ravaging our homes. He said, "God help you if I permitted them to enter your houses. Your supplies depend upon the amount that is sent in to my men." He then told me to send one or two of our prominent men to him. I replied that they had nearly all gone away, fearing that they would be seized and taken off. (I feared to give him the names of any of our gentlemen.) He then asked me to send a miller who could give him an idea of the quantity required. On leaving I asked for his autograph. He replied, "Do you want the autograph of a rebel?" I said, "General Lee, I am a true Union woman, and yet I ask for bread and your autograph." The General replied, "It is to your interest to be for the Union and I hope you may be as firm in your principles as I am in mine." He assured me that his autograph would be a dangerous thing to possess, but at length he gave it to me. Changing the topic of conversation, he assured me the war was a cruel thing, and that he only desired that they would let him go home and eat his bread there in peace. All this time I was impressed with the strength and sadness of the man.

I trust these few facts may prove of use to you. I am glad to see that you are getting up these bits of unwritten history. Of course I have just given you an outline of the affair and you are at liberty to use it as you see fit.

Mrs. ELLEN M'LELLAN.

The sequel to this visit of Mrs. McLellan will appear in the following fact: Judge Kimmell relates the following incident: On the same day of Mrs. McLellan's visit to General Lee's headquarters, or the day following, he cannot now say which, an officer of General Lee's staff came to his residence and rapped at the door. Upon opening the door the officer said, "Are you Judge Kimmell?" Upon replying in the affirmative, the officer handed him a paper, saying "General Lee sends you this." The Judge says that it had become known to some that he was engaged in sending information of the rebels to the authorities at Harrisburg, and knowing that his life would be forfeited if found out, he thought as the officer handed him the paper from General Lee that "the very mischief was to pay." His fears, however, quickly subsided when he read the paper and found that it was an order from General Lee on the guard at Stouffer's mill for ten or fifteen barrels of flour for the poor of the town. Before he could use the order, General Lee had left and it was of no use.

On this day a skirmish took place between the advance of Ewell's Corps and the Union forces at Oyster's Point, three miles from Harrisburg.

General Early entered and occupied York, and a portion of his command passed on to seize the bridge over the Susquehanna at Wrightsville.

Two regiments of Union cavalry, numbering about 2,000, under command of General Cawpland, entered Gettysburg from the direction of Emmittsburg. They had been sent forward on a reconnoissance, and after encamping over night east of the town went off in the morning towards Littlestown.

This day General Hooker was relieved of the command of the army of the Potomac, and General Meade put in his place. The whole of the Union Army was marching through Frederick northward. Generals Reynolds and Howard, with the first and eleventh corps, were sent forward in the direction of Emmittsburg.

MONDAY, JUNE 29TH.

On this day the divisions of McLaws and Hood, of Longstreet's Corps, left their encampments, north and south of the town, and proceeded to Fayetteville. The remaining division of this Corps, commanded by General Pickett, remained at Chambersburg until the morning of Thursday, July 2d, by order of General Lee, to protect the rear, and the wagon train.

Some time during this day the balance of Heth's division of Ewell's Corps left their encampment about Greenwood, and crossed the mountain, encamping near Cashtown with that part of the division which had crossed the day previously. It was this addition to the force already at that place which increased the number of camp fires of the previous evening, as seen from Gettysburg (Professor Jacob's Battle of Gettysburg, page 21).

On this day the men of Pickett's division—the only force then in or near the town—commenced to destroy the railroad. This they did by prying up the rails, piling the ties and rails from the adjoining fences into heaps with the rails across the top and setting fire thereto. When the rails became red hot they bent out of shape by their own weight and became unfit for use. This work of destruction went on until on the morning of Wednesday, July 1st, they destroyed the depot buildings. Fearing to involve surrounding buildings in destruction by setting the engine and work shops on fire, the walls were battered until they fell. Ten or a dozen soldiers would take a long iron rail, such as was used for railroad tracks, and use it as a battering ram. In this way they soon succeeded in throwing down the buildings. A large lot of lumber was carried from the carpenter shop and piled upon the turn-table and set on fire. This not only secured the destruction of the lumber, but the turn-table also.

On this day Dr. J. L. Suesserott visited the headquarters of General Lee. The object of his visit and what he saw are thus stated by the Doctor: "On the day prior to the removal of General Lee from Messersmith's woods, I visited him for the purpose of having a blind mare, the property of Col. D. O. Gehr, exempted from capture. All of the other available horses having been removed to safe quarters, I wanted to use this one for the purpose of plowing my corn. After the General had given the order to have the proper paper prepared, and whilst it was being done, having nothing to do, I employed my time in watching the features and movements of General Lee, and never since have I seen so much emotion depicted on a human countenance. With his hand at times clutching his hair and with contracted brow, he would walk with rapid strides for a few rods and then, as if he bethought himself of his actions, with a sudden jerk he would produce an entire change in his features and demeanor and cast an enquiring gaze on me only to be followed in a moment by the same contortions of face and agitation of person. The order for the safety of the horse having been finished and delivered, I made rapid strides towards town, only to find that the Medical Purveyor of the Rebel Army had taken the horse, and my corn, which sadly needed working, had to take its chance along with hundreds of acres within the county in the same condition."

On the evening of this day, some time after dark, the writer, in company with Mr. H. E. Hoke and Mr. George R. Colliflower, went up into the steeple of the Reformed church. From that elevated position we had an uninterrupted view for miles all about us. The line of the railroad could be traced south of the town by the numerous fires still burning. The sound of the drum was heard from Pickett's camp about two miles southward. Along the South Mountain for miles up and down the valley innumerable strange lights were seen flashing to and fro. That these lights were used as signals for communicating information, we well knew, but their occasion and import we were of course ignorant of. Perhaps the fact shortly to be related will solve the problem. Some time in the afterpart of that night, probably about two o'clock in the morning, I was awakened by my wife, who told me that some important movement was going on among the Confederates and that I should get up and come to the window. Peering cautiously through the half-closed shutters we saw a continuous stream of wagons driven hurriedly through the street. They were coming back from the direction of Harrisburg, and passing up Main street to the Diamond, turned east towards Gettysburg. The wagons were driven at a rapid pace, sometimes at a fast trot. They seemed to be heavily laden and caused a grinding noise upon the pike as they passed along. They proved to be Ewell's train, and contained ammunition for the great battle then near at hand. The importance of this train may be inferred from the fact that it had the precedence in the right of way over Longstreet's men. General McLaws in command of one of the divisions of Longstreet's Corps, which was kept back in its march towards Gettysburg by this train, says that it was *fourteen miles long*, (Annals of the War, page 440). Dr. Cullen, Medical Director of Longstreet's Corps, on page 439 of the same book, says that this train was in charge of Johnson's division. While passing hurriedly through our town, a rumbling noise could be heard as if the whole valley was filled with moving trains. Evidently only a part of this immense train passed through here, the balance passing up from Shippensburg along the base of the South Mountain, and coming out into the Gettysburg pike near Greenwood, as did Johnson's division having it in charge.

The hasty passage of this train through our town towards Gettysburg convinced me that Lee was concentrating his forces, and that no time should be lost in sending information thereof to the authorities at Harrisburg. Rising early to see after procuring a scout to carry a message, I was called upon by Judge Kimmell, and after interchanging a few words he left me, and in a short time procured the services of Mr. Steven W. Pomeroy, now the Rev. S. W. Pomeroy, pastor of the Presbyterian church at Mount Union, Pa. I shall, in my chapter on scouts, give Mr. Pomeroy's account of his trip with this valuable information.

But now, what was the cause of this sudden concentration of Lee's army in the direction of Gettysburg? General Longstreet in his contribution to the *Annals of the War*, page 419, says that on the evening of this day, Monday, 29th, a scout by the name of Harrison, who had been sent by him from Culpepper into the Union lines to obtain information, came to his headquarters near Chambersburg and reported that the Army of the Potomac had crossed the Potomac, and was encamped about Frederick City. Longstreet saw at once that this information was of vast importance and he sent him at once to General Lee's headquarters where he imparted to Lee the information he brought. That this was the first information which Lee received of the whereabouts of the Army of the Potomac is clearly stated by General Longstreet in the following extract from the article referred to. The General says, "We had not heard from the enemy for several days, and General Lee was in doubt as to where he was; indeed we did not know that he had yet left Virginia." In the absence of the knowledge of the position of the Union army. General Lee had issued orders for an attack upon Harrisburg by General Ewell a part of whose Corps was on the evening of that day—Monday, 29th—near the entrenchments on the west bank of the Susquehanna, but upon receiving the information brought by this scout, he countermanded that order and immediately directed General Ewell and all his other Generals to concentrate their forces ner Gettysburg. That such were the facts will appear in the following extracts from General Longstreet's article already referred to. General Longstreet says, "General Lee had already issued orders that we were to advance towards Harrisburg." Again he says that upon meeting General Lee the next morning, after the arrival of the scout, he asked him "if the information brought by the scout might not involve a change of direction of the head of the column to the right?" To this remark he says General Lee "immediately acquiesced in the suggestion, possibly saying that he had already given orders to that effect." He then adds that "the movement towards the enemy was begun at once." And that this withdrawal of General Ewell's train from down the valley and its rapid flight towards Gettysburg occurred at the time stated, is placed beyond dispute by the authorities already quoted, as well as by General Longstreet himself, who says that "about noon (Tuesday, 30th) the road in front of my Corps was blocked by Hill's Corps (the two Divisions encamped about Greenwood) and *Ewell's wagon train, which had cut into the road above*," i. e., near Greenwood, in advance of two Divisions of his Corps then near Fayetteville. (Annals of the War, page 420.)

As has been already shown, up to the night of Monday, 29th, Lee's objective was Harrisburg. But it may be said, "if Gen. Lee contemplated an attack upon Harrisburg, why did he send two corps of his army to the east in the direction of Gettysburg, and only one—Ewell's, down the valley?" This may be satisfactorily accounted for as follows:

1. General Lee no doubt supposed that Ewell's corps was sufficient to overcome all opposition he was likely to meet at Harrisburg. He knew that the army of the Potomac would not uncover the National capital to save the capital of a State, and he further knew that there was no adequate, organized force likely to oppose him in an attack upon the latter. As for raw, unorganized and undisciplined militia, he had no fear whatever for any number of them.

2. Lee may have contemplated, after making a strong demonstration in the direction of Baltimore and Washington to mislead and deceive the Federal authorities, to withdraw part of his force from that direction, and march them to reinforce Ewell before Harrisburg. If Harrisburg was his real objective, the crossing of the South Mountain and passing up northward by its eastern side of a considerable part of his force, would have been his proper route. With Early's division at York constituting his right, and Rhode's and Johnson's divisions in the neighborhood of Carlisle, constituting his left, the troops passing up to the east of the mountain would come in the centre and complete the line.

3. General Lee was too wise and cautious, in the absence of all knowledge of the whereabouts of the army of the Potomac, to leave so important a pass as the road leading from Gettysburg to this place unguarded, thereby endangering his rear in case of an advance of all his forces upon Harrisburg. He might have suspected, and certainly had sufficient reason for doing so, that his old antagonist would follow him up and strike him at the most favorable opportunity. To prepare for such a contingency was but common prudence, and to meet it adequately twice or thrice the number of men to take Harrisburg would be necessary.

But let us look at the situation, and see where the various divisions and parts of the Confederate and Federal armies were on this Monday night, before the concentration began, and we will be the better prepared to follow them in their course towards the decisive field.

1. *Ewell's Corps.* Early's division was at York; Rhode's division lay about Carlisle with its advance upon Kingston, thirteen miles from Harrisburg. Jenkin's cavalry was between Kingston and the defenses of the capital on the high hills south of the Susquehanna. Johnson's division lay in the valley between Shippensburg and Carlisle. Two brigades of cavalry under Generals William E. Jones and Beverly Robertson were somewhere in the valley with the divisions of Rhodes and Johnson.

2. *Hill's Corps.* Heth's division was east of the mountain at Cashtown; Pender's and Anderson's about Greenwood.

3. *Longstreet's Corps.* The divisions of McLaws and Hood were about Fayetteville. Pickett's division was about two miles south of Chambersburg.

Imboden's cavalry was then about Mercersburg, the Gap in the mountain west of that place, and in McConnellsburg.

Stuart's cavalry was somewhere about Hanover to the east of the Union army, and were moving about apparently without any strategical purpose other than to effect a junction with the confederate infantry.

Imagine a vast fan with its base at Lee's headquarters in Messersmith's woods, near Chambersburg, and its circumference extending from McConnellsburg its extreme left, through Carlisle and York to Cashtown, in Adams county its extreme right, and you will have some idea of the situation of the Confederate army on the night of Monday, 29th. With the exception of Pickett's division, which was to remain here to protect the rear, and Imboden's cavalry, who were to keep the way open for the divisions of Jones and Robertson, who guarded the rear of Johnson's division and Ewell's wagon train, as they fell back from down the valley, and then themselves follow on to Gettysburg, all the scattered parts of this great invading host were to be called together at one point on the right. To reach these at some of the points stated couriers must have been sent, while others may have been notified by signal. Four hours after the order was issued for concentration of these forces, a copy of it could have been carried to every point, except to Early at York, and he could have been reached before daylight on the following morning. May not the mysterious fires we saw that night, from the church steeple, have been the signals employed?

We will now turn our eyes across the South Mountain, and take a view of the grand and glorious Army of the Potomac as it marches to meet these minions of oppression and slavery. Let us mark well its movements in connection with the movements of the foe, and observe the points of contact between these two mighty forces.

The army of the Potomac at that time consisted of seven corps. The First Corps was commanded by Gen. Reynolds; the Second, Gen. Hancock; the Third, Gen. Sickles; the Fifth, Gen. Sykes, who succeeded Gen. Meade when he was made commander in chief; the Sixth, Gen. Sedgwick; the Eleventh, Gen. Howard, and the Twelfth, Gen. Slocum. The cavalry were under Gen. Pleasanton, and the artillery under Gen. Hunt. On Sunday, 28th, the day Gen. Meade succeeded Gen. Hooker to the command, these corps passed through Frederick, some forty miles south of Gettysburg. At this point they diverged, each corps taking a separate road, but all tending in one general direction northward. The Union Army, like the Confederate, spread out from the point of divergence like the sticks of a fan. The First Corps moved up the Emmittsburg road and formed the left of the army. The Eleventh Corps marched up a parallel road a little further east, through Griegerstown; the Third and Twelfth moved by parallel roads leading to Taneytown, thirteen miles south of Gettysburg; the Second and Fifth moved still further east through Liberty and Uniontown, while the Sixth, with the cavalry under Gen. Gregg, went some what circuitously by Westminster, and formed the right of the line. The Confederate Army, in its concentration, was to be swung to the right, and the fan would close upon its right support: the Federal was to be swung to the left, and would close upon its left support. The point of contact was Gettysburg, and the parts which first came in collision were Reynolds and Howard upon our left, and Heth and Pender upon the Confederate right. The reader will do well to watch in the coming details the times and places where the various parts of these two great hosts came into collision.

Col. James G. Biddle, in *Annals of the War*, pages 208, 209, says that "On the night of the 30th, after the army of the Potomac had made two days' marches, Gen. Meade heard that Lee was concentrating his army to meet him, and being ignorant of the country in front of him, he at once instructed his engineers to select some ground having a general reference to the existing positions of the army, which he might occupy by rapid movements of concentration, and thus give battle on his own terms, in case the enemy should advance across the South Mountain. The general line of Pipe Clay Creek was selected, and a preliminary order of instructions issued to the corps commanders, informing them of the fact, and explaining how they might move their corps and concentrate in a good position along the line. * * * On Tuesday, 30th, Gen. Reynolds, who commanded the left wing of the army, was sent from Emmittsburg to Gettysburg with orders to report concerning the character of the ground there, at the same time Gen. Humphrys was ordered to examine the ground in the vicinity of Emittsburg. But while thus active in his endeavors to ascertain the nature of the several positions where he could fight Lee, Gen. Meade, at the same time, continued to press forward his army, and concentrate it so that he could move it with ease toward any point."

TUESDAY, 30TH.

Early in the morning of this day Gen. Longstreet left his headquarters near this place and rode out to Messersmith's woods where, after a short consultation with General Lee, in which the latter informed him that he had countermanded his order for an attack upon Harrisburg, and had determined to cross the South Mountain and meet the Army of the Potomac, the two Generals rode together to Greenwood, where they encamped for the night. (Annals of the War, page 419, 420.)

The two divisions of Hill's Corps—Pender and Anderson—left their encampments near Fayetteville, and proceeded to Cashtown. From this place the divisions of Heth and Pender were moved to the vicinity of Marsh Creek, encamping there for the night. Anderson's division remained over night at Cashtown. McLaws and Hood's divisions of Longstreet's Corps, unable to proceed because of Ewell's wagon train and Johnson's division, which had that train in charge, and which had the right of way, remained in their encampments near Fayetteville until the following afternoon.

At an early hour this morning General Rhodes was recalled from below Carlisle, and ordered to march by way of the pike from that place across the mountain, uniting with Early's division at Heidlersburg, nine miles north of Gettysburg, the same evening. Johnson's division retraced its way, having Ewell's wagon train in charge. It and probably a part of the wagon train passed from Shippensburg to Greenwood by the country road near the base of the South Mountain, and reached Gettysburg late in the evening of the following day.

Gen. Imboden's cavalry on the evening of this day were ordered to leave their encampments about McConnellsburg and Mercersburg and proceed to Gettysburg.

About 9½ A. M. of this day a detachment from Heth's division under General Pettigrew advanced upon a reconnoisance as far as Seminary Ridge, and at 10½ withdrew again to Cashtown.

At 11¼ A. M. about 6,000 Federal Cavalry under General Buford, arrived in Gettysburg, and encamped one and a-half miles from town, on the Chambersburg pike.

In accordance with the instructions given by the commander in chief, Gen. Reynolds marched from Emmitsburg on the morning of Tuesday, 30th, and encamped that night four miles southwest of Gettysburg, and on the following morning, Wednesday, July 1st, he entered Gettysburg and found Gen. Buford with his cavalry engaged with the rebels who had advanced from their encampment at Marsh Creek, on the road leading from Chambersburg. The further movements of the Union Army will be given in connection with those of the Rebels in their proper place.

WEDNESDAY, JULY 1ST.

On the morning of this day General Lee and Longstreet left their headquarters at Greenwood, where they had spent the night, and proceeded together towards Gettysburg. After riding some three or four miles, heavy firing was heard in the direction of Gettysburg, at which General Lee rode rapidly forward to ascertain the cause of it, leaving Longstreet to see after the two divisions of his corps yet at Fayeteville. After attending to some details concerning these troops, he went forward and rejoined Lee in the rear of the line of the battle of that day about five o'clock in the afternoon. The road was not cleared of Ewell's train so that Longstreet's two corps could pass until late in the afternoon, and his artillery did not get the road until 2 o'clock the following morning. By a forced march McLaws' division reached Marsh Creek, four miles from Gettysburg, a little after dark, and Hood's division got within nearly the same distance of the town about twelve o'clock at night. (Gen. Longstreet in *Annals of the War*, pages 310 and 420.)

In order to give the precise time when the various Corps and Divisions of the two armies reached the field of conflict, and their positions in the line, and the part they respectively took in the battle, it will be necessary to go somewhat into detail of the events of those three eventful days. This detail, while familiar to most readers, still seems necessary in order to the completeness of this narrative. In grouping together the following facts, I acknowledge my indebtedness to the various persons who have written of this battle, especially to Professor Jacobs's *Battle of Gettysburg*, from which I have largely drawn.

At half-past nine o'clock this morning, skirmishing began between Buford's dismounted cavalry, which had encamped over night a mile and a half out on the pike leading to Chambersburg, and Heth's and Pender's Divisions, which had encamped the previous night four miles out on the same road. About 10½ o'clock the First Corps under Gen. Reynolds, began to come up from their encampment south west of the town. Gen. Reynolds dashed through Gettysburg and on out to Seminary Ridge, while his men moved across the fields from the Emmittsburg road and formed under cover of the same eminence. The right moved to the east of the turnpike and railroad, and formed a line behind a grove, and the left formed on the crest of the hill near the Seminary. Both wings then advanced and the cavalry gradually fell back to the rear. For over four hours these eight thousand men stood like a wall of fire against the fierce assaults of twice their number, and up to 3 P. M., the left wing was able not only to hold its own, but to drive back the enemy in their fearful charges. In an effort of Gen. Archer to flank and capture one of our brigades, they captured him and his whole brigade reduced to about 1,500 men. This took place in the rear of the Seminary, near Willoughby's run, at about the middle of the day. The right, which was comparatively weak, having been opposed by a much stronger force, although holding its position for a long while, was several times driven back through the grove and adjacent fields, down to the eastern base of Seminary Ridge. It lost heavily in killed and wounded. In these backward and forward movements, it lost, at one time, 1,900 prisoners, which were afterwards retaken, and in turn it took a regiment of Mississippians of 800 men and sent them to the rear.

"It soon became apparent that our right was the main object of the enemy's attack. As early as 10 A. M., the Divisions of Rhodes and Early left Heidlersburg, and by a rapid march by separate roads, reached the scene of conflict about noon. Arriving within a short distance of our right, and forming in a secluded valley, under cover of a hill, Rhodes' Division entered the fight and endeavored to make a flank movement upon our men. Early's Division did not participate until about 2 P. M. The Union troops being so hard pressed, were about giving way on our right, when a portion of the Eleventh Corps, which had been unaccountably delayed, came to its support. At 1 P. M., two divisions of this Corps, under Generals Schurz and Barlow, hurried through the town, and took a position on our extreme right, resting on the Mummasburg road; and by their support the tide of battle was stayed, until Early's Division took part in the fight. The other division of the Eleventh Corps, under General Steinwehr, by the prudent forethought and wise generalship of General Howard, was at once sent to occupy Cemetery Hill, on the south of the town, and to provide for the contingency which happened three hours afterwards."

After Early's Division had entered the fight, it soon became evident that our right would be turned, and our men all killed or captured, for the First Corps and the two Divisions of the Eleventh, numbering not more than 16,000, could not long stand before the 30,000 of Heth, Pender, Rhodes and Early combined. To provide for the contingency which General Howard saw was inevitable, the heavy artillery were removed to Cemetery Hill, and Steinwehr's division was arranged to receive and support our hardly pressed men when they would be compelled to retire from the unequal contest. At last the break in our line occurred, and the retreat became general. The First Corps, for the most part fell back through the southwestern outskirts of the town, and took position on the left and rear of Steinwehr. The Eleventh Corps mostly crowded through Washington and Baltimore streets to Cemetery Hill, and took position in front and on the right centre. Being badly crowded in passing through the streets, and considerably confused, they were unable to repel the enemy who pressed hard upon them; and as a consequence, about 2,500 were taken prisoners. But notwithstanding this retreat, and the confusion attending it, the brave men who had escaped to Cemetery Hill, coolly and quietly fell into position, where they found themselves supported by two lines of battle formed by Gen. Steinwehr, and by a formidable array of artillery already in place, from which a raking fire was poured upon the pressing rebels which brought them to a standstill.

Almost in the very beginning of the engagement, General Reynolds fell a victim to his cool bravery and zeal. As was his custom he rode in front of his men, placing them in position and urging them to the fight, when he was shot through the head by a rebel sharpshooter and died almost instantly. General Reynolds, it is said by those who knew him well, was the greatest soldier the Army of the Potomac ever lost in battle. General Meade said of him that "he was the noblest as well as the bravest gentleman in the army."

Major Joseph G. Rosengarten, in an article contributed by him to the *Annals of the War*, pages 63, 64, thus describes the fall of General Reynolds, and the disposition made of his body. "In the full flush of life and health, vigorously leading on the troops in hand, and energetically summoning up the rest of his command, watching and even leading the attack of a comparatively small body, a glorious picture of the best type of a military leader, superbly mounted, and horse and man sharing in the excitement of battle, Reynolds was, of course, a shining mark to the enemy's sharpshooters. He had taken his troops into a heavy growth of timber on the slope of a hillside, and, under their regimental and brigade commanders, the men did their work well and promptly. Returning to join the expected division, he was struck by a Minnie ball, fired by a sharpshooter hidden in the branches of a tree almost overhead, and killed at once; his horse bore him to the little clump of trees, where a cairn of stones and a rude mark on the bark, now almost overgrown, still tells the fatal spot."

The body of General Reynolds was at once borne to the rear and placed for a while in a little house on the Emmittsburg road. In the midst of the battle, the body of the dead chieftain was placed in an ambulance, and taken by his faithful orderly and a small escort to the nearest railroad station, whence it was borne to Baltimore, thence to Philadelphia and finally to Lancaster, his former home, where, on the Fourth of July, while the defeated and discomfitted host of rebellion and treason were seeking safety in flight, it was interred in the tranquil cemetery, where he lies in the midst of his family, near the scenes of his childhood, and on the soil of his native State.

As the little cortege which bore the body of General Reynolds from the field passed out a short distance below Gettysburg, it stopped a few minutes to give to General Hancock, who met it on his way to take command, the latest news of the day. Arriving at General Meade's headquarters at Tanneytown, the cortege again stopped where, in the midst of sincere expressions of deep sorrow over the overwhelming loss, time was taken to explain to Meade, and Warren, and Hunt, and Williams, and Tyler, all that could serve to explain the actual condition of affairs, the advantages of the position taken, and the necessity of all possible haste in sending forward troops.

General Reynolds has been charged with rashness and prematurely bringing on the battle, by leading his comparatively small force against such overwhelming numbers, and not taking a strong position and holding it until the arrival of reinforcements. The battle of that day was not so much of choice upon his part as necessity, for had he not held the rebels in check, they would have taken the position which the Union forces afterwards took and held.

Considerable discussion has taken place as to who first saw the advantages of Cemetery Hill as a suitable place for making a stand. Major Rosengarten in the *Annals of the War*, page 65, claims that honor for General Reynolds, and says that while the battle was raging, messenger after messenger was despatched to Gen. Meade, then at Taneytown, thirteen miles distant, stating the importance of the position and urging the sending forward of troops. The friends of Generals Howard and Doubleday, also claim this honor for their respective chiefs. Professor Jacobs in his Battle of Gettysburg, page 25, says that "early in the morning the hills surrounding Gettysburg had been carefully examined by the General and his signal officers. At 8½ A. M., one of these officers was on the College cupalo making observations, when his attention was specially directed to that hill by one of the officers of the College, as being of the highest strategic importance, and commanding the whole country around for many miles. Doubtless he had satisfied himself of the preeminent advantages it offered as a position of offence and defense, and therefore determined to take and hold it." Professor Jacobs does not say what General this was. It could not have been Reynolds, for as soon as he reached Gettysburg he dashed through the town out to Seminary Ridge to engage in the battle already begun between the rebels and General Buford. And it could not have been Howard, for he only reached the town at 11¼ A. M. He may refer to General Buford, but the chief credit it seems should be given to that signal officer and the Professor of the College, who pointed out the advantages of that place. To the subordinates, the Engineers, whose business it is to see after such things, the credit is doubtless due, and Buford, Reynolds, Howard or Doubleday, acted only by the suggestions these officers made.

After the fall of General Reynolds, the chief command devolved on General Doubleday until the arrival of General Howard at 11½ A. M.

Owing to the direction of the wind, the sound of Reynolds' guns did not reach General Meade's headquarters at Taneytown, and it was not until about 1 o'clock P. M., that word was brought him of the battle and the fall of Reynolds. General Meade at once sent General Hancock to Gettysburg, with orders to assume command of all the troops, and to report to him concerning the practicability of fighting a battle there. Arriving at Gettysburg, and seeing the strength of the position taken, General Hancock at once sent a despatch to Meade, in which he expressed his satisfaction with the position. Before, however, receiving this dispatch from Hancock, General Meade was satisfied from the reports of his officers returning from the field, that Lee was about to concentrate his whole army there, and without waiting for further information from Hancock, he at once issued orders to the Fifth and Twelfth Corps to proceed to the scene of action. Upon the receipt at 6½ P. M., of Hancock's dispatch, Meade ordered all his Corps commanders to move to Gettysburg, he himself breaking up his headquarters at Taneytown at 10 o'clock and reached the field at 1 A. M., of the 2d.

The new position taken by our forces after their defeat west of Gettysburg, proved to be one of great strength, and had the rebels followed the advantage gained during the day by driving them from it, the result of the next two days' fighting might have been sadly different from what it was. As to the reasons why an attack was not made upon that position that evening, the following facts from Confederate sources are to the point. Speaking of this failure, General Ewell, in his official report, says: "The enemy had fallen back to a commanding position that was known to us as Cemetery Hill, south of Gettysburg, and quickly showed a formidable front there. On entering the town, I received a message from the commanding general to attack the hill, if I could do so to advantage. I could not bring artillery to bear on it; all the troops with me were jaded by twelve hours' marching and fighting, and I was notified that General Johnson was close to the town with his division, the only one of my Corps that had not been engaged, Anderson's Division of the Third Corps, (Longstreet's) having been halted to let them pass. Cemetery Hill was not assailable from the town, and I determined, with Johnson's Division, to take possession of a wooded hill to my left, on a line with and commanding Cemetery Hill. Before Johnson got up the Federals were reported moving to our left flank—our extreme left—and I could see what seemed to be his skirmishers in that direction. Before this report could be investigated by Lieutenant T. T. Turner, of my staff, and Lieutenant Robert Early, sent to investigate it, and Johnson placed in position, the night was far advanced."

Napier Bartlett, in an article in the "*Military Annals of Louisiana*," says:—"Hays received orders, through Early, from General Ewell to halt at Gettysburg, and advance no further in case he should succeed in capturing that place. But Hays saw that the enemy were coming around by what is known as the Baltimore road, and were making for the heights—the Cemetery Ridge. This ridge meant life or death and for the possession of it the battles of the 2d and 3d were fought. * * * Owing to the long detour the enemy was compelled to make, it was obvious that he could not get his artillery in position on the heights for one or two hours. The immediate occupation of the heights by the Confederates, who were in position to get them at the time referred to, was a matter of vital importance. Hays recognized it as such, and presently sent for Early. The latter thought as Hays, but declined to disobey orders. At the urgent request of General Hays, however, he sent for General Ewell. When the latter arrived, many precious moments had been lost."

General Lee explains his failure to send positive orders to Ewell to follow up the advantages of the day by capturing Cemetery Hill as follows: "The attack was not pressed that afternoon, the enemy's force being unknown, and it being considered advisable to await the arrival of the rest of the troops. Orders were sent back to hasten their march and, in the meantime, every effort was made to ascertain the numbers and positions of the enemy, and find the most favorable point to attack."

General Longstreet, in *Annals of the War*, page 420, relates the following incident of General Lee in the afternoon of that day, which shows, as Longstreet says, that Lee was enveloped in doubt and anxiety, which seemed to have weighed him down and destroyed his equapoise. "General Anderson was resting with his division at Cashtown awaiting orders. About ten o'clock in the morning he received a message notifying him that General Lee desired to see him. He found Lee intently listening to the fire of the guns, and very much disturbed and depressed. At length Lee said, more to himself than General Anderson: 'I cannot think what has become of Stuart; I ought to have heard from him long before now. He may have met with disaster, but I hope not. In the absence of reports from him, I am in ignorance as to what we have in front here. It may be the whole Federal army, or it may be only a detachment. If it is the whole Federal force we must fight a battle here; if we do not gain a victory, those defiles and gorges through which we passed this morning will shelter us from disaster.'"

Is it not evident that the cause why Cemetery Hill was not attacked that evening was because of doubt and confusion among the leaders of the rebel hosts? Up to this point they seem to have been guided by masterly wisdom; now, and after, until defeated, their counsels seem to have been confused. The God of Nations was in it. It was not the first time that Jehovah brought confusion among the counsellors of treason and rebellion that the nation they sought to overthrow might live. (2d Samuel XVII, 14.)

In order now to have a better understanding of the operations of the following two days, and to note the time of the arrival of each division of both the confederate and Federal forces, and the positions assigned them in their respective lines, which is my purpose rather than a detail of the great battles of those two memorable days, it will be necessary to have some idea of the location and shape of these lines. General Longstreet thus describes the two positions: "Our army (the Confederate,) was stretched in an elliptical curve, reaching from the front of Round Top around Seminary Ridge, and enveloping Cemetery Heights on the left; thus covering a space of four or five miles. The enemy (the Union army) occupied the high ground in front of us, being massed within a curve of about two miles nearly concentric with the curve described by our forces. His line was about one thousand four hundred yards from ours." Divested of military parlance, the positions of the two armies may be stated thus: The Union line was somewhat in the shape of a horse shoe, its toe pointing to Gettysburg and resting upon Cemetery Hill. Its right extended by Culp's Hill to Wolff's Hill. Its left, which was considerably longer than the right, passed south-westwardly along a succession of ridges, terminating in Little and Big Round Top. Both flanks were protected by cavalry. The Baltimore pike passed diagonally through the Union line from the south-east and coming out at the centre, or the toe. The Taneytown and Emmittsburg roads, the former passing directly through the Union position, and the latter somewhat to the west of it, united near the centre. The Confederate line ran nearly parallel with the Federal line, upon ridges and eminences, and about a half to three-quarters of a mile distant. In some places, however, much nearer.

At the close of this day, Wednesday,

July 1st, the First and Eleventh Corps, or that part of them which survived the battle of the day, took their position upon Cemetery Hill. The First Corps on the left, and the Eleventh, on the front and right centre. Ewell's Corps occupied Gettysburg, and formed a line south-east to Rock creek; Rhode's Division lay on the right, occupying Middle street as far west as Seminary Hill; Early lay on the south-east of the town; and Johnson, who did not arrive until a late hour in the night, occupied the extreme left of the line. Hill's Corps took position on the Seminary ridge, in the following order: on the left, and resting on the Chambersburg road, was Heth; next came Pender, and then Anderson. The latter did not arrive in time to participate in the battle of that day. This was the condition at the close of that day, and the positions of the two contending parties. Leaving them to rest over night for the battle of the ensuing day, we come back again to narrate events which transpired here and elsewhere.

As soon as it was known at Harrisburg that the rebels who had been threatening that place had fallen back, Gen. Smith in command of several regiments of New York and Pennsylvania militia, advanced to Carlisle. At that place, in the evening of this day, Wednesday, July 1st, General Fitzhugh Lee, with a division of cavalry—a part of Stuart's force which had passed entirely around the Army of the Potomac, having crossed over from Hanover through York county with the purpose of joining Gen. Rhodes at Carlisle, came unexpectedly in contact with these militia under Gen. Smith. Lee was evidently disconcerted upon finding that place in possession of the Federals, and Rhodes gone somewhere else, and in order to lead Gen. Smith to suppose that he had purposely advanced to engage him, and thus enable him to make his escape, he at once demanded the surrender of the town. This demand Gen. Smith emphatically refused, and when a second demand for surrender was sent him, he notified Lee that he would receive no more such communications from him. A short time was allowed the citizens to get out of the town, when the rebel batteries opened upon and threw a number of shells into it. But little damage was done. Several houses were penetrated, but no one was injured. Lee then withdrew his forces and went South towards Gettysburg.

About 4 o'clock in the afternoon of this day, Imboden's cavalry entered this place. While in Mercersburg the previous evening, Gen. Imboden received a order from Gen. Lee directing him to proceed to this place and relieve Pickett's Division, which had been left here to protect their line of communications. Imboden withdrew that part of his force which was across the mountain in M'Connellsburg and all came on to this place.

Shortly after this cavalry force—called by some "Imboden's cutthroats" entered our town—an order was issued by the General for a large amount of provisions. Among the articles demanded were 5,000 pounds of bacon. Finding that no response was being made to this requisition, a Colonel in command of one of the regiments and the Major of the same, called upon Judge Kimmell and showed him the requisition. The Judge told them that our citizens had been cleaned out of all provisions, and it was utterly out of their power to furnish what was demanded. At this the Major—a little red-headed specimen of rebeldom—said to the Colonel, "Leave the matter to me, Colonel; I'll get what we want." Judge Kimmell called the Colonel's attention to Gen. Lee's order in regard to entering and plundering private houses, when the Colonel said to the little Major, "Join your regiment, sir, join your regiment." At this the little red-headed plunderer went off in sullenness and *baconless*.

Not long after this body of cavalry entered the town, they cut down the flag-pole which had been erected in the centre of the Diamond at the breaking out of the war, on Thursday, April 18th, 1861. The ropes upon this pole had been cut upon the entrance of Stuart's cavalry on the evening of October 10th, 1862, so that the rebels could not run up their hated flag upon it. No troops that entered our town created greater consternation among our people than these free-booters of Imboden. It had gotten out that they were going to search our houses for provisions, and all were in consternation and fear, when suddenly, and to our great relief, they at once withdrew and went off towards Gettysburg. The cause of their leaving is explained by Gen. Imboden himself in an article contributed by him to the *Galaxy* of April, 1871, a monthly magazine published in New York. Gen. Imboden says, "That night, (Wednesday, July 1st,) I received a brief note from General Lee, expressing the apprehension that we were in danger of being cut off from communication with him by the Union cavalry, and directing us to move next morning as far as South Mountain on the road to Gettysburg, and keep it open for Generals William E. Jones and Beverly Robertson, whose brigades of cavalry were in the direction of Shippensburg." Evidently the point where danger was apprehended in their communications was about Fayetteville and Greenwood from forces which might be sent from Harrisburg. What probably gave rise to this fear was the fact that a small body of Union cavalry did make a dash upon the rebel line at Fayetteville and captured a number of prisoners. In accordance with Lee's order Imboden moved out there that same evening.

This brings our narrative to

THURSDAY, JULY 2ND.

Early this morning Pickett's Division left its encampment South of this place, and by a forced march, reached Gettysburg the same evening. Sometime during the same day Robertson's cavalry passed through coming up from the direction of Shippensburg, and going on towards Gettysburg. These were immediately followed by Jones' brigade. Gen. Imboden in the *Galaxy* says that "about midnight of this day—the 2d—we gained the top of the mountain east of Hon. Thaddeus Steven's iron works, then in ruins. Before daybreak on the 3d, (Friday), Robertson and Jones passed us, and about sunrise we followed them and arrived before Gettysburg about noon."

An occasional straggler passed through town on Thursday, after Jone's cavalry disappeared in the direction of Gettysburg, and by the evening of that day the last of the rebels had gone through. We had been under rebel rule from Tuesday, June 23d to July 3d, a period of ten days, and were not at all grieved to be rid of them.

Wednesday night and Thursday morning were devoted by both armies to the work of preparation for the renewal of the conflict. Shortly before midnight the gallant survivors of the First and Eleventh Corps were cheered by the arrival of the Twelfth Corps, under Gen. Slocum, and a part of the Third under Gen. Sickles. Gen. Slocum placed his corps on the right flank; the second division under Gen. Geary occupying Culp's hill; the first under Gen. Williams taking position near Spangler's spring, and the third was thrown across Rock creek to Wolf hill. As soon as Gen. Meade arrived—at one o'clock—he set vigorously to work inspecting the field and posting the men. Few were the moments given to sleep by either officers or men, although they were greatly exhausted by the fighting and marching of the previous day. The full moon, veiled by thin clouds, shone down upon the strange scene. The silence was occasionally broken by the heavy tramp of armed men, the neighing of horses, and the rattle of artillery as it hurried to the positions assigned it in the line. Breast-works were constructed, rifle pits were dug, and all possible preparation was made.

At 6 o'clock in the morning Hancock's Second Corps and the Reserve Artillery reached the field; and at 7 o'clock the Second and part of the Fifth Corps—two brigades of the Pennsylvania Reserves under Gen. Crawford, and the balance of the Third Corps, arrived. Gen. Sedgwick with the Sixth Corps, and Lockwood's brigade from Maryland, temporarily attached to the Twelfth corps, arrived at 2 o'clock P. M. General Sedgwick says in relation to his march: "I arrived in Gettysburg at about 2 o'clock in the afternoon of July 2d, having marched thirty-five miles from 7 o'clock the previous evening. I received on the way frequent messages from Gen. Meade to push forward my corps as rapidly as possible. I received no less than three messages by his aids urging me on." The Union forces were now all upon the field, except the balance of The Fifth corps under Gen. Sykes, which arrived at a critical moment, about five o'clock in the afternoon. The troops were disposed of as follows: Gen. Sickles at first took position on our left centre, but when Hancock came he took the place of Sickles, whilst the latter moved his corps to our extreme left, resting on the rocky ridge immediately north of Round Top, generally called Little Round Top. The Sixth corps was placed on our left, between Hancock and Sickles, and the Fifth under Sykes placed upon Round Top joining Sickles on the right. The rebels were also busily engaged during the night in forming their line, erecting breast-works, and otherwise preparing for a renewal of the battle. As already stated, Johnson's Division, which had been delayed in consequence of having Ewell's wagon train in charge, had reached the field late in the evening and been assigned its position; and Anderson's division, of Hill's corps, which was delayed at Cashtown, and did not participate in the first day's engagement, had also arrived. The divisions of McLaws and Hood, of Longstreet's corps, which had encamped over night at Marsh creek, four miles from the town, by some unaccountable delay, for which Gen. Longstreet has been severely censured by Southern writers, did not reach their positions in the line until about 4 o'clock in the afternoon. Upon arriving upon the field, McLaws joined Anderson on the left, and Hood united with McLaws still further to the left. Detachments of cavalry guarded each flank of the Confederate line, as were the flanks of the Federal line guarded by their cavalry.

During the engagement of the first day, which lasted from 9¼ A. M., to 4 P. M., our killed, wounded and prisoners greatly exceeded in number that of the enemy. They called it a glorious victory, but when the disparity in the numbers of the two opposing armies, and the tired and exhausted condition of our men are considered, the rebels had but little to boast of.

The effect of the victory gained this day, however, had an exhilarating effect upon not only the rank and file of the army, but upon Lee himself; and it has been intimated by Southern writers that the General was under a state of subdued excitement, so that he could not see the difficulties which confronted them but which were apparent to others (*Annals of the War*, page 421). The effect upon the men was very decided and evident. They entertained the idea that they could easily annihilate the comparatively small band of Federals then in their front, and that the remaining Corps and Divisions, coming upon the field separately and worn down by long and weary marches, would be met and cut up in detail. Hence during the evening and night after this battle they were boastful. They delighted to tell of the superior skill of their officers, and to speak disparagingly of the officers of the Federal army. But when Thursday morning dawned, and they saw that the little band upon Cemetery Hill and Culp's Hill had been largely reinforced, and that breastworks had been erected, and were bristling with cannon, and that still other Corps and Divisions were arriving and taking positions upon the field, they began to give evidence that their minds were undergoing a change, and that after all they might have some hard and bloody work to do.

Daylight at last dawned, and the hours wore away, and noon came, and the afternoon came on, and yet no attack was made. Was not the overruling hand of God in this? This delay, like the failure to drive the Federals from their strong position the evening before, was the salvation of the Nation. This will fully appear hereafter. Professor Jacobs in his Battle of Gettysburg—himself a witness of the scene, says: "The morning was pleasant, the air was calm, the sun shone mildly through a smoky atmosphere, and the whole outer world was quiet and peaceful. There was nothing to foretoken the sanguinary struggle that was to close the day. During the earlier part of the day the enemy kept perfectly quiet, and not a sound was to be heard, except the firing between the pickets, and an occasional artillery shot from our guns, for the purpose of feeling the whereabouts and strength of the enemy."

In this silence and apparent idleness the morning hours passed away, and not until late in the afternoon, and until the whole of the Union Army had arrived, except part of the Fifth Corps, and had been placed in position, did the attack begin. The reason of this silence and inaction will be given hereafter. Hon. Edward Everett in his address at Gettysburg at the dedication of the National Cemetery, says: "I cannot but remark on the providential inactivity of the Rebel army. Had the contest been renewed by it at daylight on the 2d of July, with the First and Eleventh Corps exhausted by the battle and the retreat, the Third and Twelfth weary from their forced march, and the Second, Fifth and Sixth not yet arrived, nothing but a miracle could have saved the army from a great disaster. Instead of this the day dawned, the sun rose, the cool hours of the morning passed, the forenoon and a considerable part of the afternoon wore away, without the slightest aggressive movement on the part of the enemy. Thus time was given for half of our forces to arrive and take their place in the lines, while the rest of the army enjoyed a much needed half day's repose."

The cause of the delay in attacking the Federal position will be seen in the following facts: General Longstreet, who was second in command of the Confederate Army, was opposed to attacking the Federals. He says that it was agreed upon between Lee and himself before they left Virginia, that the Pennsylvania campaign was to be "offensive in strategy, but defensive in tactics." That is, that the Confederates were to invade the State, menace Washington, and then choose a strong position and force the Federals to attack them, and in no case attack the Federals in any strong position they might take. Consequently when General Lee declared on the evening of the first day's engagement his intention of attacking the Union forces in the morning, General Longstreet remonstrated against it, telling Lee that that course was at variance with the plan of the campaign that had been agreed upon before leaving Fredericksburg. Longstreet's plan was that the Confederate army should move around by its right to the left of Meade, and put itself between him and Washington, threatening his left and rear, and thus force him to leave the strong position he had taken, and attack it in whatever position it might take. Lee would not consent to this suggestion, but persisted in his purpose to renew the battle the next day. Longstreet was reluctantly compelled to accede to the purpose of his chief, and accordingly says: "On the morning of the 2d, I went to General Lee's headquarters at daylight, and renewed my views against making an attack. He seemed resolved, however, and we discussed the probable results. We observed the position of the Federals, and got a general idea of the nature of the ground. About sunrise General Lee sent Colonel Venable, of his staff, to General Ewell's headquarters, ordering him to make a reconnoissance of the ground in his front, with the view of making the main attack on his left. A short time afterward he followed Colonel Venable in person. He returned at about nine o'clock and informed me that it would not do to have Ewell open the attack. He finally determined that I should make the main attack on the extreme right. It was fully eleven o'clock when General Lee arrived at this conclusion and ordered the movement." (*Annals of the War*, pages 417, 421, 422.)

Colonel W. H. Taylor, of Lee's staff, in the same book, page 309, says: "The prevailing idea with General Lee was to press forward without delay ; to follow up promptly and vigorously the advantage already gained. Having failed to reap the full fruit of the victory before night, his mind was evidently occupied with the idea of renewing the assault upon the enemy's right with the dawn on the second. The Divisions of Maj. Generals Early and Rhodes, of Ewell's Corps, had been actively engaged, and had sustained some loss, but were still in excellent condition, and in full enjoyment of the prestige of success, and consequent elation of spirit, in having so gallantly swept the enemy from their front, through the town of Gettysburg, and compelled him to seek refuge behind the heights beyond. The Division of Maj. Gen. Edward Johnson, of the same Corps, was perfectly fresh, not having been engaged. Anderson's Division of Hill's Corps was also now up. With this force General Lee thought that the enemy's posision could be assailed with every prospect of success ; but after a conference with the Corps and Division commanders on our left, who represented that, in their judgment, it would be hazardous to attempt to storm the strong position occupied by the enemy, with troops somewhat fagged by the marching and fighting of the first day ; that the ground in their immediate front furnished greater obstacles to a successful assault than existed at other points of the line, and that it could be reasonably concluded, since they had so severely handled the enemy in their front, that he would concentrate and fortify with special reference to resisting a further advance just these, he determined to make the main attack well on the enemy's left, indulging the hope that Longstreet's Corps would be up in time to begin the movement at an early hour on the second. He instructed General Ewell to be prepared to co-operate by a simultaneous advance by his corps."

Thus it will be seen that the capture of Cemetery Hill, which might have been accomplished the evening before, was now considered impossible ; and as an attack upon the left of the Union position was determined upon, we will now turn our attention in that direction.

General Longstreet in the *Annals of the War*, page 422, says that Gen. Lee did not return to his headquarters from the conference with the corps and division commanders on his left, until nine o'clock, and that it was fully eleven o'clock when he had so far matured his plans as to issue his orders for their execution. At that hour he ordered Gen. Longstreet to move with the portion of his command that was up—McLaws and Hood's divisions—around by the Emmittsburg road on the Federal left. That would place these two divisions directly opposite Sedgwick's and Sickles' corps, with the right of Hood's division opposite Round Top. Lee's plan was for Longstreet to open the battle by attacking Sickles on the Union left and, if possible, seize and hold Round Top. Simultaneous with the advance of these troops, Ewell was to attack our right. The whole plan, it will be seen, was dependent upon the two divisions of Longstreet ; and Lee certainly had a right to expect that they were near at hand, and the battle promptly begun, for they had encamped over night at Marsh creek, but four miles from the field. But for some cause which Gen. Longstreet has utterly failed to satisfactorily explain, these troops upon whom so much depended did not reach the positions assigned them until 4 o'clock.

Shortly after the arrival of the Sixth Corps, Gen. Meade left his headquarters and proceeded to the extreme left, to attend to the posting of the troops, as also to inspect the position of the Third Corps, about which he was in doubt. When he arrived upon the ground about four o'clock he found that Gen. Sickles, instead of connecting his right with the left of General Hancock, as he had been ordered to do, had thrown forward his lines three-quarters of a mile in front of the Second corps, leaving Little Round Top unprotected, and was without support on either flank. Gen. Meade at once saw this mistake, and Gen. Sickles promptly offered to withdraw to the line he had been commanded to occupy, but Gen. Meade replied : "You cannot do it. The enemy will not let you get away without a fight." Before he had finished the sentence his prediction was fulfilled. At precisely twenty minutes past 4 o'clock the enemy began the battle by opening a terrific artillery fire upon our guns, and soon afterwards by an infantry attack upon our left. In a short time the cannonading became general along our left and centre, which was answered by the guns of the enemy of which more than one hundred were placed in a circuit of about three miles along the Seminary ridge around to the Harrisburg road, and on the hills to the east of the town. Soon large masses of infantry from Longstreet's corps were thrown upon Sickles, the enemy at the same time sending a heavy force toward Little Round Top, which Gen. Warren, Meade's chief engineer, was holding with a few men whom he had collected together. Seeing the vital importance of this position, and having no troops at hand to reinforce Gen. Warren, Gen. Meade sent one staff officer after another to Gen. Sykes, who was approaching the field to urge him forward with all possible speed. At length, at 5 P. M., when the crisis seemed to have been reached, the balance of the Fifth corps arrived, and crossing over from the Taneytown to the Emmittsburg road, at Sherfy's peach orchard, and passing to the north of Little Round Top, threw themselves upon the foe, seized Round Top, and literally carried up on it twelve thirty pounder Parrott guns, and in a short time it was transformed into a Gibraltar. In the meantime, the attack upon Gen. Sickles was continued with great fury, and after a stubborn and gallant resistance, during which Gen. Sickles was wounded, the Third corps was compelled to fall back, shattered and broken, and to re-form behind the line originally intended to be held. Still the battle raged and the result for a time seemed doubtful until about six o'clock, when our men were being driven back, and the enemy was endeavoring to come in between Round Top and Little Round Top, advancing to the summit of the latter. Gen. Crawford's division of the Fifth corps, consisting of two brigades of Pennsylvania Reserves, went into a charge with a terrific shout, and drove the rebels down the rocky front of the hill, across the valley below, and over the next hill into the woods beyond, taking three hundred prisoners. This ended the battle on our left. The fight, on that part of our lines, was gloriously ended for that day, and Little Round Top was ours. Our lines which, in the morning, had rested on or near the Emmittsburg road, had receded one-third of a mile, but the enemy had been signally repulsed and we were still intact.

A correspondent of the New York *World* furnished an account of this great struggle which is so graphic and thrilling, that I cannot refrain from inserting part of it here. His account is as follows:

"The battle begun by a heavy fire on Cemetery Hill. It must not be thought that this wrathful fire was unanswered. Our artillery began to play within a few moments, and hurled back defiance and like destruction upon the rebel lines. Until six o'clock the rush of missiles and the bursting of bombs filled all the air. The clangor alone of this awful combat might well have confused and awed a less cool and watchful commander than General Meade. It did not confuse him. With the calculation of a tactician, and the eye of an experienced judge, he watched from his headquarters, on the hill, whatever movement under the murky cloud which enveloped the rebel lines might first disclose the intention which it was evident this artillery firing covered. About six o'clock P. M. silence, deep, awfully impressive, but momentary, was permitted, as if by magic, to dwell upon the field. Only the groans—unheard before—of the wounded and dying, only a murmur, a wavering motion of the breeze through the foliage; only the low rattle of preparation of what was to come embroidered this blank stillness. Then, as the smoke beyond the village was lightly borne to the eastward, the woods on the left were seen filled with dark masses of infantry, three columns deep, who advanced at a quick step. Magnificent! Such a charge, by such a force—full forty-five thousand men, under Hill and Longstreet—even though it threatened to pierce and annihilate the Third corps, against which it was directed, drew forth cries of admiration from all who beheld it. General Sickles and his splendid command withstood the shock with a determination that checked but could not fully restrain it. Back, inch by inch, fighting, falling, dying, cheering, the men retired. The rebels came on more furiously, halting at intervals, pouring volleys that struck our troops down in scores. General Sickles, fighting desperately, was struck in the leg and fell. The Second corps came to the aid of his decimated columns. The battle then grew fearful. Standing firmly against the storm, our troops, though still outnumbered, gave back shot for shot, volley for volley, almost for death. Still the enemy was not restrained. Down he came upon our left with a momentum that nothing could check. The rifled guns that lay before our infantry on a knoll were in danger of capture. General Hancock was wounded in the thigh, General Gibbin in the shoulder. The Fifth corps, as the First and Second, wavered anew, went into the breach with shouts and such volleys as made the rebel columns tremble at last. Up from the valley behind, another battery came rolling to the heights, and flung its shot in one instant down in the midst of the enemy's ranks. Crash! crash! with discharges deafening, terrible, the musketry went on. The enemy, reforming after each discharge with wondrous celerity and firmness, still pressed up the declivity. What hideous courage filled the minutes between the appearance of the Fifth corps and the advance to the support of the rebel columns of still another column from the right. I cannot bear to tell. Men fell, as leaves fall in Autumn, before those horrible discharges. Faltering for an instant, the rebel columns seemed about to recede before the tempest. But their officers, who could be seen through the smoke of the conflict, galloping and swinging their swords along the lines, rallied them anew, and the next instant the whole line sprang forward, as if to break through our own by mere weight of numbers. A division from the Twelfth corps, on our extreme right, reached the scene at this instant, and at the same time Sedgwick came up with the Sixth corps, having finished a march of nearly thirty-six consecutive hours. To what rescue they came their officers saw and told them. Weary as they were, barefooted, hungry, fit to drop for slumber, as they were, the wish for victory was so blended with the thought of exhaustion that they cast themselves, in turn, *en masse* into line of battle, and went down on the enemy with death in their weapons and cheers on their lips. The rebel camel's back was broken by this 'feather.' His line staggered, reeled and drifted slowly back, while the shouts of our soldiers, lifted up amid the roar of musketry over the bodies of the dead and wounded, proclaimed the completness of their victory."

It will be recollected that Ewell was to attack our right simultaneously with Longstreet's attack upon our left; but for reasons as inexplicable as the delay of the latter to bring his troops into action prior to 4 o'clock in the afternoon, when they had but four miles to march to reach the scene of conflict, he was not ready for the part assigned him until near eight o'clock in the evening. Previous to that hour there had been some sharp firing on this part of our line, but no general attack had been made. Ewell began early in the evening to mass his men for attack. Rhode's division was hurried forward from the west end of the town to unite with Early's and Johnston's, then arrived from Carlisle. Early attacked Cemetery Hill. To the Louisiana Tigers was committed the task of making the charge upon our guns. They dashed forward with furious determination and although they lost half of their men in killed and wounded, some rushed up to the cannon, which were too hot to be worked, but were beaten off by the gunners with clubs and stones. If they had been successful in this charge, the battle would have been lost to us. But the enemy was successfully met, slaughtered in great numbers, and driven back with terrible loss. Ewell had directed a similar attack to be made at the same time upon the Twelfth corps, in the rear of Culp's Hill, through a valley leading up from Rock creek towards Spangler's spring. This point had been weakened by detachments sent to assist Sickles. The enemy came up under cover of the forest and approaching darkness, but with desperate courage were they met. Never did men fight with greater determination, and from the time the attack was begun to the close, about 7 to 9½ P. M., the roar of musketry was continuous and terrific. The enemy's loss was fearful, the hills in front our lines were literally covered with the wounded and dead. At length the battle ceased with only one point in our lines broken, and the rebels in possession of a plain near Spangler's Spring. With this attack the battle of the day was over. And with this slight and short-lived success, the second day's battle ended with decided advantage to the Union army. But, O, what a scene of devastation and death did this field of strife present! The dead and wounded strewed the ground everywhere. Gen. Longstreet says that of the thirteen thousand men of his two divisions which were engaged, 4,500,29—more than one-third of their number—had been left upon the field.

Two great mistakes were made by the rebels this day. The first was in delaying the attacks until so late an hour in the afternoon. Had Longstreet brought his two divisions into position early in the morning and made the attack before 6 *o'clock*, Hancock with his Second corps would not have been there to oppose them. Or had the attack been made before 2 *o'clock* P. M., Sedgwick with the Sixth corps would have been absent, and Sickles would not have had his powerful assistance, and Round Top, the key to the Union position, which up to 5 *o'clock*, when Sykes arrived with the balance of the Fifth corps, was inadequately manned, would have been taken, and the victory would have been gained by the enemy and perhaps the government destroyed. Gen. Longstreet has been severely blamed for his delay in getting up his troops, and about the only excuse he offers for his tardiness is, that he was kept back by Ewell's wagon train, which had the right of way. But this was on Tuesday and Wednesday, and his two divisions were on Wednesday night but four miles from the field. He will have to offer some more plausible reason, or history will record him as sadly delinquent. One other mistake of this day was in Ewell's failing to attack our centre and right simultaneously with Longstreet's attack on the left as he was ordered to do. Had this attack been made the heavy withdrawals of troops from this part of our lines to assist in repelling the charges made on our left, could not have been made. In explanation of his failure to attack at the time he was ordered, Gen. Rhodes, who was on Early's right, says in his report, that "after he had conferred with General Early on his left and Gen. Lane on his right, and arranged to attack in concert, he proceeded at once to make the necessary preparations; but as he had to draw his troops out of the town by the flank, change the direction of the line of battle, and then traverse a distance of twelve or fourteen hundred yards, while Gen. Early had to move only half that distance, without change of front, it resulted that, before he drove in the enemy's skirmishers, Gen. Early had attacked and been compelled to withdraw." It is charged by Gen. Longstreet that the real cause of Ewell's non-compliance with Gen. Lee's orders was, that he had broken his lines by sending two brigades off on some duty up the York road. It will thus be seen that the whole affair was disjointed and that there was an utter absence of accord in the movements of the several commands, and for this reason no decisive results attended the operations of the rebels on this day. Is it not clear that the confusion in the counsels of the rebel chieftains, which was so conspicuous in their failure to follow up the advantages of the first day's engagement by attacking Cemetery Hill, still adhered to them and caused them to blunder and stumble to their final defeat? But the end was not yet, and we will have other blunders yet to record.

With the arrival of the balance of the Fifth corps, at five o'clock, the last of the Union forces had reached the field.

Late this evening Pickett's division, which had been left at Chambersburg to protect the Confederate rear, by a forced march reached Gettysburg.

Stuart's cavalry, after making a complete circuit of the Union army, this evening united with the rebel force.

FRIDAY, 3d.

During the night there was some readjusting the lines by the rebels. Pickett's Division, which arrived that evening, was placed to the left of Anderson and to the right of Heth, and directly opposite our left centre; and at 2 A. M. Rhodes moved his division to join the rest of Ewell's corps on our right. This was done so as to be ready, by the dawn of day, to improve the advantage gained the evening before, and, if possible, obtain possession of Culp's Hill and then the Baltimore road. Thus massed, Ewell designed to throw his whole force upon our right, whilst Longstreet with his newly arrived division was to perform a similar work upon our left centre.

The Federal forces were not inactive along this part of our line, and during the night that portion of the Twelfth Corps, which had been sent to assist in repelling the rebel onslaught upon our left, was returned to its place. Shaler's brigade of the Third division of the Sixth Corps, as also Lockwood's Maryland brigade were also sent to assist in driving the enemy from the position he had captured the evening previous.

At the dawn of day our artillery opened upon the rebels at the point where he had penetrated our line, and at sunrise a general infantry attack was also made. The battle raged furiously, and was maintained with desperate obstinancy on both sides for six hours. The slaughter was fearful, as the Union forces, realizing the importance of dislodging the foe from the position they had temporarily occupied, drove them backward step by step, until the lost ground was entirely gained. At 10½ A. M. the battle ceased with complete victory to our arms, after which it was not renewed on that part of our line. In this engagement, Gen. Geary, afterwards Governor of our State, commanded the Union forces.

Gen. Longstreet, who, it will be remembered, did not force an attack upon our position, but counselled Lee to move around by our left and get between our army and Washington, went early in the morning to see Gen. Lee, and, if possible, have him adopt his plan. Gen. Longstreet says: "I did not see Gen. Lee that night. On the next morning he came to see me, and, fearing that he was still in his disposition to attack, I tried to anticipate him by saying: 'General, I have had my scouts out all night, and I find that you still have an excellent opportunity to move around to the right of Meade's army, and manouvre him to attacking us.' He replied, pointing with his fist at Cemetery Hill, 'The enemy is there, and I am going to strike him.' I felt that it was my duty to express my convictions. I said: 'General, I have been a soldier all my life, I have been with soldiers engaged in fights by couples, by squads, companies, regiments, divisions and armies, and should know, as well as anyone, what soldiers can do. It is my opinion that no fifteen thousand men ever arrayed for battle can take that position,' pointing to Cemetery Hill. Gen. Lee, in reply to this, ordered me to prepare Pickett's Division for the attack. I should not have been so urgent had I not foreseen the hopelessness of the proposed assault. I felt that I must say a word against the sacrifice of my men; and then I felt that my record was such that Gen. Lee would or could not misconstrue my motives; I said no more, however, but turned away. The plan of assault was as follows: Our artillery was to be massed in a wood, from which Pickett was to charge, and it was to pour a continuous fire upon the enemy. Under cover of this fire, and supported by it, Pickett was to charge."

From 11 A. M. to 1 P. M. all was still—a solemn pause of preparation, as if both armies were nerving themselves for the last and supreme effort. In entire ignorance of the fact that his troops had been dislodged from the position they had occupied throughout the night upon his left, Lee was making preparations for the final onslaught. At length at precisely seven minutes past one o'clock, the awful silence was broken. The enemy opened upon Cemetery Hill and our left centre a tempest of fire from one hundred and twenty guns, placed all along their line from left to right. His object was, by subjecting our artillery on Cemetery Hill to a circle of cross fire to dismount our guns, demoralize our men, and prepare the way for the final charge. Owing to the character of the ground our army could reply with but eighty guns. This artillery duel, which lasted about two hours, it is said, was the most severe and terrible experienced anywhere during the war. It produced a continuous succession of crashing sounds as if the heavens were rent assunder, and the artillery of heaven was let loose upon earth. The air was filled with whizzing, screaming, bursting shells and solid shot, causing the very earth to shake, and sending many a mortal to his last account.

Mr. Wilkinson, of the New York *Tribune*, who was at Gen. Meade's headquarters when this fire was severest, thus describes it:

"In the shadow cast by the tiny farm house, sixteen by twenty, which Gen. Meade had made his headquarters, lay wearied staff officers and tired correspondents. There was not wanting to the peacefulness of the scene the singing of a bird, which had a nest in a peach tree within the tiny yard of the whitewashed cottage. In the midst of its warbling a shell screamed over the house, instantly followed by another, and another, and in a moment the air was full of the most complete artillery prelude to an infantry battle that was ever exhibited. Every size and form of shellknown to British and American gunnery shrieked, whirled, moaned, whistled and wrathfully fluttered over our ground. As many as six in a second, constantly two in a second, bursting and screaming over and around the headquarters, made a very hell of fire that amazed the oldest officers. They burst in the yard—burst next to the fence on both sides, garnished as usual with the hitched horses of aides and orderlies. The fastened animals reared and plunged with terror. Then one fell, then another—sixteen lay dead and mangled before the fire ceased, still fastened by their halters, which gave the expression of being wickedly tied up to die painfully. These brute victims of a cruel war touched all hearts. Through the midst of the storm of screaming and exploding shells an ambulance driven by its frenzied conductor at full speed, presented to all of us the marvelous spectacle of a horse going rapidly on three legs. A hinder one had been shot off at the hock. A shell tore up the little step at the headquarters cottage, and ripped bags of oats as with a knife. Another soon carried off one of its two pillars. Soon a spherical case burst opposite the open door—another ripped through the low garret. The remaining pillar went almost immediately to the howl of a fixed shot that Whitworth must have made. During this fire the horses at twenty and thirty feet distant were receiving their death, and soldiers in Federal blue were torn to pieces in the road, and died with the peculiar yells that blend the extorted cry of pain with horror and despair. Not an orderly, not an ambulance, not a straggler was to be seen upon the field swept by this tempest of orchestral death, thirty minutes after it commenced. Were not one hundred and twenty pieces of artillery trying to cut from the field every battery we had in position to resist their proposed infantry attack, and to sweep away the slight defenses behind which our infantry were waiting? Forty minutes—fifty minutes—counted watches that ran, O so languidly! Shells through the two lower rooms. A shell into the chimney that did not explode. Shells in the yard. The air thicker and fuller, and more deafening with the howling and whirring of these infernal missiles. The Chief of Staff struck—Seth Williams—loved and respected through the army, separated from instant death by two inches of space vertically measured. An aid bored with a fragment of iron through the bone of the arm. And the time measured on the sluggish watches was one hour and forty minutes."

Said General Howard in his official report, "a single shell exploding in the cemetery killed and wounded twenty-seven men in one regiment." Said another: "A soldier was lying on the ground a few rods distant from where I was sitting. There was a shriek, such as I hope never again to hear, and his body was whirled in the air, a mangled mass of flesh, blood and bones."

The Federal commanders well understood what the object of this tremendous fire was, and calmly and with undismay prepared to meet it. After the fire had continued about an hour and a half the artillerists were ordered gradually to slacken their fire, and finally to cease altogether, with the purpose of making the enemy believe that they had silenced our guns and thus bring on the assault the sooner. The artillerists threw themselves upon the ground for rest, but were not permitted to lie there long. The ruse had succeeded and soon there went out the word all along the line, "Here they come." Two long, dark, massive lines of infantry were seen to issue from the wooded crest of Seminary Ridge, and move steadily over the intervening plain towards our left centre. These columns were composed of Pickett's division of Longstreet's corps, which had not up to that time taken any part in the battle, having only arrived from Chambersburg the evening before. This division was supported on the left by Pettigrew's brigade of Heth's division of Hill's Corps, and on the right by Wright's and Wilcox's brigades of Anderson's division of the same corps. The whole of this assaulting force amounted to 18,000 or 20,000 men. When this moving mass of men had crossed about one-third of the space between the two armies, our batteries were opened upon them, ploughing great gaps in their ranks, which were quickly closed up. For a moment they seemed to waver, and then with terrific yells pressed on again. When they had reached the Emmittsburg road, within musket range, the infantry arose and poured into their ranks a withering fire. The whole crest of the hill was lit with a solid sheet of flame before which Pettigrew's column melted away, and in five minutes were streaming back, leaving besides the dead, a third of their number prisoners. Pickett's veterans pressed on and on, and so determined were they that they fairly broke through the first Union line, charging right among the batteries, where a hand to hand fight took place. The assailants advanced a few rods, and met another line which had been formed. All that mortal men could do was done by Pickett's men, but they were met by a force equally brave and determined, and finally repulsed. Of the three brigade commanders, one lay dead, another fatally wounded, and the third borne off to die. Of fifteen field officers only one was unhurt. The ground was strewn with the dead and wounded. When the survivors attempted to retreat they were met by a furious fusilade, and they flung themselves upon the ground with hands uplifted in token of surrender. Of that gallant band three out of four were dead or prisoners. Pickett's division was annihilated. When the smoke lifted, a few hundred rebels were seen moving backward towards the place from which they came; and at last two or three men carrying a single battle flag which they had saved, and several officers on horseback followed the fugitives.

As everything connected with this great and decisive charge upon the Union line is of deepest interest, I give here the following graphic sketch by an eye witness, Charles Carleton Coffin, in his "Boys of 1861."

"As soon as the approach of the enemy was perceived every man was on the alert. The cannoneers sprung to their feet. The long lines emerged from the woods, and moved rapidly but steadily over the fields, towards the Emmittsburg road. Howard's batteries burst into flame, throwing shells with the utmost rapidity. There are gaps in the rebel ranks, but onward still they come. They reach the Emmittsburg road. Pickett's division appears by Klingel's house. All of Howard's guns are at work now. Pickett turns to the right, moving north, driven in part by the fire rolling in upon his flank from Weed's Hill (Little Round Top) and from the Third, Fifth and Sixth Corps batteries. Suddenly he faces east, descends the gentle slope from the road behind Codori's, crosses the meadow, comes in reach of the muskets of the Vermonters. The three regiments rise from their shallow trench. The men beneath the oak trees leap from their low breastworks of rails. There is a ripple, a roll, a deafening roar. Yet the momentum of the rebel column carries it on. It is becoming thinner and weaker, but they still advance. The Second Corps is like a thin blue ribbon. Will it withstand the shock? "Give them cannister! Pour it into them!" shouts Major Charles Howard, running from battery to battery. The rebel line is almost up to the grove in front of Robinson's. It has reached the clump of scrub oaks. It has drifted past the Vermont boys. Onward still, 'Break their third line! Smash their supports!' cries Gen. Howard, and Osborne and Wainwright send the fire of fifty guns into the column, each piece fired three times a minute! The cemetery is lost to view—covered with sulphurous clouds, flaming and smoking and thundering like Sinai on the great day of the Lord! The front line of rebels is melting away—the second is advancing to take its place; but beyond the first and second is the third, which reels, and breaks, and flies to the woods from whence it came, unable to withstand the storm. Hancock is wounded, and Gibbon is in command of the Second Corps. 'Hold your fire, boys; they are not near enough yet,' says Gibben, as Pickett comes on. The first volley staggers, but does not stop them. They move upon the run—up to the breastworks of rails—bearing Hancock's line to the top of the ridge—so powerful their momentum. Men fire into each other's faces, not five feet apart. There are bayonet thrusts, sabre strokes, pistol shots; cool, deliberate movements on the part of some—hot, passionate, desperate efforts with others; hand to hand contests; recklessness of life; tenacity of purpose; fiery determination; oaths, yells, curses, hurrahs, shoutings; men go down on their hands and knees, spinning round like tops, throwing out their arms, gulping up blood, falling; legless, armless, headless. There are ghastly heaps of dead men. Seconds are centuries; minutes, ages; but the thin line does not break. The rebels have swept past the Vermont regiments. 'Take them in flank,' says Gen. Stannard. The Thirteenth and Sixteenth swing out from the trench, turn a right angle to the main line, and face to the north. They move forward a few steps, pour a deadly volley into the backs of Kemper's troops. With a hurrah they rush on to drive home the bayonet. The Fifteenth, Nineteenth, Twentieth Massachusetts and Seventh Michigan, Twentieth New York, Nineteenth Maine, One Hundred and Fifty-first Pennsylvania, and other regiments catch the enthusiasm of the moment, and close upon the foe. The rebel column has lost its power. The lines waver. The soldiers of the front rank look around for their supports. They are gone—fleeing over the field, broken, shattered, thrown into confusion by the remorseless fire from the cemetery and from cannon on the ridge. The lines have disappeared like a straw in a candle's flame. The ground is thick with dead, and the wounded are like the withered leaves of autumn. Thousands of rebels throw down their arms and give themselves up as prisoners."

While this great struggle was going on upon our left centre, Stuart, who had only joined Lee the evening before from his circuitous route around the Union army, reinforced by Jenkins' brigade, led an attack upon our rear. Passing around our right he was met by the Federal cavalry, and after a desperate hand to hand fight, in which many fell upon both sides, was defeated and driven back simultaneously with the defeat on the front.

Hood's division, too, which had been annoying Little Round Top all afternoon, still kept up an occasional fire after the repulse of Pickett. It remained for the Pennsylvania Reserves to defeat this force and close the battle of Gettysburg. Led by the gallant Crawford they drove the foe, captured the battery which had annoyed them, together with three hundred prisoners, and seven thousand stand of arms. By this action the ground lost by Sickles the day before was regained, and our wounded who had lain there for twenty-four hours entirely uncared for, were recovered. This charge occurred about 5 o'clock in the evening, and with it the battle closed. The losses of the two armies during the three days' engagement at Gettysburg has been over-estimated. Some accounts place the number killed, wounded and missing at 37,000 for each army. Later and more reliable accounts place the Union loss at 23,190, of whom 16,567 were killed and wounded, and 6,643 were missing. Col. Taylor, of Gen. Lee's staff, says that on the 20th of July, after returning to Virginia, the Confederate army numbered 41,380 effective men, showing a total loss in the Pennsylvania campaign of about 29,000.

It is a singular coincidence that the rebellion should receive its most decisive defeat in the east and west at the same time, for the same shadow on the dial which marked the time of the crushing overthrow at Gettysburg, indicated also another scene in the great drama twelve hundred miles away at Vicksburg.

The battle of Gettysburg has been considered as the turning point in the war, for from it the ultimate failure of the rebellion was assured. And as that battle was the culminating crisis of the war, so the last great effort of Lee when he hurled twenty thousand of his choicest troops against the Union line, was the supreme crisis of that battle, and also of the country's history. The rebellion at that point reached its high water mark, and from that on the waters steadily receded. That charge then was the turning point of history and of human destiny. It failed, and with its failure was demonstrated the fact that a government founded upon oppression and wrong could not succeed in the advanced light and civilization of this age, and the shadow be made thereby to go backward upon the dial of human progress. The Republic was "saved, redeemed, baptized and consecrated anew to the coming ages."

CHAPTER X.

THE GREAT TRAIN OF WOUNDED FROM GETTYSBURG.

Soon after the final repulse of the rebels in their last great charge upon the left centre of the Federal position at Gettysburg upon the afternoon of Friday, July 3d, they manifested considerable fear for their safety, and some adjustment of their lines and additional breastworks were hurriedly made, to prepare for an expected counter-charge by the Union forces. Gen. Longstreet says that he expected that Gen. Meade would throw his forces against their shattered ranks, and that, to prepare for this, he at once sent his staff officers to the rear to assist in rallying the troops and preparing the batteries to receive them. But for reasons satisfactory to himself, for which he has been somewhat censured, Gen. Meade did not deem it advisable to order this charge. During the night Ewell's division was withdrawn from its exposed position in the town and upon the hills southeast of it, and placed behind the defences of Seminary Ridge. The wounded were gathered from the field and carried to the rear, and during the ensuing day a large number of such as could bear transportation were placed in wagons and sent, under care of Gen. Imboden, across the South Mountain, with instructions to take the nearest route across the country to Williamsport, and thence cross the Potomac into Virginia. This immense train, estimated at from seventeen to thirty miles in length, with its thousands of maimed, wounded and dying, the details of which shall occupy mainly this chapter, left the field about four o'clock in the afternoon, crossed the mountain by the same route it had come, at Greenwood leaving the pike and taking what is known as the "Pine Stump Road" or the "Walnut Bottom Road," leading by way of New Guilford and New Franklin to the Main road leading from Chambersburg to Greencastle and Hagerstown, coming out with the latter at or near Marion and from thence to the Potomac at Williamsport.

On the same day, Saturday, 4th, Gen. Lee withdrew from his lines west of the town and marched down near the base of the mountain by the Fairfield road, crossed the mountain at the Monterey pass and thence passed on through Hagerstown, and on the night of Monday 13th recrossed the river. The Confederates were closely pursued by Gen. Meade, who, by a flank movement through Middletown and Turner's Pass, secured for him by Gen. French, came upon the enemy on the 12th, but owing to the strength of his position did not deem it advisable to attack him. For this failure to attack Lee, Gen. Meade has been considerably censured, but in the light of subsequent disclosures as to the impregnableness of the rebel position, his course is now deemed wise and prudent. The first of the rebel infantry crossed the Potomac on the 20th of June, and recrossed on the 13th of July into Virginia. Thus it will be seen the campaign north of the Potomac lasted twenty-four days.

Leaving the army of Gen. Lee now, to which I shall not have occasion in these reminiscences again to refer, unless to detached portions, I turn to notice the wagon train heretofore spoken of. The vastness of this train, and the aggregate of woe, suffering and anguish it contained, it seems, has never been understood by the country. And now to bring it before the reader in some adequate form, I annex here the following graphic description given by Gen. Imboden, who had charge of it, in an article contributed by him to the *Galaxy* of April, 1871. After detailing his operations along the line of the Baltimore and Ohio Railroad in Western Virginia, and his passage up the valley to McConnellsburg, Fulton county, and thence by Mercersburg and Chambersburg to Gettysburg, where he arrived about noon of Friday, the 3d of July, Gen. Imboden says:

I belonged to no division or corps in our army, and therefore on arriving near Gettysburg about noon, when the conflict was raging in all its fury, I reported directly to General Lee for orders, and was assigned a position to aid in repelling any cavalry demonstration that might occur on his flanks or rear. None being made, my little force took no part in the battle. I then had only about 2,100 effective mounted men and a six-gun battery.

When night closed upon the grand scene our army was repulsed. Silence and gloom pervaded our camps. We knew that the day had gone against us, but the extent of the disaster was not known except in high quarters. The carnage of the day was reported to have been frightful, but our army was not in retreat, and we all surmised that with to-morrow's dawn would come a renewal of the struggle; and we knew that if such was the case those who had not been in the fight would have their full share in the honors and dangers of the next day. All felt and appreciated the momentous consequences of final defeat or victory on that great field. These considerations made that, to us, one of those solemn and awful nights that everyone who fought through our long war sometimes experienced before a great battle. Few camp fires enlivened the scene. It was a warm summer's night, and the weary soldiers were lying in groups on the luxuriant grass of the meadows we occupied, discussing the events of the day or watching that their horses did not straggle off in browsing around. About eleven o'clock a horseman approached and delivered a message from General Lee, that he wished to see me immediately. I mounted at once, and, accompanied by Lieutenant McPhail of my staff, and guided by the courier, rode about two miles toward Gettysburg, where half a dozen small tents on the roadside were pointed out as General Lee's headquarters for the night. He was not there, but I was informed that I would find him with General A. P. Hill half a mile farther on. On reaching the place indicated, a flickering, solitary candle, visible through the open front of a common tent, showed where Generals Lee and Hill were seated on camp stools, with a county map spread upon their knees, and engaged in a low and earnest conversation. They ceased speaking as I approached, and after the ordinary salutations General Lee directed me to go to his headquarters and wait for him. He did not return until about one o'clock, when he came riding alone at a slow walk and evidently wrapped in profound thought.

There was not even a sentinel on duty, and no one of his staff was about. The moon was high in the heavens, shedding a flood of soft silvery light, almost as bright as day, upon the scene. When he approached and saw us, he spoke, reined up his horse, and essayed to dismount. The effort to do so betrayed so much physical exhaustion that I stepped forward to assist him, but before I reached him he had alighted. He threw his arm across his saddle to rest himself, and fixing his eyes upon the ground leaned in silence upon his equally weary horse; the two forming a striking group, as motionless as a statue. The moon shone full upon his massive features, and revealed an expression of sadness I had never seen upon that fine countenance before, in any of the vicissitudes of the war through which he had passed. I waited for him to speak until the silence became painful and embarrassing, when to break it, and change the current of his thoughts, I remarked in a sympathetic tone, and in allusion to his great fatigue:

"General, this has been a hard day on you." This attracted his attention. He looked up and replied mournfully:

"Yes, it has been a sad, sad day to us," and immediately relapsed into his thoughtful mood and attitude. Being unwilling again to intrude upon his reflections, I said no more. After a minute or two he suddenly straightened up to his full height, and turning to me with more animation, energy, and excitement of manner than I had ever seen in him before, he addressed me in a voice tremulous with emotion, and said:

"General, I never saw troops behave more magnificently than Pickett's division of Virginians did to-day in their grand charge upon the enemy. And if they had been supported, as they were to have been—but, for some reason not yet fully explained to me, they were not—we would have held the position they so gloriously won at such a fearful loss of noble lives, and the day would have been ours."

After a moment he added in a tone almost of agony:

"Too bad! Too bad!! Oh! TOO BAD!!!"

I never shall forget, as long as I live, his language, and his manner, and his appearance and expression of mental suffering. Altogether it was a scene that a historical painter might well immortalize had one been fortunately present to witness it.

In a little while he called up a servant from his sleep to take his horse; spoke mournfully, by name, of several of his friends who had fallen during the day; and when a candle had been lighted invited me alone into his tent, where, as soon as we were seated, he remarked:

"We must return to Virginia. As many of our poor wounded as possible must be taken home. I have sent for you because your men are fresh, to guard the trains back to Virginia. The duty will be arduous, responsible and dangerous, for I am afraid you will be harrassed by the enemy's cavalry. I can spare you as much artillery as you require, but no other troops, as I shall need all I have to return to the Potomac by a different route from yours. All the transportation and all the care of the wounded will be intrusted to you. You will recross the mountain by the Chambersburg road, and then proceed to Williamsport by any route you deem best, without halting. There rest and feed your animals, then ford the river, and make no halt till you reach Winchester, where I will again communicate with you."

After a good deal of conversation he sent for his chiefs of staff and ordered them to have everything in readiness for me to take command the next morning, remarking to me that the general instructions he had given would be sent to me next day in writing. As I was about leaving to return to my camp, he came out of his tent and said to me in a low tone: "I will place in your hands to-morrow a sealed package for President Davis, which you will retain in your own possession till you are across the Potomac, when you will detail a trusty commissioned officer to take it to Richmond with all possible despatch, and deliver it immediately to the President. I impress it upon you that whatever happens this package must not fall into the hands of the enemy. If you should unfortunately be captured, destroy it."

On the morning of the 4th my written instructions and the package for Mr. Davis were delivered to me. It was soon apparent that the wagons and ambulances and the wounded could not be ready to move till late in the afternoon. The General sent me four four-gun field batteries, which with my own gave me twenty-two guns to defend the trains.

Shortly after noon the very windows of heaven seemed to have been opened. Rain fell in dashing torrents, and in a little while the whole face of the earth was covered with water. The meadows became small lakes; raging streams ran across the road in every depression of the ground; wagons, ambulances and artillery carriages filled the roads and fields in all directions. The storm increased in fury every moment. Canvas was no protection against it, and the poor wounded, lying upon the hard, naked boards of the wagon bodies, were drenched by the cold rain. Horses and mules were blinded and maddened by the storm, and became almost unmanageable. The roar of the winds and waters made it almost impossible to communicate orders. Night was rapidly approaching, and there was danger that in the darkness the "confusion" would become "worse confounded." About 4 P. M., the head of the column was put in motion and began the ascent of the mountain. After dark I set out to gain the advance. The train was seventeen miles long when drawn out on the road. It was moving rapidly, and from every wagon issued wails of agony. For four hours I galloped along, passing to the front, and heard more—it was too dark to see—of the horrors of war than I had witnessed from the battle of Bull Run up to that day. In the wagons were men wounded and mutilated in every conceivable way. Some had their legs shattered by a shell or Minie ball; some were shot through their bodies; others had arms torn to shreds; some had received a ball in the face, or a jagged piece of shell had lacerated their heads. Scarcely one in a hundred had received adequate surgical aid. Many had been without food for thirty-six hours. The irragged, bloody and dirty clothes, all clotted and hardened with blood, were rasping the tender, inflamed lips of their gaping wounds. Very few of the wagons had even straw in them, and all were without springs. The road was rough and rocky. The jolting was enough to have killed sound, strong men. From nearly every wagon, as the horses trotted on, such cries and shrieks as these greeted the ear:

"Oh God! why can't I die?"

"My God! will no one have mercy and kill me and end my misery?"

"Oh! stop one minute and take me out and leave me to die on the roadside."

"I am dying! I am dying! My poor wife, my dear children! what will become of you?"

Some were praying; others were uttering the most fearful oaths and execrations that despair could wring from them in their agony. Occasionally a wagon would be passed from which only low, deep moans and sobs could be heard. No help could be rendered to any of the sufferers. On, on; we *must* move on. The storm continued and the darkness was fearful. There was no time even to fill a canteen with water for a dying man; for, except the drivers and the guards disposed in compact bodies every half mile, all were wounded and helpless in that vast train of misery. The night was awful, and yet it was our safety, for no enemy would dare attack us when he could not distinguish friend from foe. We knew that when day broke upon us we would be harrassed by bands of cavalry hanging on our flanks. Therefore our aim was to go as far as possible under cover of the night, and so we kept on. It was my sad lot to pass the whole distance from the rear to the head of the column, and no language can convey an idea of the horrors of that most horrible of all nights of our long and bloody war.

Daybreak on the morning of the 5th found the head of our column at Greencastle, twelve or fifteen miles from the Potomac at Williamsport, our point of crossing. Here our apprehended troubles from the Union cavalry began. From the fields and cross-roads they attacked us in small bodies, striking the column where there were few or no guards, and creating great confusion.

To add still further to our perplexities, a report was brought that the Federals in large force held Williamsport. This fortunately proved untrue. After a great deal of harrassing and desultory fighting along the road, nearly the whole immense train reached Williamsport a little after the middle of the day. The town was taken possession of; all the churches, school houses, etc., were converted into hospitals, and proving insufficient, many of the private houses were occupied. Straw was obtained on the neighboring farms; the wounded were removed from the wagons and housed; the citizens were all put to cooking and the army surgeons to dressing wounds. The dead were selected from the train—for many had perished on the way—and were decently buried. All this had to be done because the tremendous rains had raised the river more than ten feet above the fording stage, and we could not not possibly cross.

Our situation was frightful. We had over 10,000 animals and all the wagons of General Lee's army under our charge, and all the wounded that could be brought from Gettysburg. Our supply of provisions consisted of a few wagon loads of flour and a small lot of cattle. My effective force was only about 2,100 men and twenty-odd field pieces. We did not know where our army was; the river could not be crossed; and small parties of cavalry were still hovering around. The means of ferriage consisted of two small boats and a small wire rope stretched across the river, which owing to the force of the swollen current broke several times during the day. To reduce the space to be defended as much as possible, all the wagons and animals were parked close together on the river bank.

Believing that an attack would soon be made upon us, I ordered the wagoners to be mustered, and, taking three out of every four, organized them into companies, and armed them with the weapons of the wounded men found in the train. By this means I added to my effective force about five hundred men. Slightly wounded officers promptly volunteered their services to command these improvised soldiers; and many of our quartermasters and commissaries did the same thing. We were not seriously molested on the 5th; but next morning about 9 o'clock information reached me that a large body of cavalry from Frederick, Maryland, was rapidly advancing to attack us. As we could not retreat further, it was at once frankly made known to the troops that unless we could repel the threatened attack we should all become prisoners, and that the loss of his whole transportation would probably ruin General Lee; for it could not be replaced for many months, if at all, in the then exhausted condition of the Confederate states. So far from repressing the ardor of the troops, this frank announcement of our peril inspired all with the utmost enthusiasm. Men and officers alike, forgetting the sufferings of the past few days, proclaimed their determination to drive back the attacking force or perish in the attempt. All told, we were less than 3,000 men. The advancing force we knew to be more than double ours, consisting, as we had ascertained, of five regular and eight volunteer regiments of cavalry, with eighteen guns, all under the command of Generals Buford and Kilpatrick. We had no works of any kind; the country was open and almost level, and there was no advantage of position we could occupy. It must necessarily be a square stand up fight, face to face. We had twenty-two field guns of various calibre, and one Whitworth. These were disposed in batteries, in semi-circle, about one mile out of the village, on the summit of a very slight rising ground that lies back of the town. Except the artillery, our troops were held out of view of the assailants, and ready to be moved promptly to any menaced point along the whole line of nearly two miles in extent. Knowing that nothing could save us but a bold "bluff" game, orders had been given to the artillery as soon as the advancing forces came within range to open fire along the whole line, and keep it up with the utmost rapidity. A little after one o'clock they appeared on two roads in our front, and our batteries opened. They soon had their guns in position, and a very lively artillery fight began. We fired with great rapidity, and in less than an hour two of our batteries reported that their ammunition was exhausted. This would have been fatal to us but for the opportune arrival at the critical moment of an ammunition train from Winchester. The wagons were ferried across to our side as soon as possible, and driven on the field in a gallop to supply the silent guns. Not having men to occupy half our line, they were moved up in order of battle, first to one battery, then withdrawn and double-quicked to another, but out of view of our assailants till they could be shown at some other point on our line. By this manœuvring we made the impression that we had a strong supporting force in rear of all our guns along the entire front. To test this, Generals Buford and Kilpatrick dismounted five Regiments and advanced them on foot on our right. We concentrated there all the men we had, wagoners and all, and thus, with the aid of the united fire of all our guns directed at the advancing line, we drove it back, and rushed forward two of our batteries four or five hundred yards further to the front. This boldness prevented another charge, and the fight was continued till near sunset with the artillery. About that time General Fitzhugh Lee sent a message from toward Greencastle, that if we could hold out an hour he would reinforce us with 3,000 men. This intelligence elicited a loud and long-continued cheer along our whole line, which was heard and understood by our adversaries, as we learned from prisoners taken. A few minutes later General J. E. B. Stuart, advancing from Hagerstown, fell unexpectedly upon the rear of their right wing, and in ten minutes they were in rapid retreat by their left flank in the direction of Boonsboro. Night coming on enabled them to escape.

By extraordinary good fortune we had thus saved all of General Lee's trains. A bold charge at any time before sunset would have broken our feeble lines, and we should all have fallen an easy prey to the Federals. This came to be known as "the wagoners' fight" in our army, from the fact that so many of them were armed and did such gallant service in repelling the attack made on our right by the dismounted regiments.

Our defeat that day would have been an irreparable blow to General Lee, in the loss of all his transportation. Every man engaged knew this, and probably in no fight in the war was there a more determined spirit shown than by this handful of cooped-up troops. The next day our army from Gettysburg arrived, and the country is familiar with the manner in which it escaped across the Potomac on the night of the 9th.

It may be interesting to repeat one or two facts to show the peril in which we were until the river could be bridged. About 4,000 prisoners taken at Gettysburg were ferried across the river by the morning of the 9th, and I was ordered to guard them to Staunton. Before we had proceeded two miles I received a note from General Lee to report to him in person immediately. I rode to the river, was ferried over, and galloped out toward Hagerstown. As I proceeded I became satisfied that a serious demonstration was making along our front, from the heavy artillery firing extending for a long distance along the line. I overtook General Lee riding to the front near Hagerstown. He immediately reined up, and remarked that he believed I was familiar with all the fords of the Potomac above Williamsport, and the roads approaching them. I replied that I knew them perfectly. He then called up some one of his staff to write down my answers to his questions, and required me to name all fords as high up as Cumberland, and describe minutely their character, and the roads and surrounding country on both sides of the river, and directed me to send my brother, Colonel Imboden, to him to act as a guide with his regiment, if he should be compelled to retreat higher up the river to cross it. His situation was then very precarious. When about parting from him to recross the river and move on with the prisoners, he told me they would probably be rescued before I reached Winchester, my guard was so small, and he expected a force of cavalry would cross at Harper's Ferry to cut us off; and he could not spare to me any additional troops, as he might be hard pressed before he got over the river, which was still very much swollen by the rains. Referring to the high water, he laughingly inquired, "Does it ever quit raining about here?" If so, I should like to see a clear day."

These incidents go to show how near Gettysburg came to ending the war in 1863. If we had been successful in that battle, the probabilities are that Baltimore and Washington would at once have fallen into our hands; and at that time there was so large a "peace party" in the North, that the Federal Government would have found it difficult, if not impossible, to carry on the war. General Lee's opinion was that we lost the battle because Pickett was not supported "as he was to have been." On the other hand, if Generals Buford and Kilpatrick had captured the ten thousand animals and all the transportation of Lee's army at Williamsport, it would have been an irreparable loss, and would probably have led to the fall of Richmond in the autumn of 1863. On such small circumstances do the affairs of nations sometime turn.   J. D. IMBODEN.

Leaving out of Gen. Imboden's account of this immense train that part which is but bluster and braggadocia, it will yet be seen that it comprised as much distress and suffering as was probably ever brought together in any one place on this continent. He estimates that train at *seventeen miles in length.* Other accounts, however, make it much longer. In the *Franklin Repository* of July 8th, 1863, it is said that this train commenced to pass through Greencastle on Sunday morning at 4 A. M. and continued until 11 A. M. Monday. This would make thirty-one hours in passing one point; and allowing but one mile to an hour, and we have thirty-one miles, as its probable length. In the same paper from which I have thus quoted, the number of wounded in these wagons and walking along by them, is stated at from ten to twelve thousand. Add to this vast number the seven thousand, five hundred and forty who were left upon the field who were too badly wounded to be borne away, or for whom transportation could not be given, and some idea may be formed of the extent of the losses of those three eventful days. All along the route by which this train made its way, broken wagons and dead and dying soldiers were strewn; while in and about Gettysburg, in the fields, along the roadside, and in houses and barns in the rear of the rebel line, maimed and suffering men were found everywhere. I will reserve for a subsequent chapter an account of the sad and terrible scenes I witnessed upon visiting the field on the Tuesday after the battle. Rev. Isaiah Baltzel informs me that on Monday, after the last of this train had passed, he rode along the road from Marion to Greencastle, and all along the route the terrible evidences of its passage were seen. Broken wagons lay here and there all along the route. Upon looking into one of these wagons, the occupants having been removed, the whole bottom was smeared with blood. Upon passing a house a woman called him and asked him if he was a doctor. She said they had taken two wounded men from a wagon and put them in their barn, and unless they had surgical care they would die. The men were moaning out their agony so distressingly that he could not endure it. Their wounds had not been dressed.

Rev. J. Milton Snyder, son of J. C. Snyder, Esq., of New Franklin, and now a resident of Meyersdale, Somerset county, Pa., furnishes the following account:

"I can well remember when the rebel train of wounded came from Gettysburg, by way of my father's and New Franklin. I was quite young at the time, and hence noticed many things that escaped the notice of older persons. On Saturday evening, July 4th, 1863, whilst we were quietly seated in the house, father heard a peculiar noise as the the approach of a heavy storm. This was, if I remember correctly, about 10 o'clock on Saturday night. Father went out into the darkness to listen. A short while after a body of rebel cavalry came down the road from Greenwood. They halted at father's and called him out. The night was very dark. They asked to be directed to Greencastle. They seemed to be lost or bewildered. Father not knowing whether they were Union or rebel, directed them properly. About midnight the first of the train of wounded reached our place. The wagons kept the main road as much as possible, and on either side of the train a continual stream of wounded soldiers kept moving. Thus they continued coming and going the remainder of Saturday night, all day Sunday and the last wagon passed by New Franklin on Monday at 9 o'clock. The train of wounded left the pike at Greenwood, came on the old "Walnut Bottom Road" (called also the Pine Stump road), through New Guilford by my father's, through New Franklin, thence to Marion and Greencastle. On Monday morning Gregg's cavalry came after the train, following the same route. Gen. Gregg halted at father's and 'camped' in one of our fields east of New Franklin and in our orchard. Some of our Franklin county boys were with Gregg, and Mr. Henry Flanagan visited his parents in the village of New Franklin. The rebels claimed that they were going South for ammunition. Rebel soldiers, wounded, were left all along the route of retreat. Many died and were buried by the roadside. I shall never forget those ghastly wounds, those thousands of faces dusky with powder, and that battery of black and horrid field pieces they had sent, as could be seen, many charges of 'grape' into the bosom of our brave men."

Mr. George Myers, residing near the railroad station at Marion, says that many of the teamsters did not attempt to keep the road, but took the nearest route across the fields, the wheels cutting in the soft ground up to the axles. Some of the cavalrymen having lost the road went along the railroad, jumping their tired horses over the cattle guards. All the night long groans and cries of distress were heard, and their pump was in continual use for water to bathe the wounds and quench the thirst of the wretched inmates of the wagons. In the morning some of the wagons from which groans were heard to come were closed down by curtains, the poor wretches having died.

Rev. J. C. Smith, at that time a resident of Greencastle, gives the following account:

"Saturday, July 4th, 1863, closed with a perfect quiet in Greencastle. Captain Dahlgreen and his troops disappeared as mysteriously as they had come. The stragglers, who had been bringing up the rear of Lee's army, had either all passed through or had received a hint that it would be a saving of muscle to advance no further North just then. Greencastle went to bed in entire ignorance of the results of the battle of Gettysburg, hopeful to be sure, but not assured that all was well. Four o'clock Sunday morning we awoke to hear the rumbling of wagons, the tramping of horses, the noise and racket attending an army in motion. The first question naturally would be, 'what does all this commotion mean?' And the answer came readily and earlier, "There goes another rebel army to help decide the battle in progress at Gettysburg." Hastily dressing and going out on the street, we were supremely happy in seeing the army heading the other direction. It was the army of wounded from the battlefield hastening on toward the Potomac to cross over to Virginia. No one, with any feelings of pity, will ever want to see such a sight more than once in a life-time. Here came the men who but eight or ten days before had passed through our town in the prime of health, boasting of the exploits they would do, when they would have the happy chance of seeing the Union army. A more crest-fallen, woe-begone mob may never have been seen. Hurry was the order of the day. They seemed almost to be pushing each other forward. Yet when asked about the results of the battle, the officers invariably declared that they gave the boys in blue a sound thrashing. In conversation with an intelligent officer, I asked, 'If you have thrashed our army so soundly, why are you leaving us so hurriedly? Why not stay and occupy your conquered territory?' In reply he said : 'O, we are just taking these home to have them cured up, and with these wagons bring on more ammunition and soldiers and finish up the job.' Then said he, 'did you hear from Vicksburg?' 'No,' said I. 'Well, Pemberton has captured Grant and his army.' I did not feel as though I could go into ectacies over this, but still hoped that for veracity he might be classed among those creatures whom Paul accurately describes in 1st Tit. 1: 12. The common soldier seemed to be either too stupid, or else forbidden to give a true account of the battle, but all the way through the colored portion declared that they were badly whipped. Such a scene of suffering, who may undertake to describe! No one counted the wounded. They could not be counted because hundreds of wagons loaded with them were a part of this train. All who were wounded in the lower extremities were placed into these huge and rough-rolling army wagons. When passing over any part of the street where the wagon would jolt, they would yell and groan with pain. Many had received their hurt on Wednesday and Thursday before, with no attention paid to them by surgeons, the doctors having been kept busy with the more grave cases. All who were wounded in the head, the arms, the shoulder, the non-vital parts of the body, were compelled to walk through the mud ankle deep, with no food save a little flour mixed with water and baked on a few coals. Those wounded in the arms or shoulder would tear away the garment and expose the wounded part. Such arms—swollen to twice or thrice their natural size—red and angry. When they came to a pump, one would place his wounded member under the spout while another would pump cold water on the sore. Then he would do a like service to his comrade. Thus the pumps were going all that day. I will particularize one case: this will be a sample for probably five or six thousand similar ones. He was from North Carolina ; was shot through the arm, between the shoulder and the elbow. The arm was swollen to the size of a medium sized man's thigh, very red and inflamed. Nothing had been done for him by the doctor save to press a wad of cotton into the wound in each side of the arm. He had received his wound on Wednesday. Now said he, 'I am going home, and I will never enter the army again.' Said I, 'my dear friend, I fear you can't reach home soon. I learn that our government has thrown an army on the South bank of the Potomac.' Said he, 'I never wanted to go into this war. They came to my home and drove me into the army at the point of the bayonet. The next time they come they may shoot me down at my door ; I will rather die than fight again.' We estimated the number of wounded that passed through our town at 12,000 to 15,000. It was an easy matter to trace their work of flight. Dead horses, broken down and abandoned wagons, cannon carriages and caissons, new made graves. It was simply a road covered with wrecks.

On Monday evening, June 6th, about sundown some cavalry, being the rear guard, passed through, and there ended our connection with the Rebel Confederacy."

Mr. David Z. Shook, a resident of Greencastle, and an eye witness, relates the following :

"We were awakened by a rumbling sound in the direction of Chambersburg. It was the wagon train from Gettysburg. The teamsters and guards were somewhat excited, and were hurrying through. Many of the wagons were loaded with wounded, whose cries and groans were pitiful indeed. We asked the rebels what was up? They told us that a battle had been fought at Gettysburg, but it was not at all decisive. They said too that they were only taking their wounded off and that they expected reinforcements from Virginia. They tried to hide their defeat, but we saw that there were more than wounded hurrying towards Virginia. One poor fellow begged to be lifted out of a wagon and laid on the ground as his pain in the jolting wagon was unbearable, but the teamsters hurried on and kept no account of his entreaties. The night following being very dark, many persons in town engaged in capturing horses and cattle from the train. As cattle passed by I saw many turned into alleys. Horses tied behind wagons had their halters cut and were led away unobserved. Many horses, too, gave out here and were left. They suffered greatly from not being shod, their hoofs being worn off to the quick. Many such were offered for sale—fine ones being offered as low as five dollars in Yankee money. I captured a fine bay horse, hid him in the barn, fed him well and felt proud of my possession. A few days after a citizen of Greencastle came to the barn, recognized his horse, *proved him*, and took him away. I did not smile for a week. The rebels had taken this horse on their way to Gettysburg, and I had the luck to get him as my first capture, though I was in utter ignorance of his belonging to a fellow townsman until he informed me. Many persons threw taunts at the retreating foe, such as 'How are you Gettysburg?' 'Have you been to Philadelphia already?' and 'Did you meet the Pennsylvania militia down there?' An officer rode up to a pump and asked for water. A citizen standing by said, 'Did you get enough of *Meade* over there?' The officer grew furious and called him an impudent puppy."

Some of our citizens residing upon the eastern outskirts of the town said that for a day or two they had heard cannonading across the South Mountain. During the battle of Antietam, and on other occasions when there was artillery firing down about the Potomac, the sound could be heard distinctly by persons in the country away from the noise of the town. These sounds were more distinct along the Conococheague creek, which runs into the Potomac at Williamsport, and along the sides of the mountains. During the battle of Gettysburg, the South Mountain intervening, the sound of the cannonading was not so distinct. It resembled the noise occasioned by the distant slamming of a door.

On Saturday evening at 6 o'clock, notwithstanding the inclemency of the weather, and the uncertainty as to the result of the battle which we knew had been fought, a number of our citizens gathered in front of the Court House for the purpose of celebrating our national holiday. The Burgess, Mr. Hoskinson, presided, assisted by two tried soldiers, Captains Samuel McKesson and George L. Miles as Vice Presidents. Mr. J. Porter Brown, also a soldier, was Secretary of the meeting. The *Franklin Repository* of July 15th, says that the Declaration of Independence was read by Mr. William I. Cook. My recollection is, that Mr. Upton Washabaugh read the Declaration. Speeches were made by Hon. George W. Brewer, W. S. Stenger, W. S. Everett, Esqs., and Revs. Forney and Dickson. The Chambersburg Band, under charge of Mr. H. B. Hatnick, furnished music for the occasion.

At the conclusion of this meeting Mr. H. E. Hoke informed a number of persons that he had heard from the balcony of his house on East Market street, a low rumbling noise as if an immense train of wagons were moving from the pass of the South Mountain across the country towards Greencastle. Taking several persons with him, Mr. Hoke led these persons to his dwelling, and upon going out upon the balcony and holding their ears close to the brick wall of the house, they all clearly heard the sound, and came to the conclusion that Lee was retreating.

About 10 o'clock that same evening (Saturday, July 4th) while seated upon the door step in front of my house at the north-east corner of the Diamond, Mr. Thomas Fletcher, now deceased, came along and sat down by my side. He informed me that he had just returned from a scouting service out near Turkey Foot, and that the whole way from South Mountain by Greenwood along the Pine Stump road was crowded with hundreds upon hundreds of wagons, loaded with wounded men; that they were but weakly guarded, and a few cavalry could capture nearly the whole train. From this fact of these wagons going South, we concluded that Lee was defeated and was retreating.

At the break of day on Sabbath morning, July 5th, I was called from my bed to go immediately to the School House Hospital on King street, adjoining the jail, to assist in removing from a number of wagons, which had lost their way in the night and had come to this place, a lot of wounded rebels from Gettysburg. Repairing hastily to King street I found some four or five wagons, each drawn by four horses or mules, and all laden with wounded men. Standing upon the pavement in front of the hospital was a rebel soldier with his arm off close to his shoulder. O, what a sight! Bloody, wounds undressed, almost famished for water and food, these men presented a sight such as I never wish to see again. After they were all taken into the hospital I went to the residence of Mrs. Ritner, adjoining the King street church, and engaged her to furnish them with bread. Coffee, beef tea, and such other things as they needed were furnished day after day, until General Couch, some four or five days thereafter, moved his headquarters from Harrisburg to this place, when he took charge of the hospital. Some of the wounded men told us that their army was defeated at Gettysburg, and that Lee was retreating.

The following is an account of the way this wagon train lost its way and came into Chambersburg. In the darkness of the night these wagons became separated from the train, and coming out into the Greencastle road, this side of Marion near the White Church, one of the teamsters or wagonmasters called at a house and inquired the nearest way to Williamsport. A woman looking out of a window and waving her hand towards Chambersburg said, "You had better go that way." Following her direction they came into town shortly before the break of day. Mr. John A. Lemaster, who resided at that time near the corner of Main and German streets, has furnished me with the following statement: Hearing a noise in the street he went to the window and looked out. A number of wagons were standing in the street, the front resting at German street. Cries and groans came from all the wagons. After stopping a little while a man on horseback rode up to the front teamster and said, "Why don't you drive on?" The teamster replied, "We are on the wrong road; this is not Williamsport." The horseman replied, "'Tis Williamsport; only drive on for the Yankees are just behind us." The teamster then said, "Williamsport has no church steeple like that," referring to the Reformed church. "I tell you," said the horseman, "this is Williamsport. Don't you know that just down there in that hollow is the canal and the river? Drive on as fast as you can, and after you are across the river you can take all the time you want." Another person coming up at this time and surveying the situation, said as he pointed westwardly down German street, "That looks more like the right way; down there in that hollow are the canal and river." At length a teamster from the rear was put in charge of the front team, and the whole drove on down Main street and out to the intersection of Main and Second, followed by a number of citizens, when they were convinced that they were in Chambersburg and compelled to surrender. The teams were at once driven back to the Hospital on King street, as already stated.

Mr. Jacob S. Brand tells me that when these wagons were opposite his residence on Main street, near the Diamond, the young man I have referred to as having his arm off near the shoulder, succeeded in getting out unable longer to endure the jolting. Mr. Brand said to him, "What does this mean?" "It means," said he, "that Uncle Robert has got a —— whipping."

Returning to my residence after the removal of the wounded rebels from this wagon train, I found a man at our door from the country, who had come to town to learn the latest news. His horse was hitched in front of our store. Telling him the situation, and showing him the importance of sending information of the large wagon train then passing through our county for Virginia, as quickly as possible to the authorities at Harrisburg, he consented to carry the despatch westward on the Pittsburg pike, to be delivered to the repair party who, we had heard, were somewhere between Chambersburg and Loudon repairing the telegraph line. I hastily wrote a despatch to Governor Curtin, stating the fact, and suggesting that a small body of cavalry, if a large body could not be sent, could capture a large part of that train. Handing this dispatch to the man, he mounted his horse and went at a rapid gait out on the western pike. I have no knowledge whether my despatch ever reached Governor Curtin; but it happened that the brave New York cavalry, who distinguished themselves by whipping twice their number of rebels in McConnellsburg, and also rode into the jaws of death a half mile north of Greencastle on Monday, June 22d, were at that time in McConnellsburg, and by somebody's orders they crossed the mountain, ten or twelve of them coming directly to this place, and the remainder taking across the country from Loudon towards Greencastle. When they came up to the wagon train they made a dash upon it, cut the traces, stampeded the horses and mules, and in this way by repeated efforts, they succeeded in capturing several hundred wagons with the horses and mules. Some time towards evening the ten or twelve cavalry who headed for this place entered our town. They were the first Union soldiers we had seen for a number of weeks. Never were visitors so welcome. The blessed army blue never looked so comely. We began to feel that we yet had a Country and a Government, and that after all the glorious flag of our fathers floated in triumph. Some wept for joy. Others flung their hats in the air and shouted aloud. Soon a pole was improvised, a flag drawn forth from its hiding place and nailed to the end, and the pole raised aloft and spiked fast to the stump of the pole raised on the 18th of April, 1861, and cut down by Imboden's cut throats on the Wednesday preceding.

On Monday morning about eight o'clock, while standing in front of our store, Dr. A. H. Senseny, who was just returning from a visit to the King Street Hospital, told me that already vermin had made their appearance in the wounds of the rebels, and that unless real Castile soap were procured and their wounds washed, they would all die. I purchased all of this soap Mr. A. J. Miller, the druggist, had and took it to the hospital and delivered it to the steward, telling him what to do with it. Upon coming out of the hospital I saw a man running up Second street from the depot, waving his hat in one hand and a paper in the other, shouting and yelling at the top of his voice. It proved to be Mr. J. W. Deal, the postmaster. He had spent most of the time during the invasion in Harrisburg, and having come up that morning as far as the Scotland bridge, he there took a hand car and came to town, bringing with him an extra issued by one of the newspapers of Harrisburg, giving the details of the battle. I caught the words, "Victory! Victory at Gettysburg! Lee in full retreat!!" I waited for no more but ran down King street to Main and up to the front of the Court House, calling upon everyone I saw to follow me and hear the glorious news. Mr. Deal soon reached the Court House steps, and to an immense throng he read to us the first authentic and detailed news we had yet received of the great battle at Gettysburg. The cup of our rejoicing was now full, and shouts and huzzahs rang out from almost every lip. Conveyances were at once in great demand to visit the field of carnage. Many started on foot. I was one of the fortunate ones and procuring a team, in company with three others, we started a little after the middle of the day for Gettysburg. I will resume, however, an account of this trip for a subsequent chapter.

CHAPTER XI.

SCOUTING SERVICE.

As soon as the rebel forces began to pass through our town, we saw the propriety of sending all the information of their number and movements to the authorities at Harrisburg which we could. And while we had no concerted method of operation by which information was to be gathered and sent, a number of our citizens made careful estimates of the number of troops and cannon which daily passed through the town, and in such ways as they could, forwarded the same to the Capital of the State. Hon. F. M. Kimmell, at one time presiding Judge of this district, who had acted as Provost Marshall, during the period our town was under martial law, about the time of the invasion of Maryland and the battle of Antietam, in 1862, had been requested by Governor Curtin to exercise a general superintendence here during the war. This fact was unknown to us, yet by general consent many of us cooperated with Mr. Kimmell in collecting and forwarding information during the invasion. The late Judge Paxton and Mr. Christian Stouffer were specially directed by Mr. Kimmell to take careful estimates of the enemy's force, and these estimates, with those made by others, were forwarded every day to Harrisburg by some of our young men. I am unable to give the names of all who made these perilous journeys to and from the Capital. Messrs. Shenrer Houser, Benjamin S. Huber, J. Porter Brown, Anthony Holler, Mr. Kinney, Sellers Montgomery, Thomas J. Grimison and Stephen W. Pomeroy were among the number. When anything which we deemed of special importance occurred, we made it a point to dispatch a messenger as soon as possible. Usually the facts we wished to communicate were written upon a very small piece of paper, and these papers were secreted somewhere about the person of the scout. Upon one occasion Shearer Houser, when on his way with a dispatch, was captured by some rebel cavalrymen, and to avoid the fate which surely awaited him, if his dispatch were found upon his person, pulled from his pocket a plug of tobacco and bit off the end in which the paper was secreted. While chewing and attempting to swallow it, he looked up into the branches of a tree under which he was standing, and tried to decide upon which one he would be hanged. On some occasions messages were carried verbally, which was considered less riskful. In the front room above our store, overlooking the Diamond, at a distance from the window that the person could not be seen by the passing rebels, with pencil and paper, the soldiers and cannon were counted. In almost every case the dispatches were written by Judge Kimmell. We all knew that according to the rules of war, we would be hanged if caught, and on one occasion Gen. Couch sent us this message by one of our scouts:—"Tell the gentlemen engaged in this business that the information they send us is of great importance, and I hope they will continue it, but if detected they will surely be executed." We were aware of our danger, and did our work so as to avoid detection.

It is not my purpose to put upon record here the circumstances connected with all the trips to and from Harrisburg made by our scouts. This I could not do for the reason that I could not give even the names of all the heroic young men engaged in this perilous work. I will, however, refer to but a few cases of special importance, which are as follows:

1. *Gen. Lee's arrival in Chambersburg, and his turning to the east in connection with the passage of Hill's Corps in the same direction.*

In a previous chapter I gave a detailed account of the arrival of Gen. Lee in our town, his consultation in the Diamond with Gen. Hill, and his turning east in the direction of Gettysburg. This occurred about nine or ten o'clock in the forenoon of Friday, June 26th. It should be borne in mind that Rhode's and Johnson's divisions of Ewell's Corps had already passed through and gone on down towards Harrisburg, but in the morning of this day Heth's division of Hill's Corps arrived, and instead of following the troops of Gen. Ewell down the valley, turned east and went in the direction of Gettysburg. This led us to suspect that Lee's real purpose was Baltimore and Washington, and that the demonstration down the valley was to mislead and deceive our authorities. When Gen. Lee arrived, and held that consultation with Gen. Hill, we felt anxious to see which way he would go, assured that whichever way he went would determine the real point of attack. That this opinion was shared by intelligent citizens, as well as the writer, will appear in the following note by Bishop J. Dickson, then a resident of our town:

Mr. J. HOKE: *Dear Sir:*—I stood near you in the Diamond of Chambersburg at the time Gen. Lee and staff were there, and I witnessed the council between Lee and Hill, and when Lee turned east, following that part of Hill's Corps, which had already gone in that direction, I felt satisfied that Baltimore and Washington were his destination.
J. DICKSON.

Impressed with the fact stated, and the necessity of transmitting the same as speedily as possible to the authorities at Harrisburg, I called the attention of Mr. Benjamin S. Huber, who stood by my side, to the importance of their council, when he at once volunteered, tired though he was from the trip he had just completed, to carry the intelligence. As soon as Lee and his staff turned east, Huber started on his second trip to the Capital. The following is Mr. Huber's own account of his journey: "I struck at once across the country for Roxbury, at the base of the North Mountain, and there obtained the services of S. L. Sentman, (the same person who, a few days later, furnished Mr. Pomeroy with a horse.) Under Mr. Sentman's guidance, (he being mounted and I walking) we passed through Dothan Valley to Amberson's Valley. In passing through this narrow valley we had to cross Trout Run several times. As I was on foot I had to wade the stream, which came up nearly to my knees. When we reached Amberson's Valley Mr. Sentman left me, and I pursued my way alone and passed into Perry county near Germantown. Upon entering Amberson's Valley, however, I pressed a horse, and at Germantown I got my supper and had my horse fed. About eight o'clock I left Germantown for Newport, some forty-two miles distant. This distance I rode in about seven hours without dismounting. Arriving at Newport, on the Pennsylvania railroad above Harrisburg, about three o'clock in the morning, I put my horse at a hotel and, a train coming along soon after, I took passage for Harrisburg. Shortly after daylight we reached the Capital, and when I got out of the cars I saw Hon. D. W. Rowe, then in some military service, but now Judge of this Judicial District. I told Mr. Rowe the news I brought, when he at once conducted me to the Capitol. Upon going into one of the rooms [of the Capitol, I found myself in the presence of a number of persons, among whom; were Governor Curtin, Gen. Couch and Gen. Smith. After telling them my statement I was put through a close examination by one of the Generals—I think it was Gen. Smith. After he had examined me he said: "Well, gentlemen, the information this young man brings is of the most vital importance, if we can rely upon it." Mr. William M'Lellan was there, and he said, "Gentlemen, I know this young man —you can rely upon every word he says." After a short consultation between the Governor and the military men, they commenced writing, and the telegraph operators were set to work. I sat for awhile and heard one of the officers say to another something about the army of the Potomac fighting the rebels before they could get across the South Mountain. After a little while I arose to leave when Governor Curtin took me by the hand, thanked me for the news I brought, and gave me an order for free transportation back to Newport. Returning to Newport I mounted my horse and rode home by the same way I had come. After returning the horse to his owner, I walked home, and on the way a rebel soldier stole my hat off my head. While I was away, the rebels were all about the country and my wife became alarmed, and shut up the house and went to a relative of hers. When I went into the house I found that the rebels had been in it and carried away nearly all our clothing, so that I had not a change of clothing or a hat to replace the one taken from me."

2. The dispatch carried by Messrs Anthony Holler and Mr. Kinney.

In a former article upon this subject, contributed to the Philadelphia *Times*, I associated the trip made by these two men with the rapid passage of Ewell's wagon train through this place. I wrote then from memory, but now in possession of reliable data, and correct whatever errors I may have made in that communication. The precise time when these two persons left Chambersburg for the Capital was Sunday morning, June 28th. The nature of the message which they carried I cannot certainly state. If the reader will refer to the occurrences of Saturday, 27th, as detailed in a previous chapter, he will see that on that day two of Hill's Corps—Pender's and Anderson's—passed through town, and followed Heth's out towards Gettysburg. My impression is that the information which these men carried was the direction these two divisions took as a confirmation of the inference drawn from the course taken by Heth's division and Lee's own following in the same direction. At all events the information they carried was deemed so important by both Judge Kimmell and myself that we made an effort on Saturday evening, and up as late as ten o'clock that night, to procure some one to convey it to Harrisburg. The best we could do was to secure the services of Messrs. Holler and Kinney for the ensuing morning, as Mr. Holler deemed it too great a risk to attempt to pass through the enemy's lines in the night. That I have not erred in either the time of the departure of these men, or in stating the circumstances, will appear in the subjoined note :

MR. HOKE:—*Sir:*—It was on the Sunday morning before the battle of Gettysburg that I started from Chambersburg to pilot Mr. Kinney to Roxbury on his way to Harrisburg. You came to me at a late hour the night previous and desired me to pilot Mr. Kinney, but I declined to go until morning. I conducted Mr. Kinney to Roxbury, and then left him to pursue his journey. What the information we carried was has escaped my memory.
ANTHONY HOLLER.

Mr. Holler gives the following account of their journey to Roxbury. Before starting he and Mr. Kinney agreed upon a statement to make in case of their capture. Tying in a handkerchief a number of soiled shirts and other articles of wearing apparel they decided to show these to the rebels and tell them they were school teachers going home to get their clothes washed. Mr. Kinney was a teacher in the Chambersburg Academy, and Mr. Holler's home had formerly been in the direction they were to go. Leaving Chambersburg early in the morning, they passed up along the bank of the Conococheague, on the line where the Baltimore and Cumberland Valley railroad now runs, and out over the hills above Heyser's paper mill. They were arrested three times before reaching Pleasant Hall, and to avoid detection in case they were searched, destroyed their dispatches. Their ruse about their soiled linen succeeded admirably, and when questioned closely, they maintained their composure and adhered to their story. Upon reaching Roxbury Mr. Holler returned, leaving Mr. Kinney to go on his journey.

That Mr. Kinney pursued his journey, and duly reached Harrisburg and delivered his message, will appear in the following statement furnished me by Mr. A. M. Criswell, who saw Mr. Kinney in Harrisburg on the following day :

MR. J. HOKE:—I saw Mr. Kinney at the U. S. hotel, Harrisburg, during the afternoon of Monday, 29th of June. I asked him to give me a little of his experience with the rebels, and he told me substantially as follows : "I got from a friend in Gettysburg an old blind horse, a well-worn buggy and some soiled linen which I tied in a handkerchief and placed under the seat and started for Chambersburg, intending to represent myself as a school teacher on his way home. After entering the rebel lines, I was halted frequently and my horse examined, but when his blindness was discovered they said they had no use for him, and I was permitted to pass. Near Fayetteville a rebel officer stopped me and very politely asked leave to ride with me to Chambersburg. When we reached Messersmith's woods I stopped a moment, and the officer pointed out General Lee, who was seated in front of his tent looking over some papers. Arriving at Chambersburg, I turned over the horse and buggy to a friend, obtained some very important information and started on foot for the P. R. R. Was arrested twice by the Rebs., but representing myself as a school teacher, on my way home, I got off easily. On reaching the Union lines I was arrested, and my statement that I had important information for Governor Curtin was not accepted, but at my earnest request the officer in command procured an engine on the P. R. R. and sent me under guard of two soldiers, to Harrisburg. On entering Governor Curtin's room, I was recognized by Col. M'Clure, and delivered my message to Governor Curtin and M'Clure privately. After which I saw my guard still standing at the door, and I asked them if they now thought the country safe. One replied, you are all right, and we have but done our duty.
A. M. CRISWELL.

One other important occasion when a messenger was dispatched to Harrisburg was :

3. *The rapid passage of Ewell's wagon train from down the valley and out towards Gettysburg.*

Some time in the night of Monday, June 29th, I was awakened by my wife, and told to come to the window as some important movement was going on among the rebels. Peering cautiously through the half-closed shutters, I saw a continuous stream of wagons passing hurriedly through the town. They were coming up from the direction of Harrisburg, passing up Main street to the Diamond and then turning east towards Gettysburg. They seemed to be driven in haste, and the movement clearly indicated a concentration of the Confederate forces in an eastern direction. A low, rumbling noise could be heard as if the whole valley were filled with moving trains.

It has since been learned that this train was Gen. Ewell's, which had passed through the town on down towards Harrisburg, and then was returning and concentrating at Gettysburg. It has been also shown that this train was fourteen miles in length, and that only a part of it passed back through town, the balance of it crossing from Shippensburg along the base of the South Mountain, and coming out into the Gettysburg pike near Fayetteville or Greenwood. That part of the train which passed by that route was accompanied by Johnson's division of Ewell's Corps—Rhode's division crossed directly from Carlisle to Heidlersburg, where, on the evening of the same day—Tuesday—it was joined by Early's division from York.

Whatever difficulty there may be in harmonizing the contradictory statements between the time fixed for the arrival of Longstreet's scout by Longstreet and Lee, there can be no question as to the time when this wagon train moved. Generals Longstreet and M'Laws, and Dr. Cullen, Medical Director of Longstreet's Corps, fix the time of its passage from Fayetteville to Gettysburg as Tuesday, June 30. (Annals of War, pages 439, 440.)

The importance of forwarding information of this concentration towards Gettysburg to the authorities at Harrisburg was evident, and sometime in the early morning Judge Kimmell secured the services of Mr. Stephen W. Pomeroy (now Rev. S. W. Pomeroy, pastor of Mt. Union Presbyterian church), to convey a message. That it was upon this occasion that Mr. Pomeroy was sent will undoubtedly appear from the following note from Judge Kimmell:

At the request of Governor Curtin and others, I assumed the management of matters at Chambersburg during the raids and invasions of the Confederate army, and as such I had Judge Paxton and C. Stouffer to keep account of Lee's forces each day as they passed through the town, and a good number of persons carried the result to the Pennsylvania Railroad. At the time that Pomeroy ran out, the whole of the heavy baggage and artillery trains of Lee's army that had passed over the turnpike towards Harrisburg came back again through the town on the double quick and took the road to Gettysburg, which satisfied everyone that the army was making for that point, and we knew this fact to be of the utmost importance to the government, and therefore the dispatch was sent. F. M. KIMMELL.

Rev. Mr. Pomeroy has given the circumstances of his trip in an interesting letter to Governor Curtin, and as it is desirable to preserve all such facts, I subjoin here that statement:

MOUNT UNION, Pa., Nov. 13, 1883.

HON. A. G. CURTIN—*Dear Sir:* In compliance with your request, I send you the account of how I came to send you the telegram of the concentration or the Confederate army at Gettysburg during the war. After being discharged from the nine months' service of the Pennsylvania Volunteers, I happened to be home, at my father's—Judge Pomeroy, of Roxbury, Franklin county—when the enemy were marching down the Cumberland Valley. There was, of course, great excitement, for the enemy were at our doors and taking what they would. Farmers hid their horses and other stock in the mountains, as far as possible. One day three hundred cavalry marched into Roxbury. When we learned of their coming ten of the men who had been out in the nine months' service armed ourselves as best we could and went out to intercept them; but the odds were too great, so we retired. Anxious to hear the news and render what service we might to our country, a number of us walked to Chambersburg, a distance of fourteen miles, reaching there in the afternoon. That night the rebels were concentrated at Gettysburg. Next morning Judge F. M. Kimmell, with whom my father sat as Associate Judge, learned that a son of Thomas Pomeroy was in town. He sent for me to come to him at once. I found the Judge on the street that leads to McConnellsburg, a short distance from the Franklin Hotel, where the Central Presbyterian Church now stands. As the town was full of rebels and a rebel had his beat near us, the Judge asked me in a low tone if I was a son of Judge Pomeroy. I replied in the affirmative. With apparent unconcern, he asked me to follow him. I did so and he led me into a little dark back room and told me that the rebels were concentrating at Gettysburg and Governor Curtin did not know it. He said it was of the utmost importance that the Governor should know at the earliest possible moment and asked me if I would take a telegram to the nearest point on the Pennsylvania railroad and send it to him. He added: "It is of infinite importance to him and to our country." I replied that I would try it. The telegram was already written, so he cut a hole in the buckle strap of my pantaloons and deposited the telegram to be sent there and said: "Get this safely and in the shortest time possible to the Governor." Assuming indifference, I came to the street and met the rebel guard, who did not disturb me. Some of those who came with me wishing to return to Roxbury, we set out together.

We met many at the edge of the town, returning, who could not get through the guard, who were stationed around the town.

Coming to the forks of the Strasburg and Roxbury roads we found both cavalry and infantry. On the left there was a slight hollow, also several wheat fields, and beyond these there were woods. The only way to hope for escape. At my proposal we crept along this hollow, at the end of which there was some wheat fields ; we kept these between us and the guard till we reached the woods. When getting over the fence into the woods we were seen by the enemy. They called, rode after us and leveled their muskets at us, but we ran on, and as they did not fire or follow far we escaped. Still fearing capture we kept to the fields. Before we reached Strasburg all had fallen behind but one. We must have walked about seventeen miles before we got to Roxbury. As the horses were hid in the mountains I was in dread lest I should not get a horse, but I met Mr. L. S. Sentman riding into town to get feed for his horses in the mountains. Telling him of the message I was carrying he gave me his horse. Informing my father of my errand I set out on my trip at once. It was about noon. The mountain road to Amberson Valley was, I knew, blockaded with trees to prevent the marauders from entering the valley to steal horses. On this account I crossed the mountain into Amberson Valley by a foot path, then another mountain into Path Valley. Reaching my uncle's, W. R. Pomeroy, at Concord, and telling him my business he got me another horse. The Barrens below Concord, were blockaded by citizens of Tuscarora Valley, many of whom knew me. The report having reached them that I was killed while trying to hinder the rebels from entering Roxbury, the obstacles and excitement of my friends at finding me alive hindered me about ten minutes. Free from them, I hastened down the Tuscarora Valley as fast as my horse could carry me. At Bealtown Mr. Beal, now the Rev. D. J. Beal, speedily got me a fresh horse. When I reached Silas E. Smith's I did these two things, got lunch and proved to the future Mrs. Pomeroy that I was not dead, as she supposed, but good for many years to come. From thence I rode to my uncle's, Joseph Pomeroy, at Academia, found them likewise mourning my supposed death, and he supplied another horse, the fastest he had. That carried me to within a mile of my destination, when a soldier on guard called, Halt! I told the sergeant on guard my mission and requested one of the guard to go with me, that I might get the telegram off to Harrisburg in the shortest time possible.

Getting on the horse behind me we rode in a few minutes to the office. Finding the operator, he cut the telegram out of the strap of my pantaloons and sent it at once to you. The excitement and journey being over, and the telegram being off to you, I began to look at the time and found it about midnight. I had walked that day about seventeen miles and ridden about forty-one miles. Anxious as I was about the critical state of the country, I was so tired I had to seek the house of my kinsman, Major J. M. Pomeroy, in Perryville, now Port Royal, for rest.

The above is the history of that telegram, that, I believe, gave you notice of the concentration of the rebel troops at Gettysburg, just before the famous battle in that place.

Respectfully yours,
STEPHEN W. POMEROY.

It will be seen from Mr. Pomeroy's statement that he reached the telegraph station at Port Royal about *midnight*.

That would be about twelve o'clock on the night of Tuesday, June 30th. Presuming that no time was lost in forwarding this despatch from Port Royal, and that equal promptness was made at Harrisburg in forwarding the important information it contained to the authorities at Washington, it is but fair to suppose that the fact of his concentration of Lee's forces was made known at General Meade's headquarters some time during that same night. Is there any evidence of the reception at that place of this information? Col. James G. Biddle furnishes an answer to this question in his contribution to the *Annals of the War*, page 28. Colonel Biddle says : "*On the night of the 30th*, after the Army of the Potomac had made two days' marches, *General Meade heard that Lee was concentrating his army to meet him.*" There were other ways by which the knowledge of this falling back of Lee's forces and their concentration east of the South Mountain, might be conveyed to General Meade, but it is fair to suppose that the information of this movement referred to by Col. Biddle, was conveyed from Chambersburg by Mr. Pomeroy. This honor is freely conceded to him, and in no case has it been claimed for any other. In a communication by the writer to the Philadelphia *Times*, in December last, it was claimed that while Mr. Pomeroy carried the information of this rapid concentration of Ewell's wagon train, there had been other information taken to Harrisburg previous to that which would lead the authorities to suspect that the real point of attack was east of the mountain. A correspondent of that paper, in a subsequent issue, backed by a letter from Ex-Governor Curtin, defends Mr. Pomeroy as if his claim was in question, thus entirely misapprehending my meaning. And, now, that other reliable information, such as would prove of value to the authorities in determining the real point of danger, and information upon which they acted, was carried to Harrisburg prior to the trip made by Mr. Pomeroy, will appear in the following : It is fixed beyond question that the information taken by Mr. Pomeroy could not, and did not, reach General Meade before some time in the night of Tuesday, June 30th. On Saturday morning previously Mr. Benjamin S. Huber reached Harrisburg and informed the authorities that on the preceding day Heth's division of Hill's corps, instead of following Ewell's two divisions down the valley towards Harrisburg, had turned east towards Gettysburg, and that Lee and his staff had also gone in the same direction. On Monday morning Mr. Kinney communicated the fact that the two remaining divisions of the same Corps had followed the first in the same direction. On Sunday evening the camp fires of the advance of Heth's division were seen from Gettysburg above Cashtown; and on Monday evening it was seen that these encampments at that place were largely increased. Then is it to be supposed that the people of Carlisle and York were so delinquent in patriotism as to fail to detect and report the departure of Rhodes' and Early's divisions and their march southward? This movement, be it remembered, began on Tuesday morning, about the time Mr. Pomeroy left Chambersburg for Harrisburg, and was at least sixteen hours before he reached Port Royal. That information of the departure of Rhodes' division from Carlisle, and its marching across the South Mountain towards Gettysburg, was in possession of the authorities at Harrisburg *six hours* before Mr. Pomeroy's despatch could be received, is clearly established by the annexed note:

MR. J. HOKE, *Sir:* On the day Rhodes' division fell back from Carlisle towards Gettysburg, I was in the rebel lines in the rebel uniform I captured from one of Jenkins' men at Chambersburg, and seeing the movement southward I reported the same to the authorities at Harrisburg about six o'clock the same evening.

JOHN A. SEIDERS.

With all these facts before us, was not Governor Curtin unfortunate in putting himself upon record in the following letter:

"WASHINGTON, 11th December, 1883.

"*My Dear Sir:* Your despatch was the first authentic information I received of the concentration of the army of General Lee on Gettysburg and, treating it as true, acted on it.

Yours truly,
A. G. CURTIN.

REV. S. W. POMEROY."

It might be of interest to place upon record here the following extract of a letter, written by Mr. Thomas H. McDowell, to his father, Mr. W. H. McDowell, of this place. Mr. McDowell formerly resided in Chambersburg, and, in addition to the interesting facts touching the scouting service which he relates, his letter will show the feeling of the many noble and patriotic young men who risked their lives in carrying important information of the movement of the rebels to Harrisburg, but whose services seem to be entirely ignored. Mr. McDowell says: "I have read the letters of Rev. Pomeroy and J. Hoke concerning the carrying of the news of Lee's army concentrating at Gettysburg; as also the article after the death of George R. Messersmith of his counting the troops of Lee by dropping a grain of corn in his pocket for every hundred. These statements may all be true. Each of them may have done just what they claim; but it is not the way soldiers would have done it. General Couch who was at that time in command of the Department of the Susquehanna, would never have acted on a wandering despatch, unsigned, and not knowing whether it came from friend or foe. I say I do not know what the parties above named did do, but one thing I do know, that when Lee's army passed through Chambersburg two young men were busy counting the cavalry and infantry, and taking the number and calibre of their guns. And after the conference in the Diamond, spoken of in the article of Mr. Hoke in the Philadelphia *Times*, when it was believed that Lee's army was moving on Baltimore, those two young men drew lots to decide which one was to go to Harrisburg, and which was to remain inside the enemy's lines. The trip to Harrisburg fell to the lot of J. Porter Brown, and mine was to stay in Chambersburg. Porter started, and before going far fell in with John Rodgers, and these two crossed the mountains to New Bloomfield in Perry county, where they met Col. Speakman who commanded the 133d Regiment in our Division, to whom they gave their news, and Col. Speakman telegraphed it to General Couch, informing him in the same despatch that his informant would be down on the next train. Col. Speakman furnished them conveyance to the Pennsylvania Railroad, and when they arrived at Harrisburg they met Col. A. K. McClure, who went with them to General Couch's headquarters, telling them that he would vouch for the truth of any statement Porter might make. Porter then pulled off his old boots prepared for the purpose, containing the number of cavalry, infantry, and artillery, with the number and calibre of the guns, and also the information that the army was heading towards Baltimore. This is the information that I believe General Couch acted upon, for turning to his chief of staff he remarked that if they had come on, the little earthworks and the few thousand militia he had would have been of little account. I do not think that a General of the experience of General Couch would act on a telegram unsigned, unless he had some corroborating testimony. I would wager my head that General Couch could resurrect from among his old papers the very paper which Porter Brown gave him, or at least the memorandum made by his chief of staff at the time."

But if Governor Curtin had not been put in possession of sufficient information concerning the movements of the Confederates, so as to point to the place of danger, until midnight of Tuesday, 30th, when

Mr. Pomeroy's despatch was received, let us turn our eyes to the Army of the Potomac and see if those who directed it were in this ignorance. Hon. Edward Everett in his address at the dedication of the Soldiers' National Cemetery, in November, 1863, says that the Federal army, after crossing the Potomac the day after the last of the Confederates crossed, took a position from Harper's Ferry to Frederick, so as to cover Washington and Baltimore from a flank movement by Lee, or march to any point where he might show himself. On Sunday, the 28th, that army, having abandoned its defensive position, and assumed an aggressive one, marched through Frederick, from that place diverging by different roads, but all tending in one general direction, and finally converging at Gettysburg. And so rapid were the movements of these various corps, and so defined their objective, that by Tuesday evening Reynolds and Howard with the First and Eleventh Corps, having the shortest lines of march, encamped within four miles of Gettysburg, and the next morning marched into the town and began the battle of the first day, the other corps being so near that they nearly all reached the field that night or the next morning. My authorities for these facts are the following: Charles Carleton Coffin, who was with the Army of the Potomac on this march, in his "*The Boys of 1861*," says, "All day Sunday the army was passing through Frederick." Hon. Edward Everett, in his address at Gettysburg, says that notwithstanding the change in commanders on Sunday at Frederick, "not an hour's hesitation ensued in the advance of the army." Col. Biddle in *Annals of the War*, page 208, says that "On the night of the 30th (Tuesday) *after the Army of the Potomac had made two days' marches*, General Meade heard that Lee was concentrating his army to meet him." General Pleasanton in the same book, page 453, says, "The Army of the Potomac was in motion by the 28th of June (Sunday), moving northward from Frederick." Is it to be supposed that General Hooker would depart from the policy he had adopted to maintain his position for the defense of the Capitol without positive information that Washington was not the point of attack, but some other point northward? One of the authors just quoted—Coffin—says on page 260 of his book, that "General Hooker waited in front of Washington till he was certain of Lee's intentions, and then by a rapid march pushed on to Frederick." And would General Meade, when he succeeded General Hooker in command at Frederick, take up the same policy and pursue it so vigorously, if ignorant of the real point of attack?

Thus it will be seen that the Commander of the Union army was in possession of sufficient information of Lee's objective to justify him in abandoning his defensive policy about Washington, and marching toward Gettysburg, at least *four days* before the information carried by Mr. Pomeroy was received at army headquarters. More than this, two Corps of that army in pursuance of the policy adopted by General Hooker, and taken up and continued by General Meade, when he succeeded him, were within four miles of Gettysburg on the evening of Tuesday, and other Corps close at hand, at least *six hours* before Mr. Pomeroy's message was delivered. Professor Jacobs in his Battle of Gettysburg, page 23, says that on the evening of Tuesday "there encamped that night within a short distance of our town (Gettysburg) 23,000 Union infantry and 6,000 cavalry, and 76,000 Rebel infantry and a large number of cavalry, ready to meet each other in deadly conflict on the next day." Professor Jacobs overestimated the number of men present in both armies, but the fact he states of the presence of a large force of both Federals and Confederates, six to ten hours before Mr. Pomeroy reached Port Royal, demonstrates that it was not the information he carried to Harrisburg which caused this concentration of the Union army, but information previously received. Nor will it relieve the difficulty of establishing Mr. Pomeroy's claim to have carried the first information which caused the authorities to march the Union army to Gettysburg, to say that Lee only changed his purpose to march to that place instead of Harrisburg on Monday night, for on Monday but two divisions of his army were threatening the latter place, while six were either on the eastern side of the South Mountain, or marching in that direction.

The services performed by the young men of Chambersburg and surrounding country in conveying information to the Capital of the State of the number and movements of the Confederates while passing through this place on their way to Gettysburg, if all were gathered together and placed upon record, would make a volume of thrilling interest; but as space forbids, and I am not in possession of even the names of all who performed this patriotic service, that record cannot be given. With no disposition to disparage the services rendered by any, but to place upon record the services of the many, this chapter has been written. That these services were of immense value to the commanders of our armies, and perhaps were the means, under God, of the salvation of our country, will appear in the fact that after General Couch established his headquarters here, a short time after the battle of Gettysburg, he declared to me the great value of the information sent him, and his willingness to amply reward each one who had made the perilous trips, subsequently refunding to me what I had advanced for travelling expenses to these men, and an additional sum amounting to ten dollars to each one for each trip.

CHAPTER XII.

AFTER THE BATTLE OF GETTYSBURG.—EARLY'S RAID INTO MARYLAND.

On Friday, July 10th, after the battle of Gettysburg, General D. N. Couch, in command of the Department of the Susquehanna, reached this place and established his headquarters here. Following him from day to day, came regiment after regiment of newly enlisted men, under the call of the Governor, and known as "Emergency men." They were under command of General Dana. These soldiers passed through town and went southward toward the Potomac by the Greencastle and Warm Spring roads. Another division of these emergency men, under General Smith, passed from Carlisle towards Pine Grove, some of whom turned west from the South Mountain and passed through this place. After the Confederates succeeded in recrossing the Potomac these troops returned to Harrisburg where they were disbanded.

Among the first things which demanded the attention of General Couch, after his arrival here, was the sick and wounded rebels in the King street Hospital. There were about sixty of these, some being sick and left here by Lee on his way to Gettysburg, and others wounded at that battle and brought here by the wagon train referred to in a previous chapter. The sick left by General Lee were under the care of a steward—a young man from Staunton, Virginia, and after the battle of Gettysburg the hospital was under the care of Assistant Surgeon Gamble, of the Confederate service. When he took charge of the hospital, and how he got here, I am unable to tell. The physicians of this place frequently visited the hospital and rendered valuable assistance. Up to the arrival of General Couch these sick and wounded were dependent upon our citizens. I stated in a previous chapter that I engaged Mrs. Ritner to furnish the hospital with bread each day, and that coffee and other needed articles were taken there by some of our citizens. I personally solicited funds to aid in paying for the bread furnished, and the responses were unusally prompt and willing. After the military authorities took charge of the hospital, the ladies of the town were unremitting in their attentions to the suffering men, and delicacies not furnished by the army regulations were freely given them. Not unfrequently some of the soldiers were visited by relations from Baltimore and other places within our lines. These were always permitted to enter the hospital under such regulations as the authorities deemed necessary to prevent the abuse of the privilege. In this respect Southern visitors to Northern hospitals fared differently from Northern visitors to friends in the South. Among the wounded Confederates brought here from the field of Gettysburg, was Colonel Benjamin F. Carter, of the 4th Texas Regiment. Colonel Carter had been a lawyer of prominence in Texas; he was severely wounded and died in the hospital on the 21st day of July. Some difficulty occurring as to the place of burial, his body was interred in Mr. Chas. Burnett's lot in the Methodist burial ground on South Second street. It has been, I think, subsequently removed.

The writer was sent for one day to visit one of these wounded Confederates. If I mistake not he was the youthful soldier I have previously referred to as having his arm off near the shoulder. His case was critical, and he felt he was unprepared to die. He spoke of his pious mother and his father's counsels, and deeply regretted that he had not lived a different life. Poor fellow; away from home and friends, his heart turned yearningly towards his mother and his mother's God.

Just here I will place upon record the following touching incident, for which I am indebted to Mrs. Nancy Hoover, widow of the late George Hoover, of Stoufferstown. Mr. and Mrs. Hoover at the time of the war, resided two miles south of Waynesboro, on the road leading to Hagerstown. During the retreat of the rebels, large numbers encamped in the fields around their house, and when they left many barrels of flour which they had taken during the invasion, were thrown from their wagons and left in the fields. Many of the barrels bore the brand of Mr. Jacob Stouffer, a brother-in-law of Mr. Hoover, and had been taken from his mill near this place. On Monday, July 6th, while a number of Confederate officers were seated at Mr. Hoover's table partaking of his hospitality, and discussing the great battle and pointing out the causes of their defeat and the mistakes they made, one of them took from his pocket a Testament, and handing it around to his companions, said that he had taken it from the pocket of a dead Federal captain. Upon examining it one of them remarked, "This Testament contains a request within it, which should be observed." Upon examining the book and reading the request written therein Mrs. Hoover promised that if the book were left with her she would send it to the person designated in it. The officer who had the Testament gave his name as Lieut. R. W. Wood, of Georgia. He belonged to Benning's Brigade, Hood's division of Longstreet's Corps. The request, a copy of which Mrs. Hoover kept, was as follows:

JUNE 21st, 1863.

In case I am killed and my body left on the field, the finder of this Testament will please send it to my father, John Nicoll, Blooming Grove, Orange county, N. York, and confer a great favor on me.

ISAAC NICOLL, Capt. Co. G. 124th
Regt. N. Y. State.

Shortly after the departure of these officers, Mr. Hoover sent the Testament by mail to Mr. Nicoll, with a letter containing the circumstances under which he became possessed of it. The following is a copy of Mr. Nicoll's acknowledgment, the original of which is now before me.

BLOOMING GROVE, July 24th, 1863.

MR. GEORGE HOOVER.—*Dear Sir:*—The Testament of my dear departed son, which you did me the favor to send to me, came by due course of mail. It is a precious relic of a dearly loved and highly honored son. In looking over the its pages I discover memorandums of periods up to the day previous to his death, which were devoted (notwithstanding the long marches and fatigue attending them) to its perusal. It is consoling to me to discover from scored passages that he was not an inattentive reader, that the great truths of revelation were accepted and impressed upon his mind. This Testament, conveyed by his own hand, in view of the uncertainty of life, and the necessity of preparation, constitutes to me its greatest value. I have great reason to hope that his departed spirit is now with his sainted mother who loved him so well on earth, there to enjoy with her an eternity of bliss. You can therefore appreciate the value I place upon this book—the cherished companion of his weary marches and lonely hours. As everything relating to my dear boy is interesting at this time, will you please inform me whether Lieut. Wood made any other disclosures respecting the effects he found upon the body of Captain Nicoll, and what disposition he calculated to make of them—in fact anything you heard or saw in your interview with him.

On the eve of Captain Nicolls's departure with his regiment, which was raised in this county, the ladies of this town presented him with a handsome sword. It was not a formal presentation, simply accompanied with a letter. This was in the month of September last. If that sword could be recovered I would place a much higher value upon it than its intrinsic worth. I have relatives living in Georgia, and if this uncalled for and wicked rebellion is put down, of which there is every prospect of its being speedily done, I intend to make an effort to rescue it.

My son was twenty-three years old at the time of his death; was born in the city of New York. I purchased the farm I now occupy in 1843, which has been his home ever since, with the exception of two or three years he spent in the city engaged in the mercantile business. At the call of President Lincoln for three hundred thousand men, he at once responded by raising a company in this town. The regiment left, as I have before remarked, in September last. Since then he has been attached to the army of the Potomac; was engaged in the disastrous attack of Burnside on Fredericksburg; also with Hooker at Chancellorsville, in which he lost twenty-five out of sixty men he led into action. His regiment accompanied the cavalry attack at Aldie in which he lost some of his men. Gettysburg closed his military and mortal career. It was there he yielded his life, a youthful, willing gift upon the altar of his country. He was pierced by three balls—one in his neck, one in his shoulder and one in his breast. He lived but three minutes after receiving these injuries. The regiment was making a charge at the time, was repulsed with the loss of its colonel and Major killed, and Lieut. Col. wounded, which accounts for his body being left on the field. The rebels had possession of it until the next day, when the ground was recovered. A brother officer found his body, buried where it fell, erected a board at its head with his name, regiment and company inscribed upon it. I have had it since taken up, but owing to the Government monopolizing the transportation, it proved ineffectual, and we were under the necessity of re-interring it until a more favorable opportunity offers for its removal.

When I commenced this letter it was with the intention of simply, in suitable terms, to acknowledge the receipt of the book you had the kindness and heart to send me. My mind is constantly dwelling upon my dear son—"out of the abundance of the heart the mouth speaketh"—not always with discretion, as in this case, addressing a stranger. Bear with me, and believe me to be your greatly obliged friend.
JOHN NICOLL.

Numerous touching incidents which occurred upon the field and in the hospitals might be given, but I proceed with my narrative. Sometime in the summer of 1863, George Eyster, Esq., then a resident of this place, was appointed Provost Marshall for the district comprising the counties of Bedford, Somerset, Fulton, Adams and Franklin. His headquarters were established at this place, and large numbers of persons were drawn here for enlistment or by drafting, so that during the winter of 1863-4 Chambersburg and its vicinity were swarming with soldiers. These were organized into companies and regiments, and in the spring were sent away to reinforce the armies in the field for the great struggle they were about to enter upon.

In all the history of the war, except on such occasions as when our own immediate vicinity was threatened, we never witnessed more intense and widespread solicitude and anxiety than were manifested in Chambersburg from Thursday, May 5th, to the evening of Sunday, the 8th, 1864. It was announced on Thursday that the long expected campaign in eastern Virginia had begun, that General Grant with his magnificent army had crossed the Rapidan on the evening of Tuesday previous, and that a fierce and terrible battle had been fought or was yet in progress, but we were left in ignorance as to the results. The hopes of the nation rested upon that army, and the campaign upon which it entered. The fact that the destiny of the government seemed to be at stake in the mighty struggle, was felt and acknowledged by all, and the very uncertainty as to the result increased and intensified the general anxiety. Men hurried to the bulletin boards with rapid strides and anxious countenances, and when the meagre and unsatisfactory dispatches were read, would tarry to discuss the situation and speculate as to the probable result. On Friday morning the dispatches simply told that the fearful conflict had commenced; but beyond stating that the battle raged furiously, and that the loss on both sides was heavy, no intimation was given as to which side was victorious. As the hours of the day dragged along the throng around the bulletins increased, and all seemed absorbed in the one great question—the safety—the life of the Republic. Business was practically suspended, for how could we work when the Nation—the Government, we loved so well, and around which our hopes clustered, was suspended in the balance?

On Saturday the telegraph was still silent as to the issue of the battle. Sensational reports came along the lines occasionally, but they were but speculations and rumors. In the afternoon a dispatch came stating that the battle field and the dead and wounded of the enemy were within the Union lines, and that the Confederates had fallen back, but it was unofficial. Sunday morning came and yet no news until about eleven o'clock a private dispatch announced that there were rumors floating around in Washington, but they were conflicting and unreliable. The people gathered into groups and discussed the probable issue. The fact that no definite information had been received since the morning of Friday, aroused the greatest of fears. But in the afternoon the uncertainty was measurably dispelled. A dispatch was received which stated that General Grant had driven the rebels after a terrible engagement; that he had 13,000 of their dead and wounded on his hands, and that Lee was retreating and Grant pursuing. At the reception of this news the people were greatly relieved and encouraged, but there was still too much indefiniteness and uncertainty for any outbursts of joy and rejoicing. The fact that the Confederates were falling back and the Federals pursuing, indicated that the advantages were upon the side of the Union army, but the fearful loss of life and the yet undecided struggle yet caused uneasiness and concern.

There was one day in particular during this anxious period when the excitement rose to such a pitch that by almost unanimous consent all business was suspended and the people gathered in and about the Diamond of the town. It was the day when the terrible battle of Spotsylvania was fought. We all knew from the despatches which were flashing along the wires and posted upon the bulletins, that the terrific strife was in progress. In fact it seemed that the blows that were being struck there upon the brave defenders of the Union were felt by the entire people. Despatch after despatch was received announcing the progress of the great battle. At length a bulletin was posted announcing that General Hancock had captured General Johnson and four thousand prisoners and thirty-six guns. This was soon followed by another saying that it was *reported* that Lee had surrendered. These two despatches threw our people into ecstacies and a scene of the wildest excitement ensued. The band turned out and played several patriotic airs, and the people shouted forth their glad exultation. In a short time this last despatch was contradicted. Thus day after day word was received of the terrible struggle going on, until at length it was announced that General Grant had forced the Confederates into their entrenchments about Richmond, and he had crossed the James river and besieged Petersburg. The theatre of war was now widely separated from us, and we supposed we had seen the last of invasions and raids. In this, however, we were doomed to disappointment, for the culmination of our disasters and troubles was about to fall upon us, as the sequel will show.

On the morning of Sunday, July 3d, rumors of disaster to the Union forces in the valley about Martinsburg were afloat. General Sigel was reported to have been driven across the Potomac, and rebel cavalry were threatening to cross and ravage our borders once more. Once again we set to work to pack, ship away and secrete our merchandize. During the following day, July 4th, the farmers residing in the southern part of the county again took their stock through our town and down the valley to places of safety. The occasion of this new and unexpected danger was as follows: General Grant had ordered General Hunter, who had succeeded General Sigel in the Shenandoah, to proceed up the valley to Staunton and Gordonsville and thence to Lynchburg, live upon the country as he marched, destroy the railroads, and, if possible, the James river canal. Accomplishing this, he was to return to Gordonsville and thence join Grant. General Sheridan was sent with his cavalry to join him at the latter place and assist in the work of destruction. At the same time Generals Crook and Averill, leaving Western Virginia, met Hunter near Staunton, where they had a battle with the rebels under General Jones, who was killed and his forces routed, with a loss of three guns and fifteen hundred prisoners. Hunter, instead of approaching Lynchburg by Gordonsville and Charlottsville as directed by Grant, took the road leading through Lexington and thus missed Sheridan, who, failing to find him there, returned to the White House, and rejoined Grant at Petersburg. Hunter reached Lynchburg on the 16th day of June. Lee, seeing the danger which threatened him in his rear, threw reinforcements into Lynchburg, and Hunter was compelled to retreat. Having advanced upon Lynchburg from the west, instead of from the north, as ordered, he was obliged to retreat in the same direction by the Great Kanawha Valley through Western Virginia. This left the Shenandoah Valley open, for there was no force to oppose the rebels who were at Lynchburg. Lee was quick to seize upon this apportunity to send an army northward and threaten Washington, and thereby compel Grant to let go his hold upon Richmond and Petersburg, as well as to scour the country north of the Potomac for supplies. General Ewell was sick, and General Early was put in command of the rebel troops in the Valley. Breckenridge was sent up from Richmond to reinforce him. Early was at the head of twenty-five or thirty thousand men. Mosby, with his band of guerillas, was in full possession of the knowledge of the situation, and reported the way clear to Washington, General Sigel only being in his way at Martinsburg.

Early passed rapidly down the Valley, drove Sigel across the Potomac, and followed him to Hagerstown. The people of Western Maryland and Southern Pennsylvania were thrown into great alarm. The panic was widespread. Extravagant stories were told of the force of the enemy; Lee's whole army was advancing; he had outgeneraled Grant; Washington and Baltimore would be captured, etc. General Grant understood Lee's intentions. He held on to his position about Petersburg and Richmond, detaching only the Sixth Corps to meet the enemy. Rickett's division was sent to Baltimore and the other two divisions to Washington. The Nineteenth Corps, which had just returned from the Gulf, was dispatched to Washington.

On Tuesday, July 5th, Governor Curtin issued a call for troops to serve for one hundred days to defend our border, and also the National Capitol, which, it was seen, was in danger. To this call there was a ready and considerable response. The most of the troops were sent to Washington.

On the same day the advance of the Confederate cavalry, which had crossed the Potomac into Maryland, drove the Union troops into Hagerstown, and on the afternoon of the following day, July 6th, General McCausland, who had succeeded General Jenkins in the command of that body of cavalry—Jenkins having been wounded and died some time before—entered and occupied that place.

The first invasion of Maryland, in 1862, was a political as well as a military movement. It was supposed by the rebel leaders that that State was ready to join the Confederacy, and that the people were held in subjection by military despotism. Accordingly all pillage was strictly prohibited. The troops respected this order, and but few acts of destruction or spoliation took place. But in the second invasion, when Lee passed into Pennsylvania no favor was shown to Maryland, and in this raid, officers and soldiers pillaged indiscriminately. Houses, stores, public and private buildings alike were sacked and destroyed. In accordance with this policy the rebels made the best of their opportunity. Their cavalry divided into small bodies and overran the country from Williamsport to Frederick, destroying the Baltimore and Ohio railroad, burning canal boats, seizing horses, cattle and supplies from farmers, ransacking houses, and committing all other acts of depredation which fell within their power.

Shortly after the Confederates had taken possession of Hagerstown, the authorities of that place were summoned to appear, when the following requisition was laid before them:

HEADQUARTERS CAVALRY BRIGADE,
Hagerstown, Md., July 6th, 1864.
GENERAL ORDER.

1. In accordance with the instructions of Lieut. General Early, a levy of ($20,000) Twenty Thousand Dollars is made upon the inhabitants of this city, the space of three hours is allowed for the payment of this sum in U. S. Funds.

2. A requisition is also made for all Government Stores.

3. The following articles will also be furnished from the Merchandize now in the hands of the Citizens or Merchants—viz—1,500 suits of Clothes, 1,500 Hats, 1,500 pairs Shoes or Boots, 1,500 Shirts, 1,500 pairs Drawers, 1,500 pairs Socks: Four hours allowed for their collection.

The Mayor and Council are held responsible for the execution of this order, and in case of non-compliance, the usual penalty will be enforced upon the city.

JOHN McCAUSLAND,
Brig. Gen. C. S. A.

Upon the reception of this Order, a town meeting was called in the Court House, and after some discussion, it was decided that the Council should raise the money and as much of the clothing as they could. The money was soon raised, but it was found that it would be impossible to furnish the clothing. Additional time was asked in which to raise it, but McCausland was deaf to any appeal, and swore bitterly that if his demand was not complied with within the time specified, his threat would be carried out to the letter. At length when he saw there was a disposition to do what they could, the time was lengthened two hours, telling the citizens that if the demand was not complied with they knew what they might expect. He then marched a regiment of troops into the town and stationed them in front of the Court House, evidently with the purpose of intimidating the citizens, or to carry out his threat of burning the town in case the money and goods were not delivered within the time specified. After making every possible effort it was found that but a portion of the clothing could be collected. This was taken to the Court House, and the fact of its deficiency made known to McCausland who swore most profanely what he would do if the whole was not forthcoming. He then told the citizens that he would give them a half hour to get the women and children out of the town before he would give the order to fire it. At length when he saw that the citizens had done the best they could, and that they could do no more, McCausland agreed to receive what they brought, when the following paper was given them:

"The town of Hagerstown having complied with the foregoing requisition, by paying in cash Twenty Thousand Dollars ($20,000) and having also furnished the specified articles therein mentioned to the utmost of their ability, as I hereby certify to the fact, and place the town under the protection of the Confederate forces, releasing the citizens and their property from further contributions and agreeing to shield both from further requirements.

JNO. McCAUSLAND,
Brig. Gen. C. S. A.

Memorandum of Articles Furnished.

Coats	243	Hats	830
Pants	203	Shirts	225
Drawers	132	Piece goods, 137½ yds.	
Hose	737	Clothing, 70 pieces, Assorted.	
Boots	99		
Shoes	123		

J. C. VAN FOSSEN,
Quarter Master.

Detachments from McCausland's command proceeded towards our border, and upon the evening of the same day that the foregoing requisition was made upon Hagerstown, Wednesday, 6th, telegraphic communication with Greencastle was for a time interrupted. Intense excitement prevailed throughout our town, and many of the citizens left to escape the threatened raid during that night. In the midst of the panic General Couch placed the town under martial law, and the citizens capable of bearing arms were called upon to assist the few military here in defending the place. The night, however, passed quietly, and the enemy did not advance nearer than a mile or two beyond Greencastle.

On Thursday, 7th, the rebel infantry crossed the Potomac into Maryland at Shepherdstown, and advanced eastwardly across the South Mountain; and the cavalry at Hagerstown and the detachments threatening our border, were withdrawn and followed in the same direction.

On Saturday, the 9th, a battle was fought at the Monocacy between Early and General Lew Wallace. General Wallace was in command in Baltimore. He sent what troops he could collect to meet the advancing foe. With the exception of Rickett's division of the Sixth Corps, which had been sent by General Grant from about Petersburg, Wallace's troops were men enlisted for one hundred days in response to the call of the government for the emergency, and some artillerists from the fortifications about Baltimore and invalids from the hospitals, in all not exceeding nine thousand. Attacked at the Monocacy in overwhelming numbers, General Wallace succeeded in holding the enemy in check several hours, and was at length compelled to fall back upon Baltimore with the loss of about twelve hundred men. This defeat, and the stories of the magnitude of the rebel force, put Baltimore and Washington in great excitement.

On the day following the battle of Monocacy Governor Curtin issued an address to the people of the State, setting forth the danger which threatened the National Capitol, and urging the people to turn out for its defense. This address was read by the pastors of the churches at Harrisburg that evening and telegraphed all over the State. Large numbers of volunteers enlisted for the emergency from our own and neighboring States, and hurried to Washington.

On Monday, the 11th, the rebel cavalry were near Havre de Grace, at Gunpowder river, where they burned the bridge, cut the telegraph, captured trains, and robbed passengers, entirely severing Baltimore and Washington from the loyal North. Only five miles from Washington they burned the house of Governor Bradford, and pillaged Montgomery Blair's.

On Tuesday, the 12th, the rebel sharpshooters were in front of Fort Stevens, one of the defenses of the Capitol, and after some desultory fighting they were driven off, leaving about one hundred dead and wounded. Forces were gathering around Early, and on Wednesday morning he hastily retreated, crossing the Potomac at Edward's Ferry, and made his way through Snicker's Gap, into the Shenandoah Valley, with an immense train of plunder, consisting of forage, grain, horses, cattle, hogs, sheep, groceries, clothing, etc. A requisition had been made upon Frederick for two hundred thousand dollars, which, as in the case of Hagerstown, and afterwards Chambersburg, was to be paid over at once or the city laid in ashes. The money was paid and the destruction of the place averted.

On Tuesday, 19th, Generals Crook and Averill overtook Early in the Shenandoah Valley, and, after a brisk engagement, defeated him. On Saturday, 23d, the forces of Breckenridge and Early were united, and attacked Crooks near Winchester, compelling him to retreat to Martinsburg. The Union forces were pursued to this latter place, where, on Monday, 25th, they were reinforced by General Hunter, who had brought around his army from the line of the Ohio river, whither they had gone in their retreat from Lynchburg. This retrograde movement of our forces, and the proximity of the rebels, created much uneasiness along the border and the work of sending away horses and cattle again began. In a few days the Union forces withdrew to the north bank of the Potomac, and were stationed along the river from Hancock to Harper's Ferry, the main body being located at the latter place. The Confederate army remained upon the south side of the river, with its main body near Martinsburg. Each army had cavalry stationed upon its flanks. McCauseland's cavalry was on the left of Early, and Averill somewhere on the opposite, upon the Federal right. This was the situation on Thursday, the 28th of July, and on the following day the advance was made upon our town, which will claim our attention in the ensuing chapter.

CHAPTER XIII.

THE BURNING OF CHAMBERSBURG.

As has been stated in the previous chapter, the Confederate army under General Early lay about Martinsburg, and the defeated and demoralized forces of Crooks and Hunter were strung along the north bank of the Potomac. The perilous situation we were in must certainly have been known to the authorities, but we were misled by assurances of safety. A correspondent of the Philadelphia *Inquirer*, writing from Frederick on Thursday, July 28th, said that "our troops were in such numbers, and so situated, that for the first time in the history of the war, glorious news might be expected from the Shenandoah Valley." The *Franklin Repository*, in its issue of Wednesday, 27th, probably to allay the excitement of our people, which on that day was intense owing to rumors of a threatening character along the Potomac, received the evening previous, said : "This retrograde movement of our forces, (the falling back of Crooks and Hunter), created much uneasiness on the border, and a number of persons near the river sent their stock off again; but at the time of this writing (3.30 P. M., Tuesday), no rebel demonstrations have been made on the Potomac at any point; and we do not apprehend that any will be made. Gen. Couch has the border well picketed, and the fords are all guarded, so that a surprise upon our people is hardly possible."

Such was the condition along the border and in our town up to the middle of the day of Friday, July 29th, when the news of the approach of the enemy was received. And as the destruction of our town entailed such widespread distress, and was attended with so many thrilling incidents, which could be known only to those who resided in the particular parts of the town where they occurred, this chapter will be composed mostly of the observations and experiences of a number of persons. Before proceeding, however, with these accounts, it is but fair and proper that the statements given by the principal actors in those events, as well as the reasons they assign for them, should first be heard. I will therefore quote from General M'Causland's account, written by himself and published in the *Annals of the War*, pages 770, 774:

In July, 1864, the cavalry brigade which I commanded was encamped near the Potomac river, in the county of Berkley, West Virginia. It made the advance post of the army under Gen. Early, that was guarding the approaches into Virginia through the Shenandoah Valley. On the 28th of July, I received an order from General Early to cross the Potomac with my brigade and one under General Bradley T. Johnston, and proceed to the city of Chambersburg, and after capturing it to deliver to the proper authorities a proclamation which he had issued, calling upon them to furnish me with one hundred thousand dollars in gold, or five hundred thousand dollars in greenbacks, and in case the money was not furnished I was ordered to burn the city and return to Virginia. The proclamation also stated that this course had been adopted in retaliation for the destruction of property in Virginia, by the orders of General Hunter, and specified that the houses of Andrew Hunter, A. R. Boteler, E. J. Lee, Governor Letcher, J. T. Anderson, the Virginia Military Institute, and others in Virginia, had been burned by the orders of General D. Hunter, a Federal commander, and that money demanded from Chambersburg was to be paid to these parties as a compensation for their property. It appears that the policy of General Early had been adopted upon proper reflection; that his orders were distinct and final, and that what was done on this occasion by my command was not the result of inconsiderate action or want of proper authority, as was alleged by many parties at the North, both at the time and since the close of the war.

On the 29th of July, the two cavalry brigades that were to make the dash into Pennsylvania, by turning the right of Hunter's army, were assembled at or near Hammond's mill, in Berkley county, West Virginia. During the night the Federal pickets on the northern side of the Potomac were captured, and the troops crossed just at daylight on the morning of the 30th, and moved out and formed the line of march on the National road. Major Gilmore drove the Federal cavalry from the small village of Clearspring, and pushed on toward Hagerstown to create the impression that the rest of the troops were following. At Clearspring we left the National road and turned north on the Mercersburg road. We reached Mercersburg about dark, and stopped to feed our horses, and to give time for the stragglers to come up. After this stop the march was continued all night, notwithstanding the opposition made at every available point by a regiment of Federal cavalry. Major Sweeney, with cavalry battalion, kept the roads clear, and we reached Chambersburg at daylight on the 31st. The approach to the town was defended only by one piece of artillery and some regular troops that were soon driven off, and the advance of our force took possession of the town. The main part of the two brigades was formed in line on the high ground overlooking the town. I at once went into the place with my staff, and requested some of the citizens to inform the city authorities that I wanted to see them. I also sent my staff through the town to find out where the proper officials were, and inform them that I had a proclamation for their consideration. Not one could be found. I then directed the proclamation to be read to many of the citizens that were near me, and requested them to hunt up their officers, informing them I would wait until they could either find them, or by consultation among themselves determine what they would do. Finally, I informed them that I would wait six hours, and if they would comply with the requisition their town would be safe; and in case they did not it would be destroyed in accordance with my orders from General Early. After a few hours of delay many citizens came to me—some were willing to pay the money, others were not. I urged them to comply with such reasons as occurred to me at the time, and told them plainly what they might expect. I showed to my own officers the written instructions of General Early, and before a single house was destroyed both the citizens and the Confederate officers that were present fully understood why it was done, and by whose orders. After waiting until the expiration of the six hours, and finding that the proclamation would not be complied with the destruction of the town was begun by firing the most central blocks first, and after the inhabitants had been removed from them. Thus the town was destroyed, and the inhabitants driven to the hills and fields adjacent thereto. No lives were lost by the citizens, and only one soldier was killed, and he was killed after the troops left the vicinity of the place. About noon the troops were reformed on the high ground overlooking the town, where most of them had been posted in the early morning, and the return to the Potomac was begun shortly afterward. We encamped at McConnellsburg that night, and reached the river the next day, at or near Hancock, Maryland.

General McCausland, then, in justification of the act of vandalism executed by him, says:—"I think that these facts will show that this entire expedition was planned and executed in accordance with the orders of superior officers of competent authority to order it, and, moreover, that it was an act of retaliation perfectly justified by the circumstances, and was at all times kept clearly within the rule governing civilized warfare." He thus, it will be seen, places the responsibility of his act upon General Early, his superior, and under whose orders he was acting, and in justification of the act itself quotes from Vattal's *Law of Nations*. General McCausland makes the following mistakes in the foregoing statement.

1. Chambersburg was burned on Saturday, July 30th, and not on the 31st as he states.

2. He says that his march from Mercersburg to this place was made "notwithstanding the opposition made at every available point by *a regiment of Federal Cavalry*."

The only troops to oppose the march of the rebels from Mercersburg to within two miles of this place, were a single company of cavalry under Lieut. H. T. McLean, 6th U. S. Regulars. This company made no resistance for the obvious reason that it could accomplish nothing with so vastly superior a force, but steadily fell back before the advancing foe, keeping General Couch, who was then in Chambersburg, and endeavoring to communicate with General Averill at or near Greencastle, well informed of the movements of the foe. This small body of cavalry was reinforced an hour or two before daylight on Saturday morning by a few men under Capt. McGowan and a single piece of artillery stationed here. These few troops—the two companies stated—were all that General Couch had in his department at that time, and this company was sent out west of the town only to impede the march of the rebels, and, if possible, prevent them from entering the town during the night. As the rebels stood in mass on the pike west of the hill, where the residence of Mr. Henry Greenawalt stands, a discharge from this gun killed one man.

3. General McCausland says that he waited until the expiration of *six hours* from the time the requisition was made known to our citizens, before he gave the order to commence the work of destruction.

Either the General's memory is at fault, or he wilfully falsifies. The rebels entered the town about 6 o'clock in the morning, and by 8 o'clock, as will be abundantly proven in the record to follow, the work of destruction was in progress, and by 12 o'clock, as the General himself says, he had withdrawn his forces from the town and placed them in line of battle upon the hill two miles west of the place. Their departure was hastened by the approach of General Averill's force, of whose coming their scouts brought information.

4. General McCausland also errs in saying that the firing of the town was not begun until the inhabitants had been removed from their houses. The rebels paid no attention whatever to the inhabitants, and many of them barely succeeded in escaping from their burning homes, many of which were fired in the presence of the inmates.

5. General McCausland throws the responsibility of the destruction of our town upon General Early, under whose orders he acted. Under whose orders did he act when he demanded twenty thousand dollars and a large amount of clothing, hats and shoes of the people of Hagerstown, and two hundred thousand dollars from Frederick, and in default of the payment thereof, threatened the destruction of those places? And under whose orders did he act when he demanded thirty thousand dollars of the village of Hancock, in default of which he threatened to destroy that place, and was only prevented from executing his threat by the resistance of the Marylanders under General Bradley T. Johnson and Col. Harry Gilmore and the timely arrival of General Averill? The fact is clearly established that plunder and destruction were the objects in view in the raid as is shown in the following fact: A person whose position and means of information were such as to enable him to speak understandingly, said to the writer after the invasion of our State: "When General Lee returned to Virginia after the battle of Gettysburg, the entire press of the South found fault with him for not laying this whole country in ruins; and now if ever the Confederates come again they will plunder and destroy; and my advice to you is, if ever you hear of their coming get everything out of their way that you can." The invasion of Maryland by Early, and the plunder and destruction which followed wherever he went, his demand upon Hagerstown, Frederick, Chambersburg and Hancock, and in default of the payment of his demand, the destruction of those places, prove that the bitter howl of the South against our border was to be executed, and that Early and McCausland came for that purpose, and because of their peculiar fitness for such contemptible work were chosen to execute it.

General Early in justification of the order under which Chambersburg was burned, wrote a letter of which the following is a copy, to Mr. Edward W. Bok, of Brooklyn, New York. It was written at Lynchburg, Virginia, and bears date June 6th, 1882.

Dear Sir:—In reply to your inquiries I have to inform you that the town of Chambersburg was burned on the same day on which the demand on it was made by McCausland and refused. It was ascertained that a force of the enemy's cavalry was approaching, and there was no time for delay. Moreover, the refusal was peremptory, and there was no reason for delay, unless the demand was a mere idle threat.

As to the other inquiry, I had no knowledge of what amount of money there might be in Chambersburg. I knew that it was a town of some twelve thousand inhabitants.

The town of Frederick, in Maryland, which was a much smaller town than Chambersburg had, in June, very promptly responded to my demand on it for $200,000, some of the inhabitants, who were friendly to us, expressing a regret that I had not put my demand at $500,000. There was one or more National banks at Chambersburg, and the town ought to have been able to raise the sum I demanded. I never heard that the refusal was based on inability to pay such a sum, and there was no offer to pay any sum. The value of the houses destroyed by Hunter, with their contents, was fully $100,000 in gold, and at the time I made the demand the price of gold in greenbacks had very nearly reached $3 and was going up rapidly. Hence it was that I required the $500,000 in Greenbacks, if the gold was not paid, to provide against any further depreciation of the paper money.

I would have been fully justified by the laws of retaliation in war in burning the town without giving the inhabitants the opportunity of redeeming it. Very respectfully yours,
J. A. EARLY.

The statement that the town of Frederick, Md., "was a much smaller town than Chambersburg" is incorrect, as the population of that place in 1870 was 10,000, while that of Chambersburg did not exceed 7,000.

Colonel Harry Gilmore, in his "Four Years in the Saddle," devotes considerable space in his book to a description of their march upon Chambersburg, and the terrible scenes enacted here on that memorable 30th of July, 1864. His style is so bombastic and self-laudatory that he may be suspected to be the veritable Munchausen come to life again. Colonel Gilmore after detailing his crossing the Potomac near McClay's Ford, his capturing the Federal pickets, his defeat of two Federal regiments of cavalry—the 12th and 14th Pennsylvania—with his two hundred men, and his wonderful heroism and daring in brushing aside all opposition from the overwhelming numbers of Federals who lay in ambush just specially to catch him, proceeds as follows:

By this time the brigades (McCausland's and Johnston's) were both clear of the town (Clearspring) and, in fact, two or three miles on their way to Mercersburg. I fell back to Clearspring without being followed, but did not overtake the main body till after night. They had halted about a mile beyond Mercersburg, on the road to Chambersburg. I reported at headquarters, and found Johnston and McCausland together. It was about 10 P. M., when the latter informed me he should endeavor to be in Chambersburg by daylight, and wished me to guard the rear. I had not laid down for forty-six hours, and all our men suffered terribly for want of sleep, and it was with difficulty I could keep my command together. Just before daylight I was summoned to the front. The command had halted in an oatfield to feed their horses. Day dawned as I rode up to the General. Near the edge of the town a small force of the enemy could be seen. Major Sweeney, who was in front, had run into an ambuscade of infantry and artillery, and lost one man by a grapeshot.

After making inquiry about the different roads leading into Chambersburg, General McCausland asked me to join Major Sweeney, who would attack the town with infantry. The major had a gallant command, and easily drove everything before him; in fact the enemy made no resistance at all, and we took possession without losing a man. On my entering the town I caught sight of a mounted man, and ran him beyond the limits. I then made a good reconnoisance of all that part, and in the course of it had some amusing conversations with the ladies, who exercised their tongues upon me rather freely, which I returned in good measure.

General Early's order was now published, requiring a levy of $200,000 in gold, or its equivalent in greenbacks, and in default of payment Chambersburg was to be laid in ashes. Just then some scouts returned with a prisoner from Averill's command, reporting him to be not more than two or three miles off, with a heavy force of cavalry. The citizens knew it too, and positively refused to raise the money, laughing at us when we threatened to burn the town.

After we had breakfasted at the hotel (the Franklin Hotel), General McCausland ordered me to arrest fifty or more of the most prominent citizens, and put them under guard. I had arrested about forty, when he sent for me, and said that there was no time to be lost—the town must be burned; he was sorry for it on account of the women and children, but it must be done to check the burning of private property in Virginia, and they had none to blame for it but General Hunter and their own press for extolling such fiendish acts of vandalism. He then ordered me to fire the town, and showed me General Early's order to that effect. Deeply regretting that such a task should fall upon me, I had only to obey. I then directed my men to fire the town, but be kind to the women and children and lend them all the assistance in their power. While I could remain in the streets I did nothing but assist the people, and see that no excesses were committed. Several times I received peremptory orders to make thorough work of it, and was especially directed to destroy all fine buildings.

When the town was no longer tenable, I took two men with me to fire a fine brick dwelling beautifully situated on an eminence, north-west of the town. Dismounting, I went in, and told the lady who came to the door that I was there to perform the extremely unpleasant duty of burning her house, which I much regretted; that we were obliged to resort to such extreme measures in order to prevent or check the terrible devastation committed by such men as General Hunter. I told her that the people of that town had seen us *twice before*, and that all had spoken in the highest terms of our behavior, saying that our soldiers had behaved better than their own. She was weeping, evidently much distressed, but she acknowledged the justice of my remarks, and declared that she blamed none but the administration for allowing such horrible acts of cruelty to go unpunished. She was in deep distress, and shed many bitter tears; did not beg me to spare her house; only asked time to remove some articles of value and clothing. This was readily granted. Breakfast was on the table, and she asked me to eat something while she was getting her things together. Being hungry, I accepted the invitation, and drank a glass of wine before sitting down. I delayed as much as possible, in order to afford her more time, and when I rose from the table I had half a mind to disobey orders in regard to this house. She then came in, and entered into conversation. I asked her the name of her husband. She replied, 'Colonel Boyd, of the Union Army.' 'What! Colonel Boyd, of the 1st New York Cavalry?' 'The same, sir.' 'Then, madam, your house shall not be destroyed.' I now understood why she had not pleaded for it. The reader will recollect that this officer has been already mentioned as operating in the Valley. He had ever been kind and lenient to the citizens, men, women and children, warring only against men in arms. The fact of her being the wife of Col. Boyd decided me at once. I told her that I knew her husband, and had fought against him for two years in the Valley of Virginia; that he had gained a high reputation among the citizens for kindness and gentlemanly conduct; that while we were there for the purpose of punishing vandalism, we were ready and anxious to repay acts of kindness done to our people, who, when unprotected, had been exposed by the fortunes of war to the mercy or harsh treatment of our foes. I told her that her house should not be burned, blame me for it who would, and that I would leave a guard for her protection till all were gone. She seemed to be completely overwhelmed, as though she did not comprehend what I had said; but when I assured her again that neither her house nor anything that belonged to her should be molested, her gratitude knew no bounds. To the picket near by the house she afterward sent baskets filled with nice eatables, hot coffee and as much wine as they desired.

I left a guard, and well I did, for an officer who had been drinking too much came up soon after, and tried to force the guard and burn the house.

The burning of Chambersburg was an awful sight, nor could I look on without deep sorrow, although I had been hardened by such scenes in Virginia. At one view we had, with anguished hearts, from the mountain top, gazed upon the sky reddened by the burning of one hundred and eighteen houses in that once smiling valley, a small part indeed, in the history of Hunter's ruthless raid; inflicted, too, not by an ungovernable soldiery, but under a coldly calculated mandate. Who, then, taking a dispassionate view, will condemn our government for this act of righteous retribution?

Hitherto the fires had been applied to the houses of my friends, which roused within me feelings of the sternest vengeance; still, I felt more like weeping over Chambersburg, although the people covered me with reproaches, which all who knew me will readily believe I found hard to digest; yet my pity was highly excited in behalf of these poor unfortunates, who were made to suffer for acts perpetrated by the officers of their own government.

The day was bright and intensely hot. The conflagration seemed to spring from one vast building. Dense clouds of smoke rose to the zenith, and hovered over the dark plain. At night it would have been a grand but terrible object to behold. How piteous the sight in those beautiful green meadows—groups of women and children exposed to the rays of a burning sun, hovering over the few articles they had saved, most of them wringing their hands, and with wild gesticulations bemoaning their ruined homes.

We left Chambersburg at noon, and went into camp at McConnellsburg, where we found plenty of provender and rations.

Col. Gilmore errs in his statement of the amount of money demanded of the town. He states it as $200,000 in gold or its equivalent in greenbacks. It was $100,000 in gold, or $500,000 in United States currency. His statement that soon after taking breakfast at the Franklin Hotel, McCausland told him that there was no time to be lost and that the town must be fired at once, disproves the latter's story that he gave our citizens *six hours* to raise the money demanded before he gave the order to begin the work of destruction. Col. Gilmore also says that after the town was no longer tenable, he went out to Federal Hill to burn the residence of Col. Boyd, and breakfast being on the table, and being invited to eat, and being *very hungry*, he sat down and enjoyed the proffered hospitality. Either that was a very late breakfast, or the one he had previously eaten at the Franklin Hotel did not fully satisfy him, or else he was so nearly starved out in Virginia that he did not know when he had enough, or else his memory was at fault. That the work of firing was committed to him, and that it was effectually done, and seemingly by methods well understood, and not improvised for the occasion, may be due to the fact that he was from Baltimore, where Fire Bugs have reduced their nefarious work to a science.

It will be remembered that two brigades were present in the destruction of the town, McCausland's and Bradley T. Johnston's. McCausland's brigade, although considerably reduced by the casuallies of war, was the same as Jenkins', and had been here, as Col. Gilmore says, twice before. McCausland, it is said, had been professor in the Virginia Military Institute, with Stonewall Jackson. He succeeded Jenkins in the command of his brigade. Jenkins was wounded at Gettysburg, and after his recovery, and separation from Lee's army, and his resumption of his guerilla method of warfare, he was severely wounded in a fight with General Crooks at Cloide Mountain. His wound was not considered dangerous, until one night the bandage became removed, and he bled so profusely that death ensued. Jenkins manifested some honorable traits when here, but if McCausland had any he did not manifest them.

The reasons assigned by the Confederates for the destruction of Chambersburg, it will have been perceived, were the acts of wanton cruelty said to have been perpetrated by General Hunter in the Valley of Virginia. Justice to the citizens of the South demands a fair consideration of this plea. General J. D. Imboden, in an article on this subject contributed to the *Annals of the War*, pages 169-183, details at considerable length the operations of General Hunter in his raid up the Valley upon Lynchburg, and presents a fearful record of houseburning and other acts of cruelty upon unarmed and defenseless people, that was wholly unjustifiable according to the laws of civilized warfare, *unless there were reasons for the same which have not been stated*. Says General Imboden : "If the people of Chambersburg will carefully read the record of wanton destruction of private property, this 'o'er true tale' of cruel wrong inflicted on the helpless, they will understand why, when goaded to madness, remuneration was demanded at their hands by General Early, and upon its refusal retaliation was inflicted on the nearest community that could be reached, and it was their misfortune to be that community."

Justice to General Hunter demands that he should have a hearing upon these serious charges, and I therefore give his side of the question. The depredations of guerilas and bushwhackers had become so numerous, murders and robberies so frequent, and by the aid of the residents the perpetrators so uniformly escaped justice, that General Hunter was compelled to adopt the most strenuous measures to put a stop to them. He accordingly issued and circulated the following circular:

HEADQT'S DEPARTMENT OF W. VA.,
In the Field, Valley of the Shenandoah,
May 24th, 1864.

Sir:—Your name has been reported to me with evidence that you are one of the leading secessionist sympathizers in the valley, and that you countenance and abet the bushwhackers and guerillas who infest the woods and mountains of this region, swooping out on the roads to plunder and outrage loyal residents, falling upon and firing into defenseless wagon trains and assassinating soldiers of this command, who may chance to be placed in exposed positions. These practices are not recognized by the laws of war of any civilized nation, nor are the persons engaged therein entitled to any other treatment than that done by the universal code of justice to pirates, murderers and other out-laws.

But from the difficulties of the country, the secret aid and information given to these bushwhackers by persons of your class, and the more important occupation of the troops under my command, it is impossible to chase, arrest, and punish these common marauders as they deserve. Without the countenance and help given to them by the rebel residents of the valley, they could not support themselves for a week. You are spies upon our movements, abusing the clemency which has protected your persons and your property, while loyal citizens of the United States, residing within the rebel lines, are invariably plundered of all they may possess, imprisoned, and in some cases put to death. It is from you, and your families and neighbors, that these bandits receive food, clothing, ammunition and information, and it is from their secret hiding places, in your houses, barns and woods that they issue on their missions of pillage and murder.

You are therefore hereby notified, that for every train fired upon, or soldier of the Union wounded or assassinated by bushwhackers in any neighborhood within the reach of my command, the houses and other property of every secession sympathizer residing within a circuit of five miles from the place of the outrage, shall be destroyed by fire, and that for all public property jayhawked or destroyed by these marauders, an assessment of five times the value of such property will be made upon the secession sympathizers residing within the circuit of ten miles around the point at which the offense was committed. The payment of this assessment will be enforced by the troops of this department, who will seize and hold in close military custody the persons assessed, until such payment shall have been made. This provision will also be applied to make good from the secessionists in the neighborhood, five times the amount of any loss suffered by loyal citizens of the United States, from the action of the bushwhackers whom you may encourage.

If you desire to avoid the consequences here in set forth, you will notify your guerilla and bushwhacking friends to withdraw from that portion of the valley within my lines, and to join, if they desire to fight for the rebellion, the regular forces of the secession army in my front or elsewhere. You will have none but yourselves to blame for the consequences that will certainly ensue if these evils are permitted to continue. This circular is not sent to you for the reason that you have been singled out as peculiarly obnoxious, but because you are believed to furnish the readiest means of communication with the prominent secession sympa-

thizers of your neighborhood. It will be for their benefit that you communicate to them the tenor of this circular.   D. HUNTER,
                                  Major General Commanding.

In further justification of this retributive policy of General Hunter, which, if the charges he alleges were true, was strictly within the rules of war, it should be stated that guerillas and bushwhackers, whenever caught, claimed to be in the Confederate service and should, therefore, be treated as prisoners of war. This claim the Confederate government always conceded; but General Hunter by his circular gave notice that that claim would be no longer granted. And it was the execution of the policy intimated in this order, it is claimed, that gave rise to the charges brought against him of inhumanity.

General Hunter's reason for burning the house of ex-Governor Letcher at Lexington, was the finding in a printing office in that city of the type and proof of a handbill issued and signed by Letcher, calling upon the people of that region to "bushwhack" Hunter's men. This clearly identified Letcher with this unwarranted business, and was held as a sufficient justification for the destruction of his property. What the causes were which led to the destruction of several other private residences have not been stated. If, now, the destruction of the buildings by General Hunter in the Valley of Virginia, especially of the five or six enumerated by General Early in his demand upon Chambersburg, was executed under the foregoing order, or for any other violation of the acknowledged rules of civilized warfare, the retaliation which was visited upon this place was altogether unjustifiable; if they were not destroyed for the violation of the provisions of this order, or for any other adequate reason, but from mere wantonness and revenge, then retaliation *to the same extent*, provided it had not already been visited upon some other place or places, was right and justifiable. Anything beyond this, however, would be barbarous and unwarranted. Furthermore, if the destruction of the properties in the valley by General Hunter, was in plain violation of the laws of war, as is claimed by the Confederates, the question arises whether retaliation had not already been made in the burning of the residence of Governor Bradford and the pillaging of Montgomery Blair's, near Washington, the exaction of two hundred thousand dollars from the city of Frederick, and twenty thousand dollars from Hagerstown, or in default thereof, the destruction of those two places? Judged by either of the rules stated, the destruction of Chambersburg was unjustifiable, and must forever brand its perpetrators with ignomy and reproach.

Having given the statements of the three principal actors in the destruction of our town, as well as their reasons for the same, I now proceed to narrate the same from my own observations and from those of others.

On Friday, July 29th, 1864, about half-past 12 o'clock, as I came into our store after dinner, I was informed that word had been received by telegraph that the rebel cavalry had crossed the Potomac simultaneously at Williamsport, Cherry Run and McCoy's fords. The force which crossed at the last named ford comprised the brigades of Brig. Gen's. Jno. M'Causland, formerly Jenkin's brigade, and Bradley T. Johnston. These forces took the road leading through Clearspring to Mercersburg, and evidently were aiming for Chambersburg. As soon as the information of this raid was spread throughout the town, a scene of indescribable confusion, such as had occurred several times previously during the war, at once set in. Merchants and business men set to work to remove or secrete their merchandize and valuables. I ran to the depot and learned from Messrs. Oaks and Linn that they had one empty car which I could have. This car I at once secured, and hastily packing as much of our stock of merchandize as I could find boxes for—a considerable part having been packed and sent to Philadelphia a few weeks before upon the threatened approach of the rebels—shipped the same to the depot and that night it was taken down the road. The balance of our stock, consisting of hosiery, gloves and other small articles, we secreted in the beer vault under Dr. Langhein's back building—the same in which a greater part of stock was hidden during the invasions a year previously. Other articles were placed in this vault and its entrance was walled up. I took this precaution to send off the greater part of our stock, because of the advice of the friend previously referred to—that the next time the rebels would come, it would be to burn and plunder, and that I should put everything out of their way that I could. Other business men in the town merely hid their stock somewhere in their own houses, or in the houses of others, and suffered the loss of the whole.

About dusk in the evening, about fifty or more wagons from General Hunter's command along the Potomac, commenced passing through the town, and went on down the valley towards Harrisburg. Large numbers of straggling and demoralized soldiers—infantry and cavalry—from the same command also began to pass through the town. I judge these stragglers would have amounted to one thousand or more. These men were weary, hungry and greatly demoralized. Many of them we took into our house and fed. Colonel Gilmore in his account says that while the main body of the Confederates under McCausland and Johnson left the pike at Clearspring and passed on towards Mercersburg, on their way to Chambersburg, he with his command of a few hundred men drove a force of Federal cavalry towards Hagerstown. This force was Cole's Maryland cavalry, and a member of it who participated in the operations of that day, relates that they fell back into Hagerstown and were surprised there sometime during that same day by the unexpected appearance of a Confederate force, before which they fled and became scattered. He, with some nine or ten others, in command of a sergeant, fled towards this place and spent the night within a few miles of town. On the following day, while the town was in flames, they joined Averill's force and passed through the town westwardly in pursuit of McCausland, but in a day or two afterwards rejoined their own command. It seems hardly probable that Gilmore's handful of men should drive before them a regiment of Marylanders enlisted specially for home defense, but such seems to have been the fact. But what troops were those who suddenly appeared in Hagerstown later in the day and stampeded this same regiment? The following account, furnished by Mr. J. H. Fosnot at that time, and now in the employ of the Cumberland Valley Railroad Company, may throw some light upon this question. Mr. Fosnot says: A train of cars containing a regiment of New York soldiers was taken to Hagerstown, arriving there about half-past seven o'clock in the evening. This train was in charge of Mr. Fosnot. Jacob Sweitzer was engineer, P. Zeigler, fireman and Andrew Stepler brakeman. The soldiers were sent away as soon as the train arrived. Mr. Fosnot says he had orders from Colonel Lull, Superintendent of the road, to take all the cars from Hagerstown and leave for Chambersburg as soon as possible. The rebels, Mr. F. says, were reported as between Williamsport and Hagerstown. There were several cars there loaded with forage, commissary's stores, &c.; these the officers would not permit him to take away. Notifying Colonel Lull by telegraph of this refusal, he ordered Mr. F. to leave at once with what cars he could. Just about the time the train started from Franklin street, the rebels—some fifteen or twenty—rode up to the passenger depot. Seeing the train moving, they started after it, and would have caught it but for the cattle guard at the engine house. Mr. F. was back somewhere near the rear of the train, ready to uncouple four or five of the hinder cars in case the rebels came up. At that point the grade was heavy, and the train could not go fast. Finding that they could not catch the train, the rebels rode back and set fire to all the cars left on the siding, and burned them and all their contents. Mr. F. says they left Hagerstown about 9 o'clock, and they ran through to Harrisburg that night. What became of the New York soldiers he did not know. It would seem that there was bad management somewhere, for if that regiment of Marylanders had been handled properly, or if the regiment taken to Hagerstown in the train spoken of by Mr. Fosnot, had been used, this rebel force might have been kept from entering the town and the destruction of government property averted. Evidently the purpose of the Confederates was to disconcert and mislead the Union forces, and prevent Averill from pressing McCausland and Johnson. Before these forces in and about Hagerstown Averill fell back to a short distance from Greencastle, where he went into camp for the night, and where, for the present, we will leave him, turning our attention to the force under McCausland on its way to this place.

About 6 o'clock in the evening the head of the rebel column encountered near Mercersburg Captain McLean's company of cavalry, who steadily fell back before the superior numbers of the enemy, and sent off courier after courier to General Couch giving him information of the approaching foe. General Couch sent *three dispatches* to General Averill near Greencastle, informing him of the approach of the enemy, and importuning him to hasten here with his command, but failed to receive a reply. This whole matter will be set forth from the testimony of reliable, living witnesses later on in this narrative. Failing to get a reply from General Averill, General Couch, after sending out to the hill west of the town a single piece of artillery in charge of a few men—all that he had at his disposal—for the purpose of preventing the rebels from entering the town during the darkness of the night, and knowing that his longer stay could be of no benefit to the town, and might result in his own capture, left in a special train about 1 o'clock in the morning. The few men in charge of the gun upon the hill near the residence of Mr. Greenawalt, were reinforced near daylight by Captain McLean's cavalry, and after one discharge into the rebel column, by which one man was killed and four or five wounded, the small, but heroic band, fell back to the fairgrounds, were, by skillful manœuvring, they detained the rebel advance two hours and until daylight. Then, fearing that they might be flanked and caught, they fell back down Market street to the Diamond, and down Main towards Harrisburg. Their withdrawal through the town was leisurly and orderly, and without the least appearance of fear. Nothing would have gratified that brave handful of men more than to have had about two thousand men as brave as themselves to stand by them, and wipe out once for all the whole invading crew.

While waiting along the road west of Mr. Greenawalt's for daylight, a boisterous and angry council was held by McCausland and some of his officers in Mr. Greenawalt's house. Mrs. Greenawalt overheard this contention, and says that earnest protests were made to McCausland against burning anything but public property. At this McCausland was greatly incensed, and threatened summary vengeance upon them if his orders to burn the town were disobeyed. McCausland, too, insisted upon advancing at once, and burning the town during the *darkness*. To this General Johnson and Colonel Gilmore strenuously objected. The increased horrors which must have resulted if McCausland had not been overruled in his determination, may be imagined.

Shortly after the break of day the whole command advanced, and the greater part formed in line of battle upon the hights overlooking the town, and without any notice whatever to our citizens, three shells were fired right into our town. One of these shells passed through the house standing upon the top of New England hill, formerly occupied by Mr. Jacob Eby. It went clean through the house, entering one window and passing out another directly opposite. Another shell lit in the lot in the rear of Mr. Lemuel King's carriage factory on King street. The firing of these shells, without previous notice, into a crowded and defenseless town, is against the rules of civilized warfare. And yet to avenge the alleged violation of these laws these marauding and pilfering plunderers came here to destroy our town.

The combined forces of McCausland and Johnson amounted to twenty-eight hundred by actual count as they passed through St. Thomas after the destruction of our town. About 2,000 of these, with six pieces of artillery, stood in line of battle upon the hill west of the town, and eight hundred and thirty-one came into the town, their skirmishers simultaneously investing every street and alley. I sat by an open window and saw them enter. Some five or six men on foot, with carbines ready for action entered the Diamond by Market street. At the same time I could see about the same number entering by the streets and alleys up town, and when they reached the middle of the Diamond they called to their companions further up the street, who responded by similar calls. These skirmishers were followed by the cavalry, until the Diamond was pretty well filled by them, when the work of breaking in the stores and other places of business was commenced at once. Johnson and McCausland and Gilmore, with a number of other officers, breakfasted at the Franklin hotel, after which they went out into the street to commence business. Captain Fitzhugh, who was Jeukins' chief of staff when here a year previously, recognized J. W. Douglas, and calling him communicated the information that unless one hundred thousand dollars in gold, or five hundred thousand in greenbacks were paid, the town was to be burned. As Mr. Douglas and Mr. A. Holler are the only two living persons who saw the order of General Early that I know of, these gentlemen have kindly prepared the following statements of that affair, which, because of its importance I give entire here. Mr. Douglass's account is as follows:

JACOB HOKE, ESQ.—*Dear Sir:*—At your solicitation I make the following statement with regard to my recollection of the events on the morning of the burning of the greater portion of Chambersburg by the rebel forces, under General McCausland, of which I was personally cognizant; it is now nearly twenty years since that day, and whilst many minor incidents are forgotten in the lapse of time, the great facts stand out in great vividness.

Very truly yours,
J. W. DOUGLAS.

The 30th of July, 1864, was bright and warm. A few rebel shells screamed over our heads early in the morning to warn us of the approaching foe. Near 6 o'clock, A. M., I was standing, with many others, on the veranda of the McNulty house watching the cavalry file into the square, of which they took entire possession, and commenced feeding their horses oats and corn on the edge of the pavements. Whilst thus engaged looking, I heard my name called, and just below me on the street an officer rode out of line and desired me by name to come down. When I reached the pavement the officer had already dismounted, and approaching me said: "I am Captain Fitzhugh, formerly of General Jenkin's staff. We met last year and then your Burgess directed me to you to inform your people of some things we wished done. I now ask you to be our bearer on this occasion." I told him I recollected him and asked him what he wished done. He then said we have come here to demand the payment of one hundred thousand dollars in gold, or in lieu thereof, five hundred thousand dollars in greenbacks, and if this requisition is not complied with, then to burn your town. I asked him by what authority he asked such a sum of money and threatened to lay in ashes the homes of our defenceless families if the demand was not complied with. He then unbuttoned his coat and took from a side pocket a folded paper and handed it to me with the remark: "This is my authority." The order ran something in this wise:

HEADQUARTERS OF THE ARMY OF }
NORTH VIRGINIA.   }
To General J. McCAUSLAND:—You are hereby ordered to proceed with such forces as will be detailed, and as rapidly as possible, to the town of Chambersburg, Penna., and demand of the authorities the sum of one hundred thousand dollars in gold, or in lieu thereof the sum of five hundred thousand dollars in greenbacks, and in case this demand is not complied with, then in retaliation for the burning of seven properties of peaceful inhabitants of the Valley of Virginia, by order of the Federal Gen. Hunter, you will proceed to burn the town of Chambersburg and rapidly return to this point.
Signed :   J. A. EARLY,
                        General Commanding.

"Now," said Capt. Fitzhugh, after the reading was finished, "you see we are in a hurry. I want you to go immediately and see your people and tell them of this demand and see that the money is forthcoming, for I assure you that this order will be rigidly enforced." I said this was monstrous, there were no Union soldiers here. "Oh, yes," he said, "they have been firing on us for some hours." I replied only a squad of twenty with two little pieces; they left long ago. He said there is a large force of young men in this valley, to which I did not reply. "Now go," he said, "and report to me as soon as possible." I then went up Market street and told everyone I met of the rebel demand. They generally laughed at first, and when I spoke earnestly about the terrible alternative, they said they were trying to scare us and went into their houses. I then went up Main street in the same manner and with the same result. I then went to the hotel to see Capt. F. They told me he was over in the book store buying stationary. Going to Shryock's book store, then kept where Hatnick's cigar store is now located, I met the Captain and told him most of our capitalists were out of town ; all the bank funds removed, as we knew of their advance last night, and that he couldn't squeeze blood out of a turnip. Whilst we were speaking, another officer approached us, and Capt. F. turning to him said, "General McCausland, this is the gentleman I requested to notify the people of Chambersburg of our errand." I repeated to him what I had already said to Capt. Fitzhugh. He took me by the arm, and leading me out into the Diamond, said, "are you sure you have seen your public men? I should be very sorry to carry out the retributive part of the command of my superior officer," and as we walked towards the Court House, he said : "Can't you ring the Court House bell and call the citizens together and see if this sum of money cannot be raised?" I reiterated that there was no money here; that living so near the border no large sums were kept here, and that as we knew of this advance, the bank officers had fled and taken the funds with them. I said the Court House was locked up and even the janitor had left. He then ordered some of his men to open the Court House door with the butts of their muskets and ring the bell. Then several of our citizens came and engaged in conversation with General McCausland, when I left, going to my hotel to notify my mother of the coming storm and save articles of value to no one but the family.

Mr. Holler's statement is as follows :

MR. HOKE, *Sir:* In complying with your request, I will make the following brief statement of my interview with General McCausland on the morning of the burning of Chambersburg by the rebels. Mr. John Lohr, who resided by the gate house on the Shippensburg pike, sent me word to make some arrangements for the burial of his child. Accompanied by Mr. Joseph Frey, the undertaker, I went to see General McCausland and met him in front of the Court House. I told him that we would like to have a pass to go out to see about the burial of a child at the edge of the town. He told me that he had something of more importance to attend to than burrying the dead. He then took from his pocket an order, or requisition, signed by General Early, the substance of which was, that the sum of five hundred thousand dollars in United States money, or one hundred thousand dollars in gold must be paid over to him, and if not paid in one hour's time the town would be burned. I told him that I supposed that the town would have to be burned, as the Bank had sent its funds away, and that the citizens could not raise that amount. I had some other conversation with him that I do not recollect now. I then left him for my home on Second street, and I do not think that I was over fifteen minutes on the way, and on arriving at the house I looked back and saw the smoke going up from the Court House. Thus commenced one of the most atrocious acts of the war—the burning of our beautiful town.

Respectfully yours,
                        A. HOLLER.

The citizens failing to heed McCausland's call for a conference, made through Mr. Douglas and the ringing of the Court House bell, that chieftain ordered Col. Gilmore to arrest a number of leading persons and bring them before him. Col. T. B. Kennedy says that J. McD. Sharpe and W. McLellan, Esqrs., called at his door, and while engaged in conversation about McCausland's demand and threat, Col. Gilmore rode up and told them that the citizens were treating General McCausland with great disrespect in not coming at once to the Diamond as desired. Mr. Kennedy said to him, that no disrespect was intended ; that the funds of the Bank were all sent away, and there was scarcely five hundred thousand cents left in town instead of that many dollars. Gilmore then said, "Very well, I'll take you gentlemen to Richmond, and burn your —— town." These three persons, Messrs. Sharpe, Kennedy and McLellan, with W. H. McDowell, W. S. Everett, Dr. J. C. Richards, E. G. Etter and M. A. Foltz, who were also present, were placed under guard and taken into the presence of McCausland. When brought before the General, he declared to them the order of General Early and his determination to execute it if the money was not promptly paid. Dr. J. C. Richards, acting as spokesman for the citizens repeated their utter inability to raise the money, and remonstrated against the monstrosity of burning a whole town of six to seven thousand inhabitants, in retaliation for the seven buildings named as destroyed by General Hunter. Captain Fitzhugh, who was Jenkin's chief of staff, and had made himself infamous by his conduct when here the year previously, replied with an oath, that the orders of General Early would be carried out very quickly. The citizens were then released with the order to report at the same place (in front of the Court House) at a given time, but it is needless to say that they did not "report." While these negotiations were going on, the rebels were breaking into stores and shops, plundering them of their contents. Hotels and restaurants were also visited, and liquor was drank and many became intoxicated. The robbery of the citizens along the street was commenced, and hats, caps, boots, watches, and everything of value which they could find were taken. Shortly after this conference with the citizens terminated, the work of burning was commenced, when those under arrest were discharged from custody.

As soon as General McCausland directed his men to commence the work of destruction, detachments were sent to all parts of the town; and as events of the most thrilling interest occurred all over the town that were witnessed by those only in each respective place, I will narrate those events from the various statements given me. I will commence by detailing what came within my own observation.

When I saw the doors of stores and shops broken open, I took my stand in front of our store with key in hand, ready to unlock the door and not have it broken in with the butts of their muskets as they were doing to others. When a squad came to our store I at once unlocked the door, and about twenty entered it and made a thorough search. Finding it empty they inquired where we had our goods. To this I replied that we had shipped them to Philadelphia. After they left I closed the door, and sat down by it, and entered into conversation with a gentlemanly looking man, who informed me that he was a chaplain, a Methodist minister, born in Fayette county, this State, but then residing in Virginia. His name, he said, was Johnston. While we were thus conversing, an officer rode up and dismounted and tied his horse in front of our door. Observing some of the soldiers breaking into the millinery store of Miss Mary Barnitz, nearly opposite, and coming out with bonnets, hats, feathers, flowers, and other millinery articles, I said to the chaplain, "Now, sir, you tell me you are a Methodist preacher; your men across the street are carrying from that millinery store articles which are of great value to the owner, but no use to themselves; the lady who owns them is a Methodist; can't you have them desist?" He spoke a word or two to the men, but without effect. Other soldiers passed along the pavement carrying jars of candy, handsful of cinnamon, and other articles which they had taken, and were strewing them all along as they went. Others had procured liquor, and were drinking. At length the chaplain said to me, "Do you reside in this house?" I replied affirmatively, when he said that the soldiers were rolling barrels of kerosene across the Diamond to the Court House; that they were going to burn it, and that I had better try to save what I could. Leaving the chaplain and the dismounted officer at the door, I ran up stairs, snatched up some valuable books from the parlor table, and ran down to near the corner of Main and King streets, and by permission placed them in the house of Mr. Flack. They were all burned there, and I never saw them afterwards. I next brought down to the door as much bed clothing as I could carry, and was met at the door by a man who resided on the outskirts of the town, and who volunteered to carry it to a place of safety. He took it to the house of Mr. Christian Fuller, on Second street, where it was saved. I soon followed this man with another load of bed clothing, and carried it to the same place. Emerging from our door with this load another officer who was passing by inquired why I was removing these things? I told him that they were setting fire to the Court House (I did not know that they were going to destroy the whole town) and if it burned, we too would be burned out. He said that it could not be possible that the Court House was to be burned. Returning to the house after carrying away this load, and going up stairs, I encountered a rebel officer in one of the rooms. Seeing me he inquired, "Do you reside here?" Telling him that I did, he said, "My friend, for God's sake, let me help you. Tell me what you value most, and I will take it to a place of safety, for they are going to burn the whole town." At that instant my wife appeared, and hearing the last remark, said, "If they are going to burn the whole town there is no use to remove anything for they may as well burn here as somewhere else." By this time the members of my family—myself and three others—females, had gathered together a few articles of clothing and other valued articles—my wife carrying in her hand her deceased father's photograph which she had snatched from its place on the wall, and ran down stairs. The officer followed us to the door and entreated one of the ladies to mount his horse and escape from the awful place, for by this time flames were bursting out everywhere. He declared that he did not want his horse any longer in the rebel service. At the door I found the officer already alluded to, who had rode up and hitched his horse some time before, crying bitterly. He seemed to be dazed and confused at the awful scene. Pointing here and there at the leaping, crackling flames, as they burst forth from buildings all around us, he cried out, "See! See!! Oh my God! My God!! Has it come to this that we must be made a band of thieves and robbers by a man like McCausland?" About that time another soldier came up, and unbuckling his sword placed it in our house and went away. It was found afterwards in the ruins. The officer still urging one of the women to mount his horse, another one came up, when a fierce encounter of words occurred between them. Said the first one, "The Yankees never treated our people this way." The other replied, "Yes they have; have they not been throwing Greek Fire and every other kind of fire into Charleston?" Drawing too the door and locking it, leaving the accumulated treasures of many years—furniture, bedding, clothing, books, pictures, mementoes and gifts of dear departed ones, all, all, we left lest we could not get out of the Diamond if we taried longer. Leaving the officer weeping at the door, we ran around past the Hall and Court House—the flames leaping and bursting forth everywhere, and passed out East Market street to the residence of my brother, H. E. Hoke, which was not burned and where many homeless ones gathered that day. The rebel officer who wanted one of the women to mount his horse, followed us around as far as the residence of Mr. D. O. Gehr, pleading for one of them to accept of his offer, and then turned sorrowfully away. When we reached the front of the residence of Mr. B. F. Nead, another one rode up at a gallop, and ordered me to hand him the carpet bag which I carried. I told him it contained nothing but a few articles of clothing and we could not part with them. He replied, "Have you not some things there that you brought from your store?" The villain had seen us leaving the house, and supposed that we had money or other valuables taken from the store. My wife spoke up and said, as he pressed his horse nearly upon us, "There is nothing in that bag but a few articles of clothing which we saved from our burning home, and you can't have them." This was said in so decided a tone, and with so much earnestness that the villain, fearing that he would miss other chances of plunder by longer parleying with us, turned away and left us.

The Court House was fired by placing two or three barrels of kerosene taken from a neighboring grocery, under the stairway at the southwest corner of the building. When we passed it the flames were rolling up the stairway and bursting out of the door and windows of the west end. The ringing of the bell on that building that morning proved to be its death knell. It never sounded out its familiar tones again. It, like the temple of justice over which it hung, and our homes all went down in honor; for be it known, the insulting demand to contribute money to be used for the overthrow of our grand and glorious government, to consider which, this bell on that occasion rung by rebel hands, sounded forth its call, was not even considered.

As we passed out East Market street that morning, here and there on both sides, houses were on fire, and the street was filled with the drunken and infuriated soldiers. They seemed to be as demons from the infernal pit. All along that street the occupants of the houses were endeavoring to carry articles to places of safety. The people were running wildly through the street, carrying clothing and other articles. Others were dragging sewing machines and articles of furniture. Children were screaming after their parents, and parents were frantic after their children. The feeble efforts of the aged and infirm to carry with them some valued article from their burning homes, were deeply distressing. The roaring and crackling of the flames, the falling walls, the blinding smoke, the intense heat intensified by the scorching sun, all united to form a picture of the terrible which no pen can describe nor painter portray. It was such a sight as no one would desire to witness but once in a lifetime.

Arriving at my brother's, we with several others who had fled there for refuge, sat down and for about three hours watched the awful scene. The burning mass appeared to converge toward the Diamond, forming at one time a fearful whirlwind, which, in a huge cone-shaped column, moved eastwardly from the Diamond along Market street. In the grounds around the dwelling of William McLellan, Esq., were gathered a large amount of bed-clothing, wearing apparel, &c. This column passed over some of these, and with a tremendous whirl they were taken up and carried away. A web of muslin was caught and as it unrolled, was carried up and like a huge auger or corkscrew shaped column it stood for an instant and then fell to the earth. A child, about four or five years old, was caught in this whirlwind and lifted about five or six feet from the ground. It was a grand and fearful scene and added no little to the terror of the people.

About 11 o'clock the rebels left the town fearing Averill, whose scouts captured five of the enemy near the eastern outskirts of the town. About 1 o'clock my wife and I started out to hunt up her two sisters. We found one of them after a short search at the residence of Colonel Boyd on Federal Hill. The other we did not find for several hours. She had filled two trunks with clothing, and leaving one in the house dragged the other about one hundred yards and then returned for the other, which she in like manner dragged to where she had left the first one. While thus engaged in alternately dragging these trunks up the alley leading from Market street, west of the Diamond, and southwardly across Queen street, a rebel officer riding along took one of the trunks on before him and conducted her on down one square south of the Reformed church where we found her with the little she had saved.

About 2 o'clock Averill's command passed through town, coming in East Market street and passing on westwardly in pursuit of the enemy. The men as they rode through the Diamond and saw the destruction, vowed vengeance upon the perpetrators of the dastardly act.

And now with a view to place upon record the scenes enacted in other parts of the town, I will give statements made by several of our citizens of their experiences and observations on that terrible day. In a book written by Mr. Thomas L. Wilson, entitled "The Cruelties and Atrocities of the Rebellion," I find accounts by Hon. F. M. Kimmell and Dr. J. C. Richards, which I transcribe. Judge Kimmell says: "I reside on West Market street, nearly in the heart of the town. It was known the day before (Friday) that the rebels had crossed the river and were at Mercersburg, fifteen miles southwest of the town. But we were all lulled into a false security by the fact that, when Stuart and Lee invaded the State before, strict orders were given not to molest private property or citizens. As a consequence, we rested quite easy, not dreaming that they would burn our houses, and drive us mercilessly from our home. The citizens generally were prepared to have their places of business pillaged. A little before six o'clock on Saturday morning, having heard some shells whizzing through the town, I went out to my front stoop, and was there joined by a neighbor. In about half an hour thereafter, or less time, perhaps, two men emerged from an alley next to my house, when Mrs. Aughinbaugh, another neighbor, who was standing by, thinking them citizens, asked if they were fleeing. Their answer was an oath and a coarse laugh. I remarked, 'Those are rebels.' At this moment I heard the clanking of arms, and looking westward, saw a body of mounted infantry and cavalry marching into town. As near as I can judge, there were between four and five hundred men. I then went to an upper chamber of my house for the purpose of securing some valuable papers, and while so engaged, I heard the rebels say as they passed, that they were going to burn the town. At seven and a-half o'clock, I looked out and saw a new three story building opposite in flames. Several men approached, and I heard one tell Mrs. Aughinbaugh to get out of the way as they were going to fire her house. Her prayers and entreaties for time to collect a few articles of clothing, were of no avail. With my daughter, who had got a change of apparel, I started out the back way, and conducted her to a place of safety on a hill, from which position I distinctly saw the rebels dashing in a fiendish manner through the streets and firing the houses. Women with children, each carrying little packages of clothing, were fleeing in every direction. The sight was fearful, and the horrible scene chilled my blood. The day was clear and calm, but the burning houses created a draught, and the roar was prodigious. Pickets were stationed at the street corners to prevent the people from even attempting to save their property. From intimations that we had of their approach the night previous, it was deemed prudent to remove all the records from the county Court House, and the books and money from the bank. I passed through the picket line unmolested, though many citizens were driven back. Had no conversation with any of the crowd. Finding that I could not save any of the burning property, I returned to the hill, and remained there until the rebels left. The citizens would willingly have joined in defending the place, but we had no arms and no leader, and moreover felt that it would, unless aided by some organized body, have been uselessly sacrificing ourselves to have gone out against this band of cut-throats, thieves and incendiaries. We were informed that the main force of the rebels, two thousand five hundred strong, were drawn up in line of battle on one of the hills beyond the town ready for any emergency. In my opinion the demand for money was a mere pretext. I believe they intended destroying the town in the outset."

The statement of Dr. Richards is as follows:—"Soon after the rebels had entered the town, I was standing outside of my door, when Mr. Douglas came up and said that he had just seen McCausland, who told him to call some of the prominent citizens of the town together. He demanded five hundred thousand dollars in greenbacks, or one hundred thousand dollars in coin, and said if it was not paid, he would burn the place. I was perfectly indignant at such a demand, and said I would not give a cent if they sacked and burned my property. Mr. Douglas remarked:—'They'll put the thumb-screws to us, doctor. McCausland is in earnest, for I saw it in his face.' I paid no more attention to the matter, but set out to see my patients. Between seven and eight o'clock I met Mr. Thomas B. Kennedy, and while talking with him was arrested. They also arrested J. McDowell Sharpe, William H. McDowell, William McLellan and Mr. Kennedy. At this moment Harry Gilmore rode up and said : 'Gentlemen, you are my prisoners, and I shall take you to Libby Prison, as you have made no response to the call for five hundred thousand dollars levied by General Early.' He then called for a guard to conduct us to the Court House. Knowing him by sight, I said, 'Gilmore, I wish you to understand that we are gentlemen, and that our word is as good as your guards. We will go with you without a guard.' He said he supposed it was, but a guard was customary. We accompanied him to the Court House and there he was joined by McCausland, who repeated the order of Early, demanding five hundred thousand dollars in greenbacks, or one hundred thousand dollars in coin. Some of the citizens had previously, I understood, asked to see the order, when McCausland read it, and also another order to burn the town. I did not see them or hear them read. After a short parley between McCausland and Gilmore, the latter said,' Gentlemen, you are released.' Walking up to him I put my hand on his horse's mane, and said, 'Gilmore, you know that your demand for money is ridiculous nonsense. The county alone could not pay it, let alone the town.' Straightening himself up in his saddle, he said, with an ostentatious air,'I'll tell you what it is; we came out of our regular route with the sole purpose of burning your —— town in retaliation for what Hunter did in the Shenandoah Valley.' He then galloped off and superintended the firing of the Court House and bank. My daughter escaped with only one change of clothing, and I saved only what I had on my back. Everybody in the place would have gladly joined in resisting the rebels, but we could have done nothing against such an armed band of cut-throats and thieves. The county had been so literally drained of young men that women and children had to go into the fields. We had no arms, and even if we had, we would have been indiscriminately slaughtered, and our families left to the mercy of the brutal horde.

"The town was fired in at least fifty places, and it is my belief that they designed burning the place whether or not the demand for the money was complied with. I never before saw men act with such fiendishness, and gloat on the misfortunes of the women and children rendered houseless and homeless by their vandalism. The entire scene was the most horrible I ever witnessed. The screams of the women and children, the yells of the drunken soldiers and the roaring and crackling of the burning buildings were terrible. In many instances women were compelled to throw down small bundles containing only clothing, and several of these packages I saw the rebels toss into the flames, swearing that nothing should be taken away."

Col. A. K. McClure, in the *Franklin Repository*, of Aug. 24th, 1864, relates the following:

"The main part of the town was enveloped in flames in ten minutes. No time was given to remove women or children, or sick, or even the dead. No notice of the kind was communicated to any one; but like infuriated fiends from hell itself the work of destruction was commenced. They did not have anything to learn in their hurried tirade—they proved experts in their calling. They divided into squads and fired every other house, and often every house, if they presented any prospect of plunder. They would burst in the door with iron bars or heavy plank, smash up any furniture with an axe, throw fluid or oil upon it, and ply the match. They almost invariably entered every room of each house, rifled the drawers of every bureau, appropriated money, jewelry, watches and any other valuables, and often would present pistols to the heads of inmates, men and women, and demand money or their lives. In nearly half the instances they demanded owners to ransom their property, and in a few cases it was done and the property burned. The main object of the men seemed to be plunder. Not a house escaped rifling—all were plundered of anything that could be carried away. In most cases houses were entered in the rudest manner, and no time whatever allowed even for the families to escape, much less to save anything. Many families had the utmost difficulty to get themselves and children out in time, and not one-half had so much as a change of clothing with them. They would rush from story to story to rob, and always fire the building at once in order to keep the family from detecting their robberies. Feeble and helpless women and children were treated like brutes—told insolently to get out or burn; and even the sick were not spared. Several invalids had to be carried out as the red flames licked their couches. Thus the work of desolation continued for two hours; more than half the town was on fire at once, and the wild glare of the flames, the shrieks of women and children, and often louder than all the blasphemy of the rebels, conspired to present such a scene of horror as has never been witnessed by the present generation. No one was spared save by accident. The widow and the fatherless cried and plead in vain that they would be homeless and helpless. A rude oath would close all hope of mercy, and they would fly to save their lives. The old and infirm who tottered before them were thrust aside, and the torch applied in their presence to hasten their departure. So thoroughly were all of them master of the trade of destruction that there is scarcely a house standing in Chambersburg to-day that they attempted to burn, although their stay did not exceed two hours. In that brief period, the major portion of Chambersburg—its chief wealth and business, its capital and elegance—were devoured by a barbarous foe; three millions of property sacrificed; three thousand human beings homeless and many penniless; and all without so much as a pretense that the citizens of the doomed village, or any of them, had violated any accepted rule of civilized warfare. Such is the deliberate, voluntary record made by Gen. Early, a corps commander in the insurgent army. The Government may not take summary vengeance, although it has abundant power to do so; but there is one whose voice is most terrible in wrath, who has declared, 'Vengeance is mine; I will repay.'"

Rev. Joseph Clark in an article contributed to the *Presbyterian* of Aug. 6th, 1864, says:

"The burning was executed in the most ruthless and unrelenting manner. A squad of men would approach a house, break open the door, proceed to the most convenient part of the house and kindle a fire, with no other notice to the inmates, except to get out of it as soon as they could. In many cases, five, ten, fifteen minutes, were asked to secure some clothing, which *were refused*. Many families escaped with only the clothing they had on, and such as they could gather up in their haste. In many cases they were *not allowed to take these*, but were threatened with instant death if they did not cast them away and flee. Sick and aged people had to be carried to the fields. The corpses of one or two persons who had recently died, were hastily interred in the gardens, and children, separated from their parents, ran wildly screaming through the streets. Those whose stupor, or eagerness to save something, detained them, emerged with difficulty from the streets filled with the sheeted flames of their burning homes. I should say here, that no provocation had been given; not a shot was fired on them in entering the town, and not until the full crisis was reached, did desperation, in a few instances, lead to desperate acts, and a few of the incendiaries left their bones to smoulder in the ruins.

"As to the result, I may say that the entire heart or body of the town is burned. Not a house or building of any kind is left on a space of about an average of ten squares of streets, extending each way from the centre, with some four or five exceptions, where the buildings were isolated. Only the outskirts are left. The Court House, Bank, Town Hall, German Reformed Printing Establishment, every store and hotel in the town, and every mill and factory in the space indicated, and two churches, were consumed. Between three and four hundred dwellings were burned, leaving at least twenty-five hundred persons without a home or a hearth. In value, three-fourths of the town was destroyed. The scene of desolation must be seen to be appreciated. Crumbling walls, stacks of chimneys, and smoking embers, are all that remain of once elegant and happy homes. As to the scene itself, it beggars description. My own residence being on the outskirts, and feeling it the call of duty to be with my family, I could only look on from without. The day was sultry and calm, not a breath stirring, and each column of smoke rose black, straight and single; first one, and then another, and another, and another, until the columns blended and commingled; and then one vast and lurid column of smoke and flame rose perpendicular to the sky, and spread out into a vast crown, like a cloud of sackcloth hanging over the doomed city; whilst the roar and the surging, the crackling and the crash of falling timbers and walls broke upon the still air with a fearful dissonance, and the screams and sounds of agony of burning animals, hogs and cows and horses, made the welkin horrid with the sounds of woe. It was a scene to be witnessed and heard once in a lifetime."

Rev. S. J. Nicolls, at that time pastor of the Falling Spring Presbyterian church at this place, contributed a graphic description of the great event to the Pittsburg *Evening Chronicle*, from which I quote as follows: "As McCausland released the citizens he had arrested, the smoke was rising from the doomed town, and most of them reached their homes to find them in flames. The scene that speedily followed is indescribable in its horrors. The soldiers went from house to house, bursting open the doors with planks and axes, and entering, split up the furniture to kindle the fire, or else scattered combustible materials in the closets and along the stairways, and then applied the torch. In a little over half an hour the whole town was fired, so complete were the arrangements to accomplish their hellish designs. No time was given the inhabitants to save anything. The first warning of danger most of them had was the kindling of the fire in their houses, and even the few articles that some caught up in their flight, were seized by the soldiers and flung back into the flames. Many such instances have come to the writer's knowledge, that in their dark malignity almost surpass belief. The aged, the sick, the dying and the dead were carried out from their burning homes; mothers with their babes in their arms, and surrounded by the frightened little ones, fled through the streets jeered and taunted by the brutal soldiery. Indeed their escape seemed almost a miracle, as the streets were in a blaze from one end to the other, and they were compelled to flee through a long road of fire. Had not the day been perfectly calm (not a strong breeze prevailing, as some correspondents have stated), many must have perished in the flames. The conflagration in its height was a scene of surpassing grandeur and terror. A tall, black column of smoke rose up to the very skies; around it were wrapped long streamers of flames, writhing and twisting themselves into a thousand fantastic shapes, while through it, as though they were prayers carried heavenward by the incense of some great altar sacrifice, there went upon the smoky flame-riven clouds the cries and shrieks of the women and children. But the moment of greatest alarm was not reached until some of the more humane of the rebel officers warned the women to flee if they wished to escape violence to their persons. We cannot, in this letter, describe the scenes of the sad flight which followed.

"The ferocity of the rebel soldiers during this affair seems almost incredible. With all their fierce passions unrestrained, they seemed to revel, as if intoxicated, in the work of destruction. After firing the houses, they robbed all who fell into their hands. An aged elder of the Presbyterian church (Mr. Holmes Crawford,) was taken from his house and robbed; the building was fired while his wife, aged and infirm, was still in it. Upon his return, it was with the utmost difficulty she was saved. Escape by the street was impossible, and they were compelled to flee to a little garden in the rear of the house, where they sat for hours, surrounded by fire. The rebel Gilmore forbade a lady to remove her trunks from her house, and upon her telling him to his face what she thought of his conduct, he drew his pistol and declared 'he would blow out her brains if she did not take that back.' Many such instances, and worse might be recited. There were, indeed, some among them who acted humanly, refusing to do the work assigned them, but they were exceptions.— As soon as the town was thoroughly fired the rebels fell back. On their way out they burned the residence of the County Superintendent of Public Schools, because, as they told the family, 'he had taught negroes.'

"Such is the story of the burning of Chambersburg. These outlines, however form a poor picture of the reality. The blackend ruins of this once beautiful town must first be seen to I before the calamity can be understood, and not then, for it is only by looking at it in detail, by understanding the peculiar sadness there is in each separate loss, and seeing the strange diversity of sorrow there is in this common woe, that one can realize the full extent of the ruin. Eleven squares of blackened ruins and over three millions of dollars in property consumed is the outward estimate of the loss. But who can write the history of two thousand people suddenly made homeless, dashed from affluence to poverty, torn violently from the sacred association of the past, and driven forth homeless wanderers among strangers?"

Many deeply interesting and touching incidents which occurred in various places throughout the town might be narrated, but I have room but for a few. Some of these I copy from Dr. B. S. Schneck's *Burning of Chambersburg*, from which I have taken some of the statements already given. The house of Mr. James Watson, an old and feeble man of over eighty years, was entered, and because his wife earnestly remonstrated against the burning, they fired the room, hurled her into it and locked the door on the outside. Her daughters rescued her by bursting in the door before her clothes took fire. Mrs. Conner, the widow of a Union soldier, who had no means of support, got on her knees and begged them save her and her little ones from the fury of rebel wrath; but while she was thus pleading for mercy, they fired her little home, and stole ten dollars from her—the only money she had in the world. Mr. Wolfkill, a very aged citizen, and prostrated by sickness, so that he was utterly unable to be out of bed, plend in vain to be spared a horrible death in the flames of his own house; but they laughed at his terror and fired the building. Through the superhuman efforts of some friends he was carried away safely. Mrs. Lindsay, a very feeble lady of nearly eighty, fainted when they fired her house, and was left by the fiends to be devoured in the flames; but fortunately a relative reached the house in time, and lifting her in a buggy pulled her away while the flames were kissing each other over their heads in the street. Mrs. Kuss, the wife of the jeweler on Main Street, lay dead; and although the rebels were shown the dead body, they plied the torch and burned the house. Mrs. Shryock was there with Mrs. Kuss' dying babe in her arms, and plead for the sake of the dead mother and dying child to spare that house, but it was unavailing. The body of Mrs. Kuss was buried in the garden, and the next day it was taken up and interred in the Catholic graveyard. When the flames drove Mrs.

Shryock out with the child, she went to one of the men and presenting the dying babe, said: "Is this revenge sweet?" A tender chord was touched, and without speaking a word he burst into tears. He afterwards followed Mrs. Shryock, and asked her whether he could do anything for her; but it was then too late. The babe had died and it shared its mother's sepulchre. Mrs. Louis A. Shoemaker rushed up stairs when her house was fired, and returned with some silver spoons in her hand. She found the rebels quareling over a valuable breast pin of hers, several claiming it by right of discovery. The dispute was ended by taking the spoons from her and dividing them among the squad. Mrs. Denig failing to leave her house in the Diamond in time, and finding all escape cut off but in one direction, vainly tried to cross an iron fence in that direction, and was compelled to remain in her garden for several hours because the fence was too hot. She saved herself from destruction by covering herself with a blanket, which she occasionally dipped into a cistern to keep it wet. Mr. Holmes Crawford was taken into an alley while his house was burning, and his pockets rifled. All he had about him was appropriated. Father Cullen, Catholic priest, was robbed of his watch. He was sitting on his porch, and a party of rebels came along and peremptorily demanded his watch, which he was compelled to hand over. He had been robbed by Jenkin's men a year before. Rev. H. B. Winton, while fleeing with his wife and children was compelled to deliver his shoes and hat.

Soon after the work of destruction had commenced, a squad was detailed to burn the beautiful residence of Col. McClure. It stood nearly a mile from the centre of the town, and no other building was fired within half a mile of it. The squad was commanded by Capt. Smith, son of Gov. Smith of Virginia. Passing the residence of Mr. Eyster, he supposed he had reached the object of his vengeance, and he alighted and met Mr. Eyster at the door. "Col. McClure, I presume," said Capt. Smith. "No, sir; my name is Eyster," was the reply. "Where is McClure's house?" was the next interrogatory. As the property was evidently doomed, and in sight, Mr. Eyster could only answer that it was further out on the road. Capt. Smith found Mrs. McClure quite ill, having been confined to her bed for ten days previous.— He went right up into her room and informed her of the object of his visit. He stated that she should have ten minutes to get out of the house. He then ordered her to open her secretary, the house having already been fired, and proceeded to examine its contents. In this secretary was a letter writen by a rebel prisoner, invoking the blessing of heaven upon Mr. and Mrs. McClure for kindness shown to him when here with Lee's forces a year previously. Reading this letter Capt. Smith said, "This is awful to burn this house," and then went into other parts of the house and stole Mr. McClure's gold watch, a large silver pitcher, salver and two goblets, and other valuable articles. Mrs. McClure was compelled to arise from her sick bed, and with other occupants of the house, start on foot amidst the blazing heat of the sun to a place of safety. Capt. Smith, when riding back to town, and finding the silver pitcher and salver too unwieldy, and their possession under such circumstances not entirely in harmony with his pretentions to the usual Southern chivalry, stopped at the residence of Rev. James Kennedy, and handing them to Mr. Kennedy, said, "Please deliver these to Mrs. Col. McClure, with my compliments.— She presented them to me for acts of courtesy shown her." The two silver goblets belonging to this set he had strapped to his saddle; these, the gold watch, and other articles this sorry specimen of Southern nobility carried away with him. After receiving the pitcher and salver Mr. Kennedy entreated the captain to spare his house because of his being blind. This request was complied with, and as a protection against other parties who might come along, Capt. Smith wrote and left with Mr. Kennedy the following paper which he has framed and hanging up in his house, and which he has permitted me to copy:

CHAMBERSBURG, July 20th, 1864.
Rev. Jas. F. Kennedy's house is not to be burned—positively forbidden.
By order of Brig. Gen. McCausland.
F. W. SMITH,
A. A. D. C.

Col. Gilmore says on page 218 of his book that McCausland's men "were inclined to plunder." He might have added that the officers were not excepted from this charge, of which the paper drawn by Captain Smith, and kept hanging upon the wall of Dr. Kennedy's room is a perpetual evidence.

Various causes may be stated as to why certain portions of the town were spared. One reason was the fear of Averill. The rebels were aware that he was not far away, and might come upon them at any moment. Then after firing the heart of the town, their line of retreat from the eastern part would have been necessarily circuitous. I think, however, that the principal reason was because the officers in charge of squads sent to those parts which escaped, disapproved of this wanton destruction and, contrary to their orders, refused to perform the part assigned them. This will appear in the following facts. Dr. J. L. Suesserott, in McCauley's history of Franklin county, narrates the occurrences of that memorable day, which took place on the corner of Main and Washington streets, as follows:

"South Main Street on that eventful occasion presented a scene that can scarcely be depicted. The streets were crowded with carriages, and the houses with women and children who had been driven from their homes by the fiery element, which in lambent flames licking each other, had formed a scorching archway over the streets north of Washington street. The retreating mass, still unwilling to yield their household goods without a struggle, with defiance on their countenances, withdrew inch by inch, as would a well organized army before a relentless foe. When the refugees that had collected into my house were about to depart, satisfied that it too must fall before the flood of destruction, I, at the request of a sister now deceased, went to my desk to secure any valuable papers that might have been overlooked, and finding a travelling flask of whiskey, which had been placed there after a former flight to save my horses from the raiding rebels, and feeling that I might need some medicinal agent as I expected to have a large number of helpless women and children under my care, placed it in a side pocket, but it was scarcely there until it became a source of great anxiety to me, inasmuch as the rebels were appropriating the hats and handkerchiefs, and all other moveable effects of the citizens, and as my handkerchief covered the flask, I expected that if it were taken the flask would soon follow, and become the cause of much injury. By a little extra care, however, I was enabled to protect it until my attention was engrossed by a more weighty consideration. My surgical instruments, which had been placed in a secret cupboard behind the hall door, had been discovered by the rebels, who were then swarming in and out of the office and hall, and in their efforts to force the locks of the cases they had thrown them on the floor near the open door. Noticing an officer near the front on horseback, I accosted him as Colonel, and informed him that if called upon in the capacity of a surgeon I would be unable to render any service, as his men were disabling me. The officer ordered them to lay the instruments down and come out of the house. This order was hardly complied with, and the door closed, until he countermanded it, saying that the instruments would be useful to the Confederacy; and in their eagerness to receive them the men were about to break through the door, when I, with a dead-latch key, opened the same. They had scarcely begun to gather them up when they were again ordered to lay them down and come out, and instructions were given to close the door. I was then called to the side of the officer, who informed me that there were ten men with them who did not belong to the army who would save the balance of the town if $20,-000 were immediately forthcoming. I politely informed him that it was cruel to mock a crippled foe, and that he must know that he was demanding that which it was impossible to furnish. He then demanded $10,000, and then $5,000, and was informed that not five dollars would be paid. He then replied that it would all have to go.

A man without any military insignia was noticed near by, who during a great portion of the time that the rebels had been in the occupancy of the town, was seen to exert a great influence upon the men, was interrogated as to who the departing officer was, and he replied that he was Colonel Dunn. The flask that had caused so much anxiety was politely handed to him, with a request that he would share it with Colonel Dunn, and press the petition that the fire might be stopped. With great alacrity he started, but soon returned with a flat denial from Colonel Dunn. The whiskey had, however, made a fast friend out of the individual, who proved to be a John Callon, from Baltimore, an independent aid on General Johnston's staff. Colonel Dunn soon returned to the scene and was again importuned, but was as obstinate as ever. He advanced as far in a northward direction as the flames and heat would allow, and on being driven back by the same, said to me that we might now stop the fire if we could. The houses on the northeast and northwest corners of Main and Washington streets were a mass of flames, as well as all the northern portion of the town, as far as could be judged from the locality we were in, and the cornices and roofs of the houses on the opposite corners were smoking and ready to ignite when I hurried three of my neighbors—Miss Charlotte Oyster, William H. Mong and P. Dock Frey through the house to the garret with buckets of water, who, by unsurpassed agility and energy, quenched the already developing flames, and with the assistance of a friendly rebel, we got the only remaining fire engine to the scene of conflict. After the engine arrived, on two or three occasions, heartless rebels attempted to arrest its working, but they were quickly disposed of through the agency of the whiskey-bought friend, who, together with some other rebels, who were not entirely lost to all feelings of humanity, rendered valuable assistance at the engine until the report reached them of the advance of General Averill by way of New Franklin, four miles distant, when a hasty departure of the invading fiends was inaugurated."

Mr. H. E. Hoke furnishes the following statement of what occurred about the corner of Second and Queen streets, and the way the M. E. church, Market House and other property south and east thereof were saved. Mr. Hoke's statement is as follows:

"Late in the morning when the fire in other parts of the town was well under way, Rev. Mr. Barnhart, pastor of the M. E. church, and then living in the parsonage adjoining the Market House, noticed a rebel in the act of kindling a fire in the back part of that building. Going over at once he succeeded in extinguishing it with a bucket or two of water. The act of firing this building was repeated three times in the course of half an hour, and each time was put out by Mr. Barnhart. About 9 o'clock a rebel officer came there and ordered that firing at that point should be stopped. He declared with much earnestness that if another building in that neighborhood was fired that he would bring in his brigade and unite with the citizens and drive the incendiaries out. At this time the building on the southwest corner opposite the Market House, was burning, and the roof of the hotel on the northwest corner was taking fire. This officer then ordered that the fire engine, close by, should be brought out and the fire prevented from crossing to the other side of the street. He also called together a number of rebel soldiers, who were in the neighborhood, and ordered them to assist the citizens in working the engine. The large cistern under the pavement of the Market House furnished an abundance of water, and for about a half hour citizens and soldiers worked together to keep the fire from spreading. The rebels were then called away, and our force being weakened, we found it hard work to keep the engine going, but we worked on until some of the men had to lie down on the pavement, overcome by exertion and heat. It was only through the determined effort of a few persons that the fire was prevented from crossing the street to the M. E. church, Market House and other buildings. Water was poured upon the hotel until it ran in streams out of all the doors, but the roof burned slowly away and part of the upper story, when we succeeded in extinguishing it. Just before the officer named had ordered out the engine, several ladies came out of the parsonage carrying bundles of clothing, &c. A rebel soldier seeing this, inquired of them where they wanted those bundles taken? When informed that they only wanted them removed to a place of safety, he took them up before him on his horse, and carried them out Queen street near to the Point, and then delivered them to the ladies. This man gave his name to Rev. Mr. Barnhart. He said he was from Baltimore, and was opposed to such vandalism as their forces had been guilty of that day.

"After we had succeeded in extinguishing the fire at the hotel, we felt assured that it could not spread any further—about 10½ o'clock —I noticed that the house of S. M. Armstrong Esq., and those adjoining, were just taking fire. They evidently had not been fired by the rebels, but were catching at the roof from the heat of the burning buildings on the opposite side of the street. A small force of men could have saved these buildings, but that much needed force was not at hand."

That part of the town east of the railroad along Market street was saved in the following manner. An officer detailed to fire that part of the town called at the residence of William McLellan, Esq., and notified them that their house must be burned. This was after the heart of the town was in flames, and the roads were streaming with homeless women and children. Mrs. McLellan stepped to the door and laying one hand on the shoulder of the officer, and pointing with the other to the frantic fugitives passing by, and seated all around in adjoining yards, said to him: "Sir, is not your vengeance glutted? We have a home and can get another; but can you spare no homes for those poor, helpless people and their children? When you and I and all of us shall meet before the Great Judge, can you justify this act?" The officer made no reply, but ordered his command away, and that part of the town was saved.

The large brick house which stands on the northeast corner of Market and Franklin streets, at the time of the fire, occupied by the family of Mr. Samuel Radabaugh, was saved in the following manner: The wife of Mr. B. L. Maurer was at that time quite ill and confined to her room in the house. Mr. Maurer stated this fact to a Confederate officer, who at once placed a guard at the house and prevented it from being fired. Standing somewhat isolated from other buildings, it was not burned.

Colonel F. S. Stumbaugh, who resided on Second street, between Market and King, was arrested near his home early in the morning, and with a pistol presented to his head, ordered to procure some whiskey. He refused, for the good reason that he had none and could get none. He was released, but afterwards re-arrested by another squad, the officer naming him, and was insulted in every possible way. He informed the officer that he had been in the service, and that if General Battles was present, they would not dare to insult him. When asked why, he answered, "I captured him at Shiloh and treated him like a soldier." A rebel major present, who had been under General Battles, upon inquiry, was satisfied that Colonel Stumbaugh's statement was correct, ordered his prompt release, and withdrew the entire rebel force from that part of Second street, and no buildings were burned there.

Dr. Schneck, in his *Burning of Chambersburg*, relates a few additional instances of humanity upon the part of some of the rebels, which deserve a place here. "Surgeon Budd was conversing with several citizens when the demand for tribute was made, and he assured all present that the rebel commander would not execute his threat. In the midst of his assurances, the flames burst forth almost simultaneously in every part of the town. When he saw the fire break out, he wept like a child, and publicly denounced the atrocities of his commander. He took no part in it whatever, save to aid some unfortunate ones in escaping from the flames.

Captain Baxter, formerly of Baltimore, peremptorily refused to participate in the burning, but aided many people to get some clothing and other articles out of their houses. He asked a citizen as a special favor to write to his friends in Baltimore and acquit him of the hellish work.

Surgeon Richardson, another Baltimorian, gave his horse to a lady to get some articles out of the burning town, and publicly deplored the sad work of McCausland. When asked who his commanding officer was, he answered, 'Madam, I am ashamed to say that General McCausland is my commander.'

Captain Watts manfully saved all Second street south of Queen, and with his command aided to arrest the flames. He said that he would lose his commission rather than burn out defenseless people.

One whole company was kept by its captain—name unknown—from burning and pillaging, and the southeastern portion of Chambersburg stands solely because an officer detailed there kept his men employed in aiding people."

An officer rode up to the United Brethren parsonage, in Washington street, and thus addressed Mrs. Dickson—her husband being absent: "Madam, save what you can; in fifteen minutes I will return and fire your house." He did not return.

After the rebels had left, the following note was received by Rev. S. J. Niccolls of this place. It was written with a pencil upon an envelope:

REV. MR. NICCOLLS:—Please to write to my father and give him my love. Tell him, too, as Mrs. Shoemaker will tell you, that I was most strenuously opposed to the burning of the town.
B. B. BLAIR,
Chaplain, and son of Thos. P. Blair, Shippensburg, Pa.

Many incidents of an interesting character, in addition to those already given, might be narrated, but I will only add a few: Among the hospitals in our town during the period of the war, was one in the building on the southeast corner of Main and German streets. The evening before the destruction of the town a considerable amount of government stores were in that building. These the steward and surgeon in charge turned out into the street, and desired the quartermaster to take charge of them. As these articles were all packed in boxes, and their contents unknown to that official, he refused to receive them. Seeing these valuable stores thus left to be appropriated or destroyed by the coming enemy, simply because of the *red tape* which was in the way, Mrs. Margaret Merklein, who resided on the opposite corner, had the boxes rolled into her cellar, where, her house not being burned nor searched, they were preserved. The government subsequently rewarded her in a considerable sum as salvage.

On the evening before the town was burned, and while the straggling soldiers of General Hunter's command were passing through, some of the family of Mr. B. F. Nead, who resided then and now on East Market street, were sitting on their door step. An officer of the Federal army rode up and called for one of the ladies and told her that there was every probability that there would be a fight between our troops and the enemy, and that he had a favor to ask. He said he was the possessor of a very handsome sword that had been presented to him, which he valued very highly, and that he would be under many obligations to them if they would keep it safe for him. He said his name was Lieutenant McCron, according to the present recollection of the lady who participated in the affair. The sword and scabbard were very handsome, being silver mounted, and very beautifully chased. The next day the house of Mr. Nead shared in the general conflagration, and the incident was forgotten. Sometime after the fire, Mr. Benjamin M. Nead, in hunting through the ruins in the cellar, came across the sword and part of the scabbard, fire-wrecked, but still showing the tracing of the etching on the blade. Nothing was ever heard of Liutenant McCron, but the sword still remains in the possession of Mr. Nead's family.

On the morning of the fire, Mr. David Brand, brother to our townsman, Mr. Jacob L. Brand, took the flag which hung in front of Col. Rutherford's headquarters in the Mansion House, from its staff and carried it to his home on Queen street. While the rebels were firing Queen street, Miss Louisa Brand, his sister, took the flag, and wrapping it around her, and with revolver in hand, stood in the front door of their house and dared any rebel to fire the house or disturb the flag. She passed unmolested and the house was not burned. That flag is now in the possession of the wife of Mr. A. C. McGrath, to whom Miss Brand presented it before her death.

Mr. Jacob L. Brand, relates the following: "I had in my store twenty kegs of powder. I did not know what to do with it. I fell upon the following plan: I had Mr. George Palmer clerking for me, and I had him make an excavation in my garden large and deep enough to set the kegs in upon their ends and cover them with boards and then earth thrown over. There were a large number of old boxes and barrels which we piled upon this so that no one would detect it. When the fire reached these I was expecting any moment for an explosion and got out of the way, taking my wife and child and passed up by the M. E. church. When I was on the way I was ordered to take off my boots, and hesitating for a few moments, the rebel said that if I did not take them off he would do it for me. I had $125 tied around me, and I thought I had better comply as I might be in danger of losing my money as well as my boots. I had just pulled them off and the rebel tried them on, but they were too small for him, when the Baptist preacher in town passed, and he was ordered to take off his. I took advantage of this, and picking up my boots, made my way out of the town in my stocking feet. I had no desire to wait to see the matter consummated between the rebel and the preacher. We struck out for the eastern part of the town. The next day we examined the powder we had hid, and thinking all danger past, we raised the boards and found all right. But coals of fire had passed down through the crevices and knot holes in the boards, and we could see where the fire had burnt a quarter of an inch into the heads of some of the kegs."

Upon the release of the citizens who had been captured and taken in front of the Court House by Col. Gilmore, to bear from McCausland the requisition upon the town, Mr. M. A. Foltz and Mr. E. G. Etter started out east Market street to their respective homes. When they reached the alley by Mr. D. O. Gehr's residence, Mr. Etter proposed to take that way in preference to the street as being safer because of the swarming rebels who were in it. Mr. Foltz assured him that they would be safer in the street, and pressed on that way, but Etter took the alley. When he reached his home his wardrobe had been reduced to his pantaloons and shirt, which some rebel who had met him on the way considerately permitted him to retain. This was the penalty for being one of the "leading citizens," for such General McCausland ordered Col. Gilmore to bring before him. Mr. Etter says that however he may have filled the bill when captured and taken to the Diamond, his appearance after his interview with the rebel in the alley did not specially indicate superior rank.

An incident occurred on South Main street, somewhere between Washington and German streets, which, while illustrating the humanity of one of the foe, also shows into what an unpleasant position one of our citizens was placed. Learning that a man lay with the small pox in one of the houses indicated, a rebel to whom the communication was made, fearing that that part of the town would be also fired and the sick man burned to death, went into the house, took him in his arms, bore him to the street and placed him carefully wrapped in bed clothing in a wheelbarrow, compelling a young man —Mr. P. O'Hare—who was passing by, to wheel him away to a place of safety. Mr. O'Hare reluctantly performed the duty assigned him, and reaching a place where he supposed the man was safe from the flames, he left him.

Mr. Lewis Wampler informed me that standing in the middle of the street, in front of his residence opposite the Reformed church, while the fire was raging, he could see clean down to the Diamond— nearly three squares. The flames from the houses on both sides of the street met and formed an archway. In and about the Diamond it seemed to converge and formed an immense column or dome. An hour or so after the rebels had left and the fire had subsided, I passed down Main street from Washington to the Diamond. The dust upon the street was all gone, and the stones above ground were burned white. The heat was so intense that I had to cover my face at times with my handkerchief and run.

There stand four houses on the west side of Main street, between Queen and Washington, which strangely escaped the general destruction. The inmates of these houses had means of escape which no others in other parts of the town had. They had but to pass out in the rear of their lots and take refuge in the Lutheran graveyard, where they would have been safe from the fire. Mr. A. V. Reineman informs me that hard work and the favorable wind, under the blessing of God, saved these houses. Rebels plundered his jewelry store, selecting the most showy, but the cheapest articles, leaving the fine and costly untouched. In some instances the cases containing expensive articles were taken, but the contents, which were of great value, were thrown out and left. A fancy clock in the form of a robust man, with the dial upon his stomach, kept in his show window as a sign, was carried away by a rebel, but after some time the repentant soldier brought it back and placed it where he had found it. Mr. Reineman assures me that he was impressed, divinely as he devoutly believes, that his property would not be destroyed, and his confidence was not disappointed.

Rev. S. R. Fisher, D. D., informed me that he determined to remain in his house and save it if he could. Having first explored the rear of his premises and finding that in case he were compelled to flee he could escape into the Lutheran graveyard, he accordingly carried a number of buckets of water up into the attic of his house, and watching through the trap door for any place where the shingles became ignited, immediately extinguished it and then retreated back under shelter to escape the bullets which were several times fired at him from a distance. His house was not burned.

Mr. John Jeffries relates that fire was

kindled in the telegraph office in the lower rooms of the Mansion House, then the printing establishment of the Reformed Church. Seeing this fire he ran in and kicked the blazing wood, which the rebels had split and piled upon the floor, out upon the front pavement. A rebel officer passing by caught him in the act, and led him up to General McCausland, who stood upon the corner where the lamp post stands in front of Messrs. Lortz & Wolfinger's grocery. McCausland said, "How dare you interfere to put out the fire?" To this Mr. Jeffries replied, "That, sir, is the printing establishment of the Reformed Church, and I was trying to save church property, and by all civilized people churches and church property are respected in time of war." Mr. Jeffries says he did not tell McCausland that his own property was next to the Mansion House, and that he had an eye to saving it as well as the other. To Mr. Jeffries' remark that that building was church property, McCausland replied, "Why, sir, that's a telegraph office and no printing establishment." After Mr. Jeffries succeeded in convincing the General that the property was really a publishing house of the Reformed Church, and that the telegraph office and other lower rooms were only rented to other persons, he gave permission to save it. It was, however, soon thereafter fired in the rear and entirely consumed entailing a loss upon that church of about $40,000.

Dr. Schneck in his book relates the following: "A lady well known to me, the mother of a large family of children, was ordered to leave the house in five minutes, as it must be burned. She collected her children around her to obey the cruel summons. Preparations were at once made to fire the building in the rooms above and below, and as the family group walked out of the large and beautiful mansion, the children burst into weeping. 'I am ashamed of you,' said the tenderly loving, yet heroic woman, 'to let these men see you cry,' and every child straightened up, brushed away his tears, and bravely marched out of the doomed house."

"An elderly woman, of true Spartan grit, gave one of the house burners such a sound drubbing with a heavy broom, that the invader retreated, to leave the work of destruction to be performed by another party, after the woman had left to escape the approaching flames of adjoining buildings.

"The wife of a clergyman succeeded in preventing one of the enemy from firing her house by reminding him that she had fed him during Stuart's raid in 1862, and that she had also ministered to him when he was in the hospital in this place in the summer of 1863. The man recognized her and frankly declared that he could not be so base as to destroy her house, now that he remembered her kind offices. He had been wounded and made a prisoner at the battle of Gettysburg, was brought to the hospital here and afterwards exchanged."

Those familiar with the town will remember a two story log house which stood on West Market street, between Miller's Hotel and the residence of Hon. G. W. Brewer, and which was torn away a year or two ago when the new street was cut through from Market to King. This house, it will be remembered, notwithstanding the inflammable nature of the material of which it was constructed, and the fact that every other building around it was consumed, strangely escaped. The fact itself excited considerable surprise, and many have been the causes assigned. There is a secret fact in the case which has never, so far as I am aware, been made public. That fact, with the papers relating thereto, has been laid before me by the relatives of the owners and occupants at that time, and I place them upon record here, leaving others to account for the phenomena as they can. The late Dr. Boyle frequently related that the two aged ladies who occupied that little log house at the time of the fire—Mrs. Elizabeth Smith and Lydia Etter—sisters of our former townsman, Mr. Samuel Etter, with others found their way to the field in which Reservoir hill stands, from which eminence the assembled multitude looked upon the burning of their homes. The spectacle, as may be readily imagined, was a sad one to all, but apparently less so to the two persons named. After the retreat of the rebels and partial subsidance of the flames, Dr. Boyle remarked that he would go into the town and learn the extent of the ruins. Mrs. Smith insisted upon going with him to see her house. To this the doctor objected most strenuously saying that of course her house was destroyed with the rest. "No," said she, "it can't be." The old lady consented to remain yet awhile on the hill, only on the promise of the doctor that he would be sure to go into her house and see if everything was right. Scarcely giving the matter another thought, he proceeded to town and went down West Market street amidst the yet smouldering ruins, when to his surprise and gratification there stood the little log building intact. The fences all around were clean burned up close to the house, but it was unharmed. On entering it nothing appeared to have been disturbed. Ascending the stairs to the garret, several quilts were strung on a line. These showed the marks of having been fired, and that was all. The source of the abiding confidence of these two old ladies that their home was not and could not be destroyed, was perhaps never known to Dr. Boyle, and is known to only a few to whom it was afterwards communicated. They had in their possession a paper or document on which were printed certain words, which they believed was a sure preventative against fire, and the little building, as long as it stood afterwards, was a monument to their belief. The paper itself is now before me. It is printed in German, upon coarse, heavy paper, and bears the marks of considerable age. Before me is also a translation made by, and in the handwriting of Rev. B. S. Schneck, D. D., who was long and intimately acquainted with the two old ladies and who had been let into the secret of their confidence. The doctor made the translation, but so far as I know, never gave an opinion as to the merits of the case:

(*Translation.*)

A TRUE AND TRIED ART WHICH MAY BE SUCCESSFULLY USED IN TIMES OF FIRE AND PESTILENCE.

This was discovered by a Christian Gipsy King of Egypt. In the year 1714, June 16th, there were executed six Gipsies in the Kingdom of Prussia. But the seventh, a man 80 years old, was to be executed with the sword on the 16th day of June. Fortunately for him, however, a fire broke out suddenly, and the old Gipsy was released and taken to the fire, to try his art, which he did to the astonishment of all, as the fire was extinguished in half a quarter of an hour, upon which, after having thus given such satisfactory proof, his life was spared and was set free. This was also adjudged to be so by the Royal Prussian Government and the General Superintendent at Koenigsburg, and made public in print. First printed in Konigsburg, in Prussia, by Alexander Bauman, in 1715.

"Welcome, thou fiery Guest, grasp no further than thou hast. This do I count for your penitence, O fire, in the name of the Father, the Son, and the Holy Ghost.

I command thee, fire, by God's power, which maketh all things, that thou halt and proceed no further, so sure as Christ stood at the Jordan, when John the holy man baptized him. This I reckon to your penitence, O fire, in the name of the holy Trinity.

I command thee, Fire, by the power of God, that thou allayest thy flame, as sure as Mary of all women maintained her Virginity—therefore restrain thy fury, O fire, in the name of the most Holy Trinity.

I command thee, Fire, that thou wilt abate thy heat, by the precious blood of Jesus Christ, which He shed for us, for our sin and misery. This I lay to your penitence, O fire, in the name of the Father, Son and Holy Ghost.

Jesus of Nazareth, a King of the Jews, help us in this terrible fire calamity, and spare these bounds and borders from all disease and pestilence.

"Whoever has this paper in his house, will not suffer from fire, nor from damage by lightning; and whoever has this paper in his house, or carries it with him, is safe from the fearful Pestilence."

It is, at least, a singular coincidence that in another case, which has been brought to my knowledge, another property as much exposed and inflammable as the one already referred to, was saved and stands to-day to the amazement of all who are familiar with it, and that, too, in connection with another paper on which were written the following words from Isaiah XLIII, 2—"When thou passeth through the waters, I will be with thee: and through the rivers, they shall not overflow thee: when thou walkest through the fire, thou shalt not be burned; neither shalt the flame kindle upon thee." I give these circumstances as evidences of the credulity, or as some might say, the faith of the persons, leaving each one to form his own conclusion.

When the town was fired and the people compelled to leave, some found shelter in those parts upon the outskirts which were not burned. The large majority fled to the Cemetery and fields around town, where they sat and looked upon the awful scene. Nearly every one had a bundle or some article which they had saved from their burning home, and which they kept watch over. In carrying trunks, bundles and articles of furniture through the streets to places of safety, feats of strength and endurance were wrought which seemed almost superhuman. Feeble women carried articles which, under ordinary circumstances, they could scarcely have lifted. Some climed fences, and in some way unknown to themselves or others, took with them these heavy articles. I saw myself a woman carry and drag a melodeon from her house, and upon placing it were for the time it was supposed to be safe, she left it and in a short time came dragging a heavy parlor carpet.

It has been said by some of the writers from whom I have quoted, that the women and children wept and cried and wrung their hands in anguish. Some did exhibit considerable emotion and excitement, but taking into consideration the awful circumstances under which we were placed, and the fact that many had been in a few hours reduced from affluence to poverty, not having either home or food or a change of clothing, the courage, coolness, resignation, and even cheerfulness, and in some cases, the mirthfulness, were indeed extraordinary. Two young men who were passing a yard where a considerable number of homeless ones were congregated while the fire was in progress, addressing several of their comrades whom they saw in the number, said, "Hello there! Where do you fellows get your clean shirts now?" This witticism drew a laugh from the whole crowd, and was shared in by many women and children who did not know where their next meal was to come from, or where they would lay their heads that night. This cheerfulness was characteristic of the people throughout the entire period from the burning until they were enabled as best they could to recommence the world and reconstruct their homes. Sitting down in despair, or yielding to circumstances, and suffering the tidal wave to overwhelm and paralize, were entirely unthought of. Rev. Dr. Schneck, in the *Burning of Chambersburg*, pages 34—36, records the heroism of our people in the following language: "During the whole course of my life, I have not witnessed such an absence of despondent feeling under great trials and sudden reverses of earthly fortune, never such buoyancy and vigor of soul, and even of cheerfulness amid accumulated woes and sorrows, as I have during these four weeks of our devastation. And I leave you (the reader) to imagine the many cases of extreme revulsion from independence and affluence to utter helplessness and want. The widow and fatherless, the aged and infirm, suddenly bereft of their earthly all, in many instances, even of a change of clothing. Large and valuable libraries, manuscripts, the accumulation of many years, statuary, paintings, precious and never to be replaced mementoes, more valued than gold or silver, gone forever. And yet amid all these losses and the consequent self-denial and adaptation to another and entirely different state of things, to which the great majority of the people have been subjected, you seldom see a sad or sombre countenance on the street or elsewhere. Exceptions there were, doubtless, traceable in part to feeble, physical constitution, in part also to an inordinate love of and dependence upon transitory and evanescent objects. But in a general way, the sufferers by this wholesale devastation, are among the most patient, unmurmuring, cheerful, hopeful people I have ever known. God seems to have given special grace in a special time of need. * * * I freely confess that I have never experienced in my own case, nor in the case of others, even under comparatively light and trifling losses and deprivations, such resignation, such quiet, gentle submission, and such calm endurance, amid the loss of all things, as in this instance. To such an extent have been these manifestations, that persons from neighboring towns, and strangers from a distance, who in great numbers have visited the place, almost universally remark upon it."

When the fire was over the people who had taken refuge in the cemetery and fields around the town, came back to view the remains of their ruined houses. Sad indeed were our feelings when we stood by the scene of desolation, recognizing here and there amidst the ruins some article, as the crooked and warped stoves and cooking utensils and other articles made of iron, which reminded us of the past. But when night came on and a place of shelter was needed, then only did we realize our sad condition. Such buildings as had escaped the common destruction were opened to us and occupied to their utmost capacity. Some of our people made their way on foot to the country, or to neighboring towns. And during the ensuing week hundreds availed themselves of the free transportation given by the railroad companies, and went to distant places, from which some never again permanently returned.

On the day succeeding the fire—Sunday 31st—a number of our citizens convened at the residence of William McLellan, Esq., on East Market street. Rev. John R. Warner, who was present, conducted a religious service, after which the following appeal was drawn up, signed and telegraphed over the country:

AN APPEAL TO THE BENEVOLENT CITIZENS OF THE NORTH.

On the morning of the 30th of July, 1864, the rebels under command of General McCausland, with a force of five hundred men, entered Chambersburg, Pennsylvania, and demanded five hundred thousand dollars from the citizens, under a threat of burning the town. This requisition was in writing and signed by General Jubal Early.

It is now established by indisputable proof that this demand was a mere pretext on the part of the marauders, to cover up a purpose, formed before they reached the town, to burn it the to ground without giving any time to remove the private property, and scarcely time enough for the citizens to remove their families.

They fired the houses of our citizens in perhaps fifty places. Upwards of two hundred and fifty in the heart of the town were consumed, including all the public buildings, stores and hotels, comprising about two-thirds of a town containing six thousand inhabitants. Thus a large body of citizens are reduced from comparative wealth to absolute poverty. These families have lost all their bedding, and all their clothing except what they had on their persons.

The loss will be largely over one million dollars. Without aid from abroad there will be great suffering in our community.

The Rev. John K. Warner, of Gettysburg, providentially with us at this time, is the accredited agent of the citizens for receiving subscriptions and contributions for our relief.
F. M. KIMMELL,
BERNARD WOLFF, and many others.

No sooner had this appeal been sent abroad and published, than some of the New York papers let loose their abuse upon us. The appeal stated that *five hundred rebels had entered and destroyed the town* without referring to the two thousand more, with six pieces of artillery, that were stationed upon the eminence west of the town. "What," said these editors, "a town of six thousand inhabitants, and the headquarters of a military district, and yet suffering five hundred rebels to burn them out! Why not rise up and drive the rascals away?" Thus while a large part of our able-bodied men were away in their country's service, leaving but a few hundred here, and they without arms, and discipline, and denied the use of the uniform and enrollment which would have secured to them treatment as prisoners of war, and not summary execution as guerrillas, we must not only be robbed and plundered and have our homes destroyed by the common foe, but endure the reproaches of our professed friends. And these reproaches, too, coming from a city, which, with its population of three quarters of a million, could not keep its own rabble in subjection, but had to call upon the general government for assistance, and was only saved from destruction and plunder by a detachment from the army of the Potomac at a time when these men were needed to fight rebels in their front. And here it is but right and proper to put upon record the fact that some of our people throughout the country suffered more from the emergency men sent here for our assistance, notably from volunteers from this same city which then derided and insulted us, than from the invading rebels. Were I to place upon record all the instances of plunder and spoliation by these trops sent me by sufferers throughout the county, it would, or should, cause these editors to blush with shame for their countrymen. A correspondent from Greencastle writes that they took chickens and whatever they could lay their thieving hands upon, saying that they had left their homes and come here and had driven the rebels out of the State, and they were determined to have whatever they wanted, but when the sound of cannonading was heard in the direction of Williamsport, it was with difficulty their officers could prevent them from falling back to Chambersburg.

But the appeal sent forth by our despoiled and suffering people was not treated everywhere as it was by a few of the New York newspapers. Early in the moring after the fire—Sunday 31st—people from all parts of the surrounding country and the neighboring towns, poured into Chambersburg. Many of these brought bread and other provisions. The entire population of the Cumberland Valley, even before the call of our citizens was issued, were moved by one common impulse to hasten to our relief. When the people congregated in their houses of worship for religious service, their pastors dismissed them and sent them home to gather and forward food to our suffering people. Bread and other provisions were gathered at various places along the railroad, and a special train sent from Harrisburg gathered up these much needed articles and brought them to our town. With that train on that memorable Sabbath, came large numbers of people from all points along the valley to see the ruins and to minister to our wants. These scattered all over the town and looked with astonishment upon the ruin wrought. Visitors to the town, drawn here by curiosity, or to look after friends and relatives, came in large numbers throughout the ensuing week, and loud and bitter were the denunciations of the rebels. The entire newspaper press of the country, secular and religious, with the exception of two or three of the papers of the city of New York, expressed their sympathy with our suffering people, and relief was sent from Philadelphia and other places. The immediate wants of the people were not only provided for, but provision had to be made for their assistance for the future. Provisions were not only needed, but clothing, hats, shoes and articles for housekeeping. These could only be had at exorbitant prices, and few had the means to purchase them. Muslin that can now be purchased for six and eight cents per yard, then cost sixty to seventy-five cents, and everything else in proportion. Considerable help in some of these things was sent from abroad, and housekeeping was recommenced by some on a greatly reduced scale from their former condition. Provisions were furnished daily for a week or two by the military commander of the district. The warehouse of Messrs. Wunderlich & Nead was used for the storage of these articles, and committees of our citizens who had not suffered by the destruction of the town were appointed to receive and issue these to the people. Families were supplied according to the number of persons comprising them, or the number of destitute they sheltered and fed. It was no unusual sight during these memorable days, to see some of our citizens who had previous to the fire lived in affluence, go day after day, basket in hand, to draw food for themselves and families, and many who were strangers to want before were then compelled to battle with poverty and begin the world anew. What little relief the government gave was quickly consumed by the exorbitant prices which prevailed, and hard struggling with penury marked the closing days of many whose previous life gave promise of ease and comfort. Many of the most aged of that day have gone to the grave, leaving their families to take up the bitter struggle they endured, and carry it on until the end of their days. The sad effects of the burning of Chambersburg shortened the days of many, and is yet being felt by widows and children.

On Friday succeeding the destruction of the town, August 5th, the culmination of the panics which had so frequently fallen upon us, was reached. During the intervening time since the fire, the rebels were reported to be hovering about the Potomac, threatening to return and complete the destruction of the town in retaliation for the killing of one or two of their number here on their retreat here and along the road. On that day the report was made that they were coming. The railroad company placed a large train of cars at the disposal of the people, and all who desired to go away were permitted to do so. Nearly every person whose residence was destroyed, not already gone, and many whose homes were yet intact, fled to the depot. Many carried what little they had saved in the general destruction, and placed it in cars prepared for the purpose. The people came bearing heavy burdens, panting under the heat of the day and trembling with excitement. The cars were packed with a mass of frightened humanity. Many could not get seats. At Carlisle and Mechanicsburg some got out and remained with friends. At Harrisburg they scattered, some went to Pittsburg and other places west, and others to Lancaster and Philadelphia and other places east. Large numbers tarried in Harrisburg not knowing where to go. It is said that that night Chambersburg people were laying down for much needed rest upon the floor of the depot at that place, and all about that building. Families were scattered abroad, and weeks intervened in many cases before they came together again. The panic of that day was without cause. The rebels did not make the dreaded raid; and the few houses which had escaped the conflagration formed the nucleus for the Chambersburg of to-day.

But the occurrences of what may be fitly called Chambersburg's "Black Friday," had their ludicrous as well as sombre hues, which should not be entirely overlooked. Mrs. Ellen McLellan relates that during the hurry and excitement on that day, when people were trying to conceal from the expected rebels all their valuables, which they could not take away with them in their flight, Mrs. Nixon came over to her house and said, "O, Mrs. McLellan, they say the rebels are coming back, and are not going to leave even a chicken coop; now if you have any things you want to hide, just bring them over to our house for we have a place to hide them where nobody would ever think of looking." Mrs. McLellan says she and her colored servant—a stout, heavy woman—gathered up their armsful of things and ran across to Mr. Nixon's with them and stored them away in the loft of a back building where Mrs. Nixon had already secreted a number of articles. The only entrance to this loft was by a trap door, and it was not floored. When the colored woman, who had been sent up through this trap door into the loft to place the articles, had gotten through and was hurriedly endeavoring to make her way down, her feet slipped and she sat down rather ungracefully on both sides of a joist, and with her ponderous feet brought down nearly the whole ceiling, leaving all their valuables exposed to view. They had only to laugh at the occurrence and flee, leaving the articles to the foe should he come.

Gradually the people regained their accustomed confidence, and began to return and prepare for the approaching winter. Places of business were hastily improvised. Private houses about the Market House and North Second street, which had escaped the flames, were turned into shops and stores. Sheds and temporary places of business were erected along Second street from Queen to King. The bank resumed business in the front room of the dwelling then occupied by Mr. D. K. Wunderlich, but now by Dr. McLanahan, on Second street, near Queen, and subsequently in the Masonic Hall. The Post Office was kept by Mr. J. W. Deal in his residence on Second street, adjoining the property of Mr. Christian Fuller. Families who once occupied a whole house to themselves, had to be content with two or three rooms, and many with less. But in a year or two buildings were erected in rapid succession. Mechanics from all parts gathered here, and all found ready employment. Wages and building material were high, and most of the buildings then erected were put up at great expense. Many persons who builded then involved themselves inextricably in debt, and others are reaping the benefits of their enterprise. But the Chambersburg of to-day, which arose from the ashes of the Chambersburg of the past, as is conceded by all, is the handsomest town of the Cumberland Valley. If it has its equal anywhere in any town of its size, east or west, I have never seen it.

The extent of destruction wrought by the burning of the town was as follows: Beginning at the Presbyterian lecture room on the north, the fire swept every building on the west side of Main street, but four, up to Washington street—four squares; from King street on the north side of Main, every building up to Washington—three squares; from the railroad on Third street to nearly the top of New England Hill—five squares—on both sides of the street, every building with a few exceptions; also a few buildings over the top of New England Hill; from the Market House down Queen street, both sides, to the Edge Tool Factory, and several buildings on Franklin street; also several buildings on Second street, between Market and Queen. In addition to these other buildings standing away from the line of the fire were destroyed. Among these were the residence of Col. McClure, the barn of Mr. J. Eby, and the house of Mr. McIlvain. The total number of buildings was 537. Of these 266 were residences and places of business, and 271 barns, stables and other outhouses of various kinds. As to the value of the real and personal property destroyed, the amounts received by our citizens, and also the question of who is responsible for the destruction of our town, I leave these for the ensuing chapter.

As previously stated, the rebels withdrew from our town about 11 o'clock. They proceeded westwardly by the Pittsburg pike, crossed the mountain into the Great Cove, and encamped over night at McConnellsburg. Averill's forces passed through town in pursuit about 2 P. M. They drove the enemy out of McConnellsburg on Sunday morning, pursuing them down the valley, and overtook them at Hancock just in time to save that town from destruction. McCausland had ordered a levy upon the place of $30,000 and in default of it he declared his intention to burn the town. Col. Gilmore, to whom I am indebted for this information, says that after consulting with General Bradley T. Johnston concerning this demand and threat, he brought into the town his command, and stationed two men at each house and store for their protection. But before the order to set fire to the town was issued Averill appeared and the rebels fled. (Four Years in the Saddle, page 213). Col. Gilmore details the marches of these villains until they reached Moorfield Valley, some time in August, where they were surprised one morning by Averill's men dashing in among them. The Federals slyly captured McCausland's pickets, and before the rebels were fairly aroused from their slumbers Averill's men were among them, cutting them down mercilessly to the cry of "*Remember Chambersburg!*" "*Remember Chambersburg!*" "*Surrender, you house-burning villains,*" and "*Kill every —— one of them!*" The vow made by these men as they rode through the Diamond and beheld the widespread ruin, was remembered and kept. Col. Gilmore admits, upon page 221 of his book, that McCausland's men were greatly demoralized and unfitted [for vigorous resistance "because of the amount of plunder they were allowed to carry." That plunder, which in part insured their ruin, was taken from our houses and stores. A chaplain of one of the regiments of Averill's command, a personal friend of the writer, informed me of the terrible retribution visited upon McCausland's command at Moorfield, and how regardless of the cry, "We surrender!" they were cut and shot down amid the cry of the Federal troopers, "*Chambersburg!*" "*Chambersburg!*" "*Chambersburg!!!*" He also said that nearly every rebel had either strapped to his saddle or somewhere about him a package or bundle, containing women's and children's clothing, stockings, caps, etc., while their pockets were filled with watches, jewelry and other articles of plunder.

Such was the burning of Chambersburg, so far as the history of that fearful event can be written. But there is another history of that event—a silent, secret, and unwritten record, which cannot ever be told, for each family and person had an experience which language can not portray. And it is with great reluctance that I now in conclusion reveal to my readers what occurred that never to be forgotten morning, in my own humble home—an event which a sense of duty, as well as gratitude to God, forbids me to withhold. On the morning of the fire, while the rebels were breaking open the doors of stores and shops, I was called to my breakfast, a neighbor offering to take my place and call me when the enemy approached our store. As has been my custom for many years, I read a portion of Scripture and knelt with my family in our morning prayer. Doubtless directed by the Holy Spirit, I opened at the 138th Psalm, and when I read the words: "*Though I walk in the midst of trouble, thou wilt revive me: thou shalt stretch forth thine hand against the wrath of mine enemies, and thy right hand shall save me.*" I was impressed with its extreme appropriateness. A fullness of meaning seemed to be in the words I had never seen before, and a strange and unaccountable, but very precious sense of relief, of strength, of support, stole into my heart, which stood by me throughout the terrible ordeal which followed. Desiring to remember the place I turned down the leaf, knelt in prayer, ate a hurried breakfast—the last meal in that dear place, and then in a short time, followed by my family, each one carrying some precious relic, we made our way through flame and smoke and burning buildings, and shouting, infuriated rebels, to the suburbs of the town and there looked upon the awful scene. In the evening, after the fire was over, Mr. Anthony Holler, then in our employ, came to me and told me that he had saved part of my library. He said that remembering that I had a valuable library which I prized very much, he had taken a wheelbarrow and made his way by the lower end of our lot up to the house, and filling three small boxes with my books, started back by the same way. When he was about half way down the lot, and directly under a grape arbor, he was compelled to leave it and flee to escape destruction. The Court House, Hall, hotels, and our store, and the stables and fences, were all on fire, and fearing that if he did not at once seek safety in flight he would be so hemmed in by fire as to be unable to escape, he dropped the wheelbarrow and fled. After the fire he went back to ascertain what had become of the books, and although everything combustible around was burned, the grape arbor and vines gone, the fences and out-buildings gone, and even the apples on the trees roasted and burned to a crisp, the wheelbarrow with its precious freight was safe. Upon being informed of this I inquired of him if he had saved my Bible? He at once conducted me to the residence of Mr. Christian Fuller, on Second street, where he resided, and where he had taken them, and upon examining the books I found my Bible with its turned down leaf. Some of the books which were upon the tops of the boxes bore marks of the fire. The leather binding of one or two was burned through, and one large book which was open and upon which flakes of fire had fallen, was burned and scorched through eight or ten leaves. My family that morning consisted of four persons, three of whom have since passed away, and I alone remain, but that Bible, with its turned down leaf as I turned it that morning, is still kept as a valuable and precious treasure.

Chambersburg was founded, according to the inscription upon the tombstone of its founder, Col. Benjamin Chambers, in the cemetery of the Falling Spring Presbyterian church, A. D., 1764, and was burned in the centennial of its existence, A. D., 1864. The beautiful country in the midst of which it stands was rescued from desolation by the thrift and industry of our fathers; the success of the cause for which the rebels fought would have turned the tide of its prosperity backwards towards its original wilderness. That success was denied them, and civilization and morality and religion triumphed over barbarism, immorality and oppression, and in this consummation the burning of Chambersburg bore its part. It was part of the price paid for the grand and glorious result finally achieved. The question of responsibility will be considered in my next chapter.

CHAPTER XIV.

RESPONSIBILITY FOR THE BURNING OF CHAMBERSBURG.

General Couch, the commander of the military district, as well as the people of Chambersburg, has been blamed for the destruction of the town. The injustice of this censure will be shown in this chapter.

Apprehending that the greatest danger which would threaten his department, was from raiding parties across its southern border, General Couch, shortly after the establishment of his headquarters in this place, set about making such preparations as he could to meet them. He first urged upon the citizens the necessity of forming organizations for home defense.

These calls were promptly responded to and various companies formed. The General then made application to the War Department, asking that the persons thus organized might be armed, uniformed and enrolled by the government, so that in case of their capture they would be treated as prisoners of war, and not summarily dealt with as guerillas. This request was denied. He then proceeded to organize a cavalry force for border defence from what was known as the "Six Months' Men," and many enlisted in this organization. But this force was scarcely in readiness for service before it was taken from his department and sent to the Army of the Potomac. General Couch next organized what was designed to be the "Provost Regiment," for special service along the border, and in a short time twelve hundred men were enrolled, organized and equipped. These, too, were at once ordered elsewhere by the Secretary of War. Early in the summer of 1864, when the usual time of raids drew near, the General renewed his request of the previous year for the enrollment and uniforming of the citizens, but was again refused. And during the month of July, when General Early was invading Maryland, and threatening this place, the General organized six regiments of one hundred day men who had responded to the call of the Government for volunteers specially to meet the emergency, but they too were ordered to Washington. These facts are given, not to censure the general government, for the safety of the National Capitol, then sorely menaced, was of more importance than our border, but in justification of both the General commanding this district and the people as well.

Our unpreparedness for the blow that was about to fall upon us, will fully appear in the fact, that during the time of the invasion of Maryland the whole available force in the Department did not exceed three hundred men; and at the time of McCausland's raid, when our town was laid in ashes, General Couch had but *one hundred and thirty-five* under his command. Thus it will be seen that while we had a military department, well and ably officered, we were without troops, and that too at one of the most exposed and oftenest raided places, and in one of the most threatened periods.

"But," it has been said, "why did not the citizens unite with the military, and drive the invaders away, or at least hold them in check until assistance could have been sent them?" The utmost that the town could have done would have been to have added probably four or five hundred persons to the one hundred and thirty-five soldiers here. These would have been the old and the young, and without organization or arms. The number of invaders is accurately known, for they were counted upon their retreat through St. Thomas. They numbered about 2,800. Of these *eight hundred and thirty-one*, as ascertained by actual count as they entered the town, came into the place and burned and plundered us. The remaining two thousand, with six pieces of artillery, stood in line of battle upon the hills, a mile, or a mile and a half from the Diamond of the town, their guns so planted that the place was entirely at their mercy. Now what could five hundred undisciplined, unorganized, and unarmed citizens, assisted by one hundred and thirty-one tried soldiers, with but two pieces of artillery, accomplish against twenty-eight hundred veterans like McCausland's, with their battery of six pieces? To have driven the invaders back, those hills west of the town must have been held, or once in the enemy's possession, they must have been re-taken. To have succeeded in either would have required a force at least equal to that of the foe; and to have attempted either with the few persons here, would have been sheer madness.

"But, were there not troops along the Potomac, who might have prevented this raid, or who might have been called upon to drive the invaders back?" There were troops along the river, but they were needed there to prevent the crossing of larger bodies of the enemy who were constantly threatening to cross over. Besides these troops were under the command of Generals Hunter and Crooks, and not at all subject to the orders of General Couch. That the troops failed to prevent the passage of McCausland's invaders, is for others to answer. Upon an extended line like that of our southern border, with so many fords to the river and hiding places among the valleys by which they could steal upon us, it was exceedingly difficult to prevent occasional raids.

Again it may be said, "Why did not General Couch stop the large number of stragglers from Hunter's command, who passed through the town on the evening before the fire, and unite them with the troops he had and defend the place?" Those stragglers were badly demoralized, and many of them without arms. But suppose that they had all been stopped and added to the few troops here, in connection with the citizens, would any military man risk his reputation by saying that they would have acted wisely in attempting resistance? Besides this General Couch at that early hour in the evening had every reason to suppose that Averill, of whose proximity he was aware, would come on for our protection.

"But what induced General Averill to encamp over night near Greencastle when he knew that McCausland was marching at that time upon Chambersburg? And why did he fail to respond to the repeated despatches sent him during the early evening and night by General Couch, informing him of the threatening situation, and urging him to come on at once? And why did he, the next morning, march eastwardly away from Chambersburg, and go all the way to Greenwood, nearly ten miles east of town, before he turned the head of his column toward us, and that, too, with the evidence of the foe here in the fact of the darkened heavens with the volume of smoke from our burning town?" That General Averill could have prevented the destruction of our town, had he come on here, is proven in the fact that at the mere rumor of his approach while the work of destruction was in full progress, the rebels withdrew from the town and left in haste; and when he approached McConnellsburg and subsequently Hancock, they again fled before him.

That General Couch did intend to withstand the rebels had Averil come on, and that he did use every possible effort to have him come, will clearly appear in the following statements: Col. A. K. McClure, in Dr. Schneck's *Burning of Chambersburg*, page 8, says: "General Averill possibly might have saved Chambersburg, and I know that General Couch exhausted himself to get Averill to fall back from Greencastle to this point." Col. T. B. Kennedy says that he was with General Couch at his headquarters during the whole night, until about 3 o'clock in the morning when he left town. The General was kept informed of the approach of the rebels and their progress toward town, by Lieut. McLane, who with his company of cavalry fell back from before the advancing foe all the way from Mercersburg to this place. And he was exceedingly anxious to have Averill come on here, and knowing that he was somewhere near Greencastle, he sent despatch after despatch to him, but failed to get any reply; and it was only after he had entirely abandoned all hope of getting him to come on that he left to escape capture.

Two facts must be kept in mind, which will in part explain the reason why Averill did not respond to General Couch's request. General Averill was under orders from General Hunter and was not responsible to General Couch. He was also pressed by another force, which had entered Hagerstown and was threatening him from that direction; and it was probably to prevent his being caught between that force and McCausland's that induced him to march ten miles eastwardly before he turned his column and came this way. But while not subject to the orders of General Couch, he was yet under obligations to pay some attention to the pressing despatches of the commander of the district in which he was. Military courtesy, to say nothing of the necessities of the case, would have required him to notice the despatches sent him. Why he failed in this particular will appear in the following facts furnished by Thomas R. Bard, Esq., once a resident of this place, but now an Attorney-at-Law in California. Mr. Bard's statement is as follows:

HUENEME, Ventura co., Cal., February 14, 1884.

JACOB HOKE, Esq., *Chambersburg, Penna.*, *Dear Sir:* Complying with your request contained in your letter of the 4th inst., I contribute for your use in preparing the "Reminiscences of the War," designed to preserve in a permanent form many of the incidents of the war in and about Chambersburg, the following narrative of events in which I was a participant.

Though I have no memorandum or document at hand which will in any way aid me, as a reference, these events were too full of importance to me personally, and had too much to do in directing the course of my life, to be faded in my memory, but are as fresh now as if they had happened only a year ago.

To the many readers of your Reminiscences, to whom I am unknown, it may be necessary, by way of introduction, to say that during the war I was a resident of Hagerstown, Maryland, and as one of the firm of D. Zeller & Co., was engaged in the business of Forwarding and Commission Merchants, and that being one of the organizers of a secret political society at that place, called the "Union League," designed for self-protection and aiding the Government in its terrific struggle for preservation of the Union, and very early incurred the animosity of many of the people of that place who sympathized with the Southern secessionists and rebels.

I was also the representative at that place of the Cumberland Valley Railroad Company, acting in the capacity, but without the designation, of Assistant to the Superintendent, charged with the transportation of troops and supplies—at that terminal point of the road. It was customary for me, as often as the rebel forces appeared and occupied the town, to leave Hagerstown in company with the Military telegraph operator, and to retreat up the valley by rail on a hand car. Frequently we were enabled by cutting the wires and establishing offices secretely in the woods and bushes, to receive and communicate to the military authorities important intelligence concerning the movements of the rebel forces. We were of the opinion that our capture by the rebels would be of importance to them, and rarely allowed ourselves to remain within their lines.

Therefore the rebel forces having entered Hagerstown in the afternoon of July 29, 1864, I left that place on a hand car about 3 o'clock, and arrived at Greencastle late in the afternoon of that day. I learned there that another rebel force, said to consist of 3,000 cavalry with some artillery, under command of Generals Bradley Johnson and McCausland, had crossed the Potomac river at McCoy's Ferry, and were marching in the direction of Mercersburg.

This intelligence, to the best of my recollection, was brought by one of the scouts under Lieut. McLane, of the regular army, who was in command of a squad of cavalry, mounted on the training horses of Carlisle Barracks, and operating in that country as independent scouts.

This intelligence, I was informed at the time

by the telegraph operators, D. C. Aughinbaugh and Dr. Fetterhoff, was also communicated later in the evening to General Averill, who arrived at Greencastle about 8 o'clock P. M., from Hagerstown, with a force of about 2,500 cavalry under his command.

General Averill left three "orderlies" at the telegraph office to convey to him all messages that might be received for him, and encamped his troops in a grove distant about 1½ miles north-east from Greencastle, and only 9½ miles from Chambersburg. Late in the evening General Couch, Commanding the Department of the Susquehanna, with headquarters at Chambersburg, sent a message to General Averill, which was promptly handed to one of the orderlies, who quickly mounted his horse and rode off in the direction of General Averill's camp.

Blair Gilmore, the telegraph operator at Chambersburg, kept us informed constantly of all that was transpiring at that place, and of the movements of the rebel force. It is quite probable that I was informed by one of the operators as to the contents of the message from General Couch. At any rate, at the time I understood that General Couch informed General Averill that the rebel forces were at or had passed Mercersburg, and were moving towards Chambersburg, and that being without adequate forces to check the movement, he inquired whether Averill could be depended on for assistance.

Later in the night two other messages were received from Gen. Couch for Gen. Averill and were promptly delivered to the orderlies. The last of these messages was received probably about 3 o'clock on the morning of July 30. These messages reported the rapid approach of the rebels and expressed great anxiety to learn if General Averill intended to render assistance to Couch for the defense of Chambersburg.

There had been no reply from General Averill, and learning that General Couch had made preparation for leaving Chambersburg, and that in all probability the communications with that place would be soon interrupted, I mounted a horse and hurriedly rode out to find General Averill. On the road, about half way to the camp, I met the orderlies riding leisurely towards Greencastle. In reply to my inquiry if they had delivered their messages, they said that General Averill could not be found, and that they did not know what to do with the messages. Hastily informing them of the importance of the dispatches, I took them in my own hands and telling them to follow me, I spurred my horse and was soon at the grove.

There was not a sentry or guard to halt me. All was quiet. There was not a sound save the champing of the feeding horses; there were no lights or fires except the embers where the men had prepared their evening meal. I dashed into the middle of the encampment and there found a solitary man to answer my inquiry: "Where is General Averill?" He could not tell me. An officer of a West Virginia regiment then appeared and said it would be difficult to find General Averill, but offered to aid me in the search. While he prepared to mount his horse, the booming of a cannon was heard in the direction of Chambersburg. The officer expressed surprise and asked "what can that be?" I told him it supplemented the messages which I brought, and indicated that McCausland had arrived at Chambersburg.

We rode hastily through the grove and soon found General Averill asleep by the side of a fence. On being awakened, he raised upon his elbow and heard the information I had brought. I had handed him the telegrams, but as there was no light I told him what they contained, and informed him that they had been delivered to his orderlies hours before. He made no reply and, as I thought, was about to turn over and go asleep. Minutes seemed hours to me, and growing impatient I said to him: "General Averill if you wish me to convey any answer to General Couch, I beg you to let me have it quickly, for it is barely possible I can get back before telegraphic communications will be cut off." Without rising to put his troops in motion, or without the slightest manifestation of interest in the condition of General Couch, or in the peril to which the loyal people of Chambersburg were exposed, he merely said: "Tell Couch I will be there in the morning." It was then, I think, about four o'clock, a. m.

Returning to Greencastle, I found that already the Chambersburg office was closed, having first reported that General Couch had all his military forces and supplies on cars, and that the rebel advance was about to enter the town.

I then joined Lieut. Jones and a squad of McLane's scouts, leaving Greencastle before dawn, and accompanied them as far as Green wood on the Gettysburg turnpike. On the way, the road being on the foot of the mountain and commanding a view of the valley, after passing some ore pits, I stopped in front of a house and rode up to the fence. Almost within my reach, but inside the fence, there was a well, and two or three men and some women stood near by it. I asked them for a drink, of water but they made no offer to hand it to me and sullenly told me to help myself.

After drinking, and having noticed that they were greatly excited and seemed to be looking intently at the little military force which had passed by, I remarked: "I guess you are not very loyal Union people here?" One of the men answered: "You bet we ain't, and that is what the Chambersburg people are getting for being Black Republicans," and pointed in the direction of Chambersburg, where I saw, for the first time, the dense column of black smoke whirling on its axis, erect and reaching up to the sky—it told me that I was homeless, and perhaps all that I loved and cherished had perished under its awful shadow.

It is not the province of the Annalist to record his opinions or reflections concerning the events which he is narrating. But may this narrative come to the notice of the *Historian*, who in attempting to illustrate the patriotism of the citizens of the Republic during the war, and their fortitude and loyalty under the severest trials, cannot overlook the burning of Chambersburg and the sacrifices of her people. Let him not omit to trace out the causes which led to the destruction of their homes, but let him be assured that posterity will expect him to assign *some* reason explaining why there was then withheld from that loyal people the protection which the Government is always bound to afford, and which at that disastrous time, as this narrative shows, could so easily have been provided.

Very truly yours, &c.,

THOMAS R. BARD.

The reason why General Averill did not respond to the urgent appeals of General Couch, while not plainly stated by Mr. Bard in the foregoing paper, is yet inferrable, and the reader is left to his own conclusions. Several corroborative statements as to General Averill's condition have been given me by reliable persons, but as they are not direct and the result of personal knowledge, as is Mr. Bard's, but secondary and containing information given by some of Averill's officers, I do not give them here. The facts they relate were freely spoken of immediately after the fire, and were the common talk of the people.

I subjoin a letter from Rev. J. Milton Snyder, a resident of Somerset county, Pennsylvania, but at the time of the war residing with his father, Jacob C. Snyder, Esq., of the vicinity of New Franklin, some four miles south-east of this place. Mr. Snyder's statement is as follows:

MR. J. HOKE:—*Sir*:—When Chambersburg was burned, that same morning at about 9 or 9.30 o'clock (may be 10) Gen. Averill's cavalry came from the direction of Greencastle by New Franklin. They camped south-east of New Franklin in the woods on the farm now owned by Mr. Christian Lehman, to the right of the Walnut Bottom road. Some few camped in my father's field adjoining the grove. Gen. Averill got the most of the oats and hay used on that occasion to feed his horses from father's barn. After resting awhile Averill left, passing through New Guilford, and struck the pike at Greenwood. When he passed by New Franklin the rebels were in Chambersburg, and I distinctly remember that many of the soldiers were eager to march directly to that place, and many were angry with their commander. The smoke and flames were leaping and rolling high in the heavens, shutting out the sun; and had Averill marched to Chambersburg at once instead of eastwardly as he did, your beautiful town would have been saved. I believe he is to blame for the destruction of your town, but then a civilian does not know all the circumstances; but yet he has eyes to see the conduct of public men."

Thus it will be seen that owing to the danger which threatened the National Capital, and the consequent withdrawal of the troops raised in this valley for its defense, as well as the failure for a cause which he has never yet explained of one who could and should have saved us to come on to our rescue, our town was laid in ruins, our people made homeless and many so impoverished that their lives since have been a continual struggle for existence.

But what has the government, for whose protection we were made to suffer, done in the way of compensating us for our losses? A short time after the fire a public meeting of our citizens was held, at which a committee of five persons, who had not suffered by the destruction of the town, was appointed to make a careful estimate of the value of each property destroyed. That committee was composed of the following persons viz: Wm. McLellan, Esq., C. M. Burnett, Rev. Joseph Clark, D. K. Wunderlich and John Armstrong, and the aggregate value as ascertained by them was $783,950. This was for the real estate only; the value of the personal property was not estimated by them. In response to a call issued by Governor Curtin the Legislature of the State was convened in special session, and came in a body to our town to see for itself the extent of the destruction, after which the sum of one hundred thousand dollars was appropriated for our immediate relief. This money was placed at the disposal of the aforenamed committee, and was distributed to the people, not pro rata according to the amount of their losses, but according to their necessities. The action afterwards taken by the authorities of the State in relation to the losses, the appropriations made, and the present shape of our claims, is set forth in the following concise manner by John M. McDowell, Esq., an attorney of law of this place:

CHAMBERSBURG, PA., July 19, 1884.

Mr. JACOB HOKE, *Dear Sir*:—In compliance with your request I give you a statement of the losses to property, real and personal, in Franklin county, resulting from the several raids and invasions by the rebels during the late war, and the adjudications thereof by the several commissions appointed for that purpose. Our citizens suffered in loss of property by the Stuart raid in the fall of 1862, the Jenkins' raids, and Lee's invasion of 1863, and the McCausland raid and burning of Chambersburg in July, 1864. The first action taken by our State towards adjudicating and paying our losses, was the passing of the Act of Assembly of February 15, 1866. This Act appropriated the sum of $500,000 to the sufferers by the burning of Chambersburg by McCausland on July 30, 1864—the most dastardly and cowardly act of the war—to be paid pro rata on the losses to be ascertained and adjudicated by three commissioners to be appointed by the Governor. The Governor appointed as said commissioners H. A. McAlister, Esq., of Bellefonte, Pa., Gen. Thomas J. Jordan and John Briggs, Esq., of Harrisburg, Pa. These three gentlemen entered at once upon the discharge of their duties, selecting as their clerk Col. John M. Gilmore, of Chambersburg.

The claims adjudicated by this commission

were for losses occasioned wholly by the great fire of 1864. They examined each claim separately, requiring evidence to prove the loss, other than that of the claimant himself. The total claims awarded by this commission were as follows:

Real Estate.	Personal Property.	Total.
$713,294.34	$915,137.24	$1,628,431.58

The next step taken by our State was the Act of 9th April, 1868. Under this Act the Governor was to appoint "three disinterested persons" whose duty it was "to fully investigate and adjudicate the claims of the citizens of the several counties or Franklin, Fulton, Bedford, York, Perry, Adams and Cumberland, for the amount of their losses in the late war, and to make report of same, under oath, to the Auditor General of this commonwealth." The Governor appointed D. W. Woods, of Mifflin county, Anthony T. Eby, of Lebanon county and M. T. Woods, on said commission. After a careful examination of the claims presented before them, these gentlemen reported, under oath, the total losses to citizens of Franklin county as $2,417,165.57.

Besides this they found that the citizens of the other six border counties had sustained losses to the amount of $904,617.53. The next step taken by our State was by the Act of 22d May, 1871. This Act provided that "the claims of the citizens of the seven (above mentioned) counties, as adjudicated under the two aforesaid Acts, "be subjected to a careful revision by two commissioners in each county to be appointed by the Judge of the Courts of Common Pleas of of said several counties," and that the Governor should appoint competent counsel to represent the government in the revision of said claims before the several commissions," and "that said commissions should re-examine and re-adjudicate all of said claims." These commissioners were also to revise the claims for horses taken by our Government in the organization of the Anderson Cavalry, as adjudicated by Col. D. O. Gehr and Samuel Fleisher and for losses sustained at the hands of our own soldiers during the war as adjudicated by W. H. McDowell and C. M. Burnett.

Under this Act our Court appointed as the commissioners of Franklin county, Samuel Garver and J. W. Douglas, Esqrs. The Governor appointed as counsel for the Government Thomas C. McDowell, Esq., of Harrisburg.

This commission gave every claim a thorough revision and overhauling, reducing them when found to be too high, and casting out all items of a doubtful or suspicious character. To the thoroughness of this revision the writer can testify, as he acted as clerk to this commission and knows how carefully and conscientiously these gentlemen did the work assigned them. During a short sickness of Mr. Garver, Mr. Jacob Pensinger acted, under appointment of the Court, in his stead. This commission reduced the total claims for losses to $2,471,488.85, making an actual reduction in rebel losses of about $100,000.

By the Act of 27th May, 1871, section 67—$300,000 was paid the citizens of Chambersburg upon their claims for losses by the great fire—thus making in all $800,000 to said sufferers—about fifty per cent of their claims—leaving yet unpaid $825,435.55.

Thus you will see that the claims for losses by the Burning of Chambersburg have been adjudicated, re-adjudicated and re-re-adjudicated by commissioners appointed by the State, and all other claims for losses at the hands of the rebels have been adjudicated and re-adjudicated, by said commission.

Our claims have certainly been well examined, thoroughly sifted and adjudicated. It now remains for the State to pay them all in full. It has partly paid the losses of the burning of Chambersburg. The losses outside the burning are equally as fair, just and equitable as those occasioned by the great fire of 1864, and should be fully paid and provided for by our great and rich State. A trifle from each inhabitant of this great commonwealth would pay all the claims in all the border counties in full and yet this great State refuses to be just to its suffering citizens. It is the duty of the State to protect her citizens, and if she fail in that she should pay and make good any losses occasioned by her failure to protect them, and her citizens have a good claim for damages against her. She could have protected us and did not. Hence we think she is in duty bound now to remunerate those who lost by her neglect and failure even to try to protect them.

Under the Act of 22 May 1871, the State issued to each claimant a certificate for the amount allowed in each claim in the following form:

"This is to certify that .... has on file in the office of the Auditor General, a duly approved and registered claim for the sum of .... dollars, as adjudicated under the Act entitled 'An Act to authorize the liquidation of damages sustained by citizens of Pennsylvania during the late Rebellion, and payable only when said claims shall be paid by the United States Government. In testimony whereof we have hereunto set our hands and the seal of the State this .... day of .... A. D. 1871."

Signed by the Governor and State Treasurer and countersigned by the Auditor General.

Hoping that you can obtain from the foregoing the information desired, I am

Yours, Truly,

J. M. McDOWELL.

CHAPTER XV.

LIST OF BUILDINGS DESTROYED.

The following is a list of the buildings burned in Chambersburg on July 30, 1864, and the amount of the loss sustained by each owner, as ascertained by the committee — Messrs. McLellan, Burnet, Clark, Wunderlich and Armstrong—appointed for that purpose:

SOUTH SIDE OF MARKET.

Jabob Wolfkill—Two story frame front and one story brick back building	$700
Patrick Campbell's heir—Two story brick front and one story frame back building	700
Peter M'Galligan—Two story log front and one story brick back building	600
James C. Austin—Two story brick front and back building, new	5,000
R. Austin—Two story brick front and back building and wash house	3,000
Wm. H. M'Dowell—Two story stone front and brick back building, wash house and brick stable	3,000
James M. Brown—Two story stone front and brick back building, wash house and frame stable	3,200
Jacob Sellers—Two story brick front and frame back building, brick and frame stable and ice house	4,000
J. W. Douglas—One story frame front and back building	600
Martin Brown—One and a-half story frame front and one story log back building	1,000
J. Allison & Jas. C. Eyster—Two story log front (cased with brick) and one and a-half story log back building	1,000
Mrs. Jordan—Two story brick front and back building	5,000
L. S. Clark—Two story frame front, two story brick building and frame stable	1,200
C. M. Duncan—Two story brick front and back building, frame law office and frame stable	2,000
Edmund Culbertson—Two story brick front and back building, brick law office, and two story stone barn	6,000
Mrs. Bard—Two story brick front and back building, two story brick law office, and row frame law offices	6,500
Gehr & Denny—Three story brick front and two story back building, one three story brick front and one two story brick building, &c	5,500
C. M. Duncan—Three story brick front and back building, three story brick arcade two two story brick stables, and one two story frame stable	15,000
Aug. Duncan—Three story brick front building	1,500
Henry Monks—Three story brick front building	1,500
Edward Aughinbaugh—Three story brick front building	1,500
Dr. Wm. H. Boyle—Three story brick front building	2,000
Mary Gillan—Three story brick front building	1,500
T. J. Wright—Three story brick front and one story back building	1,800
Samuel F. Greenawalt—Two story brick front and back building, frame wash house, brick smoke house and frame stable	3,000
A. H. McCulloh—Two story brick front and back building, stone stable	2,000
Rev. Mr. Nelson—Two story brick front and back building, frame building and stone stable	2,000
John P. Culbertson—Three two story brick front and one back building and wash house	5,000
Mrs. Riddle—Two story brick front and back building, wash house and frame stable	3,500
E. Finefrock—Two story front and back building, brick wash house, frame wash house and frame stable	2,000
W. F. Eyster & Bro.—Foundry—Two two story brick front and back buildings and stable	4,000
Robert E. Tolbert—Two story brick front and back building and brick stable	2,000
Matthew Gillan's heirs—Two three story brick fronts and two two story back buildings, log house, wash house and brick stable	6,000
Alex. Fritz—Two story brick front and one story frame and log back building	1,000
Mrs. Frederick Smith—Two story brick front and back building	1,200
John Burkholder's heirs—Two story brick front and back building and log barn	2,000
Hunter Robison—Two story brick front and log back building and log stable	1,200
Jacob B. Miller—Two story brick building	400
John Bigley—One and a-half story frame and two one story log buildings	500
Thomas Cook—Two story log front and two one story frame back buildings	600
Nathan Pierce—Two story log front (rough cased) and two story brick back building and wash house	1,000
Barnet Wolff—Two story frame building	600
J. M. Wolfkill—Two story brick front and two two story back buildings	2,500
Jacob Shafer—Two story brick front and one story brick back building and frame shop	1,000
Richard Woods—Two story brick front and one and a-half story log back building and brick wash house	800
John King—Two story log and one story brick building	400
Christ. Pisle—Two story brick building	500
Mrs. Elizabeth Stouffer—Two story brick front and one story brick back building	1,800
Andrew Banker—One story brick shop, two story brick house and frame barn	2,000
Mrs. Butler—Two story log building and frame stable	400
Mary Rapp—Two story log building	400
James Nill's heirs—Two story brick front and shed	500
Josiah Allen—Two story brick and one story frame building	1,000

NORTH SIDE MARKET STREET.

C. Stout—Two two story log buildings and wood shed	600
Samuel Brandt—Two story brick building	800
John M. McDowell—Two story brick front and one story back building, two story brick front building, log and frame barn hog pen and wagon maker shop and blacksmith shop and hay scales	3,500
Daniel Trostle—Two story brick front and back building, and two story brick barn	1,500
Mrs. Radebaugh—Stone and frame barn	800

Mrs. Jos. Chambers—Two story brick front and back building and brick stable	5,500
Geo. W. Brewer—Two story brick front and back building, two story brick office, spring and smoke house, brick and stone barn	5,500
Mrs. Jacob Smith—Log stable	100
John Miller, (Inn-keeper)—Two story brick front and back building, two story brick hotel, wash house, 1 brick and two frame stables, brick wagon maker and blacksmith shops	8,000
John B. Cook—Two story stone (rough cased) and two story frame buildings, bark house and grinding mill, bark shed and brick stable	5,000
C. W. Eyster—Two three story brick mills and two story brick building	15,000
Lambert & Huber—Four story stone and frame paper mill and steam house	15,000
C. W. Eyster—Two story brick front and back building and brick stable	3,000
S. M. Shillito—Two story brick building	1,500
James King—Two story brick building, frame shop and shed	1,200
Peter Brough—Three story brick front and one story back building, (unfinished)	3,000
John Noel—Three story stone front and back building and stone stable	8,000
Court House—Three story brick	15,000
Engine House—Two story brick	1,000
D. O. Gehr—Two story brick front and back building, smoke house, brick stable frame wagon shed	5,500
B. F. Nead—Two story brick front and back building, spring and smoke house, brick stable	5,000
A. D. Kauffman—Three story brick front and back building, and log stable	1,000
Mrs. Goettman—Two story brick front and back building, two story log front (rough cased) and brick back building, bake house, brick wash house, brick stable	5,500
Peiffer's heirs—Two story stone house, frame smith shop, two story frame shop, one and a half story frame front and one story brick back building, frame stable	2,000
T. B. Kennedy—Two story brick front and back building, smoke and wash house	8,000
Rev. B. S. Schneck—Two story stone front and brick back building and wash house	3,000
Levi Humelshine—Two story log front and frame back building and frame shed	600
Samuel Etter—Two story brick front and back building, and frame bake house	3,000
Rev. N. Schlosser—Two story log front and frame back building and shed	1,000
Sebastian Eckert—Two story stone front and brick back building	1,000

WEST SIDE MAIN TO SQUARE.

Benj. Chambers—Two story brick cottage and two story brick back building	5,000
William O. Reed—Two story brick front and back building, and frame and brick stable	5,000
Mrs. C. Snyder—Two story brick front and back building	3,000
Allen Smith—Two story brick front and back building, small frame stable	1,650
Christian Flack—Two story log and weatherboarded front and one story frame back building, small frame stable	1,000
Jno. Schofield—Two story log weatherboarded front and one story back building, brick shop and small frame stable	1,800
Matthew P. Welsh—Two story brick front and back building, brick wash house	2,500
Christian Stouffer (Machinist)—Two story brick front and back building, frame stable	3,000
Geo. Chambers' residence—Two story brick front and back building, brick smoke house, two story stone stable	7,000
George Chambers (Seminary)—Three story stone front and three story stone and brick back building, smoke house	5,000
George Chambers (Millinery Shop)—Two story brick front and back building	2,000
A. J. Miller—Two story stone front and brick back building, one story brick back building, wash and smoke house	4,500
James Watson—Two story brick front and back building	4,500
R. Austin—Two story brick front and two story brick back building	2,500

EAST SIDE MAIN FROM SQUARE TO KING.

Franklin Hall—Three story brick building	20,000
Jacob Hoke—Two story brick front and two story brick back building and frame stable	5,500
Dr. Langheim.—Two story brick front, two frame back building and frame stable	3,000
Widow Montgomery (Hotel,)—Three story brick front and two story brick back building, two story stone front and two story brick back building and brick stable	9,000
Daniel Trostle.—Two story Brick and stone front and three two story stone back buildings, lot of sheds and stone stable	7,000
Susan Chambers.—One story brick shop, two story brick mansion and stone stable	2,500
A. P. Frey.—Two story frame and log front and one story brick back building, two story brick shop, Coachmaker shed and blacksmith shop and log stable	3,000
A. S. Hull.—Two story brick front and one story back building and frame wash house	2,000
Mrs. Geo. Goettman.—Two story log (weatherboard) brick back building and frame shop	1,280

WEST SIDE OF MAIN, FROM SQUARE TO WASHINGTON.

Chambersburg Bank.—Two story brick front and back building, smoke and wash house, stable	8,000
Mrs. Gilmore. -Two story brick front and back building and two frame shops	5,500
Jacob B. Miller.—Two story frame front (brick cased) and story back, coal shed, stove shed and frame stable	3,000
Dr. Richards.—Two story brick front and back building, smoke house, stable	5,500
Christian Burkhart.—Three story brick front and back building, frame ice house, stable	4,500
John M. Cooper.—Three story brick front, three story brick back and two story brick back building, stone stable, &c	15,000
James L. Black.—Two story brick front and back building, spring house, stable	5,000
Dr. James Hamilton.—Three story brick front and back building, and stables	7,000
John A. Grove.—Frame shop	250
Jacob Hutton. Three story brick front and two two-story brick buildings, wash and smoke houses	4,500
John McClintock.—Two story brick front and back building, hatter shop and smoke house	3,500
Lewis Shoemaker.—Two story brick front and back building, store room, bake house and ice house	4,200
Samuel Greenawalt.—Two story brick front and back buildings, and frame shed	5,500
J. Allison Eyster -Two story brick front and one and a half story back building	5,030
J. Allison Eyster—Two story brick front and one story brick back building	1,500
J. Allison Eyster—Three story brick front and two two-story back buildings, and brick stable	5,000
Wm. Heyser's heirs—Two story brick front and back buildings, brick bake and smoke house, and brick stable	6,500
Rev. S. R. Fisher—Brick stable	500
Geo. Lehner Log stable	100
George Ludwig—Two story brick front and four two-story and one one and a half story brick back buildings, frame shed, and one story brick bake house	7,000

Charles F. Miller—Two story brick front and back building, brick wash house..... 1,500
Adam Wolff—Two story frame and brick front and frame shed.............................. 1,200
John Forbes—Two story log front and one story brick back building, frame wash and smoke house... 2,000
John Dittman—Two story brick front and back building.. 2,000
Joseph Deckelmayer—Two story brick front and back building, one story bakery... 3,000
Samuel Ott—Two two-story brick front and one two-story brick back building... 1,000
B. Radenbaugh—One story frame shop...... 150
Samuel Ott—One story frame shop............. 200
B. Radenbaugh—Two story brick front building.. 600

EAST SIDE OF MAIN, FROM WASHINGTON TO SQUARE.

F. Spahr—Two story brick front and back building... 2,500
Miss Hetrick—Two story brick front and one story brick back building............... 1,500
John A. Lehmaster—Two story brick front and back building and frame shed....... 1,500
Aug. Reineman—Two story brick front and buildings... 2,500
Samuel M. Perry—Two story brick front and back building............................... 2,000
Daniel L. Taylor—Two story log (weather boarded) front and frame back building.. 1,500
John W. Taylor—Two story brick front and back building, wash and smoke house, stable, shed and hay scales......... 7,000
George Ludwig—Two story brick front and back building, tin shop, frame sheds, brick stable.. 1,000
H. H. Hutz—Two story brick front and back building, wash and smoke house, and brick stable... 6,500
Daniel Reisher—Two story and a half story brick front and two story back building, frame kitchen, wash smoke and bake house and stable.. 1,500
Michael Kuss—Two story brick front and back building, wash house and stone stable... 2,500
Isaac Hutton—Two story brick front and two story brick back building, wood and wash house, back shop and stone stable 4,000
John P. Culbertson—One story frame front and two frame back shops........................ 800
Dr. John Lambert—Two story brick front and two story back building, brick stable and carriage house............................ 5,500
Mrs. R. Fisher—Two story brick front building.. 3,000
William Wallace (Hotel)—Three story brick front and three story back building and wash house... 9,000
Daniel Reisher—Two story brick front and two two-story back buildings and brick stable... 6,000
J. Allison Eyster (Nixon's)—Two story brick front and two two-story brick buildings, brick shed and two story brick shop... 4,500
James Eyster—Two story brick front and two story back building and brick stable 4,500
Eyster & Bro—Two story stone front, brick back building and kitchen......................... 5,500
Eyster & Bro—Three story brick front, warehouse, brick stable............................. 10,000
Brand & Flack—Two story stone front and brick back building, brick warehouse..... 6,500
A. J. White—Two story stone front and brick back building and kitchen.................. 1,500
Hiram White—Three story brick front and back building and kitchen......................... 7,500
John Jeffries—Two story stone front and brick back building, brick wash house and frame stables... 3,000
A. B. Hamilton—Two story stone front and frame and brick back buildings, frame wash house, brick stable............................ 6,000

Mansion House—Three story brick front and two story brick back buildings and stone stable... 10,000
Academy—Two story brick................................. 4,000

QUEEN SOUTH SIDE.

John W. Reyes—Two story brick front and back building and wash house................... 1,000
Wm. Cunningham—Two story brick front and back building, wash house and granary... 3,000
John Mull—Two story brick front and back building.. 2,000
J. T. Hoskinson—Two story brick front and back building.. 2,200
Jacob Flinder—Two story frame front and one story back building............................ 800
Jacob Flinder—Two story frame front and one story back building and stable......... 700
Wm. Wallace—Two story brick front and back building, wash house and wood work of spring house.................................. 4,000
Mrs. John Lindsey—Two story brick front and back building... 2,500
Barnard Wolff—Two two story brick front and back buildings, one story frame kitchen, wash house, warehouse, frame butcher shop, frame carriage house, one story brick stable..................................... 7,500
J. Allison Eyster—Two story brick front and back building... 2,200
Mrs. Blood—Two story brick front and two two story brick back buildings............ 1,800
Mrs. Clark—Two story brick front and back building... 1,800
Mrs. R. Fisher—Two story brick front and back building.. 2,000
Mrs. Sarah Stevenson—Two story brick front and one back building, wash and smoke house... 2,000
Jno. D. Grier—Two story brick front and back building.. 1,500
Mrs. Susan Nixon—Two story brick front and one story back building...................... 1,800
Robert Davis—Two story brick building..... 2,000
John Cree—Two story brick front and back building, wash and smoke house... 2,500
Samuel Myers—Two story brick front, one two and a-half and one two story back building... 3,200
Mrs. Thompson—Two story log building... 600
Mrs. Geo. S. Eyster—Two story brick front and back building.. 2,500
Andrew Banker—Two story log front and back building (rough cased) and smoke house.. 1,500

QUEEN—NORTH SIDE.

Huber & Co—Edge tool factory—Fine one story brick and one frame building........... 3,500
Brick blacksmith shop................................... 600
Baptist Church—Brick three story............. 3,000
Geo Ludwig (Brewery)—Two story stone front and back building, two story brick back building, one story office and engine house frame stable, two story shed. 8,000
Widow Grove of Wm—Two story frame front and back building, brick smoke house.. 1,500
Thomas Carlisle—Two story brick front building and two story frame front building... 3,000
Kindline's Heirs—Two story brick front and two story frame back building, two story log and brick front and two story brick back building....................................... 4,000
Widow Grove of Alex—Two story frame front and one story back building, smoke house, frame stable................................... 1,200
Jno Huber—Two story brick front building and brick kitchen frame stable................. 2,000
H. Sierer—Two story frame front and back building, two story frame wareroom, stone stable, shed, one story kitchen adjoining Stevenson's................................... 3,000
Thomas Carlisle—Two story brick front and two story back buildings.................. 2,500

Wm. Wallace—Three three story brick front buildings and three two story brick back building, two one story frame shops and two and a half story brick stable...... 8,800
Nicholas Snyder—Two story brick front and back buildings, two frame wash houses and frame stable........................... 2,500
Dr. S. D. Culbertson—Two and a half story brick front, and two story brick back building, brick spring house, and brick stable... 1,000
Mrs. Brand—Roof slightly damaged...........
J. P. Culbertson—Two story brick front and back building, smoke and spring house, and stable... 1,500

SECOND STREET.

P. Henry Peiper—New two story frame stable.. 1,800
Associate Reformed Church—One story brick building, with end gallery............ 3,000
Benj. Rhodes—Two story log front and one story brick back building............. 1,200
J. Allison Eyster—One story log shop......... 100
Charles Croft—One and a half story log building and frame kitchen.................. 800
John P. Keefer—Two story brick building and frame kitchen............................. 1,500
John Reasner—One story log bakery and frame corn crib................................ 150
Jacob S. Brown—Roof and upper floor of front and back building.................... 500
John Doebler—Two story brick front and two story back building..................... 2,000
Holmes Crawford—Two story brick front and two story back building............... 3,000
Samuel Armstrong—Two story brick front and back building, kitchen, stable and frame shed..................................... 1,000

Aug. Reineman—Two one story frame shops..

FRANKLIN.

Martin Cole—Two story brick front and back, and two story log buildings, and wash house....................................... 1,500
Philip Evans—Two story brick front and one story frame back building............ 1,200

WOLFSTOWN.

Dr. A. H. Senseny—Two story log buildings.. 200
N. Uglow—Three one story log buildings... 250

WATER.

Geo. Kindline—One and a half story brick wagonmaker and blacksmith shop, one brick stable...................................... 800

ALLEY.

Widow Palmer—Frame stable................ 150
Nicholas Garwick—Frame stable............ 100
Henry Greenawalt—Brick stable............ 300

KING.

George Chambers—Three two-story brick front and one one-story brick back building.. 2,500
Upton Washabaugh—Two story frame front and brick back building, stone brewery, brick granary wagon shed, two brick stables and frame shed.......................... 8,000
Conrad Harman—Stone and frame butcher shop and dwelling, frame stable.......... 800
A. K. M'Clure—House and barn............ 9,500
Jacob Eby—Barn................................. 2,500
Andrew M'Elwaine—House.................. 100

CHAPTER XVI.

CAUGHT WITHIN THE CONFEDERATE LINES, AND WHAT CAME OF IT.

On Monday, July 6th, when the retreat of the Confederate army was certainly known in our town, a large number of our citizens started to Gettysburg, and others to Hagerstown. The persons going to the latter place expected to witness a battle at the crossing of the Potomac. After walking from Chambersburg to Middletown at the State Line, where they remained over night, the following persons resumed their journey to Hagerstown along the Cumberland Valley Railroad, viz:—Dr. James Hamilton, his brother, A. B. Hamilton, John P. Culbertson, Dr. George R. Kaufman, Jacob N. Snider, Allen C. McGrath, Charles Kinsler, Thomas H. McDowell, George S. Heck, J. Winter Tritle, Levi D. C. Houser, J. Porter Brown, D. M. Eiker, and Rev. Charles Steck. When passing through the deep cut along the railroad, a short distance this side of Hagerstown, the party overtook two rebel soldiers who had been out in the country foraging. One of them carried in his hand a tin bucket in which he had sausage and butter. Mr. Tritle took the musket from one of them and proposed to break it, but was prevented by his companions, who told him that they might get into trouble by doing so. At length the musket was returned to the soldier, and they were permitted to go on into Hagerstown. Arriving at that point on the railroad where the Western Maryland railroad crosses the track of the Cumberland Valley, the party stopped and held a consultation. They did not know whether Hagerstown was in possession of Federals or Confederates. At length Messrs. Steck, Tritle and A. B. Hamilton proposed to go on into the town and if all was right and it was safe to enter, they would come back and show themselves upon a hill near the cemetery within sight. After waiting a while and the party not appearing upon the hill, Mr. Houser proposed that he would go forward and reconnoitre. When he entered within the limits of the town he found it in possession of the rebels. The streets were filled with army wagons and the pavements crowded with soldiers. Things began to assume an unhealthy appearance, and when he reached the Round House belonging to the railroad company he met a woman with whom he had some acquaintance, and while conversing with her he saw his companions coming around the corner in the road escorted by a guard. They had waited but a short time after Houser started, and determined to proceed, but had not gone far before they ran against a lot of rebels, among whom were the two they had stopped out on the road. When Houser saw that his comrades were prisoners, he gave a gum blanket and haversack, which he had brought with him, to this woman to keep for him and went back to his party, supposing that the two they had stopped would not recognize him. In this he was mistaken, and he was at once placed under arrest and compelled to fall in at the rear. He told the guard that they had mistaken their man, that he was a citizen of the place, and did not like to be marched through the street, and be recognized and laughed at, but they would not let him go. They were first taken to the front of Doyle's hotel, and sat there for a while, when they were again put upon their feet and taken to the Washington hotel, where the guard inquired for the Provost Marshal. The office of this person was directly opposite the hotel, and when they crossed the street and halted before the office, Houser left the rear and went to the front, and motioning to Snider, they walked away and were soon lost sight of in the crowd. After proceeding a short distance they crossed the street between the wagons, and proceeded towards the residence of Mr. Lewis Heist, a former resident of this place, but before reaching the dwelling of Mr. Heist they met him in the street. Mr. Heist expressed his surprise at finding these men there, and they soon saw that he did not intend to do anything for them. They next concluded to proceed to the residence of Mr. John Hutton, another former resident of Chambersburg, but just before arriving at Mr. Hutton's, they discovered their own party in the hands of their guard before his door. They at once left, and remembering that Mr. Jacob Keller, long a resident of this place, and then and now in the employment of the Cumberland Valley Railroad, at that time occupied the building at the depot which was then used as a ticket office, they determined to try and find their way there. Arriving at Mr. Keller's, they tapped at the back door, which was immediately opened by Mrs. Keller, who at once took in the situation, motioned them to be silent as rebels were in the front part of the house, and pointed to the stairway. They were not slow in taking the hint, and went softly up into the attic, where for several days the family of Mr. Keller—he being absent—showed them all possible kindness. That evening after it became dark Mr. Houser disguised himself in Mr. Keller's clothes, putting on his head a fur cap, and went out to obtain information of his comrades. Passing along the street he saw another party of five or six of our citizens in the hands of the rebels, among whom were Mr. Mong and Kitzmiller. When passing the party, who failed to recognize him in his disguise, he overheard one of the rebels declare that they were not satisfied for they had not yet caught that fellow with *the white vest* who wanted to break their gun. Finding it was not safe thus to expose himself upon the street, Mr. Houser went back to their place of concealment. One day while in their hiding place, they heard the sound of sawing. Upon making investigation, they found that Mrs. Keller had taken it into her head to provide a kind of underground railroad from the room they occupied to the cellar by sawing a hole in the floor into a closet. To their assurances that this would not likely be needed, their kind hostess desisted.

On Friday morning Snider and Houser determined that they would endeavor to pass through the lines and make their way home. And as a ruse to deceive the rebels they borrowed a market basket and some napkins of Mrs. Keller, determining to pass themselves as persons in search of butter for sick soldiers. They accordingly went out by what is called the Mud road, which leads from Hagerstown to Mercersburg. They had not proceeded far from town until they came upon a rebel encampment. The rebels stopped them and asked them who they were and where they were going. They told their story and were permitted to pass on. Seeing a farm house they went to it and found the women engaged in churning. They inquired if they could purchase butter. They were told that they could not as it was already engaged by the soldiers who were standing there and waiting for it. They said that they were eat out, and had some sick soldiers who must have butter, and offered one dollar a pound in gold, but were still refused. Houser says he had not a cent of money in his pocket, but they determined to put on a bold front to deceive the rebels. Their conduct entirely deceived the rebel guard, and they inquired where the main line was, which was told them and they were permitted to pass on. They had not proceeded far until they saw the glitter of bayonets over the brow of a hill, when they got over the fence and sat down under a tree. There were five rebels in this party, and when they came up to them they got over the fence, and when asked what they were after and where they were going, they told their butter story. "That's just what we are after," said one of the soldiers. They then proposed to the rebels that they would take a circuit among the farmers, and would meet them near the town, and whichever party succeeded in procuring butter should divide with the other. To this the rebels assented, and again they passed on. In a little while they were halted by five cavalrymen, to whom they repeated their story. These soldiers did not seem to credit their story, but after a parley Snider drew from his pocket a flask containing some whiskey. At the sight of this flask their eyes fairly danced, and one of the soldiers was about putting it to his mouth when he hesitated and said, "Perhaps it is drugged." Snider said, "Hand it back to me and I'll drink first." Seeing that Snider was willing to drink, and there was only enough for about four, the soldier said, "No, it's too precious," and took a drink and handed it to his comrades who drained it of its contents. After they had drank Snider said, "Well what are you going to do? Are you going to let us go on?" One of the soldiers replied, "Wait till we reach the top of that hill," pointing to a hill top near at hand, "and when we pass there you may go on." As soon as the hill was passed they passed on. In a little while they heard firing across a wheat field, and by taking a circuitous route they escaped and soon struck the road leading from Williamsport to Greencastle, which they followed and without further molestation reached the latter place. Leaving their basket there with a friend to send to Mrs. Keller, they at once set out for Chambersburg. On their way they saw the broken down wagons and other debris of the wagon train of wounded which had passed that way from Gettysburg a few days previously. When within about three miles of Chambersburg they met a number of men on horseback who proved to be reporters for several of the New York papers. When these men found out that Snider and Houser were right from Hagerstown, they plied them with questions, and returning to town they forwarded their dispatches to New York. The next day, Mr. Snider says, the New York papers contained important news from Hagerstown from their own special correspondents. Arriving home in the evening, tired and weary, they retired to bed, but Gen. Couch having that day removed his headquarters to this place and hearing of their return from within the enemy's lines, sent and had Mr. Sni-

der get up and go to his headquarters and tell him all he knew.

Such were the adventures of Snider and Houser as related by themselves, but what became of their companions who were left in the hands of the rebels? The three men—Steck, Tritle and Hamilton, who had gone into Hagerstown—upon entering the town and finding it occupied by the rebels, secreted themselves and escaped capture. The other party consisting of Mong, Kitzmiller and three or four others were taken along by the rebels. When about crossing the Potomac, at Falling Waters, Kitzmiller made his escape by running away, but narrowly escaped a shower of balls which were sent after him. The others were released at Bunker Hill, near Winchester, and permitted to return home. The fate of the remaining nine, viz., Dr. James Hamilton, Dr. George R. Kaufman, John P. Culbertson, George S. Heck, Thomas H. McDowell, J. Porter Brown, Charles Kinsler, Allen C. McGrath and D. M. Eiker, was as follows, as related by Mr. Eiker: "After Snider and Houser left us, and not finding the Provost Marshal in his office, we were taken to the porch in front of the house of Dr. Dorsey, on Washington street, and while sitting there the head of the column of Union soldiers captured at Gettysburg—about four thousand in number—came up, when we were ordered to fall in with them. In company with them we were marched towards Williamsport, and encamped that night in a wheat field. Throughout the night it rained heavily, and we got wet to the skin. The next day we were ferried across the river, and started on our long and wearisome journey to Richmond. Reaching Staunton by foot, some one hundred and twenty-five miles, about the 18th of July, we there embarked upon the cars and were taken to the Capital of the Confederacy, accomplishing what many others had for some time tried to do—take Richmond—or, rather I should say, Richmond had taken us,

"We arrived in Richmond, July 21st, about 4 A. M. Our first halt in the city was in front of 'Castle Thunder,' formerly a tobacco factory, but then used as a prison. We were then moved on down Carey street about two blocks, and halted in front of that noted place, 'Libby Prison.' Here we were taken to the office, where our name, age, and where we came from and what we had been doing to bring us there, were taken down, and after being searched, quarters were assigned us. Our quarters were in a room that was on a level with Carey street, and in the rear was one story high—the building standing on a slope—running back to the canal, and overlooking James River. The basement room was used as a cook house, where our rations were prepared. And such rations! It almost makes my teeth water to think of them. As to the manner of their being served to us—in the morning any time from 8 to 11 o'clock, a sergeant with a guard would come into the room and call for six, eight or ten men (as the case might require) and a blanket. When they returned, two to four men would have the blanket and in it our rations of bread for 24 hours, consisting of about 8 ounces for each man. The rest of the men would bring buckets containing meat—any kind from beef to mule. About 2 to 3 ounces constituted a ration. After cleaning the bones of all the meat, some of us turned our attention to manufacturing ornaments of jewelry, which we had no difficulty in disposing of to the rebels. In the evening, generally about dusk, we were furnished about a pint of soup. This soup was made of cow peas, a prolific crop in the South and used as food for cattle; hence their name. As this savory dish was brought in after it was dark, we ate it in *faith*, not knowing exactly all it was composed of. But one evening it was issued before sundown, and upon examining it I found that it contained bugs. I began to throw them out with my spoon—a wooden one I had whittled out of a piece of rail—but I soon discovered that if I took them all out I would have but little soup left. After that I took mine *straight*, bugs and all, concluding that as the bugs had come from the peas, they properly belonged there, and it was not right to separate them.

"The room overhead contained Federal officers; and in the dusk of the evening we would build a platform with barrels, and climbing upon it, hold conversation with them. On one occasion Dr. Hamilton passed a note up to an officer. One of the rebel authorities happened to be in the room at the time and signed the note. He then came down to our room, and in an insolent manner inquired, 'Where is this man Hamilton?' When he found him he was taken out and placed in a dungeon for several days. On another evening when the scaffolding had been put in place, and several parties had been up talking, an officer inquired for some one from Chambersburg, Pa. I happened near at the time, and was called and mounted the platform, when the following conversation took place: 'Are you from Chambersburg?' 'I am; my name is Eiker.' 'I am Captain Ed. Schroeder, of York, Pa., and a relation of the Nitterhouse family of Chambersburg. How are you off for grub?' 'Not very well.' 'Wait and I will pass you something?' In a few minutes he came and passed me some bread and crackers. The officers were allowed to buy, which we were not. This conversation was carried on through a hole in the floor that had been made for a large rope to pass through to hoist goods. After the war I met Capt. Schroeder and renewed the acquaintance and have visited him at his home in York, and have found him to be a genial, whole-souled gentleman. He shall always have a place in my memory.

"Frequently a squad of prisoners from Belle Isle, for transfer to another prison, would be brought in and turned into our room for the night. On such occasions we would be packed 'like herring in a box.' During the part of August that we were there, when the room would be crowded, we would be almost suffocated from heat. One day a citizen passing by stopped and looked up at the window. One of the prisoners looking out called to him, 'Come out from under that hat. I know you are in it. I see your feet sticking out.' The citizen reported this to the officers and charged it to our room. The consequence was, we were put on bread and water until the offender could be found out. This punishment was kept up for several days when it was suggested by some one of the prisoners that if someone in the room would acknowledge himself the offender they would give him a certain number of rations of bread. Finally one of the men agreed. He was taken out and put in the dungeon. After that we received our usual rations. A guard was stationed at a stairway in our room, and one day a surly fellow was on this post. He took a bayonet and marked a line on the floor with the remark, 'Now, ——— you, stay outside that.' Owing to the crowded condition of the room I, by some means, got on this line, when he gave me a bayonet thrust on my left cheek just below the eye.

"Sometime in the latter part of August I was transferred to 'Castle Thunder,' another of the prisons of Richmond for Union prisoners. Castle Thunder—classic name! How or where it came by that name I never learned. It was a tobacco factory prior to the war. When it was made known to us that the 'Castle' was our destination we felt rather blue. During our sojourn in Libby we heard all sorts of tales of the horrors and cruelties of that place, but we were agreeably disappointed. The discipline was not as rigid as in Libby, and rations were better. In the morning we received good bread and beef in fair quantities. In the afternoon good vegetable soup. But as there is an end to all things under the sun, the end came to our good fare. Towards the end of summer our rations began to diminish, until they consisted of a small piece of corn bread and about a pint of boiled cow peas.

"When first taken to the 'Castle' we were confined in what is termed as the 'Court Martial Room'—a room in the rear of the main building. On Sunday the post chaplain by the name of Carpenter—a very poor carpenter of theology he was—came in to preach to the "Heathen Yankees.' I will give a specimen of his preaching and the reader can judge how much his services were appreciated. Discoursing on the glories of Heaven, he remarked, 'Why, my hearers, the Confederacy in all her glory is nothing in comparison with the glory of heaven.' Had he taken *the other place* for the comparison the bill would have been much better filled. Prisoners were from time to time taken from the Court Martial Room and distributed in other rooms in the building. Dr. Kauffman, J. Porter Brown and myself were put in what was termed 'The Citizens' Room,' because all confined here were political prisoners. In other rooms were rebel convicts and Yankee deserters. These deserters were the worst used of any prisoners that came under my observation. They were the only prisoners I ever saw flogged. A little colored boy from York. Pa., captured during the invasion, was in Castle Thunder, but was allowed to go and come at his pleasure. It was Joe's—that was the only name we knew him by—business to conduct fresh arrivals to their rooms, and whenever we heard his cry of 'Fresh Fish,' we knew that some other unfortunate ones were to be added to our number. Joe usually before leaving his charge would caution them to 'Look out when you get in there or them fellows will mug you.' That is, go through them and steal whatever might be worth stealing. In some parts of the building this was generally the case with fresh arrivals.

"Divided by a plank partition from the room we were in was the 'Condemned Cell,' and it was supposed that all persons put there were under sentence of death, which was no doubt true. A fine looking young man, known in prison by the name of Cole, said to be from Kentucky, was one day brought into the corridor and placed in double irons—that is wrists and ankles were manacled. I witnessed the ironing and never saw, apparently, such cool indifference in any one. Whilst the irons were being riveted on he stood and whistled, paying no more attention to what was being done than if the irons were being put on some one else a thousand miles away. There were one or two others in the cell where he was put. In a short time after Cole was put in this cell; throughout the day and night considerable noise was heard, such as the clanking of chains and thumping their balls upon the floor. This was kept up for some time and to us it seemed mysterious. One night the mystery was explained. About eleven o'clock we were aroused by the discharge of a musket in the corridor below us, followed by groans. We soon learned that Cole and a fellow prisoner had made their escape from the cell, disarmed the guard and shot him, one of them taking his musket and accoutrements, the other marching by his side as though a prisoner. They went out through the streets and it was reported that they got out of Richmond and finally reached the Union line. Of the truth of their final escape I cannot vouch. While the noise we heard was going on, they were engaged in getting off their irons and sawing a hole in the floor, through which they escaped. Next morning I went down stairs, and looking in the corridor saw the poor fellow that had been on guard lying there dead. It made me feel very sad, but I could find no fault with Cole or his companion for what they had done. No doubt it was with them, 'Your life or ours.'

"While in the Castle I met Alexander Lewis, a colored man, from this place, known to many of our citizens, and now employed, I think, at the National hotel. Alex. was captured and taken to Richmond and sent to the Castle and put in charge of the culinary department. We could buy something at the Sutler's called coffee, but none of us could tell what it was composed of. But after we had this 'coffee,' the trouble was to make it, for there was neither stove nor fireplace in our room. We finally bargained with Alex. to prepare it for us in the cook house. In the morning you could have seen parties with cords of every description waiting their turn at a certain window to lower their vessels and receive their coffee (?) from Alex. This was in the fall when the mornings began to be cool, and a cup of this stuff served to warm us up after we had slept on the soft side of the floor. This was before I was lucky enough to own a bunk.

One evening about the time the elections were held in Pennsylvania, two cavalry officers—a Captain and Lieutenant of the Rebel army were brought to the Castle and placed in the Citizen's room. During the evening the Captain joined our group, who were discussing the topics of the day, among others the elections in Northern States that were about that time held. Not knowing who we were, or where we came from, he began to spread his views, and make assertions which we knew to be utterly false. I kept quiet until he asserted that at elections held in Pennsylvania, Democrats were either not permitted to vote, or were marched to the polls at the point of the bayonet, and compelled to vote the Republican ticket. That was more than I could stand, and I said to him, 'Excuse me, sir, but you have been asserting some things in regard to the elections in Pennsylvania that are incorrect. I have seen elections held there, and I never saw anything like what you say.' At this he became very angry, and turned towards me and said, 'Where did you come from, and who are you?' I told him who I was and where I came from, when he said, 'I know you, and have seen you many a time.' About that time I began to feel a little shaky, and thought, 'Is this fellow going to trump up something against me to get me into more trouble?' I said to him, 'I think you are mistaken; I have no recollection whatever of ever having seen you?' By this time his indignation had somewhat subsided, and he said, 'Do you remember a person by the name of Glenn, who accidentally, one night in a fracas in Chambersburg, shot a friend named McLaughlin?' I said, 'Of course I do.' 'Well, I am the man.' Some of our citizens may remember the occurrence. It took place, as near as I can remember, between 1857 and 1859, on North Main street, at a house of questionable character. After this the subject of elections was dropped, and he began to ply me with questions thick and fast in regard to Chambersburg and the people he knew, among others, what had become of his friend McLaughlin? I told him that he had lost his life at Fredericksburg fighting for the old flag. At this he seemed much affected. The conversation by this time had taken a very pleasant turn, and was continued until late in the night. In a day or two the Captain and his Lieutenant were taken away and I never heard of them afterwards. I understood that they had been placed under arrest for some breach of discipline. When I retired to my bunk I asked Porter Brown, who shared my bunk, if he recognized the man I had been talking with? He said 'Don't tell him I am here; my father was Sheriff when he was in prison for that shooting.' But by some means Glenn found Porter out, and they had long chats together."

"Some time in October, 1863, in company with many others, we were sent to Salisbury, North Carolina, to be held as hostages for a like number of persons held by our government for bushwhacking, bridge burning, &c. Salisbury at that time, considered as a Rebel prison, was not the worst place in the Confederacy. During the winter of 1863 and summer of 1864, we got along pretty fairly considering that we were 'in jail.' The number of prisoners was about five to six hundred. The larger number were Rebel convicts, sentenced to 'solitary' confinement with 'ball and chain,' both of which were 'thin,' for they had the same privileges of going out and coming in that others had. As to balls and chains, a large cistern upon being cleaned, revealed about a cart load of them that had been taken off and thrown in by the prisoners. The building used as a prison had been a cotton factory. It was large and four stories high. It, with a number of small buildings, formerly used for offices and operatives, afforded shelter for all. The stockade contained about three acres enclosed by a high board fence near the top of which a platform extended. On this platform the sentries were placed. A well of good water and a number of forest trees were inside the stockade. Every morning the rebel convicts were made to sweep the greater portion of the grounds. At one time Dr. Curry was surgeon in charge. He was also a Doctor of Divinity and frequently on the Sabbath preached to us.

"From October, the time of our induction to Salisbury, nothing of special importance transpired, until near Christmas. A number of sailors—merchantmen, who were prisoners—had a lot of bunting, and it was agreed that a flag should be made and at Christmas we would have 'a jolly, good time.' The sailors went to work and made a flag and on Christmas eve the good time began. One of the prisoners had an old violin, and the 'Grand March' began after dark, the fiddle leading, and every fellow that could sing 'Rally around the flag boys,' joined in the procession. Round and round the room we went, singing and cheering the old flag, which attached to a stick, was carried at the head of the procession. We kept this up until about midnight. By some means the authorities learned that we had a United States flag in our room, when a search was made and our flag taken from us and placed upon the top of the building with the Union down—a sign of distress. It was certainly appropriate for us, for we were in distress. How long it was allowed to remain there I have forgotten, and what became of it afterward I never knew.

"Some time in the winter some of the boys conceived the idea of tunnelling out. Among the number was J. Porter Brown and Thomas McDowell, both well known citizens of Chambersburg. The lower floor of the building, in which we were confined, was not occupied. It was under this floor that it was decided to tunnel. A plank was taken up and through the opening one went below. There were from two to two and a-half feet between the floor and the ground. The men were divided into working parties, so many for each day. As a guard was stationed at the door leading into this room, it took some time before the number detailed could all get through, but as each one got down through the floor he went to work. The tools used were anything in the shape of iron, from a case-knife to an old gate hinge, as much twine as could be got and a couple of small boxes. The mode of operation was this,—as many as could get in dug loose the earth. Another filled it into the boxes; others with the twine drew them away. They would stay down under the floor the greater part of the day working like beavers. The work had been going on in this way for some time when, as the boys said, some one 'blowed' on them, and those who had been engaged at it were taken out, 'Bucked and Gagged' and afterwards put into a dungeon. After their release from the dungeon, the commandant had the floor taken up and compelled them to carry stones and fill up the hole. And such a hole as it was—large as an ordinary sized cistern. After the hole had been filled the floor was nailed down again.

Not long after this, notwithstanding this failure, another party took it into hand, and after working awhile they too were discovered and had to fill up the excavation they had made. Still another party —some rebel convicts, undertook to open the tunnel. They did not calculate distance correctly, for when they made the opening out as they supposed into liberty, they found that they were still inside the stockade. The opening was one foot short from the fence. After this the authorities ordered the entire floor taken up. The room afterwards was used without a floor for a hospital."

Up to this point I have followed the narrative given principally by Mr. D. M. Eiker. I will now introduce some important facts related by Mr. Eiker and A. C. McGrath, and also culled from a record kept by Mr. McGrath. The manner of subsistence was as follows: The men were divided into messes of two and four, or more, just as parties suited each other. One of the messes consisted of A. C. McGrath, D. M. Eiker, Dr. Kaufman, Alexander Harper, (now of Greencastle), and Captain May, of Pittsburg. Mr. McGrath was made commissary or caterer. He was also made commissary for the hospital, as the following paper shows, the original of which is now before me.

Mr. McGrath, citizen prisoner, is hereby constituted commissary agent for the distribution of commissary supplies within the Prison Hospital, and will be allowed the extra ration usual under such circumstances. He will receive the rations issued for the prison hospital and see that they are properly prepared and distributed according to the number of patients in each ward. He will also see that the supply of hospital wood is properly distributed according to the number of prisoners, and the size thereof in each ward.

JNO. WILSON, JR.,
Surgeon in charge of C. S. Military Prison Hospital, Salisbury, N. C.
Jan. 26th, 1865.

In the execution of his duties as set forth in the foregoing paper, Mr. McGrath was allowed the privilege of going outside of the prison into the town, as is shown in the following copy of his parole:

(Duplicate.)

CONFEDERATE STATES MILITARY PRISON,
SALISBURY, N. C.,
No. 38.   Jan. 31st, 1865.

I Allen C. McGrath, a political prisoner, do hereby give my PAROLE OF HONOR not to attempt to ESCAPE, OR AID OR ABET others in making their escape, or do anything contrary to the *Honor or interest of the Confederate States until duly exchanged*, or this PAROLE shall be cancelled.

I do further declare that I will confine myself to such limits as the commandant of the Post or Prison shall designate—to the limits of Salisbury, N. C.   A. C. M'GRATH.
Witness: J. L. LYERLY.
Approved: JNO. H. GEE, *Maj. Commanding.*

The following is Mr. M'Grath's pass:

CONFEDERATE STATES MILITARY PRISON,
SALISBURY, N. C.,
No. 21.   January 31st, 1865.

The bearer, A. C. McGrath, will be allowed to pass the —— of the prison during the day time only for 30 days.

JNO. H. GEE,
Major Commanding.

That those of our citizens associated with Mr. McGrath in the prison would be benefitted by the liberty allowed him in procuring articles of food and other conveniences, which the prison regulations did not supply, will appear in the facts yet to be related. The Post Sutler, Mr. L. Taff, who took a kind interest in our citizen prisoners, agreed to furnish them with such articles as they needed, receiving his payment as they earned money in the way hereinafter designated, or at some future time. Mr. McGrath run up accounts with him amounting to as high as twenty-eight hundred dollars, and in one case over three thousand dollars. At the time of their departure from the South, Mr. McGrath's account was over two thousand dollars, and a year or two after the close of the war Mr. Taff visited Mr. McGrath at this place and enjoyed his hospitality and renewed old acquaintance for a week or two, when this account was adjusted by the payment of some three hundred and seventy-five dollars in greenbacks, which was entirely satisfactory to Mr. Taff, for the prices charged for the articles were proportioned to the market value of Confederate scrip at the time of the purchase.

Mr. McGrath's method was to keep an account of the expenditures for the mess for a month, at the expiration of which each person was charged for his share, as well as for any extra luxuries, as will be shown presently. To give an idea of the manner of living, as well as the prices paid, I copy a few items from Mr. McGrath's book now before me: 2 lbs. coffee $20; box shoe blacking $3; 2 lbs. sugar $20; stockings $13; flour $16; pepper $1.50; beef $18; chicken $10; goose $30; apples $1; dried apples $5; soda $3; cabbage $10; potatoes $20; turnips $6; bacon, 5 lbs. $30; chicken $20; parsnips $5; envelopes $5; onions $5; sausage $5; eggs $30; butter $60; molasses $13.50. Judging from the frequent charges for potatoes, tobacco, onions and such luxuries, with an occasional goose at thirty dollars, and chickens at from seven to ten dollars, with all the other necessary "fixins" for the table, it will be seen that McGrath was the right man for the place. The occasional charges of several dollars for needles and thread suggests the idea of sewing on buttons and mending clothes. In the individual accounts charged to the persons composing the mess, I find one person, whose name I withhold lest he be charged with gross extravagance, charged with tobacco $6; tooth-brush $5; share in mess $36.55; tobacco $10; thread $1.80; tobacco $6; stockings $6.50; salt $2.50; chicken, (perhaps he was an invalid and needed something extra), $10; pie $2; envelopes $5; apples $5; medicine purchased in town $25. About the only article of luxury charged to Mr. Eiker, other than his share in a goose at thirty dollars, chickens at ten dollars, and other things in proportion, is twenty dollars for a *breastpin*. Mr. Eiker explains this purchase in this way: Some impecunious prisoner had this article of jewelry and needing tobacco or some other things more than it, traded it to him for twenty dollars in Confederate scrip. Mr. Eiker yet has this breastpin and says it is a very valuable one.

It would be injustice to Mr. McGrath to pass by his skill as a caterer to his mess without referring especially to his abilities in making pies and Indian puddings. It might be that some of our hotels or restaurants need a first-class cook or baker, or some of our lady readers might desire to take lessons in these desirable acquirements, and justice to them as well as to Mr. McGrath requires that he be placed upon record here. Coming into the prison one day, he was asked what he had procured for dinner? "Nothing," he replied, "but I'll see about that." Going out again for a little while he returned with some blackberries and flour. Procuring some water, he put in the flour and began the process of making pies. With the rim of his cap turned up so as not to interfere with his sight, and all eyes turned upon him as he proceeded to knead the dough, and occasionally stopping in the interesting process to answer some question, or to attend to some other duty, at the same time endeavoring to disentangle his fingers from the sticky stuff by wiping them upon his pantaloons, he succeeded in placing before his hungry, but admiring mess, several delicious blackberry pies. True, they were not very short and crisp, for they were composed only of flour, water and blackberries, but short pie-crust was not wholesome for persons accustomed to so little out-door exercise. The subject of discussion while at dinner was, whether the jolly baker had not as much dough upon his trousers as in the pies! "Ah," says Eiker, "my mouth watered when I looked upon those pies, and water yet whenever I think of them." But if McGrath had one specialty over another it was in making Indian Puddings. Coming in one day with near a peck of blackberries, we inquired what he was going to do with them? The delectable idea of blackberry pies danced before our imagination. "Never you mind," said he, "I'll show you." After mixing the meal and making up the dough, and putting in the blackberries, a halt was called. A bag was necessary to boil it in. What was to be done now? Mac set his wits to work to get over this difficulty, and after considerable "beating around," a happy thought suggested itself to him. A pair of drawers belonging to some one of the prisoners was seen hanging on the wall. No sooner did these come under his notice than he was out of his trouble. What use has a person for the luxury of drawers in jail? and why put on such appendages of civilization and gentility when all could not have the same? Taking out his knife he cut off one leg, washed it and put the pudding in and soon it was boiled and ready for use. "Mac" says the pudding bag was not exactly to his liking when he put it in the pot, but when he took it out it was clean and white. But now another dilemma confronted them. Indian pudding, even though so artistically made, was not a savory dish without sauce. Where was that to be had? Wine was out of the question, but Dr. Kaufman thought commissary whiskey would answer, and as he was acting as assistant surgeon and had access to the drug and medicine department, he *borrowed* of the Confederacy a small quantity and the bill of fare was complete. When the pudding, flavored with the doctor's captured whiskey, was set before the admiring mess, it was unanimously decided that it was an improvement even upon "Mac's" pies. Surely such genius as Mr. McGrath displayed in catering to his mess is worthy of everlasting remembrance, and so far as I can do so I give him this immortality of fame.

After this pleasant digression, I return now to Mr. Eiker's account. "As a matter of recreation, and with the view to turning my opportunities to the best account, I turned my attention to making jewelry out of bones. I usually made two finger rings a day, which I sold to the Johnnies at fifteen dollars a piece in "Confederate shucks." These I used to defray expenses or turned into Greenbacks, at the rate of from three to ten, and sometimes twenty dollars in currency for one dollar Federal money. Brokers in the prison were sometimes as plentiful as in Wall street. In the morning they were usually "on 'Change," with fists full of Confederate scrip. The usual inquiry was, "How much are you paying to-day?" "Five for one. How much do you pay?" "Ten for one." It is said that in some cases Confederate officers furnished this scrip to exchange into Greenbacks, they paying a commission to the persons negotiating for them. At one time a broker from Richmond, said to have been sent by the Confederate Government, came to Salisbury, and advertised through the stockade by posters that on the following day he would be on hand to purchase greenbacks, and would pay three dollars for one. Among the prisoners was a sailor from Philadelphia, and although a Norwegian by birth, he was one of the truest and shrewdest of Yankees. This man's name was Jack Lovell, and he acted sometimes in the capacity of a broker. After seeing the Richmond broker's advertisement, Jack swore that he would make him pay for Greenbacks. True to his threat, Jack went next morning "on 'Change," and "bulled the market" so that before the Richmond chap came upon the board Greenbacks were up twenty for one in Confederate scrip. The consequence was the Richmond fellow could not get a single dollar. One of the Yankee prisoners had brought with him some two dollar bills, also some fifty cent fractional currency. These he raised to larger amounts so adroitly that he "shoved" them upon the Johnnies for sums ranging from three to six hundred dollars. At length the fraud was discovered, but the perpetrator was not.

"What I have been saying may be termed the bright side of our prison life at Salisbury, and I will now give the reader the other or *dark side*. Some time during the month of October, 1864, about 11,000 Federal prisoners were sent to our prison. Then what had been, during the summer, all things considered, a tolerably fair place—perhaps one of the best regulated prisons in the Confederacy, was turned into a pandemonium. Men were turned into the stockade like cattle into a field, without shelter. Winter coming on, and the rations poor, their condition was unpromising indeed. The authorities did finally furnish a few tents. All the buildings, with one exception, were appropriated for hospital purposes. For about eleven months I was placed in the hospital department, and my duty was to keep the books up to the time of my escape. It was my duty to visit all the hospitals each morning after "Surgeon's Call," to report deaths, convalescents, discharges, and to assign the sick to vacant places in the wards. Discharges, other than those made by the grim reaper, were rare. Eight o'clock has arrived, and I am about to start on my morning round. Will the reader go with me and witness the sad sights? Here we are at Hospital No. 1, a frame building one and a half stories high, and about seventy-five feet long, and wide enough for a row of cots on each side. There is a chimney in the centre with two fire places facing from the centre. But what is the use of fire places without wood—for such frequently was the case for several days at a time during the winter? The building was on a slope, and built on pillars of brick ten or twelve feet apart. Between these pillars the prisoners had built up with clay, leaving small spaces to crawl in and out. This was a place of shelter for all that could get in. Of course at the upper end the space between the ground and floor was not higher than barely to allow a man to crawl under. Poor fellows! Many were glad to crawl in there to seek shelter from the cold, and there many died. I have seen many a poor fellow cold in death dragged from under that building and carried to the dead house. But what means that crowd gathering at the end of the building? Some are borne on the shoulders of comrades, others in blankets. This is "Surgeon's Call," and these poor fellows are coming with a vain hope that something may be done to relieve them of their sufferings. Some are begging for medicine; others for admission to the hospital. It was indeed a sad duty for me—these morning rounds. Of all these poor fellows—brave defenders of their country —this will be their last sick call for some of them. To-morrow's sun will not arise for them. They will have gone where sickness and pain can never more reach them. It may be thought that I exaggerate when I say that *scores of them* are making their last appeal for help ere they close their eyes forever to earth, but such is not the case. During the winter the death rate reached as high as sixty a day. The burial squad with a wagon in which the bodies were piled like so many pieces of wood, many of them stripped of every particle of clothing, their arms dangling over the sides of the wagon and against the wheels, would daily pass around and carry the poor fellows who had died during the night to the place of burial. In some cases so many died that they could not all be buried in one day. But as there are five or six more hospitals to visit, we will not tarry here to look inside to see the innumerable cases of wretchedness and suffering, but move on. We are now at Hospital No. 2. This is a small building, 16 by 24 feet, having a chimney at each end. Ranged side by side, on a little straw spread on the floor, along the sides of the room, lay the poor fellows shivering with the cold, their only covering being rags, filth and vermin. As this hospital is a fair sample of all the others, and the narration of the horrible may not be agreeable to the reader, I will not enter into any description of them.

A great deal of the terrible suffering endured by our prisoners might have been avoided, had the authorities given us tools and the privilege to use some of the timber which was convenient and plentiful. Comfortable quarters could have been made for both the sick and the well. Frequently the hospitals would be without wood for a day or two at a time. At one time our well of water failed to supply the demand, when the commandant of the Post furnished some picks and shovels for the men to dig wells. But not being furnished with other implements, they were not very successful in procuring water. I have seen men so pressed for water that, scant as their rations were, they bartered bread for a drink of water. The earth taken out of these wells was utilized by the men by making it into large, square blocks, and with them building huts for their shelter. Any that were fortunate enough to have a piece of tent, or a blanket for a roof over these huts could thus make a tolerably good shelter. Some dug caves in the ground and lived in them. The rations, never amounting to much, became smaller and worse in quality. At one time the bread furnished appeared to have been made of corn—cobs and all—and sorghum seed ground together.

"Some time in the month of November, 1864, an attempt was made by a small squad to break out and capture the garrison—they by some means having learned that two regiments had been ordered away and left. The regiments had left the garrison, but were yet at the depot in Salisbury awaiting a train to take them to their destination. The squad began their work by attacking the relief and the guard and capturing their arms. The first intimation I had of it was in this way: I was sitting by a window in Hospital No. 1, and hearing the report of a gun, I supposed that there had been some thieving going on at the Sutler's, or among the men, as was often the case. On looking out I saw a Federal prisoner with a gun, when I knew what was going on. In a short time the "Long Roll" was sounded, and the two regiments, which it was supposed had left the town, "double quicked" back to the stockade. These with the other soldiers on duty, and two pieces of artillery, opened fire upon the prisoners. After a time the firing ceased when an order came from the commandant to return all the guns taken within a certain time, and if not returned by the time specified, he would open fire again and keep it up until they were returned. This order could not be complied with for by that time some of the guns had been thrown into a cistern that was about forty feet deep. The consequence was the order to open fire was given, and it was resumed by the infantry and the artillery. It was indeed a fearful experience. It would not have been so bad had we been permitted to fire back. The building I was in was weatherboarded, and the bullets whistled through it. Fortunately no one in the building was struck. Some balls struck the chimney and fell back on some bunks that were occupied by sick men. I do not now remember how long the firing continued, but it seemed to me at the time to be ages. And I have forgotten the number killed and wounded. A number of men lying in a tent at the lower end of the ground, who had nothing to do with the outbreak, were torn to pieces by the artillery. I worked with the surgeons almost the entire night caring for the wounded. The artillery was charged with boiler punchings, and they made ugly wounds. I remember one poor fellow, quite a boy, from whose hand and arm we cut three of these boiler punchings. For several nights after this outbreak, whenever a person was seen moving about, some too-willing rebel was ready to fire upon him. Numbers of poor fellows secured their last furlough in that way. The "Dead Line," an imaginary line about five feet from the fence, was the limit set to the men, and none were allowed to pass it. Many poor fellows unthinkingly approached too close to this line and were shot down like wild beasts. And any rebel who had a desire or ambition to excite a little notoriety by killing a "Yankee" would watch his chance and make an approach to this line a pretext to fire. I forgot to say at the appropriate place that the guns thrown into the cistern, twenty-four in number, were taken from the cistern the day after the revolt.

Attempts were made at different times after the fruitless and costly effort, to escape by tunnelling and other ways, and for doing so I have seen men bucked and gagged, tied up by the thumbs, stripped to the waist and flogged until they would faint and hang limp in the cords that bound them. These punishments inflicted upon our men for their efforts to escape from their miserable bondage, were ordered by Post Commander, Captain Alexander, a deserter from the United States Navy. This Captain Alexander had with him the finest specimen of a canine I ever saw—a Russian blood hound. Whether he was used for hunting escaped prisoners or not I never knew. If he was I did not find it out.

"Some time in Dec. 1864, Dr. Kaufman, J. Porter Brown, T. H. McDowell, a North Carolinian by the name of Anges, and myself, (Eiker), managed to effect our escape from our prison, and for a time tasted the sweetness of freedom. It was accomplished in the following manner: Brown had been selected by the surgeon in charge to go outside the stockade to the Dispensary for medicines for the prisoner's hospital, and a pass was furnished him for that purpose. The idea suggested itself to some of us that if that pass could be duplicated we could effect our escape, and accordingly McGrath was applied to. The result proved that he could cook passes as well as bake pies and Indian puddings, and in a short time each of the four persons named, besides Brown, had the needed paper. Perhaps I ought not to have said anything about this for McGrath might yet be indicted for forgery. The arrangement was to pass out of the prison separately between daybreak and sunrise and meet at or near a certain designated point located by observation from the stockade. We accordingly presented our passes which were duly honored—the intervals between each one were short. I was the last to go; Dr. Kaufman was next before me. He could not have been more than one hundred yards before me when I passed out, and yet strange to say, I saw nothing of him or any of the party from that time until the 18th day of Jan. 1865, when we met again in our old quarters. And what was unaccountably strange at the time, they failed to wait at the designated place for all to come up. This was explained afterwards when we were returned to prison. It was noticed by each of us on passing the barracks that there was a considerable stir amongst the guard and frequent calls for 'corporal of the guard.' This caused a suspicion that information of our departure had been given. The first four managed to keep in sight of each other, and when they came together, they concluded that it was not safe to wait for me and at once moved on. This I afterwards considered fortunate for me, for the following week I was taken sick and remained ill for about two weeks. When I gained the place designated, I looked for my companions, in all directions, and called them as loud as I thought advisable, for I was scarcely out of hearing of the men in the barracks. After some time spent in wandering up and down the banks of a small stream, and through the bushes looking for them, I sat down on a stump to meditate. Well do I remember the morning, such as we usually have here in October—bright, crisp and frosty—just a morning to make one feel as though a new lease of life had been given. There I sat on that stump 'cogitating,' enjoying the bright morning and my freedom—the first time in a year and a-half that I had gone anywhere without a man and gun to accompany me. After due and deliberate consideration, I came to the conclusion that the boys were not to be found, and I would not undertake the trip alone. I then concluded that I would take a stroll into Salisbury, which was only a short distance away, take a look at the place, and then go back to my old quarters. No one molested me until I reached the entrance to the stockade after returning from the town, when I experienced my first trouble. As I had destroyed my pass as soon as I had gotten outside, I had none now to show to get in again. The guard for awhile refused to let me enter, but at length I succeeded in pushing open the gate and going in. Of course I was not glad to get back again, but rather than take the risk of finding my companions, or taking the tramp alone, I went back. The reader may imagine, if he can, what were my feelings upon again entering this 'Prison Pen,' after a few hours of freedom, and the thought that the boys were on their journey home and I left behind. It made me sick to think of it. This feeling was not decreased as I thought day after day of my escaped comrades as nearing 'God's country' and soon being at their homes.

"On the 18th day of January, 1865, towards evening, three dirty, ragged and smoke-begrimmed men were turned into the stockade, and the word soon passed around that Kaufman, Brown and McDowell had been recaptured. In a short time this report was confirmed by the appearance of the men themselves. They had gone towards Newbern, travelling about three weeks, and when within about six miles of the Union lines were recaptured. The North Carolinian who was also captured at the same time, was not immediately returned to our prison, but in a short time after the return of the others, was also brought back and placed in his old quarters.

"Having had a brief experience of liberty, we immediately after our return, began preparations for another escape, which was effected February 18th, just one month after the return of these men. This was accomplished in this way: In the afternoon of Friday, February 17th, Dr. Kaufman said to me that that night there would be an opportunity for four persons to escape, and asked me if I would be one of them? The doctor, it will be remembered, was an assistant surgeon to the prisoner's hospital, and had opportunities for mingling with the guards and ascertaining their feelings and sentiments which none of the rest of us enjoyed. And in his secret conferences he ascertained that a certain Corporal of the guard was willing for a compensation to permit a limited number of his prisoners to pass out. The Doctor had arranged with him that when it came to his turn to be on guard he would pass four of us out for twenty-five dollars each in Greenbacks, and that night was his turn. When the proposal was made to me by the doctor to be one of the four, I at first hesitated, for I had been unwell for sometime, and was afraid I could not endure the fatigue of the journey. But after considering the matter for sometime I agreed to go. Accordingly at the time agreed upon, Dr. Kaufman, J. Porter Brown, a man by the name of Galbraith from Centre county, Pennsylvania, and myself, passed out of the stockade handing the guard the sum agreed upon. Referring to my Diary, I find it reads thus:—"Left Salisbury at 11 o'clock A. M., homeward bound." After passing out we travelled until daylight, and then laid in the woods during the day. After dark we started again, and reached the south branch of the Yadkin river, and as it was very dark we concluded to lie down and sleep until the moon would rise. As soon as the moon rose we set to work to build a raft on which to cross the river. Fortunately we had brought with us all the rope and twine we could find before we started, and having gathered a lot of rails and driftwood, we soon had the thing ready, when to our amazement we found that it would not swim. Daylight coming on we had to abandon the raft and seek a place of concealment for the day.

In the evening we again started, but before reaching the road we heard a person coming up the road singing. One of our party went out to see who it was and met a colored man who told him that we were close to the Ferry, and that if we would go to the river and call, the ferryman on the opposite side would come over for us. After reaching the river we called for sometime before any one answered. Finally we heard the ferryman unchain his boat, and then came the words, 'Is you walkin'?' When the boat reached our side we stepped in and without a word from either party he pushed off from the shore. When we got out at the other side I said to the colored man (for such he proved to be), 'Uncle do you know who we are?' 'No, I dosent,' he replied. 'We are Yankees,' I said. 'Is you? I se put about sebenty of your men across dis winter," he replied. He then took us to his house and gave us our supper for which we paid him ten dollars in Confederate scrip. He then directed us to take the road and travel on as there was no danger. We intended flanking Mocksville during the night, but one of our party gave out and so we had to stop. We lay in a woods during that day with nothing to eat. During the afternoon of that day an old colored woman, gathering wood, came close to us, when Dr. Kaufman went out to see her in regard to something to eat, and for news. When she saw the doctor, her first words were, "Don't come near me; I's afraid of you." When the doctor got close enough to her he told her who we were, when her fears were gone. In conversation with her she informed us that we were close by Mocksville, and that her master lived in the first house going into the town, and if we would call at a small house in the yard close by the fence and tap on the fence, she would give us something to eat. She also told us that about 300 rebel cavalry were lying close by on the left side of the town—the side we intended taking had not one of our party given out. This was certainly a providential interposition, for had he not given out we would have gone that way, and would most certainly have run into their camp and been captured. In the evening we followed the old lady's directions and tapped on the fence. She came out bringing a loaf of corn bread and a piece of boiled bacon. After thanking and bidding her good-bye, we flanked the town on the right, stopping in a field to take supper off of old auntie's corn bread and bacon. I must say here that I never ate supper that tasted better. We travelled all that night, and the next day we lay in the woods near Farmington. In the evening we started again and were frightened from our course by what appeared to be a rebel officer on horseback. When we left Salisbury we intended coming by way of West Virginia, and had been travelling in a northernly direction up to that time. This circumstance changed our course, and we turned westward. We travelled until morning when we lay down and slept, and when we awoke we found we were among a range of hills in which we travelled all that day. Towards evening it began to rain, and we stopped on one of those hills and began to make preparations to spend the night, gathering brush and leaves to make a shelter. While engaged in that way, a woman came up a road that wound around the hill, when Dr. Kauffman went to the foot of the hill to meet her. On meeting her he asked her if there were any Union men about there? After eyeing him sharply, she replied, 'If you are what I think you are, I can tell you all you want to know in a very few minutes.' After further conversation with her, the doctor repeated the question, when the reply was the same. Finally the Doctor told her that we were Yankees. She then said that the man who lived at the hill was a good Union man, and so were his boys. After further telling us that she had just come from the house, and left one of the boys there, she passed on up the hill. Dr. Kaufman then went down to the house to see about getting something to eat. The woman had been gone but a short time until she returned to the top of the hill and called to us that one of the boys was up there and if we were 'all right,' he was also, and would meet us. I accordingly met him, and very soon discovered that he was what the rebels called a "Bush Boy"—that is a Union man, and conscripted, and having deserted the army had come home and was living among the hills, mountains and caves. In a very few minutes we were joined by some six or eight more, who had been notified and came to see us. After talking awhile, I suggested that we go on with our preparations for spending the night, when one of our friends said that it was unnecessary, as it promised to be dark and rainy and he did not think any guards would be out that night. They also said that they would risk to take us down to their barn to sleep. After dark we were conducted down to their house and had a good supper. As soon as we were done eating we were taken back over the hill to their camp, where we remained until about 9 o'clock, when we went to the barn and laid down in the hay. Before daylight we were called up for breakfast, and as soon as we were through with it we went back to the hills before it became quite light. After some more consultation it was agreed that some of the boys should go with us two or three miles to put us in the right way. They accordingly did so and when they had put us right and given us all the information they could, and directed us where to find the next friends, they bade us farewell. We started on and travelled all that day through a drenching rain, and towards evening we stopped and gathered some brush and leaves to make a shelter under which to spend the night. That night was the longest I ever experienced. The rain continued to fall all night long. It was rain above us, below us—rain to the right of us, and rain to the left of us. But that night, like all other nights, came to an end, and we made a start, and after wandering around for some time concluded that we were completely lost. We accordingly retraced our steps until we came in sight of a house we saw the evening before. Brown was of the opinion that this house was the one our friends of the morning before, when about taking leave of us, directed us to call at for information for other friends. The rest of us hooted at the idea of its being the same, for they told us it was six miles from where we parted from them, and we had been travelling hard all day and supposed we had at least made twenty miles. At last to settle the matter Brown and I went to the house and sure enough it was the place we had been directed to. So with all our long and painful walking the day before, we had been zig-zagging, and perhaps been walking in a circle and made about six or eight miles in a direct course. The persons we found there were friends, but could not entertain us as it was on a public road, and cavalry were passing back and forth, and some rebels lived close by. They, however, gave us something to eat, and all the information they could in regard to the country and the people we were travelling amongst. They also directed us to an old lady—"Auntie Lucinda D——"—living some distance beyond and near Hamptonville. Whilst travelling on we saw an old gentleman riding through the woods, and tried to dodge him, but in this we failed. He came riding up to us when, as near as I can remember, the following conversation took place:—'Well, boys, you home from the army?' 'Yes,' we replied. 'Well how are things going on there?' 'All right.' we said. 'Some of our leading men around here think that it is not going as it should.' 'Never mind about that; we've been fighting the Yanks for four years, and if necessary will fight them four years longer.' (How was that for '*yarning*.') I don't know whether it was any consolation for the old gentleman or not, but he bid us good-bye and rode on when we again started on our tramp to find Aunt Lucinda D——. Towards evening we came across a colored man and two white boys. The man was working; the boys hunting. When we got close to the colored man he said to us, 'You does not want to be seen, does you?' Of course we answered that we did not. Just then the boys' dog began to bark some distance from us, when the colored man began peering through the woods, saying, 'I done see a squirrel down thar.' This took with the boys, and away they went. We then had some conversation with our colored friend, asking him if he could direct us to Aunt Lucinda D——'s? He replied 'that is her home over there,' pointing to a house in sight. He then said that one of those boys was her nephew, and calling the boy he asked him if his aunt was at home. He said she was not. He then said to the boys, 'Here are some gentlemen who wish to see your aunt—will you show them to the house and go for her?' To this he readily agreed, and we were at once conducted to her house and the old lady was sent for. When she came home and we told her who we were, and that we had been directed to her house, she said she was glad to see us, and if we were not afraid to stay she was not afraid to keep us over night. It was a public place by the road side. The old lady prepared supper for us, after which she made a roaring fire in a large fire-place in her best room. We sat by the fire drying our wet clothing and chatting pleasantly with her until it was time to retire, when she made us 'shake-downs' by the fire, where we enjoyed a good night's rest. The friends who had directed us to this old lady told us she was what they termed a 'soothsayer'—in other words a 'fortune teller, of which she gave us proof during the evening. Whilst sitting by the fire she brought out a pack of cards which she began to shuffle and 'run off,' talking all the while. She told us, 'you will get through all right, but will have some trouble.' She also cautioned us to beware of 'a dark-haired woman.' She further said that one of our party would take sick on the way. Of the 'dark-haired woman' we saw nothing, but think we heard of her before we reached the Union lines, of which I may speak further on in another connection. The sick man proved to be Dr. Kaufman, for he actually was sick for several days. We discovered that the old lady's house was a kind of headquarters for loyally disposed persons residing in that neighborhood. A young woman, whose husband was in the Union army, and her brother spent the same night at her house. In conversation I discovered that her fame as a soothsayer, or fortune teller, was her safeguard for the superstitions of her neighborhood avoided her house. She said to me, 'they don't bother me much, I have sent a great many through, and you will get through all right.'

"Feb. 25. This date covers one week since we escaped. After breakfast we bade our kind hostess good-bye, and again started out in the rain. The young man who had spent the night with us went along some eight or ten miles as our guide. He took us to a family by the name of T-b-r. The old gentleman was not at home when we arrived, having "gone to town." The mother and her daughter prepared dinner for us. While they were thus engaged we entered into conversation with them, and told them we had been directed to find a man living in that locality by the name of Boggus, who perhaps could give us some information in regard to friends, route, &c. They expressed great surprise that we had been so directed telling us that this man Boggus was one of the worst men in that neighborhood. He employed his time, they said, in hunting out citizens who were loyal to the old flag, and escaped prisoners. All this was certainly unaccountable to us, as it was the young woman whose brother had been our guide of that morning who had directed us to find this man Boggus. But I thought then, and think so still, that Aunt Lucinda's dark haired woman had something to do with it, for a little incident that occurred at 'Crab Orchard,' Tennessee, about three weeks afterward seemed to look that way. Of this, however, I will speak when I get to the place. After dinner we started again, the rain continuing to fall, and wandered, as we supposed, until towards evening, when we came to a new, unoccupied, and as we discovered after effecting an entrance, an unfurnished house. We thought ourselves fortunate in coming across this house, and concluded to get in, build a fire, dry our clothing, and have a good sleep. Before leaving Salisbury, each one of us provided himself with all the keys he could get, to be used in unlocking boats, &c. Stepping up to the door of this house each fellow whipped out his keys and found one which unlocked the door. What was our dismay when we pushed the door open to find the house filled with straw! Of course that put us upon our guard, and making a fire was out of the question. The next best thing we could do was to bury ourselves in the straw and try to keep warm, which was hard to do with our clothing soaking wet. A short time before dark we heard a noise at one of the doors, as if someone was trying to get in. We thought our time had come, and when the door opened expected to see Boggus and his gang. But instead of this dreaded man the newcomer proved to be one of the young women who had prepared dinner for us. To our astonishment we learned that we had been wandering around nearly the whole afternoon, and had not gotten off of the plantation. This young woman, in the absence of her father, had come out to this house to feed some cattle that were in the field near by and opened the door to get provender for them. Sometime after dark a second party came to one of the doors, and having opened it, called us. This proved to be the owner of the premises, a kind old gentleman, and a friend. Upon his return home he was informed of our being there and he came through the darkness and rain to—I was about to say, to see us, for see each other we could not. But the old gentleman came in, sat down on the straw and spent perhaps an hour with us. When about to leave he kindly invited us to come to his house in the morning and take breakfast with him. Bidding us good night he went out and locked the door.

"Sunday, Feb. 26th. According to instructions last night from our friend, when he invited us to take breakfast with him, we were out before daylight and on our way to his house. This was necessary for his safety as well as ours, that our movements should be guarded. After breakfast, in company with the old gentleman, we returned to our quarters of the night before—the straw house—where a council was held. Our friend did not know much about the situation, but concluded to send us to some friends further on who, he thought, could give us information that would be of benefit to us. We accordingly bade him farewell, and with our guide of the day before started. We arrived at the place sometime during the forenoon, and received a hearty welcome from this friend and his good wife, who prepared dinner for us. During the afternoon we dried our blankets and clothing, and I did some darning of stockings and mending of clothes for the boys. In the evening this friend took us a few miles further on to other friends—a relative of his named W-b-n, a man loyal and true. A number of families of the same name lived in this neighborhood, all loyal. After supper we were conducted to a barn some distance away where we spent the night. The next morning we learned from our friend that a number of escaped prisoners had traveled this road before us. Among the number was Junius Henri Brown and Albert D. Richardson, both of the New York *Tribune*, and had made their escape from Salisbury in December. I might say here that these two men, Brown and Richardson, were prisoners with us in Salisbury, and that we were well acquainted with them. They effected their escape in about the same way we did. Both of them wrote books detailing their experience in Southern prisons and the incidents of their escape to the Union lines. We were also informed that a noted scout, a native of North Carolina, whose name I cannot now recall, was traveling back and forth to Knoxville, Tennessee, conducting escaped prisoners and recruits for the army. Of this scout's whereabouts at this time our friend did not know, but he promised to try and find him. We spent Monday and Tuesday among these families, expecting to hear something of this scout. On Tuesday night, not having heard of the scout, our friend conducted us to another friend—Esquire B.— from whom he thought we might learn some information. We arrived at the place about 11 o'clock; the family had retired. Our friend tried the door and found it unlocked, and went in and called to the man of the house—an old gentleman, who was in bed in another part of the house— "Squire B——, I have some friends with me who wish to stay with you to-night." His reply was, "God bless you, friends, lie down by the fire and make yourselves as comfortable as you can until morning." Our friend and guide bade us good bye and started home, when we laid down and soon were fast asleep. When we awoke in the morning and met the family, which consisted of the "Squire"—an aged gentleman, two daughters and a son—a splendid looking fellow—and wearing the uniform of a rebel soldier, they welcomed us to their home. This young man had been in the army, but like many others had grown tired and disheartened and was home on a furlough. When breakfast was ready we were invited to the table, and while eating one of the daughters came in and told us that a number of armed men were coming towards the house. In less time than it takes to write it there were five young men going from the house in an opposite direction about as fast as they could, keeping the house between them and the approaching soldiers. We ran a considerable distance through a lane and then took to the hills. After gaining the top of a hill we stopped to reconnoitre, expecting to see the men coming after us. Seeing no one pursuing us, we waited sometime for something to turn up, when the 'Squire's son, who had run with us, said he would return to the house and see who they were. He did not return for perhaps an hour or more, when we began to feel uneasy. We were laying under a large pine tree. I arose and upon looking around saw seven rebel soldiers fully armed and equipped coming directly toward the tree. I thought that our time was surely come. They circled around the tree and came to a halt. By this time the rest of our party were sitting up—the Johnnies looking at us, and we at them. They stood looking at us for perhaps a minute, and not a word passed between us, when they wheeled and marched down the hill. We were dumbfounded, and it took some little time to realize that we had not been recaptured. We knew that seven men armed could easily have captured four unarmed persons. It was not long until the mystery was made clear. Our friend came back to us and reported them to be seven deserters from the rebel army on their way home to Mississippi. Their errand to the 'Squire was to get something to eat. When at breakfast they told the 'Squire that they had been in the army almost from the beginning of the war, and could never get a furlough to go home, and now they had left intending to go home "peaceably if they could, forcibly if they must." After learning who they were I regretted that we did not make known to them who we were. After hearing the report from our friend, and our recovery from our fright, we proceeded to interview him in regard to the situation, when he informed us that the circumstances under which he was at home rendered it very necessary for his safety that he should keep "out of sight" as much as possible, and that consequently he had no information to give us. After consulting a while as to what was best for us to do, we concluded to return to the friend who had conducted us the previous night to his house. Bidding him farewell, we at once set out upon our return, and finding our friend of the previous day, we spent the day with him and had three square meals, sleeping in good beds that night. Whilst sitting by the fire in the evening chatting with our host, a little girl of the family came running in greatly excited (we found that the children understood the situation) saying, "Man's coming." That was enough. It did not take us five minutes to get away from that house and do some fast walking. After proceeding a considerable distance from the house, we concealed ourselves and waited to see what would next turn up. It was not long until a peculiar whistle brought us from our hiding place, when we met our friend who informed us that the strangers consisted of four persons, three of whom were escaped prisoners from Salisbury and a rebel soldier on horseback. The three prisoners had escaped from the stockade the same night we did. The whole four were under the influence of apple jack. They were a jolly, roystering set and such as we did not wish to travel with. Accordingly we did not put in an appearance. After they left we returned to the house and retired, sleeping well after the scare we had.

"The following day, March 2d, we spent at the house of our friend, and the morning after he piloted us across 'Brush Mountain' to another friend whose name was B-l-y. From him and his family we were the recipients of much kindness, and owing to rain and high waters we were compelled to remain with them three days. Part of this time we spent in the house and part in the woods. Our principal object now was to find the scout previously referred to, and our host, Mr. B., gained for us all the information he could. The friends here all knew him, but could not tell where he was at that time. Mr. B. had a son who was working in a cotton factory on the Yadkin river, about six miles distant. He was expected home on the following Saturday evening if the river was not too high to cross, and from him it was supposed we could get the information we desired. Whilst staying here a little incident occurred, and I think if I could at the time have got hold of Galbraith's throat, I would have stopped one snorer for that time at least. Some time during the day a woman was reported coming towards the house. Hearing this we started for a ladder leading to a loft overhead—the house being but a story and a half high. Dr. Kaufman, Brown and myself ascended the ladder, expecting Galbraith would follow, but instead of doing so he stepped into another room in which were two beds. When we discovered that he was not coming up after us we drew up the ladder and closed the trap door and disposed of ourselves upon the loft—Brown lying down upon a bed on the floor. We were but barely fixed before the woman came in. I was sitting in a chair directly over her, and through a crack in the floor could see her and hear the conversation carried on between her and Mr. B. By and by I heard a snore and concluded that Brown had fallen asleep, but on looking around found that both he and Dr. Kaufman were awake. Presently another noise, followed by others, and each successive one louder than the previous one, until the last grand finale—a real, tearing snort was reached. Then all was quiet, but there were three uneasy fellows in that loft during the 'overture.' I could see and hear from the conversation below that the visitor heard the snoring. She inquired of Mrs. B. what it was? Mrs. B. evaded by remarking that she supposed it was one of the dogs under the house. Her visitor looked very suspicious and prolonged her visit until I thought she never would go, but at length she left, when I hastily descended from the loft and went for Galbraith, but he denied that he had snored at all. After the scare was over we had considerable fun at his expense, and that night made him sleep in the woods, as we did not think it safe to stay in the house.

"Saturday, March 4th. This day Abraham Lincoln was inaugurated the second time President of the United States. This day we lay in the woods during a heavy rain. In the evening Mr. B.'s son came home from the factory, and upon being informed of our whereabouts, came out to see us. Sometime on Sunday he returned to the factory to make arrangements for crossing us over the river that night. In the evening with his father for our guide, we started for the river, and on the way we had to cross a road that was frequented by rebel cavalry. Before coming to this road we stopped to reconnoitre as best we could in the dark, and heard the tramp of horses. Secreting ourselves until they passed us, we crossed over on a run and continued running until we gained a woods, when we again stopped to listen. This time we did not hear the tramp of horses, but of men, and they seemed to be in about as great a hurry as ourselves. We did not stop to ascertain who they were nor what their haste was about, but again took to our heels. The moon was shining but it was somewhat cloudy. Whilst running we became separated, and at our first halt managed to get together again. We agreed that our guide, Mr. B., should lead and we would follow, and as we went on we could still hear the party coming after us. We again started, stopping occasionally to listen. Each time we could hear our pursuers. Finally we heard one say, 'Well, let them go.' We were close to each other, but a fence between us. After a short consultation we concluded to make ourselves known to them. Dr. Kaufman and myself, both armed with a club, marched up to the fence and challenged—'Who are you?' The reply was, 'Friends, and we have friends of yours with us.' During this conversation they were advancing toward the fence when we ordered them to 'Halt,' which was promptly obeyed. We then inquired who these friends were. He replied, 'I have their names on a piece of paper in my pocket and will give it to you.' Coming to the fence he handed me a paper, and in the moonlight I managed, with his assistance, to decipher the names. There were three of them, all from Salisbury, two of whom we knew. After parlying awhile they were brought forward and proved to be as represented, and the same party we ran away from a few evenings before, excepting the rebel soldier. Of course we were in for it now, but we did not care much for their company.—Scare No. 3.

"We continued on to the river, and were met by friends who ferried us over. The river was very turbulent, but we got over safely. Here we found a supply of good rations, provided by friends—the employees of the cotton factory, who had been apprised of our coming by the young man, B.l.y. After spending a short time very pleasantly with these kind friends, and receiving such information as they could give, we bade them farewell, and with one of their number as a guide, took up our line of march. This guide took us to a point about ten miles on our way to another friend, in whose barn we spent the remainder of the night.

"March 6th. We spent this day in the woods communicating with some friends in regard to a man living in the neighborhood (William D——) whose services we secured as a guide, and who finally decided, not only to conduct us, but also to go through into the Union lines himself. This latter, however, he did not succeed in doing for the reason that after travelling some time with us, it was reported that the Yankees were likely to advance into the locality where he lived, and he returned home so that he could 'settle' with some of his rebel neighbors some 'old scores' he had against them. During this day we were joined by John W-b-n, a Lieutenant of the Rebel army, who had been on duty at Salisbury. He was at home on furlough, and we had met him a week previously at his cousin's, a friend with whom we had stopped. He joined us for the purpose of coming through to a friend of his in Iowa, and he finally succeeded in getting to him. At dark, with William D—— as our guide, we again took up our line of march—our number having been increased to eight persons. During the night we travelled through some very rough country, crossing several hills and two branches of Roaring River To cross this we had to undress ourselves, tie our clothing in bundles, and plunge in the water—not a very pleasant experience for a night in March. At about 3 o'clock a. m., a halt was called and we all went to bed—that is laid down and slept.

"March 7th. At daybreak we arose from our bivouac, and started again on our march, and after proceeding about six miles, we found a friend who kindly gave us our breakfast, after which we took to the woods and spent the day and started again at dark. Having a mountain to cross, we experienced considerable difficulty in doing so. Before reaching this mountain we called at the house of a friend to whom we had been directed, who told us of other friends further on.

When we asked him how we were to get to them, he said 'Do you see yon mountain?' We looked in the direction indicated, and discerned a huge pile looming up in the darkness. Pointing with his finger, he then said, 'You cross in that direction, and at the foot, on the other side, you will find friends I have told you of.' Bidding him farewell we went on towards the mountain, reaching which we found no road, no path, but an abundance of rocks, brush, &c. But we managed to reach the summit, and pretty well down the other side, by about 3 o'clock a. m., when we were brought to a halt by the squaking of chickens and lights flitting back and forth. A halt was ordered and a consultation held, and we came to the conclusion that we had run into some rebel soldiers who we engaged in robbing hen roosts, and that we had better retire and sleep until daylight, which we accordingly did.

"March 8th. We arose early, made our toilets, and resumed our march down the mountain, and finding the friend to whom we had been directed, a widow lady—Mrs. V——, enjoyed a good breakfast which she kindly prepared for us. This lady informed us that the commotion among the chickens, which we had heard during the night, was caused by other 'varmints' than rebel soldiers. After paying our respects to the good breakfast prepared by our kind hostess, and receiving her best wishes, we moved on. The mountains having become numerous, we crossed another one, and arrived at the home of other friends where we had dinner. In the afternoon, in accordance with instructions from the friend with whom we took dinner, we crossed another mountain. This mountain, by the way, is the one which caused considerable excitement during the past year or two by various eruptions. There had been eruptions before we crossed it. Our guide, William D——, whilst crossing, called our attention to several places which gave evidence of volcanic disturbances, but as it was raining, and we were in search of liberty and not on scientific explorations, we did not stop long to inspect the phenomena. In a little ravine between two small mountain ranges, we found a good log house unoccupied, which we took possession of, and made preparations to spend the night there. We gathered wood and made a roaring fire, and with some straw we found on the floor, made beds and slept well.

"March 9th. The friend with whom we took dinner yesterday, according to a promise made us before leaving his house, joined us this morning to conduct us several miles, and show us where to cross the Blue Ridge. After taking us out of the wilds, where we spent the night, he brought us to a public road which crossed the Blue Ridge, but as it was unsafe for us to cross by this road, he directed us to a point on the summit, saying, "There is where you must cross; it is some ten or twelve miles distant, and the only way to reach that point is to go straight to it regardless of paths or roads.' When the poet wrote

'Tis distance lends enchantment to the view,'

he did not have ten or twelve miles to walk to reach a mountain top, and no road or path to travel on. I tried to catch the 'enchantment,' but could not. It did not enchant worth a cent. Our friend here bid us farewell and turned back, and we began our march, keeping the road for a mile or two, until we came to the foot of the mountain. When we were about to leave the road, we heard some persons coming in our rear. We ran into the bushes and took a survey and saw what we supposed to be—and what a friend the next day told us we had every reason to think they were—a squad of Rebel cavalry—'Price's Guerrillas,' he termed them, who, he said, had been operating in that country. We laid flat on the ground until they had passed. They passed within a hundred yards of us, and we could tell by their conduct that they were a jolly set and in a jolly mood, singing and shouting as they passed. After they had gone by, we moved on a spur of the mountain, hiding them from us, but we could hear them for a mile or more. After we had gotten pretty well up the side of the 'Spur,' we concluded to lay by and let them get well out of our way before we ventured to the top. The morning was beautiful. The sun was shining, bright and warm. Whilst lying by some pigs came along, and fearing that we might run short of rations, we confiscated one of them. After slaughtering and dressing it we started for the summit. During the afternoon a change came upon the air indicating rain, and by the time we reached the summit we were in a terrific storm of rain, which soon turned to snow. After wandering along the top a short distance, we came to an old house, the roof of which had fallen in and the chimneys were down to within a few feet of the ground. Here we crawled in for shelter, but fearing the rebel cavalry might be lurking somewhere near, we did not venture to make fire at first; but going out in different directions to reconnoitre, and seeing or hearing nothing of them, and the storm growing fiercer and the cold increasing, we at length became desperate, and determined to build a fire. The house was built of logs, and the plastering between them had fallen out, so that the reader can judge how successful we were in making ourselves comfortable that night. We started our fire and piled on wood, causing the flames to shoot up into the air and out through the crevices of the chimney, and when we had a good bed of coals we laid on our (or somebody else's) pig and roasted it. After a hearty repast on roast pig, we retired to sleep—well, rather to freeze, for that night I really thought we would freeze to death, but by going to the fire every few minutes to warm up, we at length worried through the night.

"Friday, March 10th. Arose early, much the worse for the storm. After shaking ourselves to become fully aroused, we started down the western slope, in the meantime looking out for our breakfast After travelling some distance we espied a small house on the mountain side. A couple of our party went to this house to see about getting something to eat, and in a short time a signal was given for the rest of the party to follow. Arriving at the house we found an old gentleman by the name of P——, his wife and daughter with himself, composing the family. They prepared us breakfast consisting of corn bread and bacon, and I can assure the reader it was to us a royal feast. Large plates of 'sizzling' bacon, crisp and brown, and corn bread, sweet and hot. It would have made a boarding house keeper weep to see how rapidly things disappeared at that table. But our good friends did nothing of the kind, but busied themselves in frying bacon and baking corn bread to meet the unexpected drain upon their larder. After breakfast we 'interviewed' our host in regard to getting over the mountain, &c. He volunteered to go with us to a brother-in-law of his, some twenty miles distant on New River, which place we made about 8 o'clock p. m. Here we were introduced to Mr. S—— and his family, which consisted of his wife and several daughters. They prepared supper for us, after which we adjourned to the barn and laid down to sleep.

"March 11th. We were awakened about daybreak by our friend, who informed us that 'guards' had been seen on the opposite side of the river. Upon receiving this news we did not deem it prudent to wait for breakfast, but started at once for the river. When over this stream we found another friend, a Mr. W——, who gave us breakfast and directed us to some high bluffs on the river, where we could pass the day in safety. In the evening he came to us and conducted us to the top of 'Snake Mountain'—a local name for one of the ranges which divide North Carolina and Tennessee. Arriving at the top of this mountain, he gave us directions where to find friends on the other side and then bade us farewell and turned homeward. We were now on our march downward on a good mountain road into Tennessee, and at about 2 o'clock Sunday morning arrived at the place to which we had been directed. A knock at the door brought out an old gentleman, who asked us who we were? We told him who we were, and that a friend on the other side of the mountain had directed us to him, and that we desired to get to a place of safety to spend the day. He at once said he would conduct us to such a place, and would get ready at once to go with us. At this point a woman in another part of the house who had overheard our conversation, came forward with an emphatic 'No, you shall not go, but I will.' Men caught in secreting, aiding, or conducting escaped prisoners, by the rebels were hanged. This woman was the wife of the old gentleman—Mr. M.—and she did not wish to have her husband exposed to this danger. She got herself in readiness and we started—the old lady—God bless her—acting as our guide. She led us up hill, and down hill, and through ravines until about the break of day, when she arrived at the place intended, when she turned back and left us, we going to some friends to whom we were directed. Whilst travelling along with this woman, I remarked to her, 'It is rather hard that you should get up at this time of night, and undertake to do for us what you are doing.' To this she replied, 'This is nothing. I have been out on business of this kind before when the safety of the 'Boys' required it.' The Boys referred to were termed 'Bush Boys' —persons who had been conscripted, but deserted and returned home. These were living amongst the hills, mountains, and in caves. We sometimes spent nights in their camps and hiding places. It was not long after our arrival at this place, until quite a number of friendly persons were with us, of whom some were ladies, and some of them fine looking young ones. We spent the day with them very pleasantly, and at night slept in a Bush Boys' cave, with a loaded musket by each one's side.

"Monday morning, March 13th. Started early and went about two miles before breakfast. During this day we forded Elk River, crossed Flint Mountain, and reached Crab Orchard, Tennessee. Here we were informed by a friend that it was reported that a body of rebels were marching on that place. Whilst consulting as to what we should do, and where we should go, a lady came to the house we were in, and told us that she lived on the mountain side, about a mile and a-half from the place we were. She further said that she had an unoccupied house on the top of the mountain, and that no rebels had ever been seen there, and that we were welcome to occupy it, and would be perfectly safe there. By this time it began to rain and we concluded to find her house, which we reached before dark. We gathered a lot of wood, made a fire, and laid down to sleep.

"March 15th. This day we remained indoors; some of the party went down the mountain to see what could be had to replenish our commissary. On their return they reported that they had bought bacon and flour; some of the latter they had left to have baked into bread. On the way up they had 'borrowed' a skillet, and I at once, in the absence of our friend McGrath, turned my attention to the culinary department for that day. It was nothing, however, but to fry, bake, and eat, and eat, bake, and fry, all day long. When night came I was glad to lie down to rest. We lived that day, as the saying is, 'on the top of the pile,' as well as upon the top of the mountain.

"March 16th. Brown and I went down the mountain this morning for the bread that had been baked for us. Reports still said that the Rebels were coming. We got our bread and returned—had a jolly good time that day.

"March 17th. St. Patrick's day in the morning. Brown and I again trudged down the mountain for *more bread*. Our capacity for fried bacon and fresh bread was truly remarkable. The report this morning was that no rebels were about. Whilst down in the valley we met two Yankee officers, named respectively Samuel B. Piper, Adjutent 3d Ohio Regiment —now postmaster at Barnesville, Ohio, and Lieutenant George W. Bailey, Co. A. 3d Ohio, now editor and publisher of the Hamilton county *News*, Aurora, Nebraska. They had escaped from Charolotte, North Carolina. We gave them an invitation to go with us to our mountain home, which they readily accepted, and together we trudged up the hill. As our family had increased more rations were needed, and Dr. Kaufman and Galbraith started on a foraging expedition. At this place we also met the scout previously referred to, and we arranged with him to conduct us to Knoxville, Tennesee, which was at that time in possession of the Union forces. It was arranged that we were to start on our journey on the following morning, and after completing some arrangements, he left to visit some friends and expecting to remain away over night. The next morning, March 18th, when he returned to our camp, he informed us that there was to be a "Log Rolling" on the farm belonging to the woman whose house we occupied, and suggested that as she had been kind to us, we ought to stay and assist. Postponing therefore our departure until the following morning, we readily consented to his proposition. Up to that time we were in ignorance of what a log rolling was, but we found it out that day. In that region of country when a farmer wishes to break up a piece of timber land for agricultural purposes, he does not do it as we do in Pennsylvania—that is, go to work and cut off the timber, but girdles each tree with an axe, and as a consequence they soon die. The ground is then ploughed and cultivated and in the course of time the storms break down these trees, when they cut them into pieces that can be handled.— These are rolled together in piles and set fire to and burned up. It was at a party of this kind that we attended that day, and with some eighteen or twenty neighbors, who had gathered together, we had a jolly good time, although the work was hard.

"Whilst in conversation with our scout that day, I remarked to him that I had spent a night close by the place where his wife was staying, and that I thought of calling to see her. He gave me a significant look, but said nothing. In conversing with another person, I mentioned this to him and said that I thought it very strange conduct, when he replied : "I can enlighten you in regard to that : When the war began this man and his wife took opposite sides, she telling him that a man that would not fight for his country did not deserve a country." The consequence was, he did enter upon the services of his country—the country whose flag was the glorious stars and stripes, and his wife remained at home sympathizing with the stars and bars. He further informed me that the night we spent with aunt Lucinda D——, the soothsayer or fortune teller, this woman was at her father's who was a near neighbor of aunt Lucinda's. Here then, as I then thought and have ever since believed, was aunt Lucinda's "dark haired woman." I think, too that this woman knew of our being there, and managed to have our friends—innocently to them—send us on the hunt of 'Bogges.'

"March 19th. "Break camp fall in, and forward march," was the order this morning, and down the mountain, and into the valley, and onward we went. During our halt of the last few days, our squad had been increasing and we now numbered twenty three, all escaped prisoners from various places. In the evening we found an empty house, which we too possession of and spent the night there.

"March 20th. We sent some of our party out after rations for our breakfast, after which we resumed our march. In the evening we reached a place called "Greasy Cave" in Washington County, Tennesee. Here we had supper and spent the night. Our squad was too large to be accomodated at one place, consequently we divided and went to different places. Our original party of four, however, never separated and we always remained together. This night we were assigned to a family named P——, and when the time for retiring came one of the family having a pine torch made his appearance and said that he was ready to conduct us to our sleeping quarters. He led, we following and crossing a small stream in front of the house; he struck a by path through the bushes and began to ascend a hill, and in a very short time stopped at the entrance to a cave on the hill side. When we reached this place our guide said 'Here is where you are to sleep, add I think you will be safe.' Leaving us the torch he bade us good night and left. After going into the cave some distance we found straw, indicating that others had occupied these quarters before. Before we laid down, Brown and I determined to do a little exploring, and taking the torch we started and had gone but a short distance when we discovered several avenues branching off from the main one. We entered one of these and had not proceeded far until we noticed still others branching off from this one, when we concluded that we were at a dangerous business and had better retrace our steps. After returning a short distance back, we came to a point where we disagreed as to which was the right way and after some parleying I yielded to Brown, and it was well I did for it proved to be the the right way and soon we were at our starting point. Had we taken the other avenue, there is no doubt but what we would have been lost and our bones might now be bleaching in that cave. The next morining when we came out of the cave, we found that we were but a little distance from the house, but considerably elevated above it. We told our friends of our adventure in the cave, and they said it was well we returned when we did for the cave led to no one knew where and no person had ever succeeded in finding its end.

"March 21st. Before starting this day we had to provide rations, and the baking of bread detained us until about ten o'clock. It rained some during the day, and toward evening we crossed Chuckee river in a canoe and encamped on Indian creek.

"March 22d. We broke camp at 8 o'clock and soon reached 'Boss Mountain,' and the last one we crossed on foot. It is one of the Allegheny range and by the natives it is called the 'Big Butt.' We began the ascent of this mountain about 9 o'clock and after climbing long enough to reach the top as we supposed, we ascertained it proved to be a plateau of perhaps two or three hundred feet, and then another ascent. This was succeeded by still another plateau and a rise and these by another until the top was reached. From this summit we had a view of magnificent grandeur. The whole valley lay spread out before us for miles upon miles. The Cumberland Mountains were visible in the distance, and directly below and parallell with the one we were on were other ranges which appeared to us as though we could have dropped stones down upon their tops. It was indeed a reward for the toil we had endured in scaling these heights. Penmar and High Rock seem but pigmies when compared with them. We reached the foot of the the mountain in the evening, having spent almost the entire day in crossing. That night we encamped in an old house.

"March 23d. We were now out of the mountains, and concluded to spend that day in camp and rest.

March 24th. After marching about five miles on the morning of this day, we were informed that 'the rebels were coming.' Upon receiving this unwelcome news we concluded to halt and lay by for the day. In the evening some friends brought us rations, and at this point our scout left us.

"March 25th. We lay in camp during the day, expecting to resume our march in the evening, but during the afternoon we were informed that the rebels were within ten miles of the place we were at. Hearing this we separated into squads and went to different places to spend the night. The squad I was with consisting of Dr. Kaufman, Brown, Galbraith, Adjutant Piper, Lieut. Bailey and myself, remained together. During the evening a man—a relative of the family with whom we were staying—came there from Greenville, ten miles distant (the home of President Andrew Johnson,) and informed us that the Yankees were in possession of the place. This information made us feel pretty good, and Adjutant Piper, who had became impatient because we had not gotten through the rebel lines, declared that on the following morning he was going to Greenville, if no one else would go. But he did not succeed in carrying out his purpose as soon and easily as he expected.

"Sunday, March 26th. During the last two days we had been within but a few miles of the expiration of the rebel lines, and had done but little less than advance and then fall back, making but little, if any advancement. Knowing that we were so near the lines of our friends, we could scarcely restrain ourselves, and act as cautiously as the circumstances demanded.

This morning we all gathered together, after our night of separation, and started for Greenville, every one of us as determined to go through as was Piper the night before. Between us and Greenville there was a road and a river which we had to cross. On this road was our greatest danger, for rebel cavalry were patrolling it, and we were in constant danger, and that was the reason we did not get to Greenville that morning as we so confidently expected. In company with some friends we started, and after proceeding two or three miles, we were informed that rebels had been seen but a short time before on the road, at the precise point we were to cross. We at once fell backward again pretty quickly—Piper retreating with us. Towards evening, with a friend to pilot us we again started, and succeeded in crossing the road, and at once hurried on to Nolchucky river. We had not proceeded far after crossing this road until we were invited to stop for supper, which invitation, with our thanks, we declined. No supper for us now, hungry though we were, until we had once more seen our dear old flag and the friends who defended it. Reaching the river, we were put over by some friends in a 'Dug Out,' they giving us directions to travel by. Bidding them farewell, we moved rapidly on and about 8 o'clock we struck the Union lines and were challenged by Federal pickets. As our squad had by that time increased to twenty-six, it was not considered safe for us all to advance at once upon the picket line, and we thereupon halted some distance before we reached it and sent two or three forward to report our presence. In a short time they returned, saying that it was all right, when we all advanced and crossed the line and found ourselves in the camp of the 4th Tennessee Infantry, and without much ceremony distributed ourselves amongst the different companies for something to eat and a place to spend the night. These we had no difficulty in obtaining, and we lay down that night under the sweet consciousness that we were once more under the protection of our dear, glorious old flag, and that in a short time we would return to our homes and to our friends from whom we had been so long separated.

"Monday, March 27th. This morning we reported to the Colonel commanding the regiment, and after telling him who we were, where we came from, and where we wished to go, he informed us that a detail would leave for Knoxville in the afternoon with a number of prisoners, and that we could fall in with them and proceed to that place. When the guard came around to take charge of the prisoners, we recognized among them Mr. Edward Ferry, a fellow-townsman; and when everything was in readiness to start, and the order to "forward march" was given, we moved along with them. The guards were mounted and formed a hollow square, with the prisoners in the inside and we along with them. We were allowed to go as we pleased, either before or behind as suited us best. After proceeding along until towards evening, we met the advance of the army of General George H. Thomas, which was moving towards Virginia. After passing a number of regiments, we saw a battery about going into camp a short distance from the road, and stopping to take a look at it, discovered to our great pleasure that it was battery B, formerly commanded by the lamented Captain Samuel McDowell, of this place, and composed largely of men from Chambersburg. I cannot now recall the name of the Captain who then commanded it, but the Lieutenants were Camp and Shatzer. The only privates I can remember were Jesse Richter and Frank Yeager. The boys were astonished at seeing us, and glad to meet us, and we were no less surprised and gratified to meet them. They gave us an invitation to spend the night with them, which we gratefully accepted. After going into camp with these men, and the troops yet passing along, we went to the road side to look at them, when by and by along came the 77th Pennsylvania regiment, which had been partly recruited at this place, and had been commanded successively by our former fellow-townsmen, Colonels Stumbaugh and Housum, the former distinguishing himself at Pittsburg Landing, in which his regiment took an active part, and the latter falling at Stone River. The name of the Colonel commanding the regiment at the time I saw it, I do not now remember, and it was composed of but a handful of battle-scarred veterans, the only one of whom I recognized being Sergeant William Eaker, of this place, and known to many of our older citizens.

"March 28th. This morning Lieutenant Camp rode with Dr. Kaufman to General Stanley's headquarters, and after stating our case the General gave the necessary passes and orders for transportation. At this place our party separated, Dr. Kaufman, J. Porter Brown and myself pursuing our way homeward together, and with but one exception—Galbraith—who, sometime during the summer after our return, paid us a visit, we have not met since.

"After partaking of a substantial dinner with the officers of the battery, and having our haversacks filled, we bade our kind friends adieu and started for Bull's Gap, six miles distant, from which place trains were running to Knoxville. When we reached the Gap, a train was about to start and finding an empty box car we took possession of it and, night coming on, we spread our blankets and laid down and slept.

"March 29th. When we awoke in the morning our train was standing still near a town, and upon inquiring were told that it was Knoxville. After breakfasting from our haversacks we got out to take a look around and ascertain when our train would go on. The conductor, engineer and fireman had gone off, and we could find no one that could give us any information. Whilst waiting for the return of these men, and the starting of our train, we learned that a train, with a passenger coach attached, was about to start for Chattanooga, and as the place of its standing was some distance from us, we did not succeed in reaching it in time to get aboard. The only thing we could do then was to wait. By and by our engineer returned, and finding that the fire in the engine had gone out, he started on the hunt for the fireman, but by the time he was found and the fire started up, the engineer was missing and some one went to look him up. At length all were found and at their posts, and when the familiar and welcome 'All aboard' was called, we pulled out. Towards evening our train came to a halt —some one said, I think, near Sweet Water river—and upon getting out to ascertain the cause, we were informed that there had been a wreck on the opposite side of the river, and that several trains ahead of us had been delayed—a part of some of them standing on the bridge spanning the river. We climbed up to the top of the car, and passing from one to the other and over the bridge to the wreck, we found that the track was being cleared as rapidly as possible. The engine was lying with its wheels up, in a gully, and it required no immediate attention. When waiting and walking about among the trains, we discovered the one which had passed out in the morning in advance of the one we were on. Hunting up the conductor, we asked him if we might get into his train? He inquired where we had been riding, and after telling him, he said "Well, why can't you ride there again?" We told him that we were tired of riding in house cars. He then inquired who we were and where we were going? In replying to his inquiries, we showed him the papers given us by General Stanley, and after carefully looking at them a change occurred in his manner, and he said, 'Ah! I see that you are escaped prisoners. Gentlemen, there is my car, step in and make yourselves comfortable.' This man was a lieutenant and military conductor, but strange to say, neither of us thought of asking his name, which we greatly regretted. Upon entering the car we found it pretty well filled with both ladies and gentlemen ; and in a short time our newly made friend came in, and coming to where we sat, he said, 'Well, boys, I suppose you have not had *too much* to eat?' We replied, 'Hardly ever,' when he went out and in a short time returned with a good sized parcel done up in paper, which he handed us, saying, 'Boys, that's the best I can do for you here.' Upon opening the package we found that it contained crackers and cheese. Whilst the train stood there parties in our car began to pay their respects to certain lunch baskets, and when in a short time it began to be known throughout the car that we were escaped prisoners from Southern prisons, both ladies and gentlemen pressed us with invitations to partake with them. In a very short time we were well supplied with cold chicken, sandwiches, cake, &c., luxuries we had been strangers to for the past year and nine months.

"At length the track was cleared and the train started for Chattanooga and we arrived there about 2 o'clock, A. M. We stopped at the Soldier's Home and after breakfast repaired to headquarters for a pass that we might go around sight-seeing without being molested by patrols. Whilst strolling around the city, we had the pleasure of meeting Mr. A. F. Smith, now Chief of Police of this place, and his brother Dr. John. Adam was in charge of Government iron works, and I don't know which was the gladder party—the Smiths or us. After congratulations, Adam said, 'Boys, how are you off for funds?' We told him we were just about out, having spent our last cent shortly before reaching the Federal lines. Taking out his pocket-book, he handed each one of us a five dollar bill, at the same time saying that he was sorry that it was not more— that he had not received pay for sometime and was a little short. He then told us of several other Chambersburgers that were in Chattanooga, and proposed to conduct us around to see them. Arriving at the place we met Henry Bowers, now an engineer on the Mont Alto railroad, and one of the Cline boys—Frank, I think. They told us of several others who were there, but at that time were away on duty. Bowers and William Murray were running engines at Chattanooga—Murray at the time was home on a furlough. When meal time came we took bean soup with Henry —pure bean soup without the usual accompanyment of *bugs* to which we had been accustomed to on our prison life. At 1:30 P. M. we left Chattanooga for Nashville. We occupied a box car, the seats of which extended acrosss the entire car, and about dark a number of soldiers were taken aboard as a train guard for the night. I had a seat entirely to myself, and wrapping my blanket around me, lay down to sleep. About 2 o'clock in the morning I was awakened by a thumping and bumping, and before I could rightly take in the situation, I was sprawling on the floor of the car. Instantly all was confusion and the guards were ordered to the front. It was supposed that the rebels had purposely thrown the train from the track, as one had been wrecked by them in that same locality but a short time previously. We got out of the car and found the engine and three cars off the track, but no rebels about. We were detained until about 11 o'clock, when the track being cleared we proceeded upon our journey and arrived at Nashville at 2 P. M. The next morning we went to headquarters to see about having our passes for transportation renewed, but were informed that nothing could be done for us. We now for the first time were brought to face the inconvenience of being far from home in a strange place without money. As already stated we had spent our last cent just before entering the Union lines. Our guide, who had engaged to conduct us to Knoxville, when he found that we were within ten miles of the lines at Greenville, said that we could then do without his further services, and if we would pay him the sum stipulated for he would return. The amount we paid him was, I think, seventy dollars, which entirely cleaned us out. But as long as we travelled on military roads--roads controlled by the military authorities--we managed to get along, and Adam Smith's five dollars did not go very far towards bringing us from Chattanooga to Chambersburg. We accordingly telegraphed for remittances to be sent us at Cincinnati, and then started out on the hunt for the Christian Commission, hoping that it might do something in the way of assisting us on our way. At length we found it, and communicated our story to the person in charge, a kind hearted, fatherly old gentleman, whose name has escaped my memory. I told him that when at home in Chambersburg I had done considerable work for the ladies of the Commission in the way of assisting in making, packing and nailing boxes. After listening to my statement he said, 'That being the case, the Commission won't go back on you now. I will arrange to send you to Louisville, Kentucky, and will give you a letter of introduction to Dr. Newberry, of that place, who is also a member of the Commission.' In the afternoon, sent on our way by this noble Commission, which did so much for our brave soldiers during the war, as well as for unfortunate persons like ourselves when far away from home without money, we left for Louisville, and arrived there about 4 o'clock on Sunday morning. After breakfasting at the Soldiers' Home, we started out to look for Dr. Newberry, and finding him at his place handed him our letter of introduction. He was a pleasant old gentleman, ready and willing to assist us. He told us that a boat was to leave at 12 o'clock for Cincinnati, and gave us enough money to pay for first-class passage to that place. On our way to the landing Dr. Kaufman said, 'Boys, we now have money enough to pay our passage, but nothing for 'grub'; let us go aboard and bargain for cheap fare and spend what is left for something to eat.' To this proposal we readily agreed, and went aboard, and bargained accordingly, after which the doctor started out foraging and after some time returned with a good supply. What cared we for first-class cabin passage now that we had plenty to eat? The boat left on time, and the afternoon being very fine, and we on our way home, we had a delightful trip. When night came on we got behind the smoke stack, wrapped ourselves in our blankets and laid down and slept soundly, and arrived at Cincinnati shortly before daylight on Monday morning. We intended to remain here until our remittances would come, but being again without money and knowing not where to find lodging and food, we concluded once again to apply to the Christian Commission. Going to its place, we stated our case, when we were taken to the 'Refugee's Home' on Longworth street. The Superintendent's card reads thus:

L. V. LOOKER,
Sup't. of Refugees,
52 Longworth St.

This place, as its name indicates, was a home for Southern refugees. There we remained until the following Wednesday morning, when we left to seek more congenial quarters, as the place was not to our liking. The Superintendent was a first-rate old gentleman, but our objections were on account of some of the inmates and other matters connected with the institution. Early this morning we left the place and started out to look for some other place to stay at until we could hear from home, and in passing along the street I espied a hotel with the following sign over the door—'Pennsylvania House' —at which I said, 'Boys, that must be our house.' We at once went in and inquired for the proprietor, to whom we related our situation, informing him that we were expecting a remittance from home and wished to stop with him until it came.

Whether out of pity for us, or seeing honesty beaming from our features, he at once took us in and ordered breakfast for us. We spent the balance of that day in strolling around the city sight seeing, and furnishing sights for others, for we were certainly an interesting looking trio—rags and tatters, and—, well I was about to say something else but had better not. I shall not enter into any description of our outfit, for Dr. Kaufman is somewhat fastidious, and I would not like to place him upon record here in an unfavorable light. The news of the fall of Richmond was received that day, and I think the excitement of the people of Cincinnati that night was never surpassed excepting perhaps during the recent riots there. Wherever you would go, and from every person you met, men, women and children, the cry was, 'Richmond's gone up!' 'Richmond's gone up!' Bands of music were parading the streets and speeches were being made.

"Every day we remained in Cincinnati we went to the office of the Express Company expecting to hear from home, and on Thursday morning after breakfast, as usual, Dr. Kaufman and myself started for that place. As we passed into the office a man was standing in the doorway, but looking up the street in an opposite direction from the way we came and consequently did not see us. When in the office Dr. Kaufman said, 'That is George Balsley, of Chambersburg.' I replied, 'Yes, I think it is;' but neither of us really supposed it was him although the resemblance was striking. Passing on down to the proper desk and making our usual inquiry—'Anything for us this morning?'—we received the usual reply, 'No;' at the same time glancing toward the door, he said, 'Wait a moment,' and walked forward. In a short time he returned with the gentleman we had seen upon passing in, and sure enough, to our great joy, he proved to be Mr. Balsley, a brother-in-law of J. Porter Brown. He had been sent here by our friends to see after us, and upon seeing him the thermometer of our feelings indicated at least summer heat. The first thing done was to visit the clothiers, then a bath and next the barber. After we had undergone the process of ablution, and put on our new garments, we could scarcely recognize each other; and when we went back to the Pennsylvania House, our host did not recognize us, but when he at length did, we all took a good laugh together. Paying our bills and thanking him for his kindness, we went to the Burnett House, where Mr. Balsley was stopping. At the table we met some gentlemen who recognized us as the party that had attracted so much attention in strolling around the city in our Salisbury garb, and we had considerable joking over it.

"At 10 o'clock on Thursday night, we left Cincinnati for home. We arrived at Pittsburg in the afternoon of Friday, and making close connection with the train east, left at once, stopping at Latrobe for supper. Whilst there Mr. Balsley said, 'I promised to telegraph home as soon as I found you, and have forgotten it until now.' Hurrying into the office he sent a despatch which was received in Chambersburg about two hours in advance of us. We arrived at Harrisburg about 3 a. m., and took the 8 o'clock train for home. In all my wanderings I had never become impatient to get on, but could take things as I found them, and make the best out of them I could, but after taking my seat in the familiar Cumberland Valley train, it did seem to get along rather too slowly. At 11 o'clock the train came in to where the depot stood when we left (the town had been burned during our absence) where we were met by an immense crowd to welcome us home, and with the crowd was the old Chambersburg Band, of which I had been a member from its organization in 1851. After some considerable hand shaking we started up town, the Band playing a quick step entitled 'Eiker's Return,' which had been composed specially for the occasion by the late Professor F. J. Keller, at that time leader of the Band. They marched up Second street to Brown's Hotel, on the northwest corner of Second and Queen streets, where Brown once more entered his home; but as there was a little woman whom I had called 'wife' but six months before I had left, and who, I knew, was watching and waiting for me at the corner of Market and Franklin streets, I did not stop but proceeded quickly there. And now just here I want to say that if any of my friends would like to know the why and how I got into all this trouble I have been telling of, if they will call at No. 148 East Washington street, I think she will explain it all—I've heard her do so many times, and she always makes it clear as well, I was about to say, clear as mud. Be sure, however, that I am at home when you call, for it seems that she always enjoys a little secret satisfaction when I am present 'in giving me away,' as we used to say in prison parlance. But, I suppose I deserve it, for it was mean in me to go over to Hagerstown with the boys to see the elephant, leaving her alone. But, I resume. In company with my brothers-in-law, Dr. J. S. and B. L. Maurer, we wended our way from Brown's hotel down Queen street to Main, thence to Market, and out to Franklin. Passing through the burnt district, with the ruins all about me, a feeling of sadness came over me, but meeting the little woman who was waiting for me, I soon regained my cheerfulness. We were captured in Hagerstown on Tuesday, July 7th, 1863, and after a prolonged tour through the South, returned to Chambersburg on Saturday, April 8th, 1865, having been absent one year, nine months and two days.

Dr. Kaufman, J. Porter Brown and myself were the last of our party to return to Chambersburg. Dr. Hamilton and J. P. Culbertson came home in August, 1864; A. C. McGrath, T. H. McDowell, Charles Kinsler and George Heck were taken from Salisbury to Richmond a few days after we left, and from thence were sent to Washington, reaching home several weeks before we did. They were all exchanged, and their way home was not attended with the privations and hardships we endured, but I had an experience which they had not, and it proved of great benefit to me. Previous to leaving Salisbury I became much reduced by a severe attack of that terrible scourge amongst the prisoners, diarrhœa, and when the proposition to escape was made I hesitated, fearing I was unable to endure the fatigue of the journey, but after a little encouragement from Dr. Kaufman consented to go, and after being out a few days I began to improve, and by the time we reached home my weight had increased from one hundred and twenty pounds to one hundred and forty-two, and I felt as though I could walk with any one and beat him every time. It was out door living, pure mountain air, and, sometimes, good corn bread and bacon that did it. And now if any of my readers are troubled with dyspepsia, and desire an effectual remedy, and have the money to foot the bills, I might find the time to join them in a trip over the same route, in the same way, and feel safe in guaranteeing a cure. 'No cure, no pay.'

"I feel that before closing these recollections, that there is one other person who shared our prison life, that should be mentioned, for although not of our party, he is well known to many of our citizens. I refer to Mike Latus, who, a few years ago, conducted a bakery here, but at present resides in Reading. At the time of Milroy's rout at Winchester, Mr. Latus was captured, and when taken to Libby prison he had about six hundred dollars in Greenbacks, which he managed to conceal from the rebels. Mike is one of the largest hearted men I ever knew, and while his money lasted he spent it freely for the benefit of others less fortunate than himself. After spending some time in Libby he was sent to Salisbury, and on the first Christmas we spent there he conceived the idea of giving us a Christmas treat. Buying such articles as could be obtained, he set about baking cakes, and on Christmas morning, with a piece of board for a tray, he went around among the prisoners dispensing his good things. That treat, at the prices he was obliged to pay, cost him, I have no doubt, several hundred dollars in Confederate scrip, into which he exchanged his greenbacks. He made his escape from Salisbury in December, 1864, and succeeded after a long and toilsome march, and after enduring great hardships, in entering the Union lines in Western Virginia. Mr. Latus visited Chambersburg in 1865—the year succeeding his escape—and being much pleased with what was left of the town after its destruction by the rebels, he determined to return in the fall of that year, which he accordingly did and carried on his business as a baker.

"When we left home on Monday, July 6th, 1863, it was our purpose to go to Gettysburg by way of Waynesboro', but owing to circumstances which we could not control, our route was by Richmond, Salisbury, Knoxville, Cincinnati and Pittsburg. And after a lapse of two years, less two days, and several thousand miles of travel through seven different States, both in and out of the Union, we succeeded in reaching our destination, and was present at the laying of the corner stone of the monument in the Soldiers' National Cemetery at Gettysburg on July 4th, 1865. Our object in going was to see the '*elephant*,' and we did see it, and a real Jumbo it proved to be before we got done seeing it. And now 'Taps,' 'Lights out,' and 'good night,' I subscribe myself,

D. M. EIKER."

Chambersburg, Aug. 18th, 1884.

CHAPTER XVII.

ANGELS OF MERCY IN THE HOSPITALS.

Reference has been made in previous chapters of these reminiscences, to the work done by the ladies of Chambersburg and other parts of Franklin county, in the hospitals established here during the war, as well as for sick and wounded soldiers elsewhere; and desiring to place upon permanent record these transactions as far as they can be recollected by the survivors, and gathered from such papers as escaped the conflagration of our town, I have secured the services of Mrs. J. S. Nixon to prepare that account. Mrs. Nixon was a prominent actor in the work she records, and being conversant with the details thereof, as well as in possession of some important papers relating thereto, she is perfectly competent to perform the task assigned her. Many of the actors in the events she relates have passed away, but the facts are of public interest and worthy of perpetual remembrance. Her account is as follows:

The interesting articles, gleaned from the thrilling events of the late war by Mr. Hoke induced me to look over almost forgotten papers in my possession. I copy from the Secretaries book. In accordance with notice given in the churches on the previous Sabbath, the ladies of Chambersburg met in the United Presbyterian church on Monday, July 14th, 1862, at 4 P. M. The meeting was organized by the election of Mrs. Dr. Schneck, President; Miss Susan B. Chambers, Treasurer; Mrs. J. Sharpe Nixon, Secretary. Managers: Mrs. S. M. Armstrong, Mrs. Nead, Mrs. J. Shryock, Mrs. Burnett, Mrs. Glosser, Mrs. Hershberger, Miss Sarah Wright, Mrs. Blood, Mrs. Jacob Hoke, Mrs. J. Armstrong, Mrs. John Culbertson, Mrs. Harry Stoner, Miss M. Heyser.

Mr. Nixon was present and offered the church as a regular place of meeting, and it was arranged that meetings would be held every Wednesday and Friday morning at 8 o'clock. Met again on Wednesday, A. M., and committees were sent out to purchase goods, when articles were given to the following persons. I think the list should be on the "roll of honor:" Mrs. B. Early, Miss Sarah Early, Mrs. S. E. Huber, Mrs. Gettys, Miss Helen Reid, Ellie Lambert, Emma Smith, Mrs. Joseph Chambers, Mrs. Senseny, Mrs. J. Kennedy, Mrs. Cree, M. A. Armstrong, Alice McCulloh, M. McCulloh, Mrs. M. J. Nixon, Mrs. Schneck, Mrs. Dr. Fisher, Mrs. Gilmore, Mrs. H. M. White, Mrs. Ritner, Mary Hull, Mrs. Dr. Lane, Mrs. Wallace, Mrs. Dobler, Sallie Brown, Lizzie McLanahan, Mrs. John Reed, Mrs. Welsh, Lou. Bard, Mrs. Davis, Miss Heck, Mrs. Nelson, Louisa Smith, Mrs. E. D. Reid, Miss S. A. Chambers, Miss S. B. Chambers, Miss Kimmell, Mrs. Shillito, Mrs. Reasner, Mrs. Melhorn, Emma Stuart, Josephine Kochenour, Miss Nancy McCulloh, Miss Prudy McCulloh, Miss Nesbit, Florence Brown, Mary Cree, Mrs. Hoskinson. Lizzie McDowell, Mrs. Nill, Maggie Nill, Miss A. Radabaugh, Mrs. Johns, Mrs. Caufman, Anna Watson, Kate Heck, Mattie Watson, Eliza Irvin, Mrs. Jacob Brown, Mrs. Heyser, Mrs. E. Culbertson, Lide Tolbert, Mira Black, Lizzie Watson, Mrs. John Nill, Mrs. McFadden, Maggie Scibert, Hallie Beatty, Mrs. Etter, Mrs. Dr. Montgomery, Jennie Kirby, Mrs. Kimmell, Miss Reily, Theresa Armstrong, Miss Flory, Nancy Early, Mrs. Duncan, Mrs. Clark, Sallie Smith, Mrs. Wood, Jennie Davis, Mrs. Captain Brown, Miss Lizzie Nill, Miss Kindline, Mrs. Mull, Mrs. T. B. Kennedy, Miss Ritner, Miss J. Gilmore, Miss Gillan, Miss Detrich, Mrs. J. Eyster, Mary Eyster, Mrs. Allie Eyster, Kate Davis, Miss Sellers, Mrs. Everett, Miss Sallie Miller, Miss Radabaugh, Mrs. Berger, Miss Work, Mrs. Carlisle, Miss L. McLellan, Sarah Reynolds, Alice Senseny, Mrs. George Eyster, Sr., Ellie Eyster, Mrs. Britton, Mrs. P. Smith, Miss Oaks, Miss Stirk, Miss Kuhn, Mrs. Bankard, Kate Kirby, Mrs. Heyser, Mrs. Dechert, Mrs. Lull, Mrs. Sharpe, Mrs. Dr. Snesserott Mrs. Guthrie, Annie Reed, Mrs. Wolfkill, Mrs. Hazlet, Mrs. Hull, Mrs. Myers, Miss Hoffman, Helen Early, Mary Black, Miss Bechtol, Miss Stouffer, Mrs. H. Greenawalt, Alcesta Lull, Mrs. Julie Grove, Mrs. McDowell, Sophia Clipper, Miss Yager, Mrs. Fritz, Mrs. Shepler.

In giving a list of the workers it is impossible to give work done by individuals. Suffice it to say that during the months following over *fifteen hundred* garments were made, sent away and used in our own hospitals, consisting in part of sheets, shirts, drawers, pillows, pillow cases, carpet slippers, double wrappers, flannel sacques, towels, handkerchiefs, bandages, &c. Mr. H. refers to the memorable Sabbath that we met in the old church, and spent the afternoon in packing boxes, making bandages, &c. None who were present will ever forget that day, when messages went from house to house, and people moved by one impulse, came to aid in the good work.

Included in the number of garments named was an order, received from Dr. Henry H. Smith, for the following articles, after the battle of Antietam, the materials to be paid for by the government, the work gratuitous by our society. The following is a copy of items of bill in Dr. Smith's writing:

SEPTEMBER 22nd, 1862.

The United States To Mrs. Rebecca Schneck, Dr.

To bedding furnished Academy, School House and Franklin Hall Hospitals for U. S. troops, wounded at Antietam and located at Chambersburg, by order of Medical Inspector Cuyler, through Henry H. Smith, Surgeon Gen. of Pennsylvania, and acting Medical Director U. S., and by command of Brig. Gen. Reynolds, as follows:

To 265 bed sacks	$347 15
" 195 yds. check for spreads	43 39
" 83 yds. ticking (pillows)	15 62
" 135 sheets	85 25
" 175 pillow cases	21 00
	$512 41

I cannot go into particulars, but after a lapse of four months and an interminable amount of "red tape," Mr. Nixon and myself visiting Philadelphia, going from office to office, we succeeded in getting the amount and paying our own merchants for goods ordered. I copy a note from Dr. Smith:

"Dr. S. desires to say in reply to Mrs. N's communication, that the better plan will be to put the bills into the hands of an agent to collect at the Surgeon General's office, Washington. Stating the fact of refusal to pay of parties in Philadelphia. Dr. Cuyler's approval would be all that is required, and he is probably in Washington. Dr. Smith regrets the want of faith apparent in the non-settlement of a bill contracted under full orders of the proper U. S. officers, and if not paid would recommend a legal course. Jan. 13th, 1862."

When these hospitals were opened, committees were formed to visit each day to furnish such articles of food as the government could not, and wounded and convalescent soldirs required, and supply many little luxuries.

The School House Hospital committee for Thursday, was Mrs. Lull, Mrs. McKinley; Friday, Mrs. Ritner, Mrs. Hull; Saturday, Mrs. McCullgh, Miss Wark; Sabbath, Mrs. Emblich, Miss L. Flack; Monday, Mrs. Beatty, Mrs. Erhart; Tuesday, Mrs. K. Eyster, Mrs. Auld; Wednesday, Mrs. Wood, Mrs. S. M. Armstrong. Franklin Hall, Thursday, Mrs. Nead, Mrs. Hoke; Friday, Mrs. Reeves, Mrs. Culbertson; Saturday, Mrs. Clark, Mrs. Douglas; Sabbath, Mrs. Allie Eyster, Mrs. Huber; Monday, Mrs. Nelson, Mrs. Cauffman; Tuesday, Mrs. Bard, Mrs. Paxton; Wednesday, Mrs. Gilmore, Watson, Messersmith.

Academy, Thursday, Mrs. John Armstrong, Mrs. Nixon; Friday, Mrs. Burnett, Mrs. Wallace; Saturday, Mrs. William Seibert, Mrs. Wright; Sabbath, Mrs. John Reed, Mrs. J. Culbertson; Monday, Mrs. Hoskinson, Mrs. Guthrie; Tuesday, Mrs. Brown, Mrs. M'Dowell; Wednesday, Mrs. McLellan, Mrs. Hershberger.

There were many boxes of fruit, jellies, &c., &c., received from other towns. I am very sorry there is no record of them. One large one I remember from the L. A. Society of Lancaster. Our committee took charge of and made proper distribution of such things. It will not be deemed improper to mention some things that were donated by different persons and prepared. One time I remember thirteen chickens were stewed at my house, and a bushel of sweet potatoes roasted for a dinner. At one of my neighbors hot corn-bread was baked for supper, frozen custard one day for eighty men then in the Academy, and various articles of that sort. I will give a quotation or two from the Sanitary Commission:

PHILADELPHIA, May 14th, 1863.

The Woman's Penna. Branch of U. S. Sanitary commission acknowledges with pleasure the receipt of five very valuable boxes of clothing and hospital stores from L. A. Society of Chambersburg. Ladies, your society has done nobly. We have received few as valuable contributions from any society.

Another of May 8th.

The ladies of Chambersburg are known far and wide for their devotion to the cause of the Union. Their patriotism will *never* be forgotten.

Some of the Philadelphians forget it very soon. It is to be regretted that we have no record of money raised for this one object, Miss Chambers' papers being all destroyed by the fire. I find a slip cut from a newspaper of Miss Douglas' *second report: Balance in Treasury, Aug. 1863, $146.18. Feb., 1864, Rev. John Warner's lecture on Battle of Gettysburg, $78.55; donations from gentlemen, $269 50, making $494.23. On another page of my book this record:

Received from Mr. Watson from Presbyterian church	$70 00
Mrs. McKinley	2 00
Mr. McLellan, from Quincy	66 75
Miss S. Chambers	5 00
Mrs. Nelson	5 00
Kitty Lindsay	1 00
Miss Denny	5 00
Mr. A. Stouffer	2 00
Odd Fellows	25 00
J. & W. Eyster	20 00

Mr. Nixon.......................... $10 00
Capt. Brown.......................... 5 00
Dr. Platte.......................... 2 00
Mr. Jacob Hoke.......................... 20 00

*Miss Douglas succeeded Miss Chambers.

This, of course, is a very imperfect sketch, as all churches and many individuals gave just as liberally. It may serve to show coming generations how nobly the people responded to the country's call.

The following is an editorial notice in the *Valley Spirit* of July 30th, 1862:

We visited on Friday last the United Presbyterian church which is occupied by the "Ladies' Aid Society." We found the room pretty well filled with ladies engaged in the noble, patriotic and christian duty of providing clothing and other comforts for our sick and wounded soldiers. We might say much in praise of our ladies, but this is an age in which noble deeds bring their own reward. We will say this much, however. The ladies of Chambersburg will compare with any in existence, in their efforts to provide for the wants and relieve the sufferings of our soldiers. They have enlisted in the good cause their nimble fingers and their noble, warm hearts, with a will. All honor then to our ladies who have thus nobly evinced their patriotism, and vindicated that judgment which the poet has pronounced upon their sex, and which the world has applauded:

"When pain and anguish wring the brow
A ministering angel thou."

From the *Valley Spirit* Aug. 6th, 1862:

Most of the churches in this place have taken up collections for relief of the sick and wounded. During the last week, the Lutheran church moved in this matter and on Sunday after a sermon by the pastor "on the blessedness of giving," completed their work. The result was a contribution of three hundred dollars.

Much of the credit for this successful result is due to the zeal and activity of B. F. Nead, Esq., in soliciting from the congregation during the week.

Sept. 3d, 1862.

The following dispatch has been issued from Washington by the Surgeon General:

To the loyal women and children in the United States:—The supply of lint in the market is nearly exhausted. The brave men wounded in defence of the country will soon be in want of it. I appeal to you to come to our aid in supplying us with the necessary article. There is scarcely a woman or child who cannot scrape lint, and there is no way in which they can be more useful than in furnishing means to dress the wounds of those who fall in the defence of their rights and homes.

In response to this call, Mrs. Schneck, the president of the ladies' society here, issued the following appeal:

In behalf of the Ladies' A. Society, I appeal to all friends of our country in the town and surrounding community, to prepare lint and send it in as soon as possible. Also old shirts, sheets, &c., suitable for bandages to dress wounds.

I would also add that onions, tomatoes, potatoes and dried fruits are much needed, and will be thankfully received and forwarded. In behalf of the society.

R. R. SCHNECK, *President*.

Persons who reside in the country can leave such articles as they wish to go to sick and wounded soldiers at the drug store of J. S. Nixon.

The following is copied from the *Valley Spirit* of March 5th, 1863:

The box of hospital supplies made up at Nixon's drug store by some ladies of this place, was forwarded last week to the 77th Reg. in Kentucky. This box will reach the place most needed at the right time, and its contents will prove acceptable to sick soldiers. When the 77th left Camp Wood for Nashville, it had over one hundred sick in hospital at Munfordsville. To this point the box was sent.

From the *Valley Spirit*, Sept. 24th, 1862:

The second and third floors of the Franklin Hall are occupied at present for hospital purposes. Several hundred sick and wounded have already been brought over from the battle field and everything that can be done by skillful physicians and a humane community is being done to render them comfortable.

The following is Surgeon General Smith's acknowledgement:

SURGEON GENERAL'S OFFICE, }
Chambersburg, Sept. 25, 1862. }

The undersigned, on behalf of a large number of soldiers of the Penna. militia, as well of the United States volunteers, respectfully tenders his thanks to citizens of Chambersburg for refreshments liberally furnished by them to these men arriving in the town during the late emergency. He also tenders to the ladies of the Christian Association assembled in the United Presbyterian church, *his grateful acknowledgement of the valuable assistance they have rendered the U. S. troops in the General Hospitals of Chambersburg*. By their untiring efforts in preparing bedding and other articles urgently required by the wounded soldiers on their arrival from the field of battle, they have greatly contributed to their comfort and welfare, and diminished the labors of the surgeons in charge.

HENRY H. SMITH,
Surgeon General Penn'a.

The following is the action taken by the soldiers for favors shown them:

Headquarters Co. F., from Huntingdon.
The following resolutions were adopted:

Resolved, That the thanks of this company be tendered Mrs. Wm. McLellan for the magnificent dinner she has furnished us to-day.

Lieut. WM. LEWIS.
R. MILTON SPEER,
Secretary.

The officers and members of Capt. Thomas W. Lynn's Co. (5th Pa. Regt.) return their sincere thanks to ladies who contributed to our comfort on our arrival from Hagerstown while

quartered in the Court House. They will be held in grateful remembrance.
1st. Lieut. W. A. CONAHAY,
2d Lieut. WM. L. DAVIS.

From the *Valley Spirit* of Dec. 17th, 1862:

About one hundred and twenty of the sick and wounded soldiers who have been in our hospitals, were removed on Thursday last to Philadelphia in charge of Dr. J. R. Rodgers, Medical Director. Most of the men are convalescent, and seemed to leave Chambersburg with regret. The ladies of our town were untiring in their attentions to these men, whilst in our midst. They no doubt have their reward in the heartfelt gratitude of the soldiers and the approval of their consciences.

Valley Spirit, of Nov. 12th:

The following donations were received and distributed at the "School House Hospital" during the past week. From Mrs. McGrath, pies, rusk and sundries. A large donation of potatoes, cabbage, onions, pumpkins, green and dried apples, apple butter, &c., by Mrs. Mahon (collected from Scotland and vicinity). Milk, flour and eggs, through Mrs. Auld. Corn starch from Mrs. Caufuman. Cider and apples from Mrs. Senseny and Davis. Blancmange from Mrs. Chambers. Apples and milk, Mrs. Dr. Fisher. Baked beans, Mrs. Lull and Ritter. A liberal donation of fruit, butter, &c., from Lancaster, through L. A. S. Mrs. Nead, apple butter. Cherry butter, Mrs. Sprecher. From Fayetteville, through Miss Horner, Miss McGowan, Miss Colby and Miss Mattie Brown, pies, cakes, bread, apples, milk, jellies, butter. Donors, Mrs. Barr, Mrs. Dr. Hartzell, Mrs. Oyler, Mrs. Greenawalt, Mrs. Weldy. Pies and apples from Mrs. Richards and Miss Henderson. Mrs. Duncan, blanc-mange and cream. Vegetables, Mrs. Kline. Prepared farina and milk for the whole house from Radebaugh, Brewer, Culbertson and Nead. Farina in package from Boston through Mrs. Clark. Mrs. Montgomery, Mrs. Grove, Mrs. Reed, Mrs. Anderson, Mrs. Ehrhart, Miss Stouffer, private meals to patients.

A very agreeable musical entertainment by a party of ladies and gentlemen ought to have been mentioned. Then follows names of committees for this hospital (given in a former part of this article) and the Steward says: "To these are to be added others, among whom must be specially named Anna Newman and Nettie Flack. Nothing can exceed the devotion with which these ladies have addressed themselves in catering to the wants of the soldiers, made more laborious by the inconvenience of a hospital, designed for mere temporary use. Even when the building was threatened with destruction on the morning of rebel invasion, when all other help had fled, some of these ladies were found at their posts. It is surely no infringement of the delicacy of the sex to send forth this humble record as a greeting to the noble band of mothers and sisters in other towns engaged in similar labors. It indicates an army of brave hearts at home as well as in the field, and furnishes the best guarantee of the ultimate triumph of the Government we love.

GEORGE BAYNE,
Hospital Steward."

Again on Nov. 19th: "A large list of delicacies, fruit and vegetables, from contributors named, and Mrs. Ebbert, Thomson, Newman, Nead, Brewer, Jordan, Reeves. From Fayetteville. Also, Mrs. Britton, Trostle, Linn and E. D. Reid. With a mention of shirts, towels and handkerchiefs from L. A. T. A week later Mrs. Chas. Eyster, Mrs. Wood, Lizzie Lester, a liberal donation again from Fayetteville from Mrs. Crawford, consisting of chickens, pies, rusk, &c. A movement to furnish the entire house with mush and milk was effected in great profusion, by about thirty ladies, most of whom have been named. A concert by the sweet voices in Presbyterian choir was among the luxuries enjoyed last week."

Another article, Dec. 3, 1862. "A dinner was given to the inmates of the Hospitals here on Thanksgiving day. Never before did soldiers sit down to such a dinner. Turkeys and ducks and chickens and roasts and bakes and stews and puddings and pies in endless variety. Nothing was lacking which the valley could supply. Great anxiety was evinced by the citizens lest there should not be enough, and many families sacrificed entirely their own private entertainment. The overplus lasted the remaining days of the week. It was an ovation to the *everlasting* credit of Chambersburg. At the close the men gave three roaring cheers, and subscribed to a card which reads thus:

The undersigned, for themselves and associates, take this method of tendering thanks for the magnificent entertainment of Thanksgiving day. They are aware this is but a feeble return for the kindness extended. But it is all a soldier has to give. These are his cherished memories easily impressed but never forgotten. When duty calls it is ours to obey. But we shall carry the remembrance of Chambersburg to every camp. It shall be our watchword on every field." Signed by JOHN C. LEWIS, M. D., and eighty others.

The following is taken from one of our town papers of Feb. 22d, 1862:

A few days ago the Rev. Rebaugh, of near Chambersburg, dropped into headquarters of the 46th Pa. Vol. and presented to Col. Jos. Knipe, for the use of his regiment, a very handsome and acceptable gift, in the shape of a box of mittens knit by the fair hands of Chambersburg ladies. We tender the cordial thanks of all for the kind remembrance of Pennsylvania's stout-hearted and brawny-handed sons, by pious mothers, loved sisters, and sweet daughters of the hospitable town of Chambersburg. 'Tis gratifying to the soldier, as he walks his lonely beat, amidst the storms of winter, to know that the loved ones at home are mindful of him, and labor so zealously to make him comfortable as he vigilantly guards the homes and lives of those whom he *knows* little but *loves* much. We feel the kind remembrance of us exemplified in this timely gift by the fair ladies of Chambersburg and venture the hope that when the fortunes of war bring us home again they will not, as now, give us the mitten.

A SOLDIER OF 46TH REGT. PENNA. VOLS.

From another paper :

The Quarter Master General acknowledges a large box of Hospital supplies, and adds : Noble deeds the test of beauty, and in this respect the ladies of *Mercersburg* will come up to the standard of loyalty, and a little beyond. Also a notice of 80 pairs of woolen socks having been received from ladies of Guilford township, signed by Capt. D. G. Thomas, and another of 150 pairs from Greencastle, through Mrs. D. F. Robinson. Acknowledged by

CAPT. WILL HOUSE.

In this same connection I copy from the same paper of May 4th, 1864 :

In pursuance of notice given, the ladies of Chambersburg convened at the residence of J. S. Nixon, on Tuesday, April 26th, to consider the propriety of holding a fair for the benefit of the Christian Commission. After a short address by Rev. S. J. Niccolls, Rev. F. Dyson was called to the chair, and Miss Mary McCulloh appointed Secretary. On motion it was decided to hold the fair, and the following officers elected : President, Mrs. General D. N. Couch ; Vice President, Mrs. Wm. McLellan : Treasurer, Mrs. J. L. Dechert. Managers, Mrs. L. S. Clark, Mrs. J. K. Shryock, Mrs. John Armstrong, Mrs. H. S. Stoner, Mrs. Wm. Mitchell, Mrs. B. T. Fellows, Mrs. Hoskinson, Mrs. McClure, Mrs. S. G. Lane, Miss Reynolds, Miss Helen Seibert, Miss Sarah Wright, Miss M. Stevenson, Miss Ellen Cook, Miss Kate Wilt, and Miss Maggie Glosser.

Collectors were appointed to solicit from citizens. Ladies of neighboring towns were invited, signed by Mrs. Couch. June 18th. Committees appointed : Fancy tables, Misses M. Seiders, Maggie McCulloh, Kate Miller, Mary Black, Mrs. Wm. Stenger, Mrs. Wm. Carlisle, Mrs. Y. McCoy. Toys and books, Mrs. Shryock and Mrs. Foster. Ice cream, Mrs. Wunderlich, Miss Stevenson. Cake, Mrs. Mitchell, Mrs. Fellows. Confectionery, Mrs. Lane, Mrs. Platt, Miss S. Wright, Major Bert. Restaurant, Mrs. Lull, Mrs. Early, Mrs. Clark, Mrs. A. H. McCulloh. Strawberries, Mrs. Wm. McDowell, Mrs. Nixon. Floral, Misses Mary and Lucy Chambers, and Capt. Sweringen. Silverware, Mrs. H. S. Stoner, Miss Wampler. Lemonade, Mr. and Mrs. Kinney, and Mrs. Duncan.

June 22d. The fair held by the ladies of Chambersburg and vicinity for the benefit of the U. S. Christian Commission, opened in Franklin Hall, on the 13th inst., and continued until Saturday evening last. The Hall and Court House were both used for the display of articles for sale, and were thronged during the entire period with an interested and delighted crowd of visitors, who dispensed their cash with commendable liberality. The Halls were decorated with much taste and the display of articles in various departments spoke well for the industry of our ladies, when excited to action by charitable objects. The Old Folks' Concert attracted an immense crowd from neighboring towns and villages, and on each evening the Hall was packed with delighted though perspiring auditors.

No one who attended this, by far the grandest, in every sense of the word, affair that was ever given in our town will ever forget it, and though twenty years have rolled away, and many of the familar names are recalled only with a sigh, as the thought comes, they too have passed away. Memory takes me back to the old Court House, with its decorations of flowers, banners, flags and other patriotic emblems, the stirring music of drum and fife, the sweet strains of the Chambersburg Cornet Band. The men in uniforms, etc , and the delicious lunches. How soon after was it all laid waste by the rebel torch. In the paper published three days before the fire I find the following :

July 26th, 1864. Receipts and expenditures of Ladies' Fair for benefit of C. C.—June 14th. To subscription of committees in Chambersburg, $953.55. The managers acknowledge the following donations :

Miss R. Walk (Upper Path Valley) .	$ 159 74
Mrs. Wm. Burgess (Loudon)	14 50
General S. Cameron	10 00
Mrs. Monn and Miss Welty (Quincy)	164 30
Mr. Pomeroy (Roxbury)	44 06
Mrs. John Eberly	1 00
John Wallace	5 00
Henry Wills	2 00
Mrs. S. R. Fisher	5 00
Mrs. Dr. Reamer (Bedford)	10 00
Mrs. Dr. Wright	3 00
G. Deitz, wood	11 04
Ladies' Aid Society, Chambersburg . .	20 00
Capt. Jos. Ege	5 00
Cash from Fair	2,627 93
Cash from Old Folks' Concert	557 43
Cash from Museum	77 00
Cash from Fayetteville table	161 05
	$4,831 96
Expenses	1,304 19
	$3,527 77

The managers return thanks to the Franklin Hall Co., Commissioners, &c., &c., to the citizens and vicinity for generous contributions and encouragement, and thanks to all who have aided in making up the amount. Signed

Mrs. J. L. DECHERT,
Secretary.

In the following days these same "loyal," kind, patriotic, hospitable people were homeless and penniless. When blackened walls and hearthstones were all that remained of our homes, when sad memories of the past were of hourly recurrence, when the problem of how to keep "the wolf from the door" was ever pressing upon us, this large amount of money was sent to the Christian Commission. Part of it *after* the town was in ashes, and the people had not bread to eat. The money had been raised for our suffering soldiers and we did not feel as if we had any right to it; and yet that which should have gained us favor, was only an injury. It was received with the utmost coolness by the Treasurer of that Commission. I remember well the acknowledgment but do not the exact date. I also recall a *tirade* of abuse I received when doing some shopping for a widowed mother some months after, in Philadelphia, which reflected very bitterly on *our* treatment of the soldier, &c. While we bury the wrongs of the past, we gratefully remember those who came to our relief in our time of need.

Mrs. J. S. NIXON.

Chambersburg, Aug. 7th, 1884.

CHAPTER XVIII.

THE NATION'S SHRINE, OR THREE VISITS TO GETTYSBURG.

On the afternoon of Monday, July 6th, 1863, when the fact of the defeat of the Confederate army at Gettysburg and its retreat southward was fully assured, a considerable number of our citizens started out for sight seeing. Several went to Hagerstown expecting to witness a great battle there. How they fared and what came of it have been stated elsewhere. Many others went to visit the field of carnage at Gettysburg. Conveyances were scarce and in demand, and the majority had to walk. I was among the few who succeeded in procuring a seat in a spring wagon, which had been kept from being taken off by the rebels by taking off its wheels and secreting them under a house half a mile out of town. We left Chambersburg about two o'clock in the afternoon, and reached Gettysburg a little while before dark. All along the road from this place to Gettysburg the evidences of encampments were visible. At Fayetteville we saw some Federal cavalry who were gathering up straggling rebels. These stragglers were foot-sore, tired and greatly discouraged. We found them all along the road. One of them, a North Carolinian, we gave a seat in our wagon and hauled him several miles. He was so foot-sore and weary that he could scarcely walk and we pitied him. This man told us the usual story of nearly all the men we conversed with from his State that he was opposed to the war, was in favor of the Union, had been dragged away from his family, and was resolved never again to fight in the cause he detested. Of his sincerity we had not a doubt. Poor fellow, his heart yearned for his absent wife and children and he desired to know if there was any way by which he could have them brought north so that he need not ever return to his southern home.

At the top of the mountain a line of breastworks was thrown up, with an opening in the middle of the pike for artillery. These fortifications were evidently for the protection of their rear in case of an advance of any hostile force in that direction. Reaching Cashtown we saw the evidence of large encampments. Broken down fences, the remains of slaughtered cattle and other debris of military encampments were visible on every side. When nearing Marsh Creek, four or five miles this side of Gettysburg, we saw in the bottom lands skirting that stream, a large number of tents. This was one of the Confederate hospitals, and these tents and the woods around were filled with wounded men. From this place on to Gettysburg, every house, barn and other outbuildings was improvised into a hospital. Men wounded and maimed in almost every conceivable way lay along the roadside, in yards and gardens. Some were propped against the houses, or supported against the backs of chairs with an arm or leg off, and some having lost both arms. Dead horses lay along the road, and the people, in some instances, were piling wood upon and burning them. In the fields west of Seminary Ridge, where the battle of the first day occurred, hundreds and even thousands of empty boxes were strewn. The contents of these boxes, in the shape of shot and shell, had been hurled against the gallant defenders of the Union, and sent hundreds into eternity and crippled and maimed others for life. Along the crest of Seminary Ridge breastworks were thrown up, and from that place to the town dead Union soldiers were seen partially covered with earth. Several had been put into the gullies made by water along the roadside, and their toes, hands, noses and, in some cases, their faces protruded from their slight covering of earth scraped from the pike. New made graves were in the fields on both sides of the road.

Arriving at Gettysburg, we procured lodgment for the night, and then sauntered out to see whatever we could. In the Court Hosue sickening sights met our gaze. Every available place in the rooms, halls, vestibule and stairway was crowded with suffering heroes. Many had lost an arm or a leg. Groans of agony were heard on every side. The churches and other public buildings were also crowded with wounded men. The amputating tables were yet standing, and arms and legs were thrown indiscriminately upon piles and covered with earth.

In the morning at an early hour we started out to visit the field of battle. Teamsters and ambulance drivers, overcome with excessive labor, were laying asleep under the shadow of churches and other buildings. We made our way first towards Culp's Hill. The line of breastworks along the crest of East Cemetery Hill was plainly visible. After going a short distance we found in a field a man's leg, and a little distance from it a partly buried confederate. This leg was evidently separated from the body by a piece of a shell, for its torn and mangled edge showed this. Near by we picked up part of a pocket Bible. It had been cut nearly in two by some missile, the irregular edges and angles of which corresponded with both the marks upon the Bible and the soldier's leg. The soldier had evidently carried this Bible in the pocket of his blouse, and the same shell which had severed his leg had cut through his Bible. That he was a rebel was evident in the place where he was found, and in the fact that a rebel song was enclosed within his Bible. The leaves of the Bible were stained with the blood of its owner. It may have been a gift from some devoted mother or wife. We divided the leaves among us, and sometime afterwards, while in the city of New York, I gave a number of them to a friend, who placed them on sale at the great Fair held there for the benefit of the Sanitary Commission. A minister of one of the city churches, to whom my friend presented one of these leaves, took it into his pulpit and took his text from it.

Within the lines where the brave defenders of the Union had stood, were, here and there, places where wounded men had lain. Branches from the trees and leaves were gathered together for a bed, and these were saturated with blood. Paper, envelopes, bits of letters, shreds of clothing, pieces of photographs, muskets, bayonets, ramrods, knapsacks, haversacks, caps, old shoes and blankets, and many other articles, were scattered everywhere. The trees were riddled with balls. We saw an iron ramrod so fastened in a tree that we could not pull it out. It had evidently been fired from some musket, and buried itself so deeply that we failed, as did several others, to extract it. Long trenches, heaped over with fresh earth, told where tens, twenties and fifties of rebels were interred. They boasted that in coming into our State they had got back into the Union,— Many who thus boasted occupied these trenches. Their boasting had met a fearful verification. Upon Cemetery Hill, within the enclosure where rest many of the former residents of Gettysburg, the evidences of the terrible strife were painfully visible. Many of the tombstones and monuments had been laid down, either to prevent their being defaced and broken, or to form sheltering places from the iron and leaden hurricane which had concentrated from one hundred and twenty guns upon that place. The silent sleepers in that city of the dead, all unconscious of the terrible conflict going on all about them, uttered no protest against the temporary and necessary desecration of their last resting place. Several of the monuments in this cemetery were defaced by shot and shell.

Passing on down along the Union line, we saw where Pickett's great charge was made in the afternoon of the third day's battle. Muskets were piled up along a fence like cord wood. There must have been ten thousand in one of those ranks. Dead horses lay all about the house where General Meade had his headquarters, and from that place all along down to Round Top scores of them were seen. Some had great holes in them, and pools of blood had formed in the hollow places. They were swollen and putrid, and the stench was horrible. Arriving at Little Round Top we ascended to its summit, and the scene of the second day's engagement was before us, in which Sickles' corps, perhaps injudiciously posted, was pushed back step by step from the Peach Orchard, a half mile to the west, to the base of this hill. Leaving Round Top, we passed by the Devil's Den, seeing here and there among the huge boulders, unburied confederates. They were black and bloated, eyes open and glaring, and corruption running from their mouths. I had seen similar sights before upon the field of South Mountain, but some of our party had not seen the like before. They were shocked and horrified. Over the ground where the most desperate fighting that ever occurred upon this continent took place—the historic Wheat Field and Peach Orchard—we passed and returned by the Emmittsburg road. In this field and orchard the evidences of the great struggle were numerous. The ground was covered with the debris of battle, while blankets could have been gathered by the wagon loads. All along the Emmittsburg road pools of blood were seen. When passing where Pickett's assaulting column crossed the road, the ground was like the floor of a slaughter house. In the low ground beyond Codori's, dead confederates yet lay unburied. One lay dead in a stable near Codori's house, and a grave was being dug for him when we passed. Returning to town we saw at the depot three or four disabled cannon. They were broken in various ways. One had been struck squarely in the muzzle by a solid shot one size larger than its calibre. The ball stuck fast in the muzzle and broke a piece out of it. Shortly after the middle of the day we left for home, bringing with us, as did almost every one else who visited the field, some relic in the shape of bullets, bayonets, &c. Bullets could be gathered everywhere, and we saw persons engaged in collecting them by the bucketfull. During a recent visit to Gettysburg we were informed that these bullets, gathered by different persons from the battlefield, were bought up by dealers, and one firm alone shipped fifty tons of them. This seems fabulous and we leave the reader to discount the statement to any extent he pleases. Even yet many are found, and to visitors they are the objects of diligent search.

On Wednesday, Nov. 18th, 1863, four months after the battle of Gettysburg I again visited that place to witness the ceremonies connected with the consecration of the SOLDIER'S NATIONAL CEMETERY. The occasion being one of national importance, persons were there from all parts of the country, among whom where President LINCOLN, several members of his cabinet, foreign ministers, governors of States, distinguished military men, and other persons of note. The President and his suite arrived by rail early in the evening and proceeded to the residence of Mr. David Wills on the southeast corner of the public square, where they were entertained. Shortly after dark the Marine band from Washington proceeded to the front of Mr. Wills' residence and played several excellent pieces of music, while the crowd which had gathered, loudly called for the President. A gentleman appeared at the door and announced that Mr. Lincoln was at supper, but would, as soon as he had eaten, respond to the call of the people. After a little while the door was again opened, and ABRAHAM LINCOLN stood before us. The appearance of the President was the signal for an outburst of enthusiasm that I had never heard equalled. While the people cheered and otherwise expressed their delight, he stood before us bowing his acknowledgments. At length silence was restored, when his face relaxed its appearance of careworn sadness and anxiety, and a kind and genial smile overspread his countenance. He then said that we had doubtless expected a speech, and he would be happy to gratify us, but he dare not do it for Mr. Seward would not let him, and he could only thank us for the respect shown him and bid us all good night. Amidst a tremendous outburst of applause he withdrew, when loud calls were made for Mr. Seward. Mr. Seward soon made his appearance and favored the audience with a speech of considerable length, in which he referred to the great issue before the country, and the part of the great drama which occurred in and about that place.

In the morning of the following day, Thursday, 19th, the whole population of the surrounding country seemed to be crowding into Gettysburg. Almost everyone wanted to see the President, and the house where he lodged was beseiged by an immense crowd, watching for his appearance. At length the time arrived for the procession to move from the town to the ground set apart for the burial of the fallen heroes and the President emerged from the house and mounted a horse. It was with difficulty that he could move with the procession, for the crowd pressed upon him and sought to grasp his hand. Desiring to get an eligible position upon the ground in company with my wife and several others, we proceeded to the cemetery. An immense crowd had already gathered there and were waiting the arrival of the President. When the great and imposing pageant entered the ground, the thunder of the artillery again shook those hills ; and when at length, as one distinguished man after another mounted the platform, the tall form of the Nation's President was recognized, a shout went up to heaven like that which occurred when the hosts of treason and rebellion were defeated and thrown back from those hills a few months previously.

Throughout the whole of the services, which occupied several hours, we were compelled to stand, and between the wearisomeness of the long-standing and the crowding and jostling of the people, several persons fainted and with difficulty were removed from the throng. At the conclusion of Mr. Everett's address, and after some excellent music, President LINCOLN arose, and amidst the thunder of artillery and the tremendous applause of the immense multitude, advanced to the front of the platform, his tall, gaunt form and sad but amiable face within the view of thousands who beheld the memorable scene. When silence was secured he proceeded in slow and measured tones to deliver his dedicatory address. His words were not heard by the larger majority of the people present, but during his address the most profound silence was observed. When he uttered the closing words, which have become immortal, emphasizing each sentence with a brief pause and a significant nodding and jerking of his head— "*that the government of the people, by the people, and for the people, shall not perish from the earth*"—it occurred to me (for I stood within a few feet of him and heard all he said) that I had never heard or read anything like them, and that they were destined to an imperishable immortality in the hearts of the American people. When the exercises closed the President's horse was brought near to where I stood, and taking the arm of Marshal Lamon, he came down from the platform and passed close by us. As he approached us my wife said, "O but I would like to shake his hand." Hearing this remark he turned and smiled, when I said, "Mr. President, will you have the kindness to permit this lady take you by the hand?" "Most certainly," he replied, "if my horse will let me," for by that time his attendants were urging him to mount, and his horse was prancing. Mounting his horse he turned full around towards us and extended his hand. My wife clasped it and exclaimed, "God bless you, Mr. Lincoln! God bless you!" The people standing near seeing this, made a rush for a shake of his hand, and his attendants, seeing the difficulty he was about getting into, interfered and led him away amidst the cries of "God bless you, Mr. Lincoln! God bless you, Mr. President!"

The admiration and esteem of the people for President LINCOLN exceeded any ever bestowed upon any other man within my knowledge. It was evidently not so much for him personally, as *representatively*. He was recognized as the embodiment, the personification of the cause which was enshrined in every patriot's heart, and for which the armies of the Union were contending. To love the Union was to love ABRAHAM LINCOLN. To hate and defame ABRAHAM LINCOLN was the acknowledged evidence of disloyalty. The honored head of the Nation, standing upon the ground where one of the greatest struggles of modern times occurred for its very existence, and where its destiny was in part decided, that humble man of Illinois modestly received the willing homage of the assembled thousands. The Man—the President—the Government—the yet undecided peril to which it was exposed—the ground we were on—the sleeping thousands all about us, whose blood had been poured out that the Nation might live, all, all conspired to make the occasion one never to be forgotten.

The Soldier's National Cemetery at Gettysburg is situated upon Cemetery Hill, so called because upon it and immediately in the rear of where the heroes of the Union lie, the local cemetery of the town is located. It is composed of about seventeen acres, and occupies the position where the centre of the Federal line upon the second and third day's engagements rested. Around it occurred desperate fighting, and upon it, during the terrific cannonading of the afternoon of the last day's fight, prior to the advance of Pickett's great assaulting column upon our left centre, the fire of one hundred and twenty guns was concentrated. In it are interred the bodies of 3,555 Union soldiers. They were from the following States: Maine, 104; New Hampshire, 48; Vermont, 61; Massachusetts, 159; Rhode Island, 12; Connecticut, 22; New York, 866; New Jersey, 78; Pennsylvanion, 526; Delaware, 15; Maryland, 22; West Virginia, 11; Ohio, 131; Indiana, 80; Illinois, 6; Michigan, 171; Wisconsin, 73; Minnesota, 52; United States Regulars, 138; Unknown, 979. These heroic men having gathered together from the East and West, and stood side by side under one flag, fighting for one cause, and pouring out their life blood together, it is but right and proper that they should not be divided in death, but rest upon the ground hallowed by their valor. For them there are no more hardships, no more weary marches, no more digging of trenches, no more charging into the yawning chasm of death, and no more cheering the old flag. They have fallen, but victory is ours—theirs enrollment upon the scroll of undying fame. They have not fought in vain. They did not die for nought. Not for themselves, but for their children; for those who may never visit their graves or hear of their undying valor; "for humanity, righteousness, peace; for Paradise upon earth: for Christ and for God, they have given themselves a willing sacrifice. Blessed be their memories forever." On that "Altar of Sacrifice," then, that "Mount of Salvation," that "Field of Deliverance," guarded by the Nation they saved, let them sleep until the Archangel's clarion shall sound with a louder blast than that which summoned them to that field of heroic deeds.

"On Fame's eternal camping ground
Their silent tents are spread,
And Glory guards, with solemn round,
The bivouac of the dead."

The month of April, 1865, was memorable in the history of the Nation. From the first day of the month until the ninth, bulletin after bulletin announced victory after victory for the Union arms. On Sabbath night, the 9th, we were aroused from our sleep by the ringing of bells and thunder of artillery. We at once knew what it meant, for the air during the previous day was fragrant with victory. Rushing into the street we heard cheer upon cheer. "*Lee has surrendered*," was heard upon every side. "*Thank God*," cried some, "*the Union is saved and the war is over*." A company of artillerists quartered in the field opposite to where the new depot stands, brought out their guns, and discharge after discharge announced to the people throughout the country that joyful news had been received. The long pent up feelings of the people at last had an outlet, and the methods of expression adopted by some were ludicrous in the extreme. Handshaking, embracing each other, and lifting some of our citizens upon brick piles or into the hind end of a cart, and compelling them to make speeches, were not unusual.

But this period of rejoicing was destined to be soon supplemented by a great revulsion. On Saturday morning, the 15th, while seated at the breakfast table, my wife, who had gone into the street to purchase some marketing, hastily returned with terror in her countenance, exclaiming: "*Oh, they have killed the President!*" Rushing into the street I ascertained that the report was but too true. Upon the bulletin board was posted the announcement, "*The President was shot last night at Ford's Theatre*." A little later came another, "*The President died this morning at twenty-two minutes after seven o'clock*." Still later another announcement was made that Secretary Seward was dead. This was soon after contradicted. At 11 o'clock a. m,, the Burgess of the town issued a proclamation announcing the death of the President and recommending that all business should be suspended during the day. In accordance with his recommendation all business houses were closed, flags were draped in mourning, and the church bells tolled all day. In the evening the pulpits of the churches were hung in mourning, and during the following week the demand for low priced black material for draping buildings was so great that the entire stock throughout the country and in the cities was exhausted.

During the week ensuing the assassination of the President I was in the city of New York, and while there the body of our loved and lamented chief was brought there on its way to Springfield, Illinois, its final resting place. The body was placed in a room in the second story of the City Hall, and the doors thrown open to visitors. There was one entrance by Chatham street and Park Row, on the east, and another by Broadway, on the west. Visitors passed in by one door, ascended a flight of stairs, passed along by the corpse as it lay in its casket, surrounded by General Dix and several other military men, and on down another flight of stairs, and out of the building by a different door from where they entered. Persons desiring to see the corpse had to take their place at the foot of the column, which extended for several squares from each place of entrance. Shortly after dark I took my place at the end of the line—some three squares from the City Hall, and amidst the crowding and jostling of the people who blocked up the entire street for squares, and who tried to break the line, in about an hour came up to the entrance of the Park where the crowding and pushing were so great that notwithstanding the efforts of the police, many were compelled to leave the line, and several fainted and had to be carried out over the heads of the people. At that point I came near being thrown down and trampled to death, but finally reached the building and passed by the lamented President. These lines were kept filled, and until four o'clock the next morning did that living tide of humanity thus press its way to get a last look at the lamented dead. No one was permitted to linger at the casket, but pass on. Tears and sobs were frequent, and expressions of affection involuntarily fell from many lips. At midnight a German Singing Society—about two hundred in number—gathered in front of the City Hall and sang a solemn funeral dirge.

Shortly after daylight the throng again besieged the City Hall, and long lines stood along the streets and waited their turn to see the dead President. This continued up to 10 o'clock, the time for the procession to move. Leaving the neighborhood of the City Hall I went up Broadway, above Canal street, and accepting an invitation to a place upon the flat roof of a store house, I stood there *four hours* watching the moving mass of humanity as it bore our dead Chieftain to the depot, and then becoming tired, and seeing no end of the procession, I came down and went to my hotel. Long before the end of that procession passed the place where I stood, the train which bore the corpse and funeral party had left the city and was miles away along the banks of the Hudson river towards its destination.

The war opened with the firing upon Fort Sumpter, April 12th, 1861, and virtually closed with the assassination of its most illustrious victim, ABRAHAM LINCOLN, April 15th, 1865, but in the language of another of the Nation's martyrs, JAMES A. GARFIELD, "*The Government at Washington still lives.*"

July 2d, 1884. The noise and excitement of war have ended, and on this twenty-first anniversary of the Battle of Gettysburg, I am again upon that field. The evidences of the great battle fought at that place which greeted me when I visited it a day or two after the mighty conflict, in the form of dead and loathesome corpses, mangled and suffering men, pools of human gore, and the wreck and waste of war, are no longer visible. The breastworks and other defensive works are still standing, and the marks of balls and shells upon trees and rocks yet remain. Upon the eastern slope of Little Round Top is one of the most beautiful and attractive pic-nic grounds. Here are gathered people from a distance, who have come to this place to renew their devotion to the cause for which the heroes who sleep in the cemetery upon that hill offered up their lives. In the pavillion, which is situated upon the ground over which brave men moved to charge upon the foe down in yonder fields, the voice of thanksgiving and prayer is heard. Christain ministers are telling of the deeds of heroism wrought upon this field, and deducing lessons of instruction therefrom. Ascending to the brow of the hill, but a little distance away, we see tablets marking the places where this and that regiment fought, and where Vincent and Weed and Hazlitt and O'Rouke fell. In those fields and amongst those boulders below you, within a space scarcely a mile square, fifty thousand men, like two mighty giants, wrestled for victory. That enclosed field to your right—the first beyond that open space, and south of that lane which runs westwardly—is the historic "Wheat Field," and a half mile further west, where the lane intersects the Emmittsburg road, is that other historic place, the "Peach Orchard." In these two places the battle raged most furiously, and the ground was covered with the slain. Now the growing crops have obliterated every trace of the mighty conflict. Along that lane, in the Wheat Field, and among those boulders east and south of it, tablets mark the places where heroes yielded up their lives that their country might live. Chief among these are General Zook, Col. Taylor, of the Bucktail Regiment, and Col. Ellis, of the 124th New York. Around the noble monument to the latter are gathered a few survivors of his regiment, who have come from their homes to dedicate this memento to their fallen chieftain, upon the twenty-first anniversary of his death. Upon the ground where they are gathered to listen to a masterly oration by General Woodford, of New York, twentyone years ago;on this day they stood and fought. In that sunken place in the ground, where that board is planted, their comrades who fell on that day were interred. Their bodies have since been removed and re-interred, either among their comrades upon Cemetery Hill, or in the distant cemeteries of their former homes. All along the Avenue, which runs along the Union line, tablets are placed which mark where Corps, Divisions, Brigades and Regiments stood, and where distinguished men fell. That board by the fence designates the place where Sedgwick of the 6th Corps and Warren of the 5th, had their headquarters during the terrible strife. There consultations were had and measures taken to check the assaults of the foe, who were pressing our men back from the Peach Orchard almost to the place where they stood. East Cemetery Hill and Culp's Hill yet show the marks of the strife in the breastworks and cannon which still remain. But it is in the National Cemetery where the greatest interest centres. Here are gathered the heroes from the whole field. That monument which rears its top above the surrounding trees, stands upon the spot where LINCOLN stood when he delivered his memorable dedicatory address. And that bronze statue near by the entrance is for Reynolds, who fell about a mile to the west, in the grove behind the Seminary. But it is all hallowed ground. Although in extent covering twenty-five square miles, it is all hallowed by patriot blood. Upon it the destiny of the Nation was decided. It is the Nation's shrine, and to it lovers of liberty will continue to come while the Republic lasts, and the heroic dead who lie there will be the Nation's care.

> "'Tis holy ground—
> This spot, where, in their graves,
> Are placed our country's braves,
> Who fell in Freedom's holy cause,
> Fighting for liberties and laws;
>   Let tears abound.
>
> Here where they fell,
> Oft shall the widow's tears be shed,
> Oft shall fond parents mourn their dead;
> The orphan here shall kneel and weep,
> And maidens, where their lovers sleep,
>   Their woes to tell.
>
> Here let them rest:
> And summer's heat and winter's cold
> Shall glow and freeze above their mould—
> A thousand years shall pass away—
> A nation still shall mourn their clay,
>   Which now is blest."

APPENDIX.

Since the publication of these reminiscences of the war upon our border, facts and incidents have been brought to my notice which I place upon record in this appendix. Additional information has also been received in regard to some incidents already published, which add to their detail and interest. These I also give here. In a few instances I find by additional data subsequently received, that I erred in fixing dates. These corrections are also given. Historical accuracy being all important in this record, I have availed myself of all possible means of correct information, and I can assure the reader of the entire reliability of the facts and dates given. In a contemplated revision of this work, which was somewhat hastily written, these additional incidents and modifications will appear in their respective and appropriate places.

CHAPTER I.

On page 8 reference is made to a meeting of our citizens in the Court House upon the evening of Thursday, April 18th, immediately upon the breaking out of the war, to take into consideration the condition of the country, and to express their appreciation of and sympathy for the Chambers Artillery—the first troops from Franklin county to respond to the call of President Lincoln, who were, on the following morning, to proceed to Harrisburg. The proceedings of that meeting were given and reference made to the resolutions it passed. The following are those resolutions:

RESOLUTIONS offered by I. H. McCauley, Esq., at the town meeting held on Thursday evening last.

WHEREAS, A band of traitorous spirits, regardless of their allegiance to the country of their birth, have for years past been plotting the dismemberment of our glorious confederacy, the hope of struggling Freedom throughout the World, and the asylum of the oppressed and down-trodden of all Nations:

And Whereas, Their hellish efforts have resulted in inducing the people of seven of the Southern States of our Confederacy to declare that they will no longer continue under the same Government, under the title of the "Confederate States of North America," which Government has stolen the treasure, seized the fortresses and taken possession of the National Vessels, Arms and Munitions of War belonging to the Union, and placed in their midst for the defense of our common country:

And Whereas, The said "Confederate and Rebel" Government, without just cause, has marshalled its armies and treasonably made war upon the Government of the Union, by attacking an unoffending but gallant soldier and servant of his country, Major Robert Anderson, and his forlorn hope of seventy noble rank and file, and by the aid of starvation and exhaustion has caused him to surrender his post, though not without honor to himself and those who so faithfully stood by his side, but yet to the great chagrin of all true lovers of the Constitution and Laws.

And Whereas, The Arch Traitor of them all—the Benedict Arnold of the South—Jefferson Davis—the President of the so-called "Confederate States," has boldly and openly threatened to march upon the Capitol of our country at the head of 25,000 men, and drive out the Constitutional Authorities of the land and seat himself in the mansion and Chair of State, sanctified by those noble Executives who have presided in past times over the destinies of the Republic.

And Whereas, The President of the United States of America, in view of these undeniable facts, in view of the hostile attitude of the said "Confederate States" towards Fort Pickens and the other National Stations South, and in view of the wide-spread treasonable sentiments that surround the city of Washington, has called upon the soldiery of the nation, who are faithful to their country, without respect to party feelings or predilections, to the number of 75,000 to rally in defense of the Constitution and the Laws. Therefore—

Resolved, By the people of Chambersburg, in town meeting assembled, without respect to party, that we cordially endorse the action of our National Executive, believing that the late and present National Government has been forbearing in the extreme towards those traiterous spirits who have been plotting to overturn our beloved and blood-cemented institutions, paralyze the arms of our national authorities, degrade the flag of our affections, and deluge the land of our nativity and adoption in the blood of its citizens.

Resolved, That the time has come for all men

to sink the *Partisan* in the *Patriot*, to forego political principles and party animosities, until the danger that threatens our national existence is past, and to rally *as one man*, with *one heart, one mind* and *one purpose*, at the call of the constituted authorities of the land, for the maintenance of the Constitution and the laws as they now are.

Resolved, That we cordially endorse the recommendation of our Executive and the prompt action of our Legislature, in placing the Old Keystone State on a proper war footing, as one of the surest and most certain means of "conquering a peace," and restoring our lately happy land to prosperity.

Resolved, That we hail, as one of the most unerring evidences that we have a government, and that that government possesses the confidence and affections of the people, the fact that the gallant soldiery of our noble State and the country generally, have so speedily and so cheerfully responded to the call of their Country, in numbers far over the aggregate desired.

Resolved, That our gallant and patriotic fellow-citizens, the members of the Chambers Artillery and other Volunteers of our county, who on to-morrow's morn are to go out from our midst, and from their families and friends, at the call of their country, have our most sincere, heartfelt wishes for their individual preservation from death or grievous injury during their absence, and our ardent prayers that they may each and all be speedily restored to the arms of those who so patriotically part with them at the call of duty.

Resolved, That we hereby pledge to each one of these our friends, our sacred honors, that we will see that their wives and children, and whoever else is dependent upon them, shall not, during their absence, lack for anything temporal that money and willing hearts can provide.

During the great demand for flags immediately upon the breaking of the war, as stated upon page 7, the following occurrence, related by Mr. A. N. Rankin, at that time editor and proprietor of the *Franklin Repository*, took place. The part the writer bore in the transaction is but imperfectly remembered. Mr. Rankin says:—"Immediately upon the breaking out of the war the demand for flags was so great that in order to procure one for the office of the *Franklin Repository*, of which I was, at that time, editor and proprietor. I directed Mr. Jacob Hoke, one of our dry goods merchants, to telegraph to Horstmans, of Philadelphia, to send one of their best flags by express. Two days thereafter the flag arrived, but it proved to be entirely too large to be suspended upon the pole above the office, and it was hung from the upper windows and covered nearly the whole front of the three-storied building. Another flag of proper size was made for our flag-staff under the supervision of Mr. Hoke, and in a short time the large flag was folded up and put away. Some months thereafter the seventy-seventh Pennsylvania Regiment was organized, when Capt. Samuel M. McDowell, a cousin of my wife, asked me to present the large flag to that Regiment, which was freely done. The Regiment was called to Harrisburg, and from there was sent to Pittsburg, and while in camp at or near that place, the formal acceptance of the flag was forwarded to me of which the following, which appeared in the *Repository* of October 23d, 1861, is a copy:

CAMP WILKINS, Oct. 10th, 1861.

A. N. RANKIN, Esq., *Dear Sir*:—Allow me to return you the sincere thanks of my Regiment for the beautiful American Flag you were so kind to present to us. It is too large to be carried into battle, but wherever the Seventy-Seventh encamps, it shall float proudly over our temporary place of repose. It will be our pride and pleasure to protect its graceful folds from harm. In behalf of my regiment, I again thank you for the elegant present.

F. S. STUMBAUGH,
Col. Com. 77th Regt. Penn. Volunteers.

Subsequently the 77th joined the Army of the Tennessee, and while in camp after the battle of Shiloh, or Pittsburg Landing, Gen. Sherman seeing this flag, and having but a regimental flag for his own headquarters, requested Col. Stumbaugh to exchange with him which, by my consent, obtained by telegraph, was done, and that flag was carried by Gen. Sherman throughout all his campaigns. Thus it will be seen that Chambersburg contributed the flag which floated over Sherman's headquarters wherever he led his triumphant hosts, which followed him in his grand march from Atlanta to the sea, and thence to North Carolina, where he received the surrender of Johnson, and from thence to Washington, where it is now stored amid the sacred relics of the terrible rebellion."

CHAPTER II.

In the roll of honor, page 10, Co. A., 2nd Regiment, Pennsylvania Volunteers, 3d Corporal John F. Snyder should be J. Frank Snyder. Private Ed. E. Fairweather should be Ed. E. Fairbrother.

CHAPTER VI.

The account given on page 22 and 23 of the ringing of the Court House bell to give notice of the approach of the rebels, the declaration of Martial Law, and the erection of breastworks and the planting of cannon about the Diamond, should be placed in Chapter XII, page 103, in connection with the excitement which occurred upon the evening of Wednesday, July 6th, 1864, when McCausland's Cavalry advanced from Hagerstown to near Greencastle, during Early's raid into Maryland.

For this incident I had no written data, and fixed it from personal recollection; but I subsequently found data for it in Dr. Schneck's *Burning of Chambersburg*, page 49, and also in the *Franklin Repository* of July 13th, 1864. Martial Law was proclaimed by General Couch, then commander of this military district. Judge Kimmell was not Marshal at that time.

In referring to the danger which threatened our border during Lee's invasion of Maryland and previous to the battle of Antietam, in Chapter VI, I omitted to state that among the military preparations made at this place was the mounting of what was known as the "Anderson Cavalry." Horses were procured for these men in the following manner as stated by Samuel Reisher, Esq., one of the old and well-known citizens of this place:

CHAMBERSBURG, July 26th, 1884.

MR. J. HOKE, *Sir* :—It will be remembered by some that when the rebels were invading Maryland in Sept., 1862, Governor Curtin authorized William McLellan, Esq., to publish a call to the people of the county for horses to mount the Anderson Cavalry, and also for other issues during that threatening period. He was directed to say in that call that he would give certificates to all persons bringing in horses certifying to their value. After said horses were approved, forty cents per day for their use was to be allowed, and in case the horses received any injury, an additional sum was to be allowed to cover said damages; and in case the horses were not returned to their respective owners they were to be paid for. As the farmers at that time were busy preparing to put in their fall crops and had need of their horses, but few were brought in. As the danger increased and the necessity for horses became more pressing, the Governor directed and empowered me to impress all horses found fit for military purposes. I immediately sent out press gangs of able and judicious men into all parts of the county with instructions to take all horses they could find for the service without respect to persons or party. Among those sent were Messrs. F. A. Zarman, Jacob Hollinger and Sam'l Myers. These persons went out throughout the county and gathered the horses needed, unhitching them from wagons and ploughs, however pressing the needs of their owners. The people saw the necessity for them and were generally satisfied, but many were unable for the want of them to prosecute their fall work. A certificate signed by me was given for each horse taken, in which its value was stated, and all were assured that in due time they would be paid for their use, as well as for any damage which might result to them, or their full value in case they were not returned. These horses had to be fed by us until delivered over to the military authorities, and this feed we had also to take from the people. Then followed the stripping of shops of saddles and bridles. These, like the horses and feed, we had to take wherever we found them. It was indeed a hard duty to perform, but the condition of our border seemed to require it, and we did it under the authority of the Governor and his pledge that the State would make it all right.

These horses, when delivered into the care of the troopers, in some cases were traded off for others of less value, and money was received as the difference by the men. When this fact was brought to the notice of General Reynolds, who had command here, he isssued an order requiring every one of these horses to be branded "U. S." so as to prevent this trading. When the emergency under which this property was thus taken, had passed, some of these horses were returned to their respective owners, but some were in such a condition that they were of but little use. Many were never returned, and such also was the case with the saddles and bridles.

After the property was ordered to be returned, Mr. D. O. Gehr and myself were appointed to hear and determine all claims, which was accordingly done, and our report was sent to Governor Curtin where it was approved and placed in the archives of the State at Harrisburg. In some cases when the horses were returned to their owners, I was frequently called upon to relieve persons of difficulty for having horses in their possession bearing the brand of the government. These arrests were made at both Carlisle and Harrisburg when the owners fled to these places during subsevqent raids. And now, notwithstanding the assurances given by the Governor, under whose authority we acted, these horses and the feed and saddles and bridles have never been paid for. It seems to me that our suffering people should be paid for their property thus taken in a time of public need, and I feel the more interested in this matter for the reason that I was made the unwilling instrument of taking it. If not, I am yet young enough to inquire, for what use governments are instituted. Hoping that the State will yet see its obligation to do ample justice in this matter, I subscribe myself

Yours, &c.,

SAMUEL REISHER.

CHAPTER VII.

In giving the names of persons captured and taken away by the rebels during Stuart's raid on page 32, I was led into error by the information given me. Mr. G. G. Rupley who was one of the persons captured has given me the true account. Messrs. Perry A. Rice, Daniel Shaffer, C. Louderbaugh, G. C. Steiger, John McDowell, James Grove, Wm. Raby, Dr. Blair, and G. G. Rupley were taken at Mercersburg; Joseph Winger at Clay Lick Hall, and William Conner at St. Thomas. Steiger made his escape near Bridgeport; McDowell and Louderbaugh at Chamberssburg. Wm Raby and Dr. Blair escaped in Montgomery county, Md., before crossing the Potomac, and Rice, Shaffer, Conner, Winger, Grove and Rupley were taken to Richmond and incarcerated in Libby prison. Winger and Rupley were paroled about the first of December, 1862. Rice died in January or

February, 1863, and Grove, Shaffer and Conner were exchanged in March, 1863.

CHAPTER VIII.

In referring, on page 33, to John S. Oaks, who was wounded at the battle of Fredericksburg and afterwards died and his body brought here for burial, I omitted the names of others of our Franklin county soldiers who were killed and wounded in that battle, for the reason that space forbid me to give the names of all the gallant men from our county who fell in their country's service. I should have added as another victim of the battle of Fredericksburg, who was brought here for burial, D. Augustus Houser. He, too, was a member of Capt. John Doebler's company, and received his wound in the same battle and while in the act of tying up the wound of Capt. Doebler. His body was brought to this place and interred the day after the funeral of John S. Oaks.

On page 31 mention is made of the excitement in the town upon the reception, in the evening of Sunday, June 14th, of the news of the disaster to our forces at Winchester and the probable appearance of the rebels in our midst, and the packing and sending away and secreting of merchandize and other valuables. Mr. John F. Glosser, who was then an assistant in the office of the Prothonotary of the county, quoting from his diary of events of that time, says: "Saturday evening, June 13th, 1863, our town was thrown into great commotion occasioned by a rumor that the rebels were coming. Matters quieted down however until the following Sunday evening (14th) when I was summoned to the office (Prothonotary) to aid in packing the records preparatory to shipping them off to a point of safety. Finished our work about 2 o'clock Monday morning. During this day our merchants were busy packing and shipping off their goods.

On page 39 I speak of an engagement in McConnellsburg between what I supposed was a detatchment from Jenkins' force and a company of the 1st New York Cavalry under Capt. Jones. I have since learned that that engagement was not with Jenkins' men, but a part of Imboden's force and occurred several days after the visit to McConnellsburg of a detachment from Jenkins. The detachment which Jenkins sent into Fulton county consisted of about two hundred and fifty men and was under command of Col. Furguson. It was detached from his main force after he fell back from Chambersburg to below Greencastle on Wednesday, June 17th. This was the first rebel force that visited McConnellsburg during the war, and it was the same which captured ex-sheriff Taylor's cattle, which were grazing in a field about two miles north of McConnellsburg. They also succeeded in taking away about eighty valuable horses from the town and immediate neighborhood which, with the cattle, were delivered to Rhodes' infantry at Greencastle the week following.

For the following additional facts I am indebted to W. Scott Alexander, Esq., an attorney, resident in McConnellsburg, who gathered the facts he has communicated from some of the older inhabitants of the place. During the week before the battle of Gettysburg, from Wednesday until Saturday, General Imboden's force, which entered the valley at Hancock, plundered the whole lower end of the valley. They penetrated it as far as Webster Mills, and then crossed the mountain by Hunter's road to the Cap. While in the Cove they took everything that came in their way that they could in any way use, and afterward destroyed what they could not take along. The farmers lost nearly all their stock, and Robinson's store at Big Cove Tannery and Patterson's at Webster Mills, were completely stripped of their contents. In many cases houses were entered and private property taken.

On Sunday, June 28th, a company of the 12th Pennsylvania cavalry was surprised on the east side of the Cove mountain, and several of their number captured by a detachment of Imboden's men. In the afternoon of the same day a company of Imboden's force, thought to have been the same that had the skirmish in the morning with these Pennsylvanians, dashed into McConnellsburg. Finding no Federal soldiers there they did not dismount but returned by the way they came, in the direction of Mercersburg.

The engagement which occurred in McConnellsburg was on Monday, 29th, and was as follows: Early on Monday morning Capt. Jones with Co. A, 1st New York cavalry, entered the town from Everett or Bloody Run. Shortly afterwards a company of newly organized militia cavalry arrived from Mount Union. Capt. Jones's men had dismounted and were in the vicinity of the "Fulton House," while Capt. Jones himself was in the hotel. The militia were in the neighborhood of the Court House, but before they had dismounted some of Jones' scouts came dashing into town and reported the approach of a rebel force along the Mercersburg road. Jones inquired of his scouts concerning their number and when informed that they did not exceed seventy-five men—double the number of his own force—declared his intention to fight them. He at once ordered his men, who were nearly all Irishmen and fond of a fight, to examine their arms and then fall into line. The men examined their pistols and then stuck them into their boots. He then consulted with the commander of the militia, and the part assigned them was to remain in the cross street until the rebels were drawn down opposite to them, when they were to make some demonstration merely to frighten the foe by the show of their numbers, leaving whatever fighting was to be done to him and his command. Jones then hastily formed his men in line—but 38 in all—he taking the rear, and as the rebels approached the town by the east and showed themselves in the street in the upper end of the town, he leisurely fell back to the lower or west end. When he had drawn the foe to the Fulton House Captain Irvine, who was in command of the rebels, ordered them to charge, but this order was not obeyed. But about the time this command was given, a member of the militia cavalry ventured down to the main street to take a look at the situation, and when he reached the corner, about one hundred feet from the head of the rebel column, his sudden appearance caused Capt. Irvine to suppose that Jones's retreat was intended to lead him further into the town, so that the force in the cross street could come in on his rear and cut off his retreat. Instead, then, of charging as ordered, the rebels, without orders, suddenly wheeled about and made a hasty retreat. As soon as they had turned, Capt. Jones ordered his men to "Right about face—charge." But as soon as the member of the militia company notified his associates of the approach of the foe, the entire company broke ranks and made a more hasty retreat than did the rebels. Reports say that they did not stop until they reached Burnt Cabins, 12 miles distant. Capt. Jones, however, followed up the rebels and commenced firing before they got out of the town. He continued the pursuit for about one mile east of the town when the greater part of the rebels surrendered, not however, until two of their number had been killed and one or two wounded. Jones captured 32 men and 33 horses. A few of the rebels having fast horses escaped. Jones had but one man wounded. When they returned to McConnellsburg the citizens seeing about as many rebels as Federals did not at first know who had been victorious—whether the rebels had captured Jones, or Jones the Confederates. The prisoners were at once taken westward to Everett. The rebel killed were put in coffins by the citizens, and in the afternoon of the same day were interred near the place where they fell. While the interrment was taking place a rebel force of cavalry came down the Mercersburg pike, while a similar force, which had crossed the mountain six miles down the valley by Hunter's road, and crossed the valley, entered the pike about a mile west of the town. Thus the town was surrounded and again in possession of the foe, but Jones with his booty was not there. The entire rebel force numbered about 400 men, and belonged to Imboden's command. They had with them three pieces of artillery, which they planted at the east end of the town. Expecting to find Union soldiers, arms, &c., secreted in the houses, a search was made, but failing to find anything they left about dark towards the Cove Gap. This engagement should be transferred from page 39 to page 67, and recorded among the occurrences of Monday, June 29th.

On page 39 reference is made to Jenkins' cavalry after it fell back from this place to below Greencastle, where, during the intervening few days before it again advanced at the head of Rhodes' division of infantry, it was divided into squads, which scoured the whole southern part of the county plundering and robbing the people. On Sunday, June 21st, that party of about two hundred and fifty men under Col. Furguson, who had visited McConnellsburg, in Fulton county, robbing and plundering the people there, entered Greencastle and pillaged that place. The *Pilot* of July 28th, 1863, says that on that day a systematic pillage was made. "In some stores a great quantity of goods were destroyed. The order given by an artillery captain, in front of Messrs. S. H. Prather & Co.'s store, was to 'dismount and ransack the store.' Mr. Reilly's store had, a day or two previously, suffered heavily by these men. The losses it is impossible now to state. If it had not been that our merchants had a portion of their stock sent East, there would have been a clean sweep made. Maj. Paxton took possession of the warehouses and loaded the Confederate States' wagons with flour and grain, &c."

CHAPTER IX.

In further confirmation of the correctness of the estimate of the number of Lee's army, which invaded our State, as given on page 41, the following additional testimony is given : Mr, William A. Reid, of Greencastle, in an article contributed by him to the *Pilot* of that place, in its issue of July 28th, 1863, says : "The Rebel force that passed through town (Greencastle) has been estimated at about 50,000 or 60,000 men, accompanied by 192 pieces of ordnance. The force that went by way of Waynesboro', it is said, numbered between 20,000 and 30,000, making a total force of about 90,000 or 100,000." The only force which passed by the way of

Waynesboro' was Early's Division, which did not exceed 8,000 men. Mr. John F. Glosser, at the time of the war a resident of this place, but now of Philadelphia, from a diary written at the time, furnishes the following estimates: Ewell's Corps 15,000 men, infantry, artillery and cavalry, with 60 pieces of artillery and about 1,000 wagons; A. P. Hill's Corps the same; Longstreet's Corps 20,000 men, 80 pieces of artillery and over 1,000 wagons. "The entire army," he says, "did not number over 48,000 or 50,000 men—Infantry, Cavalry and Artillery, 200 pieces of artillery and 3,000 wagons." Add to the 50,000 which the *Franklin Repository*, Greencastle *Pilot*, and Mr. John F. Glosser say passed through Greencastle and this place, Early's 8,000 which passed by way of Waynesboro' and Greenwood, and Gen. Stuart's cavalry, 12,000 to 13,000, who passed around east of the Union army, and we have a total of 70,000 or 71,000 as claimed by the Confederate authorities.

Add to this immense host the three thousand wagons and 200 pieces of artillery with their caissons and forges, as stated by Mr. Glosser from notes made by himself at the time, and the droves of cattle and other plunder taken along the way, and we have confirmation of the estimate of the probable length of the whole Rebel column as stated on page 54.

Reference is made on page 45 to the fact that Stuart's brigade of Rhodes' division of Ewell's Corps was, on the morning of Wednesday, June 24th, at Greencastle, detached from the main column on its way to this place, and sent westward through Mercersburg to McConnellsburg. This brigade consisted of about 2,500 infantry and 300 cavalry, and was under command of General Stuart. Its object in crossing the mountain was to look after that part of Milroy's force, which had escaped from Winchester and crossed the Potomac at and above Hancock. They reached Mercersburg about the middle of the day, and at once made themselves at home. Learning that a theological Seminary was located there, General Stuart placed a guard around the property for its protection. The soldiers were forbidden to enter either the Seminary or private houses under penalty of severe punishment. The stores were ordered to be opened, and the soldiers permitted to purchase whatever they needed. To their credit be it said that everything was in an orderly manner. No pillaging was permitted. What they took was taken by officers who made out bills and paid in Confederate scrip. Major Goldsboro, of Baltimore, was Provost Marshal. He was afterwards killed at the battle of Gettysburg.

This force reached McConnellsburg shortly after dark on the evening of this same day. When about half a mile east of the town, they formed in line of battle, and the cavalry dashed into the town on a charge, expecting to find Milroy's force, but in this were mistaken, as the small force which had been there during the day had moved westward before dark, after having had a slight skirmish with the advance of the rebels at the top of the Cove mountain. As soon as the infantry entered the town it was placed under guard and the citizens ordered to remain in their houses. A few, however, who were anxious to see what was going on, ventured out into the streets, and were arrested and placed under guard until the next morning. The invaders disturbed nothing during the night, but in the morning they entered the stores and shops and helped themselves to whatever they wanted, and in some cases, it is said, offered Confederate scrip in payment for what they had taken. About one-third of the cavalry went north, up the valley as far as the Burnt Cabins, gathering a great many horses from the farmers along the way, and picking up others that had been sent to that valley from Franklin county. From Burnt Cabins they crossed to Fannettsburg and thence on to Chambersburg, or joined the rebel forces somewhere in Franklin county. The infantry and the remainder of the cavalry remained in the vicinity of McConnellsburg until early on Friday morning when they finally left, crossing the mountain and passing through Loudon and St. Thomas and rejoining the main column at Chambersburg.

Rev. B. Bausman, D. D., at the time of the war a resident of our town, in an article in the *Guardian* of Sept., 1874, of which he was editor, says that in the absence of the Town Council, who had nearly all left town upon the approach of Lee's invading army, a meeting of some six or eight of our leading citizens, with the resident pastors of the place who had not followed the example of the town fathers in putting themselves beyond the reach of the dreaded foe, was held in the Cashier's office in the Bank, about 11 o'clock on Monday night, June 22d, to decide upon some course to be pursued when the expected demand for the surrender of the town would be made. At this meeting it was decided that in the absence of the proper authorities, the pastors should serve as the representatives of the town and make such terms with the rebels as they thought best. Rev. B. S. Schueck, D. D., was constituted president of this committee. On Wednesday following, 24th, this clerical committee found it necessary to call to its assistance some eight or ten of our business men. The town was taken possession of, but its surrender was not asked for. But when the heads of the Commissary and Quartermaster's departments laid in their requisitions for a large amount of stores, among the rest for twenty-five barrels of sour kraut, this committee found it necessary to call to their aid a number of the business men. This transaction is referred to on page 48.

When writing the account of the skirmish between a small body of Federal cavalry and Jenkin's force and the advance of Rhode's infantry, which occurred on Monday, 22d, a short distance north of Greencastle, which is found on page 45. I was not certain whether that engagement or the one spoken of on page 39 which occurred in McConnellsburg, was the first battle of the rebellion on Pennsylvania soil. I have since learned by undoubted authority that the battle in McConnellsburg occurred on Monday, June 29, one week later than the engagement near Greencastle. The engagement then near Greencastle was clearly the first one of the war upon the soil of our State. In my former account of this battle I stated that the Union force engaged was a company of the 1st New York cavalry, commanded by Capt. Jones—the same who fought the rebels at McConnellsburg. Subsequent information has shown me that that company was commanded by Captain, and afterwards, Col. Boyd. The 1st New York cavalry, like the other Federal forces engaged in the disaster at Winchester under Gen. Milroy, on Saturday and Sunday, June 13th and 14th, were scattered. Part of this regiment escaped into Pennsylvania at Hancock and fled to Everett, or Bloody Run, in Bedford county. Captain Jones' company was among these, and he advanced eastwardly to the neighborhood of McConnellsburg, giving the rebels much trouble, and subsequently crossed the mountain and cut off part of the great wagon train of wounded from Gettysburg as related elsewhere. One company of this same regiment—company C, commanded by Capt. Boyd—covered the retreat of the wagon train, which escaped from Winchester and dashed through our town on Monday, 15th, as related on page 34. It was this company, not the one commanded by Capt. Jones, which engaged the rebels near Greencastle. The Union force consisted of forty-three men, and the engagement occurred between 12 and 1 o'clock in the middle of the day. Mr. D. G. Shook, who investigated this matter for me, consulting some of the older citizens, says that a portion of Rhodes' infantry, in connection with Jenkins' cavalry, was engaged in the fight. The infantry were concealed in a wheat field,

and fired upon the Federal cavalry when it had been drawn within their range. Mr. Reid, in an article in the *Pilot* of July 28th, 1863, says two rebels were killed in this engagement. Sergeant Rhile, who was killed was interred by the rebels in a shallow grave, having been first stripped of hat, shoes and coat buttons. A few days afterwards he was disinterred by the citizens of Greencastle. placed in a neat coffin, and, accompanied by a large concourse of citizens, was buried in the Lutheran graveyard of that place. Sergeant Cafferty, who was wounded in the leg, was taken to the residence of Mr. George Ilginfritz, where his wounds were dressed and where he received the kind attentions of the family and citizens. Dr. Carl, one of Greencastle's most eminent physicians attended him.

On this same day, Monday 22d, General Rhodes' Division encamped in the vicinity of the town (Greencastle) in a field belonging to Rev. J. Loose. Col. Willis, of the 12th Georgia regiment, was appointed Provost Marshal. Assisted by Captain Carson and the Adjutant, with a detail of men from his regiment, the Colonel maintained excellent order throughout the town.

To the occurrences of Tuesday, 23d, as given on pages 46 and 47, the following should be added. Requisitions were made upon Greencastle by Ewell's corps, which remained over this day at that place, as follows:

HEADQUARTERS 2D ARMY CORPS, }
June 23d, 1863. }
To the Authorities of Greencastle :
By direction of Lieut. General R. S. Ewell, I make requisition for the following articles :
100 saddles and bridles.
12 pistols.
These articles are to be furnished at 2 o'clock P. M.

J. A. HARMON,
Maj. and Q. M. 2d Corps de Armie.

Following this requisition came another for onions, sourkraut, potatoes, radishes, &c., signed by A. M. Mitchell, Maj. and Ch. Com. Then another demanding
2000 pounds of lead.
1000 " " leather.
100 pistols.
12 boxes of tin.
200 curry combs and brushes.
Signed, WM. ALLEN, M. and C.

The chief of the Topographical Engineers also demanded two maps of Franklin county.

These demands were so heavy that the Council felt it impossible to fill them, and no effort was accordingly made. The rebels however, secured some saddles and bridles, and about $2,000 worth of leather from Mr. A. Stiffel.

On pages 46 and 47, I give the time of the entrance of the rebel infantry into our town as Tuesday 23d. I there stated that this was a disputed point, and I decided upon that day because of the weight of evidence in favor of it. That decision was against my own written record made at the time, which placed it on Wednesday, 24th. Additional evidence since received, clearly proves that the latter date is correct. That additional evidence is as follows: Mr. Wm. A. Reed, in his article contributed to the Greencastle *Pilot* of July 28th, 1863, says that "Gen. Rhodes' Division left here, (Greencastle), and marched direct to Chambersburg." In another place he says, "On the 24th, General Ewell passed through town in a carriage, and was engaged in closely examining a map."

Mr. David Z. Shook, another resident of Greencastle who, at my request, specially investigated this matter, says, "Rhodes' Division left Greencastle early in the morning of Wednesday, June 24th."

Mr. John F. Glosser, quoting from a record made at the time by himself, says, "Wednesday morning, the 24th, the army commenced their entry in the following order: Lieutenant General Ewell's Grand Division, or Corps, (Jackson's old corps) headed by General Rhodes' Division." The entrance of Jenkins' cavalry, he previously placed on Tuesday. I have no hesitation in placing the first entrance of the rebel infantry into our town on Wednesday 24th, instead of Tuesday 23d, as published on pages 46 and 47. The weight of evidence is so decided that it cannot be doubted. Besides this day coincides with the time fixed in my own record, made at the time and with great care, and also with my own recollection. The references made of the entrance of Ewell's men on Tuesday by the *Franklin Repository* and Professor Jacobs in his Battle of Gettysburg, must be to Jenkins' cavalry, which, at that time, formed part of Ewell's corps.

In further evidence of the ludicrous conduct of the New York soldiers in fleeing from their position half mile south of town on Monday, June 22d, at the rumored approach of the rebels, as given on page 46, the following statement by Mr. Solomon D. Swert, who was an eye witness of what he relates, is given:

MR. J. HOKE, *Dear Sir:*—According to promise, I give the following concerning the inglorious retreat of the New York militia, which came here during the war as upon a holiday excursion. Upon Sunday, June 21st, 1863, a regiment of New York soldiers reached our town and after a short rest in the Diamond, proceeded to the woods of the late Mr. Messersmith, about half a mile south of the town.

On the following day, Monday 22, when a rumor reached the camp that the rebels were coming, these soldiers hastily gathered their camp equipage together in a large pile near the railroad. After doing this they left it and went pell-mell to town and down to the depot, taking nothing with them but the clothes they had on and their muskets. The two howitzers belonging to this regiment were left behind in their panic, but they were hauled to town by our home guard and delivered to their owners at the depot.

But what I wish more particularly to bring to notice is the cowardly conduct of the Colonel of the regiment. This officer came up the railroad from the camp, and instead of turning off at the Waynesboro' crossing and coming through town by second street, kept on by the railroad. Passing along the track his horse fell into a cattle-guard, and the Colonel, failing to get him out as quickly as he desired, drew his pistol and shot him in the head. I myself and two or three citizens passing along shortly after, saw the horse. He was a noble animal. Whether the Colonel stopped long enough to take off the saddle and bridle, I cannot say, but it is altogether likely that some person got a first-rate saddle and bridle cheap. The Colonel either walked or ran from where he shot his horse to the depot, where they took the train and got safely to Shippensburg. Meanwhile many persons helped themselves to what they pleased of clothing and other articles left at the camp, all of which was new and good. Mr. Abram Metz in the goodness of his heart loaded a one-horse wagon full of pantaloons, blouses, blankets, buckets, camp kettles, pistols, etc., which he hauled after the panic-stricken party, which lay over at Shippensburg, where he delivered them to their owners. Upon returning, when near Chambersburg, he encountered the advance of the rebels who relieved him of his horse. This he got for his services, and our brave defenders got safely back to New York without the loss of a man.

On page 45 I speak of General Early's movement to the east through Gettysburg to York. Upon reaching Gettysburg on Friday 26th, he issued the following requisition upon the town, viz, for 60 barrels of flour; 7,000 lbs. of pork or bacon; 1,200 lbs. of sugar; 100 lbs. coffee; 1,000 lbs. salt; 40 bushels of onions; 1,000 pairs of shoes; 500 hats; or $10,000 in money.

To this demand the Town Council, through its President, Mr. D. Kendlehart, made the following reply:

GETTYSBURG, June 26th, 1863.

GENERAL EARLY, *Sir:*—The authorities of the borough of Gettysburg, in answer to the demand made by you upon the said borough and county, say that their authority extends but to the borough and that the requisition asked for cannot be given, because it is utterly impossible to comply. The quantities required are far beyond that in our possession. In compliance, however, to the demands we will request the stores to be opened and the citizens to furnish whatever they can of such provisions,

&c., as may be asked. Further we cannot promise.

By authority of the council of the borough of Gettysburg, I hereunto, as President of said Board, attach my name.

D. KENDLEHART.

General Early received orders that evening to proceed to York, and the requisition was not further pressed.

On page 57 I say the only instance in which armed resistance to marauding parties of rebels during the invasion, was made was by the inhabitants of Horse Valley at the Strasburg pass. The following additional case has been brought to my notice by Mr. Christian H. Deck. Mr. Deck says : Every nook and corner from Mercersburg to Newburg, along the entire mountain, was searched by the rebels and many horses were captured and taken away, with one exception, and that was at Keefler's Gap. Mr. Christian Deck, the father of the informant, at that time lived on what is known as the Keefer farm in Hamilton township, Franklin county, and close to the gap where the old path crosses the mountain to Horse Valley. Mr. Deck conceived the plan of putting his horses at a good place in the mountain, and to get as many of his neighbors as possible to join and have a regular camp and to organize a band of men to protect the horses. Accordingly several tents were erected and all who would were invited to join. About twenty or twenty-five persons responded, among whom were the following, being all Mr. Deck can remember. William Finney, Abraham Weaver, George Weaver, Henry Clay Keefer, Franklin Deck, Augustus Deck, Jonas Keefer, Harry Deck, Daniel Heckman, Jacob Pugh, John Bossart, Jerome Keefer, David Timmons, Emauuel Weaver, Frederick Golden and John Weaver. Some of these at that time were but boys, but they shouldered their guns and went into camp to protect the property of their parents and neighbors. From one hundred to one hundred and twenty-five horses were taken there, belonging to the following named persons and others whose names have escaped Mr. Deck: Christian Deck, Henry Keefer, William Bossart, Daniel Hull, John Heckman, Daniel Kunkle, Henry Allen, John Gelwix, Geo. Brake, Henry Treper, William Melhorn and Frederick Deck. The persons first named were all well armed with their trusty guns and revolvers. Some fifteen or twenty were kept on duty continually while the rest attended to the horses and brought in supplies, mostly from Mr. Deck's whose farm was the nearest at hand. The roads and paths were guarded and when a suspicious person would come along, two of the guards would take him in charge, escort him to the top of the mountain, and with orders not to be seen around there anymore again would be let go. Mr. Deck advised that about every five minutes a gun should be discharged. Accordingly a continual booming was kept up, and while every other gap in the mountain was visited by the rebels, and horses taken, not a visit was made to this gap nor a horse taken.

To show what dread the rebels had of being bushwacked the following incident is to the point. Many rebels were almost continually passing within about a mile of this camp, but none ventured to the gap. One day a party inquired of a farmer if there were not horses in the gap? "Yes," he replied, "come and I will show you." Just then bang went a gun, at which one of them said, "Oh, you can't fool us," and away they rode, remarking, "There, the d——d Yankees have killed another rebel." On another occasion five rebels ventured as near as Mr. Deck's residence. It happened just as they came up the road that Daniel Heckman, one of the scouts, was at Mr. Deck's and another scout about two hundred yards from the house. Mr. Heckman at once made a dash towards the camp, but the rebels saw him as he ran in an opposite direction to escape from them. One of the rebels dismounted and laid his carbine on the fence and taking aim fired. The ball went hissing close to Mr. Heckman's head. Three others then dashed after him, but by that time he had reached another fence along which trees, bushes and vines were thickly grown. Among these bushes Mr. Heckman made his escape while the rebels rode on furiously for about a mile thinking to capture him. Failing to find him they became enraged. In the meanwhile as these were after Heckman, the two rebels who remained at the house took hold of Mr. Deck, who was at his barn, and placing their revolvers to his head demanded to know who the bushwhacker was and where he lived. Mr. Deck refused to tell them. The rebels then again and again threatened with oaths to shoot him, but could not frighten him into telling them. They then accused him of harboring bushwhackers and declared that they would kill him and burn all his buildings. Finding that he would not tell they threw him to the ground and then left declaring that they would return the next day and bring a whole company and plant a battery on what is known as the Big Hill, situated about a half mile off, and would shell the gap and kill every bushwhacker they would find. While these things were transpiring with Mr. Deck the other scout, Abraham Weaver, had reached the camp and reported what was going on. Here now was an opportunity for the boys to show their courage. The following ten persons at once went on the double quick, well armed, down the mountain to rescue Mr. Deck, viz: William Finney, as Captain, Abraham Weaver, George Weaver, Henry Clay Keefer, Franklin Deck, Augustus Deck, Harry Deck, Jacob Pugh, John Bossart and David Timmons. On reaching Mr. Deck's they found that the rebels had just left. Again they double quicked across the fields to intercept them, but the rebels had gotten ahead of them and went straight for Chambersburg. This ended the first and only trouble at Keefer's Gap, and every horse which was kept there was safe. One farmer becoming dissatisfied with this staying in the mountain, left the camp one evening with his horses, The next day his six horses were taken. They were good horses and the six were worth from a thousand to twelve hundred dollars. Mr. Heckman, the scout they shot at, was afterwards killed by the explosion of a shell while he was attempting to take out its contents.

Dr. McClay, of Greenvillage, quoting from his journal written during the war, furnishes the following:

During the night of Tuesday, June 23d (1863), a large body of rebel cavalry passed through the Village on down towards Shippensburg. Their arms and accoutrements seemed to be all muffled so as to make no noise.

Rhodes' infantry took up a position about Shirk's Hill (about two miles south of the Village on the Chambersburg road) and planted a large number of cannon there. It was their intention to fortify this hill and wait the coming of the Union army. Rev. Wesley Howe, who at that time lived in the Village, had this from the officers, many of whom he knew when preaching in Virginia.

On the morning of the 26th (Friday), before daylight, the rebel infantry commenced to pass down the valley and continued passing until after night. (This was Rhodes' division.)

Several of the officers were much interested in the Presbyterian churches of the valley, and made inquiries concerning church matters, and but little about politics or the war. A religious service was held by them on Sabbath, 28th, in Mr. John Immell's woods near the Village. Fine discourse, attentive congregation and good singing. Three of the soldiers who stood guard about my house had been students of Dr. Shoemaker's, at Academia, Juniata county, at one time.

June 30th (Tuesday) rebel army began to return from down the valley. They went out the Scotland road.

Walked to Shirk's Hill after the rebels had left. The woods and fields all around were covered with hundreds of hides cut to pieces to render them useless. The rebels were passing right over the fields in a direct line for Fayetteville, regardless of roads, and evidently in a great hurry. From Monn's down to Hargleroad's mill and over the old camp meeting ground, the rebels lay in immense numbers. They were all moving when we looked over the fields from the highest point on the hill. Drums were beating and the ear-piercing fife and the shrill notes of the trumpet were all calling to arms. We gazed on the scene and silently invoked the great God of battles to protect our Army and Nation from this great force of misguided men. (This was Johnson's division. Part of his wagon train came up the pike to Chambersburg and passed out towards Gettysburg. The balance of his train with Rhoads', passed across the county by Scotland and the road leading from Shippensburg to Greenwood.—J. HOKE.)

But little is known of the circumstances connected with the retreat of the Confederate army from Gettysburg. Dr. H. G. Chritzman, who was with Kilpatrick's cavalry at that time, furnishes the following interesting account, which we gratefully place upon record here.

MR. J. HOKE, Sir:

At your request I have prepared the following statement of events connected with Kilpatrick's pursuit of Lee on his retreat from Gettysburg, of which I was personally cognizant. So far as I know the incidents related have not been yet published.

H. G. CHRITZMAN.

A great deal has been written and spoken about the battle of Gettysburg, but I have never read anything concerning Kilpatrick's dash across the mountains through Monterey Pass, after the battle.

I will state the doings of the 8th Pa. cavalry, of which I was a member before and after the fight. The 8th cavalry was originally commanded by David M. Gregg, but at the time of the movement on Gettysburg, Gregg was a Brigadier General commanding the 2d Division of Pleasanton's cavalry corps, and was considered one among the ablest cavalry commanders in the army of the Potomac.

June 28th, 1863, the 8th cavalry was at Frederick, Md., it was then detached from Devin's Brigade, and united with Kilpatrick's old brigade. Col. Huey of the 8th cavalry was assigned to the command of the Brigade, consisting of the 2d and 4th New York, 6th Ohio and 8th Pa. cavalry, also battery C, 3d U. S.

From Frederick we pushed on to New Market. June 29th. Still on the march through the night, arriving at Westminster at daybreak, June 30th.

A little incident took place during this night march which will go far to show how indifferent soldiers may become to danger, even in the face of the enemy, by the exhaustion of long and fatiguing marches. The command had halted from some cause and the writer of this becoming somewhat weary in the saddle dismounted and sat down in a fence corner to rest. How long he had remained in that position he is now unable to say, but on awaking from a fitful slumber all seemed dark and still, not even the sound of a restive horse or the clank of a sabre disturbed the silence. Getting upon my feet and peering out into the uncertain light, I could just discern my regiment still there, seeming like some phantom column of men and horses. I walked up to the officer commanding and spoke of this ominous silence, expressing my fears that the column had moved on. He told me to walk up the line and ascertain if there was anything in front of us. I soon discovered that the column had moved on with the exception of a battery in our immediate front, the men of which were fast asleep. There sat cannoneers and drivers forgetful of duty, perhaps many of them dreaming of far away homes and brighter scenes than the stern and relentless strife in which they were soon to engage. I immediately reported the fact that the column with the exception of the battery had moved forward. I can assure you there was some lively traveling for a time until we caught up to the rest of the brigade, about daylight. During July 1st, 2d and 3d, our brigade did picket duty on the right and rear of the army, and guarded the trains.

July 4th, moved to Emmittsburg and reported to Kilpatrick; moved same evening to intercept Ewell's wagon train which was reported to be near Monterey Springs. The brigade moved rapidly up the mountain road striking Ewell's wagon train about 3 a. m., July 5th, in the midst of a furious thunder storm, whilst on its retreat from Gettysburg.

"Then arose so wild a yell
Along that dark and narrow dell,
As if the fiends from heaven had fell,"

Combined with the Plutonic darkness made it one of the nights long to be remembered. When we came up with the wagon train, Union and Rebel cavalry, wagons, ambulances, drivers and mules became a confused mass of pursued and pursuing demons whose shouts and carbine shots, mingled with the lightning's red glare and the thunder crash, made it appear as if we were in the infernal regions. Especially so as the cries of the wounded often rose high above the din of the conflicting forces.

Frequently a driver would be shot or leave his mule team, when the unrestrained animals would rush wildly down the narrow road, and in many instances the wagons with the mules attached would be found at daylight at the bottom of some deep ravine crushed to pieces and the mules dead or dying. It was a fearful ride suiting well the fearless intrepidity of our daring commander. First a rebel brigade, then a long train of wagons and ambulances, then our brigade in the centre, with Ewell's corps in our rear, going down that narrow mountain road upon the principle of the devil take the hindmost, and you have Kilpatrick's dash across Monterey Pass.

The result of this brilliant movement was the capture of a large number of wagons, ambulances and mules with fifteen hundred prisoners. The brigade reached the foot of the mountain about daylight, leaving the Baltimore pike where it turns towards Waynesboro', the column moved on to Smithsburg, Md., where the wagons and ambulances were burnt. The command rested at this place during the day. As the shades of evening drew nigh we were treated to a compliment of shot and shell by Stuart, who appeared at Raven Rock Gap, above the little vallage. Soon our battery got into position when Stuart was compelled to retire, when our brigade took up the line of march for Boonsboro, where it arrived about midnight without further interruption.

A great deal more might be said of this brigade and especially of the gallant Kilpatrick, who figured so conspicuously in Sherman's march from the mountains through the two Carolinas to the sea, but time and space forbid. General Hooker's prize, offered for a dead cavalryman, would soon have depleted his exchequer, for many brave troopers bit the dust during the Gettysburg campaign.

We thank God for Gettysburg, for it was there the very heart and flower of the Southern confederacy dashed itself to pieces against the Union lines on the "Rocky Heights of Gettysburg."

It was there our God-given liberties were perpetuated. The 3d and 4th days of July, 1863, witnessed the defeat of Lee and the capitulation of Vicksburg. They have aptly been suggested as days of destiny for America. A century before, on the 4th of July, the tocsin of American independence was sounded, and now again the 3d and 4th of July became critical and decided epochs in the history of the war for the Union.

CHAPTER X.

In addition to the accounts of the great wagon train of wounded Confederates from Gettysburg passing through our county to Virginia, given by various persons, the following interesting statement by Mr. Jacob C. Snyder, of New Franklin, is worthy of preservation. It should come in on page 88. Mr. Snyder says:

About 10 or 11 o'clock on the night of Saturday, July 4th, 1863, we heard a great noise of horses feet chattering and tramping along on the road. It was at first supposed that another detachment was passing along to Gettysburg. After a little the rumbling of wagons was heard. I at once arose, struck a light, opened the door and went out, and in less than fifteen minutes the large hall in my house and the yard in front were filled with wounded Confederate soldiers. They at once set up the clamor to my wife and other members of my family, "Water! Water!! Give us Water!!!" They also begged to have their wounds dressed. O, what a sight! I at once came to the conclusion that something unusual had taken place, and as the rain was falling in torrents, I put on my overcoat and walked out to the barn-yard at the roadside with a staff in my hand. I there found that some cavalrymen were driving some of my young cattle out of my barn-yard. I walked up to the gate and closed it to prevent any more from being driven out. The officer in charge, sitting on his horse, and seeing the staff I carried, supposed it to be a gun and at once rode away. At about 1 o'clock, A. M., a man with a short leg rode up to the yard gate in company with five or six others. He very politely asked Mrs. Snyder for a drink of water. He seemed to be strapped to his horse. When riding away one of the men said he was General Ewell. I afterwards learned that his amputated limb had gotten sore. (It seems to me that this could not have been General Ewell. Unless positively unable he would certainly have remained at the head of his corps. —J. HOKE.) The long-wished for daylight at length dawned, and revealed to the farmers along the road that their fences were torn down and ambulances and wagons, together with hundreds of cavalry, were making their way through their fields and their wheat, corn and grass were being ruined. The narrow road in many places was so badly cut up that the wagons could scarcely get along, and many had to take the fields. Broken down wagons and caissons, yet containing large amounts of ammunition, were strewn all along the route. Oh, what a sight! The groans of the wounded and shrieks of the dying beggar description. I said to several of the men—Major Throckmorton and others who had been at my house on their way to Gettysburg, "What does this mean? I think you have received a most terrible whipping." They replied that they were only going back to get more ammunition and would come back and clean out the Yankees. I then said: "It looks to me as if the Yankees have completely cleaned you out, and I think, and I presume you think so yourselves, that you had better stayed at home and remained under the Old Flag." At 2 o'clock, P. M., a battery of six brass pieces drew up in front of my barn and fed their horses. This battery was supported and accompanied by about 100 cavalry and some infantry. The cavalry dismounted in a ten acre field of prime wheat, all out in head. At the same time during the halt the men were slaughtering cattle at Mr. Jeremiah W. George's. At this place some of the men died and were buried, and others unable to go any further were left with Mr. George. The graves of some that died there can yet be seen along the road; others are farmed over. Among those that were buried was Major McDine, of South Carolina. He was buried close by the well in a beautiful grove, and his grave was marked by a head-board bearing his initials. On the 20th day of April, 1866, three persons came to Mr. George's in search of this grave. One of them was the Major's brother-in-law, who was accompanied by a friend of the deceased, and the two were under the guidance of a colored man who had been the Major's servant, and was with him when he died and was buried. In a conversation with these persons I learned that Mrs. M'Dine, the Major's wife, had partially lost her mind upon hearing of the death of her husband, and at her urgent solicitation and with the hope to relieve her, they had come in search of his body. They came from South Carolina to Hagerstown, thence to Gettysburg, and then under the guidance of the colored man, followed up the way of the disastrous retreat until they came to Mr. George's, where the guide at once recognized the place and took them to the grave. The remains were taken up, carried to near my spring and there prepared and enclosed in a box and taken along.

Among the wounded left at Mr. George's was Lieut. Col. Benjamin F. Carter, of General McLaw's Division, Longstreet's Corps. I visited Col. Carter frequently during his stay there. He was a man of more than ordinary ability. He had enjoyed the advantages of a fine education and had great conversational powers. He was a Texan and had served two years in the legislature of that State. He had two daughters living. The one was Mrs. M. C. McLove, residing in Burnettsville, Marlboro District, South Carolina. In the discussion of "the principles of the secession heresy" as he termed it, which he often did with his companions, and in my presence, I learned that he was of the Alexander H. Stephens stamp. He was taken to Chambersburg by Dr. A. H. Senseny in an ambulance, where he subsequently died.

From Col. Carter I obtained much information in relation to the battle of Gettysburg. He had received his wound in the first charge made by McLaw upon little Round Top, from the "Devil's Den." They had met a heavy repulse from that place, and when General Longstreet ordered General McLaw to charge the second time, the latter replied in these words, "General Longstreet, I regard a second charge a needless sacrifice of human life—to lead men against one of nature's impregnable barriers so well manned and so bravely defended—I disobey the order." These, said Colonel Carter, were the precise words used by General McLaw.

"On Monday morning, the 5th, about 3 o'clock, four men drove into my yard with a two-horse carriage. They asked to have their jaded horses fed and breakfast for four persons, for all which they proposed to pay. I said that if they paid in greenbacks and not in Confederate scrip, they could be accommodated. They were evidently civilians and not soldiers, and the higher grade of Southern aristocracy. They were cursing and swearing about the Yankees getting one of their blooded horses for which they said they were offered $1,500. Their great trouble seemed to be, "if the Yankees only knew what kind of a horse they had." They paid my son a five dollar government note. I told them that they had better get away or the Yanks would get them and their old rips of horses. It was about daylight when they left. It was evident that they expected the Blue Coats to be after them. Just as they were about to leave some colored persons, who came along, began to sing,

I'se gwine back to Dixe,
No more I'se gwine to wander,
My heart's turned back to Dixie,
I can't stay here no longer;
I miss de old plantation,
My home and my relation,
My hearts turned back to Dixie,
And I must go.

Chorus :—I'se gwine back to Dixie,
For I hear the children calling,
I see the sad tears falling,
My heart's turned back to Dixie
And I must go.

Never shall I forget that scene, and never did I see a more forlorn and disgusted party than those five men when, in their old rickety two-horse carriage, drawn by two old rips, they drove away amidst the singing of those colored persons.

In a few hours the Boys in Blue, under General Gregg, were on hands and took hundreds of prisoners.

When writing the account given in a previous chapter of the dash made upon the great wagon train from Gettysburg by the gallant Captain Jones between Greencastle and Williamsport, I was ignorant of the way by which Captain Jones was ordered to cross from McConnellsburg to Mercersburg at that eventful time. Mr. W. Scott Fletcher, who was a resident of McConnellsburg during the war, and well informed of all the events which occurred there, relates the following: That part of General Milroy's force, which had escaped into Pennsylvania after his defeat and route at Winchester, and had congregated at Everett or Bloody Run, composed of the 14th Pennsylvania Cavalry, several companies of the First New York Cavalry, some infantry and other parts of regiments and companies, had advanced to McConnellsburg and occupied that place on Saturday, July 4th. The whole of these forces was under command of Colonel Pierce of the 14th Pennsylvania. Mr. James O. Carson, of Mercersburg, on the evening of that day, being ignorant of the approach of that great wagon train, but seeking protection from the numerous straggling rebels who were prowling about the country, sent a letter to Mr. W. S. Fletcher at McConnellsburg, asking him in case there were any Federal soldiers there to have some sent across the mountain to Mercersburg. Mr. Fletcher received this letter late on Saturday evening, and at once showed it to Col. Pierce and asked him to send Captain Jones with about two hundred men. Mr. Fletcher selected Captain Jones because of his well known bearing and efficiency. To this request Col. Pierce agreed and sent Captain Jones with his own company and about one hundred men from the 14th Pennsylvania. These left McConnellsburg early on Sunday morning, and upon reaching Mercersburg, or probably before reaching that place, they learned of the great wagon train and at once proceeded to intercept it.

The following account of the dash upon and capture of a part of this train was given by Lieut. David Irwin to Rev. J. Spangler Keiffer, who was an intimate friend and school-mate of his. Lieut. Irwin was from Union county, Pennsylvania, and a graduate of Amherest College. He is now a captain in the regular army, of the United States. Mr. Keiffer, at the time of the war, was teaching in the Academy at Mercersburg, and obtained his information from Lieut. Irwin at the time of the occurrence. It has been transmitted to me by Mr. Keiffer through Rev. Mr. Cort.

Lieutenant Irwin's statement is as follows: A cavalry force of about two hundred men, under command of Captain Jones, of the First New York cavalry, hearing on Sunday, July 5th, of the great wagon train on its way from Gettysburg to Virginia, advanced upon it by way of Mercersburg and intercepted it at Cearfoss's Cross Roads, nearly midway between Greencastle, Pa., and Williamsport, Md. After a sharp skirmish with the guards, who were scattered somewhat thinly along the line, the wagons were turned into the road leading to Mercersburg. The train was cut out from Hayde's down to the farm formerly owned by David Zellers. The wagons cut off south of the Cross Roads were turned around in the barn-yard of Mr. Zellers, and hastily driven back to follow the other part of the captured train to Mercersburg. Hugh Logan was along with the Confederate escort and made a very narrow escape from capture by leaving his horse and hiding until the Union cavalry had left. Mr. Henry Zellers saw him and says he was in great dread of capture. Great gallantry was displayed by Captain Jones and his brave troopers in this affair, as well as in all other affairs he had with the rebels. One of his troopers rode gallantly as far as the Broad Fording Road, but finding himself unsupported he was obliged to make his escape by turning off at that point.

In this gallant affair about one hundred wagons—as many as this small body of cavalry could handle—with about 600 or 700 hundred wounded Confederates who were in the wagons, were captured. The head of this captured train began to pass through Mercersburg about dusk, and continued passing until late in the night. It was hurried on through the town towards the Gap for fear of an effort to recapture it. At or near the Gap the head of the train met a large detachment from the 14th Pennsylvania cavalry under Col. Pierce. Upon believing themselves strong enough to protect themselves from capture, they returned to Mercersburg, where the wounded were taken from the wagons and placed in the Seminary and other buildings. In addition to over one hundred wagons, and 600 or 700 prisoners captured, there was also one cannon. Mr. Keiffer overheard a sharp discussion and dispute between Col. Pierce and Captain Jones in relation to the results of this affair. It appeared that Captain Jones was not satisfied with the result, and wanted to make another dash upon the train, but was overruled and prevented by Col. Pierce. Had Capt. Jones been in command, and been permitted to have his own way, with the increased force then at his disposal, greater captures would have resulted. It is necessary only to say that Col. Pierce was subsequently discharged from the service for his entire incompetency.

Lieutenant Irwin related to Mr. Keifler the particulars of a personal encounter he had with a rebel officer when the dash was made upon that train at the Cross Roads. The officer was mounted on a fine charger and dashed upon Lieutenant Irwin in such a way by a semi-circling charge, that the Lieutenant was unable to use his sabre. As this semi-circling charge was made, the officer fired his pistol rapidly, and one ball struck the rim of Lieutenant Irwin's hat. Turning partly around in his saddle and resting his pistol on his left arm or shoulder, he fired backwards at his assailant, when he fell from his horse, which afterwards became the property of the Lieutenant. Irwin immediately dismounted and offered assistance to his prostrate foe, but he was in no mood to accept of it. Judging that he was mortally wounded, Lieutenant Irwin left him. Dr. Victor Miller says that he was called upon to dress the wound of a Captain Zaine, who was fatally wounded in the same engagement along the pike not far from Hayde's, several miles from Greencastle. General Jenkins also came along sometime after, and dismounted to take a look at the wounded officer. He ordered that he be taken to Williamsport, where he afterwards died. From all that can be learned this Captain Zaine was the officer with whom Lieutenant Irwin had the contest. General Jenkins had Dr. Miller to examine and dress a wound he received at Gettysburg on the top of his head, caused by a piece of a shell.

A very romantic occurrence took place in connection with the wounding of this Confederate officer. At a later period of the war Lieutenant Irwin was stationed at Williamsport as Provost Marshall, and as gallant young men were in the habit of doing, he made the acquaintance of some of the young ladies of that place. Among others he frequently visited a family to which several interesting ladies belonged. They were strongly Southern in their sympathies, and had much to say of a dear friend of theirs—a certain officer of a Virginia regiment, who had been killed in the war. One day these ladies showed the Lieutenant a picture of the deceased friend, which he saw at once was a striking likeness of the officer whom he had met in bloody combat in the raid upon the wagon train. He said nothing, however, but proceeded to read a funeral discourse which they handed him and which had been preached and published on the life and character of the lamented officer. Reading the circumstances of his death as detailed in this sermon, he saw that he was indeed the identical officer he had fatally wounded. Of course he did not shock the sensibilities of his fair friends by telling them what part he had played in the death of their friend.

CHAPTER XII.

In further illustration of General McCausland's brutality and profanity, as referred to in his conduct at Hagerstown on page 103, I take the following from an article contributed to the Philadelphia *Record* of August 4th, 1877, by a correspondent signing his name as "*Franklin*." It is only necessary to say that this person resided in Hagerstown and knew whereof he spoke. That correspondent says of McCausland :

Entering the town, he demanded a sum of money which astounded the rebel sympathizers in the place. Hamilton, Alvey, Menley, Syester and other leading "secesh" were constituted a committee to wait upon the General for the purpose of getting him to withdraw his demand upon the town. They did so, and in response to their expressions of sympathy for the cause in which he had unsheathed his sword, he swore that he wanted money, and cared nothing for their sympathy ; that if his demand was not complied with in the time specified he would "burn the —— —— town to ——." The committee retired for consultation, and were in dismay. In their extremity they summoned Captain Isaac Nesbit, a prominent Union man, and implored him to wait upon their guest and endeavor to bring him to such terms as could be complied with. Nesbit demurred from attempting negotiations after the failure of the committee, but was finally prevailed upon to call upon McCausland, who had quartered himself in the Court House. When Nesbit approached the General, he was in the act of changing his shirt in view of the people in the square. Repugnant in his appearance, surly in his manner, someone remarked that he looked like "a lion with a hat on." Nesbit walked up to McCausland after he had somewhat adjusted the shirt (a red one it was) with which he had just adorned himself, and remarked to the General that he was "steep in his demands upon the town." Taking his watch from his pocket and looking at it McCausland replied that "if his demand—steep as it might appear—was not honored he would burn the —— town to —— in one hour from that time." Nesbit kept perfectly cool and self-poised and, seemingly, did not notice the words of McCausland. He answered that the merchants had removed their goods, the banks their deposits, on the approach of the Confederates, and it was an utter impossibility, however much the people might feel disposed to comply with his demands. McCausland then looking at his watch repeated his threat. Nesbit, looking McCausland full in the face, replied with considerable vehemence, that he (McCausland) had the power, as he well knew, to burn the town and he might just as well begin the work at once, as there was not the remotest possibility of his preposterous demands being met by the handful of citizens remaining in Hagerstown. McCausland changed his manner to Nesbit immediately and told him that he "talked like a man," and wanted to know what could be done. Nesbit, in return, remarked that the General was becoming rational. He (Nesbit) could not promise what booty would be raised, but all that was possible.

On page 106 I give as evidence that the sentiment of many of the Southern people demanded the laying waste of our border, the remark made to me by a gentleman familiar with the people of that section, that after the return of the Confederate army to Virginia, after the battle of Gettysburg, the press of nearly the entire South found fault with General Lee for not laying this whole country in ruins; and, said my friend, "if ever the Confederates get back here again, they will burn and plunder." That this sentiment prevailed among General Lee's army during the invasion of 1863, and his men were only held from executing it by his orders forbidding it, is apparent in a statement hereafter to appear by one of the Confederates, who was with Lee's army during the invasion, and also at the burning of the town, one year afterwards. This fact is further proven in the following extract from an editorial which appeared in the Richmond *Express* (Jefferson Davis' official organ) conveying to its readers the intelligence of the destruction of Chambersburg by McCausland:

"We love to hear those cries of anguish. This howl of desolation and despair from the quarter in which it is heard comes upon our ear like 'music on the water.' It is sweet beyond all earthly gratification. Glad are we that retribution has at last put forth its terrible arm and assumed its most terrible shape. We hope it will be pushed to the furthest extremity to which it is capable of going. We should be glad to hear that the whole valley of the Susquehanna was one long, unbroken, irresistable flame, not to subside as long as a house, or a tree, or a blade of grass, or a stalk of corn, remained to testify that it had ever been inhabited by man. No sight could be more agreeable to our eyes than to behold every part of Yankeedom within reach of our armies, converted into a mass of ashes—to see every beast that walked on four feet, and could not be driven off for our own use, slaughtered and left to rot on the ground."

A touching incident which occurred on the day of the burning of Chambersburg, is related by John Jeffries, Esq., as follows: Mr. Jeffries says he was returning from Harrison Avenue, whither he had carried some articles for a friend to save them from the flames, when he was accosted somewhere near the Market House by a Confederate officer, or soldier, in the following language: "I am told that there is an old gentleman somewhere in this street (Queen) who is sick in his house and will be burned up unless he is taken out. Can you take me to him?" Concluding that the person referred to was Dr. S. D. Culbertson, Mr. Jeffries led the soldier to Mr. Culbertson's house, and passing through it and not finding him in, they ran into the adjoining house of Mr. E. D. Reid, Mr. Culbertson's son-in-law, thinking he possibly might be there, and in passing through a door in the back part of the house the soldier struck his head against the upper part of the door frame, and owing to the great speed at which he was running he was knocked down. Mr. Jeffries sprang to his assistance when he said, "Never mind me; for God's sake find the old gentleman that we may save him." Passing out into the street they met Mrs. Lindsay, daughter of Mr. Bernard Wolff, who was lamenting concerning her father and saying that he was in his house on the southeast corner of Main and Queen streets, and refused to leave it. Rushing through Mrs. Lindsay's yard to the rear of Mr. Wolff's residence, they found that venerable man standing by a somewhat antiquated bureau, and declaring that he would not leave the place while that bureau remained as it was his mother's. Assisted by the soldier Mr. Jeffries bore the bureau out of the house and placed it in the adjoining lot as far away from the house as they could where they left it, when Mr. Wolff followed them to a place of safety. The object of his solicitude, however, was burned there.

A couple of hours after the subsidence of the fire, the writer met the venerable Judge Chambers at Main and King streets. He had been up taking a look at the ruins of his residence, and was on his way out North Main street where he had gone when the town was fired. While conversing with him a person passing by informed him that the rebels had been making inquiries for him, and that it was rumored that they were coming back to complete the destruction of the town. Hearing this the Judge said that he thought it prudent for him to proceed at once to his place of lodging and he passed on out North Main street. The rumored return of the rebels proved to be Averill's men, who shortly thereafter entered and passed through the town.

In an article contributed to the *Franklin Repository* of July 30th, 1884, by Mr.

W. A. Reid, exception is taken to the statement of Thomas R. Bard, Esq., upon page 134, as to General Averill's whereabouts and condition during the night previous to the burning of Chambersburg, when General Couch was attempting to communicate with him by telegraph from this place and failed to elicit any reply. Mr. Reid's statement is substantially as follows:

Late in the afternoon of Friday, July 29th, 1864, General Averill with his command of cavalry came into Greencastle from Williamsport, Md., to escape a force under General Vaughan, which crossed the Potomac at the latter place. Some time was spent by the commanding officer in looking at the topography of the country, examining Long's Hill (and perhaps another point, John Wilhelm's field, near the C. V. warehouse) doubtless with the view of selecting a place for battle in case he was followed by the enemy, then at or near Hagerstown. During the forenoon many stragglers had hurried on, but it was after the middle of the afternoon that the cavalry, jaded with their recent hurried marches in West Virginia, filed by, passing through Carlisle street. That evening General Averill made his headquarters at the residence of Archibald Fleming, Sr., about one mile north on the Chambersburg road. It will be remembered that, on that evening a body of new troops enlisted for a short term, six months we believe, had been sent here by General Couch. They rested on the Square and along Carlisle street, while Averill's cavalry bivouacked on Fleming's farm. The telegraphic news throughout the afternoon and evening was most unwelcome intelligence. Mr. H. R. Fetterhoff was local operator at that time, and D. C. Aughinbaugh operator from Hagerstown who in those perilous days was frequently here and along the line, was also in the office at least during part of the evening. With the wires working badly and the news, as read in the faces of the operators and their friends, always getting worse, our people were left to wonder "what next?" Orderlies carried messages to the commander at Fleming's. At about half-past eleven that night intelligence was brought in showing that McCausland, who had crossed at McCoy's Ferry, was on the Warm Spring road. Whether later news was received by telegraph from Chambersburg, I am not prepared to say, as, of course, the despatches were for the commanding officer they were not shown to citizens. Now as to Mr. Bard's statement in his letter published by Mr. Hoke in the last number of *Public Opinion*, that the orderlies bearing messages could not find General Averill, and his own search for him, I cannot understand. General Averill, as already said, had his headquarters at Mr. Fleming's house. Mr. William Fleming informs me that General Averill and some of his officers took supper at his father's house, that he lay down at a late hour to rest in the yard (which is immediately on the public road). The General inquired of him the distances from McCoy's Ferry to Mercersburg, to Chambersburg and other points. Before 3 o'clock in the morning the troops were up. General Averill with Captain Crawford of his staff, and Messrs. William and Jacob Fleming examined a map of Franklin county which hung in the hall of their father's house. Wishing to move on a line east of the Chambersburg road, Mr. Jacob Fleming complied with the request made of him to pilot them out to the Brown's Mill road and there leaving them (on account of the serious illness of his father), he directed them as to the route chosen to come out near Fayetteville, on the Baltimore turnpike road. Mr. William Fleming thinks that General Averill was under the impression, after learning the distances which the rebels had to march, that they could not reach Chambersburg so early as they did; and next, as to going eastward, he expected, at least he expressed the thought, that the rebel force from Hagerstown would closely follow him, and pursued by a force in the rear, with McCausland on the left flank in front, he took the route northeast to have a clear field on the Gettysburg turnpike road; as Stuart had made this circuit in 1862, it is probable that General Averill would recall that event, and perhaps this too had some influence to shape his course. This, however, is only conjecture.

I have certainly no desire to do injustice to General Averall, for he was considered an excellent officer, but the truth of history requires that the facts in regard to his failure to march to the relief of Chambersburg, or at least to take some notice of the frequent and urgent appeals of a superior officer in such an emergency, should be known. Now can the statement of Mr. Reid be harmonized with Mr. Bard's? Let us see. Mr. Reid says that General Averill after supper at Mr. Fleming's "lay down at a late hour to rest in the yard, which is immediately upon the public road." Mr. Bard says that he found the General "asleep by the side of a fence." Mr. Reid further says that "before 3 o'clock in the morning the troops were up" and that "General Averill with Captain Crawford of his staff and Messrs. William and Jacob Fleming examined a map of Franklin county which hung in the hall of their father's house." Mr. Bard says that the last of General Couch's despatches was received about 3 o'clock, and upon the reception of which he at once proceeded to General Averill's camp and after a short time spent in search found the General. Is it not fair to suppose that, informed of the contents of the three despatches from General Couch, and the approach of the foe, the staff, if not the General himself, would bestir themselves; and that the cause of their early rise was the visit of Mr. Bard, and the consulting of a map with a view to escape being caught between General Vaughan's forces from Hagerstown and that of McCausland at Chambersburg, was the result of the information just then received of the approach of the foe in this direction? If they knew of the new danger which threatened them from this direction before, why defer consulting the map until that late hour? Mr. Reid says: "Orderlies carried messages to the commander at Fleming's." Whether they were delivered to General Averill or not, is not stated. Mr. Bard says they were not, and he ought to know, for he had personal knowledge of what he affirms. The statement of Mr. Bard was made immediately after the destruction of our town, and up to the publication of Mr. Reid's account, so far as I know, was never denied. Would it not be more creditable for General Averill to say that he did not receive General Couch's urgent despatches than that he did receive them, and took no notice whatever of them? His obligations to the General commanding the District, to say nothing of the peril threatening a loyal people, whom it was his duty, if not his pleasure to protect, would have compelled him to at least acknowledge the receipt of the despatches sent him, and inform him that he could not do anything for him.

It may not be generally known that the town of Ringgold, in the State of Georgia, was burned partly in retaliation for the destruction of Chambersburg. During General Sherman's campaign through that State, Ringgold was captured with a considerable amount of Confederate stores. Soon after the burning of Chambersburg General Geary who was in command in that place, was ordered by General Sherman to burn whatever of the supplies they could not bring away and then evacuate the place. Whether Sherman's order contemplated the destruction of the whole town, I cannot say, but General Geary gave it that interpretation and the whole place was laid in ruins. General Geary's command was composed in part of Pennsylvanians, and to the cry of "retaliation for Chambersburg" they applied the torch.

As everything relating to the battle of Gettysburg will prove of increasing interest in all the years to come in the Nation's history, I place upon record the following account of a visit to the field of battle a few days after its close, by Rev. C. Cort, now pastor of the Reformed congregation at Greencastle. Mr. Cort's account is as follows:

MR. JACOB HOKE, *Dear Sir:*—I have been greatly interested in your reminiscences of the war, and as Gettysburg was the great and decisive battle in the great contest between freedom and slavery, everything relating to it will be a matter of increasing interest to all students of history and of military tactics. And as I had a few experiences in connection with that battle, which will help to illustrate some features of the conflict, I herewith submit them for your use. These recollections are written from notes taken in my diary at the time.
Yours, &c., C. CORT.

GETTYSBURG AS HEARD AFAR OFF AND AS SEEN NEAR AT HAND.

On Friday afternoon, July 3d, 1863, I was returning to Somerset, Pennsylvania, from a trip to Mt. Pleasant, in Westmoreland county, same State, Rev. George H. Johnston, then pastor of the Reformed church in Somerset, but now pastor of a congregation in West Philadelphia, was my traveling companion. We stopped for a late dinner at the hotel of a Mr. Hay at the eastern base of Chestnut Ridge in Ligonier Valley, Westmoreland county, and while we were at dinner the landlord entered the room and remarked that a terrible battle must be going on somewhere. We replied that the latest telegraphic despatches received at Mt. Pleasant before our departure indicated that the invading army under General Lee had met the Union forces at Gettysburg, and a great battle would, no doubt, be fought there. Mr. Hay replied, "It must be going on now; we can hear the cannonading." Expressing our astonishment at his statement, he led us out to the end of his porch, where we distinctly heard what we regarded as heavy and continuous discharges of artillery in an eastern direction. This was about 2 o'clock, and the precise time when the great artillery duel took place preparatory to Pickett's great charge upon the Federal line. Upon going out to the turnpike the sound was still more distinct. We listened at the portentous sounds for some time with great interest and anxiety, for we knew that to a great extent the destiny of our government depended upon the battle then in progress. The following entry in my diary indicates the thought which was uppermost in our minds at the time: "May the Lord of hosts give victory to the army of the Union, and may the hordes of rebeldom be discomfitted in the valleys of our noble old Keystone Commonwealth."

Mr. Hay told us that the cannonading had been going on more or less for several days. We afterwards learned that hundreds of people had heard the same all along the south-eastern border of Westmoreland county, and that during the battle of Manassas the sound of the cannonading was also distinctly heard throughout the same localities. The distance from the place we heard this cannonading to Gettysburg, in a straight line, was not less than one hundred and forty miles, and the configuration of the intervening country—the numerous transverse ridges of the Allegheny mountains—would seem to be unfavorable for the transmission of sound to so great a distance. And yet, while the fact is established beyond dispute that the sound of the great conflict at Gettysburg was distinctly heard in some of the western counties of the State, it was not heard in many intervening localities not one-third that distance from the scene of the conflict. Even in Chambersburg and Greencastle, but about twenty-five miles distant, but few heard the cannonading and the few who did hear it say it was very indistinct. Here is a question for scientists to solve. Some military men to whom

I had stated the fact a few days later at Gettysbug, hooted at the idea of what I said, and supposed, I have no doubt, that I was telling an untruth, or was mistaken. *And yet the fact is true beyond question*, and upon the strength of what I heard, I at once prepared to start for the scene of strife which shall next claim our attention.

Hearing the sound of battle from afar, filled me with a desire to proceed at once to the scene of action, to do whatever I could to relieve the sufferings of the wounded, but my pulpit duties on the following Sabbath prevented my going until after these duties were discharged. Accordingly on Monday I hastened east by coach to Johntown and the Pennsylvania railroad to Harrisburg, at which place I took passage on the train for Carlisle by the Cumberland Valley railroad. On Tuesday morning I procured a pass to go through the picket line, but before I reached it, upon the suburbs of Carlisle, the permit was countermanded on the ground that it was considered unsafe for citizens to venture across the country while so many stragglers from the Confederate army were prowling about. I however determined, notwithstanding this danger, to run the risk, and succeeded in getting through the lines in the following manner : A number of gentlemen connected with the Christian Commission had engaged a carriage to take them from Carlisle to Gettysburg for which they were to pay fifty dollars, and through the kindness of Mr. John Wiest, of Philadelphia, who was one of the number, I was permitted to take a seat with them until we passed through the lines, we all passing upon the strength of the special pass given them. After getting safely through the lines, and thanking the party for the favor done me, I set out on foot, and proceeded on my way, doing some fast walking that excessively hot afternoon and evening. Owing to the heat those having horses had frequently to stop under shade trees to rest them, but I passed on and overtook and out-travelled a number of high-priced teams such as the one hired by the gentlemen of the Christian Commission. I went by way of Papertown and Whitestown, and part of the road led through a gloomy forest, where, I was told, I would be apt to meet straggling rebels, but I saw none. I met many of the country people returning from the battle-field carrying guns and other things which they had picked up and smuggled through the lines. At length at 8 o'clock in the evening I reached Conewago creek, where I had considerable trouble to find the foot-log in the gathering darkness, but at length succeeded in getting over. Meeting a man with a gun on his shoulder and a cross dog by his side, I asked him for lodging for the night, when he put me off with the remark that they had smallpox at his house and it would not be safe for me to stay there, but at Floi's mill, near by, he thought I could get lodging for the night. In a little while I called at the house of Mr. Floi and asked to be permitted to remain over night which was after some little time granted. I had walked twenty miles in five hours, and felt that I needed rest. Beside this a heavy thunder storm was near at hand and it was very dark. With a thankful heart I sat down to a table on which were placed some books, and taking up one—a hymn book of the Reformed church—found that I was among my own people. They now, upon being apprised of who I was, felt free to converse with me about the stirring events of the past week, which they would have been loth to do to an entire stranger, and as they had seen much of the effects of the battle upon the enemy's side, they gave me much interesting information.

I had gotten ahead of my friends of the Christian Commission and their high-priced conveyance, who were obliged to seek shelter in a farm house before reaching the Conewago. Before morning I had additional reasons for feeling grateful over the results of my forced march, for a terrible thunder storm broke upon us and seemed to vent its fury upon that battle-scarred region. The rain descended in torrents, and soon the Conewago was an impassable stream. It was said that it was never known to be so high as on that occasion. A number of carriages approached the flooded bottoms on the opposite side, but were forced to lie over an entire day, or make a detour of many miles to reach a bridge. My host took me some six miles to Gettysburg in his carriage after the rain had somewhat subsided. This was on the morning of Wednesday, July 8th, 1863. Soon after starting we saw a couple of Confederate soldiers coming out of the flooded bottoms, and I proposed that we should stop at a house near by and get a gun and march them along back with us to Gettysburg as prisoners, but my host deemed it too risky. We then drove up to a squad of neighbors not far off and informed them of our discovery, and advised the capture of the rebels, which they set out to accomplish. My friend then took in some supplies for the wounded, and in due time we reached Gettysburg, where I at once reported to the Christian Commission who directed me where to work. Ascertaining where help was most needed, I proceeded to give such assistance and relief as I was able during the remainder of the week. The supplies my friend brought with him were eagerly received by the poor, suffering men. Our butter and chickens were taken in a hurry. One poor fellow came out of a tent on one leg without either a crutch or cane, and bore back in triumph a dressed fowl.

The scenes of suffering among the many thousands of wounded of both the Union and Confederate armies which came under my observation in the few days I spent in and about Gettysburg on that memorable occasion, are altogether indescribable. Human language is inadequate to do it justice. The horrors of war were revealed in a way that was sickening to the heart. The ghastly wounds, the moans and cries and screams of anguish, the ravings of those whose reason had been dethroned, and the appeals for water to allay thirst and morphine to ease pain, were such as to move the stoutest hearts. One of the streams had overflowed its banks, and a number of wounded confederates were drowned and their bodies swept away by the raging waters. Great piles of amputated limbs lay around. Experienced surgeons and medical students fresh from the schools were at work like so many bloody butchers. The putrid and swollen remains of slaughtered men and horses filled the air with malaria, which soon brought disease and death to visitors from all parts of the country, as well as to the inmates of the crowded hospitals. Suffering and death were everywhere, and the efforts put forth for alleviating the latter, though rendered by hundreds of willing hands, seemed as but drops to a bucketfull when compared to the vast aggregate all about us.

The fratricidal nature of the strife was frequently brought vividly to our minds as we ministered to the suffering men of both armies. In the Lutheran Seminary building I met Lieutenant Harry Hoffman, of the Union army, who had been severely wounded by the explosion of a shell in the first day's battle. He was much rejoiced to see an old college friend, and I was no less glad and surprised to meet him. Out on the Hunterstown road some distance I met another college friend, Major Kyd Douglas, formerly an aid to Stonewall Jackson, but afterwards Adjutant of General Johnson's division of Ewell's corps of the Confederate army. He had been severely wounded in the left shoulder while leading a brigade into action near Culp's Hill. He had passed unscathed through forty-three battles and skirmishes previous to the great conflict at Gettysburg. In one of the twelfth army corps hospitals I found a young Mr. Hockman of the Stonewall Brigade, and having visited his relations near Woodstock, in the Valley of Virginia, in company with another of my classmates, Rev. M. H. Hockman, when General Shields first went up the Shenandoah Valley in the spring of 1862, I felt a deep interest in the wounded youth. With the assistance of another collegemate, (now Rev. E. H. Dieffenbacher), I relieved his bodily wants and ministered such spiritual advice as was necessary. He was shot twice through the lungs and also through one arm. He calmly spoke of his wounds as being necessarily fatal. I sent a telegram to his brother, then pastor of a Reformed congregation in Lancaster, Ohio. I learned some time afterwards that at that very time his Ohio brother was absent from home sick from exposure endured in helping to head off and capture General John Morgan during his famous raid into Ohio. A few days later this young man died, and his grave was marked by Dieffenbacher, who had known him in his southern home. Lieutenant Mace, another college friend, was severely wounded and his body was burned up in a barn. Thousands of slightly wounded soldiers were transported to hospitals in the cities and other places as soon as they could be moved, or transportation could be had for them, while large numbers of persons from all parts of the North came on to see after and care for those in and about Gettysburg.

I found by conversing with the southern soldiers in the hospitals, that the men from Georgia and North Carolina generally expressed great abhorrence of the war into which they had been forced against their will. "War is a very mean way to settle disputes," was the remark of one of these men.

On Saturday afternoon, July 11th, I concluded to cross the mountain to the vicinity of Hagerstown where, it was expected, another battle would be fought between the Federal army under General Meade and the Confederates under Lee. Accordingly in company with Rev. Jas. A. Schultz, I set out about half-past two o'clock by Fairfield and Monterey Pass. A. M. Hoover and his wife were going on a visit to his father-in-law, Johnstons, on the old Harbaugh farm, near where Pen Mar station on the Western Maryland railroad in now located. We had the privilege of riding in their spring wagon a good part of the way. For half a dozen miles west and south of Gettysburg, hospitals were continually in view, and everywhere from farm houses, barns, tents, &c., the red flag streamed out. After passing Monterey we saw frequent remains of the wagon train which had been raided and destroyed by General Kilpatrick the week before. It was dark when we arrived at Mr. Johnstons, and upon arriving there we found the family in distress on account of the abduction of Mr. Johnston by the rebels. He and some of his neighbors were watching a passing train of wagons, when some mountaineers imprudently came down carrying their guns with them. The whole party was arrested as bushwhackers, although no overt act had been committed, and a number of them were unarmed and inoffensive persons. They were marched off to Williamsport and experienced a trying time before they were permitted to return to their homes. In fact Mr. Johnston never fully recovered from the shock and exposure to which he was subjected. In the evening of this day I went with Rev. Mr. Schultz to Waynesboro', where we stayed over night, and called at the Reformed parsonage, where we learned that Rev. Mr. Krebs had kept his horse concealed three weeks in the wash-house and the rebels failed to find him. Almost every person had stories to tell of how they had succeeded in concealing horses and other valuables from the rebels. On Monday, July 13th, we footed it to Greencastle and thence to Mercersburg. At this place we found the Theological Seminary and other buildings filled with wounded rebels who had been captured by Captain Jones and his brave command of the First New York Cavalry from the large wagon train of wounded in charge of General Imboden. There were about six hundred of these prisoners; among them were about a dozen officers, including Col. Leaventhorpe, of the Eleventh North Carolina regiment; Captains Chambers, Williams, Archer, Belts, &c. Col. Leaventhorpe, was a very intelligent and candid man. He had been eight years with the British army before becoming a resident of North Carolina. He said the southern leaders had no faith in Republican institutions, and as soon as their independence was secured they would modify the form of the Confederate government, and introduce more of the monarchial and aristocratic elements into it. Many of the private soldiers among the North Carolina and Georgia prisoners denounced the war as the wicked work of ambitious politicians. They said they had been conscripted into the confederate service against their will, and hoped that the war would soon end. Such expressions were very common among this class of prisoners both at Gettysburg and Mercersburg.

Mercersburg, because of its proximity to the border, had been frequently visited by rebel soldiers during the war. Stuart's raiders on their way to Chambersburg in Oct., 1862, a detachment of Jenkin's command under Colonel

Ferguson, on its way to McConnellsburg, in June, 1863, the brigade of General Stuart on its way to the same place a week afterward, the cavalry command of Imboden a few days later, and finally McNeill's gang some time about the battle of Gettysburg, successively visited this place. Some of these commands were under good discipline and conducted themselves tolerably well, but the last to visit this place—"McNeill's Border Ruffian Slave Hunters"—were the most ill-behaved of any. This gang made it their especial business to hunt up poor colored persons and drag them South into slavery, and not content with carrying off colored refugees who had escaped from the South during the war, they carried away a number of free colored persons, among whom were Samuel Brooks, Little Cotton and other noted characters.

Rev. Mr. Keiffer relates the following occurrence, which he copies from his diary written at the time, July 3d, 1863. "Two Union scouts came in from Hagerstown, who reported that General Hooker was sick and McClellan had taken command of the Union army on Tuesday morning, June 30th. Shortly after the arrival of these scouts three rebels dashed into Mercersburg in pursuit of Mr. Wolf. The two soldiers fired on them, killing private Alban and slightly wounding Lieut. William Cane, of the 12th Virginia cavalry, both of Captain Shaver's company. The Lieutenant's horse was killed and he was captured. The other rebel made his escape."

It was not until Wednesday, July 15th, that we learned definitely at Mercersburg that Lee had escaped with his army across the Potomac. In the meantime we were hourly expecting to hear the roar of a decisive battle along that river, and were in hopes that he would be either captured or so crippled as to virtually end the war. But this was not to be for long and weary months yet to come.

The phenomena related by Mr. Cort in the foregoing of hearing the sound of the cannonading at Gettysburg in Westmoreland county, not less than one hundred and forty miles from the scene of the conflict, may seem incredible, but the fact rests not upon his unsupported evidence alone, but is attested by the following additional testimony. Rev. Dr. C. R. Lane, at present a resident of this place, relates the following, as well as gives the reasons why the sound of the guns at Gettysburg was heard so far away, and so very indistinctly in this valley and other intermediate places:

CHAMBERSBURG, Aug. 19th, 1884.

JACOB HOKE, Esq., *Dear Sir*:—The facts referred to in our late conversation, as I understood the matter at the time, are the following: The sound of the artillery at the battle of Gettysburg, was heard on a mountain in the southwestern part of Wyoming county, a distance measured in a straight line of at least one hundred and twenty (120) miles. Supposing the alleged fact to be true, this was a very remarkable propagation of sound and requires,

1st. A very favorable state of atmosphere for the propagation of sound.
2nd. A favorable current of air, and
3d. Perhaps there was a cloud so situated as to reflect the sound to the particular locality where it was heard.

Thanking you for your efforts to collect and preserve information in regard to the war, I remain Yours truly,
C. R. LANE.

That the phenomena referred to was not confined to the battle of Gettysburg, but occurred at other great battles, will appear in the following from Rev. Bishop J. J. Glossbrenner, a resident of Churchville, near Staunton, in the Valley of Virginia:

CHURCHVILLE, VA., June 19th, 1884.

MR. J. HOKE, *Dear Sir*:—In your note you desire me to state in writing what I communicated to you verbally some time ago. That fact is as follows: During the great battles about Richmond, which is upwards of one hundred miles from here, we distinctly heard the report of the cannonading.
Respectfully yours,
J. J. GLOSSBRENNER.

Hon. F. M. Kimmell, at present a resident of this place, furnishes the following in relation to the sound of cannonading at the first Bull Run engagement.

CHAMBERSBURG, Sept. 12th, 1884.

Mr. J. HOKE, *Dear Sir*: On the 21st of July, 1861, I lived at Somerset, Somerset co., Pa., being Sunday, distant from Cumberland, Md., 37 miles by turnpike road. This latter place is 190 miles by rail from Baltimore, and as I now understand the geography of the country 190 would carry you from Cumberland to either Washington or Bull Run in Virginia. This would make a distance of some 230 miles by the roads from Somerset to the battle field, or as the bird flies, or as sounds carry—200 miles. Standing on a hill which overlooks the town, in company with others, we distinctly heard the "thuds" of the cannon of the battle, not once only nor for a short time, but often and at intervals extending over hours. We, having previously learned of the army having moved South, conjectured that a battle was being fought between the Federal and Confederate forces, and we were on the tip toe of expectation. When the news came we found our conjectures fully verified, as to time and direction. Somerset lies on the west of the main ridge of the Allegheny, 14 miles from the Summit. The waters of the eastern slopes of the mountain at that point are carried by Wills creek to the Potomac at Cumberland, and thence flow to Washington City, D. C. The clouds during the day were impending so far as we could see. We learned that this was the case along the river, and my theory was, whether right or wrong, that the clouds confined the sounds to the valley of the Potomac, and sent them to the mountains upwards, as through a funnel. Along the Alleghenies above Cumberland, the sounds were heard by multitudes. Our congregation near the Summit adjourned the sermon to listen.

On the days of the Gettysburg fights I lived at Chambersburg, 25 miles from the contest, in which there was immense cannonading and never heard it at all. I don't remember the condition of the clouds, and only remember the facts of the first fight, because the matter was the subject of discussion.

I heard or read somewhere that the sounds of Waterloo were heard 200 miles away.

F. M. KIMMELL.

Deeming the facts of this phenomena so well authenticated that they could not be questioned, and desiring to be informed of the reason of the same, I communicated them to the officers of the Smithsonian Institute at Washington, D. C., and received the following replies. The first is from that eminent scientist Spencer F. Baird, and is as follows:

WASHINGTON, D. C., Sept. 6, 1884.

Dear Sir: The irregularities of sound transmission referred to in your letter of August 30, have been repeatedly observed, and may be thus explained: With a gentle wind, the current of air is of course considerably retarded near the surface of the earth by friction with its irregular out lines; and as we rise higher the speed is ordinarily found to gradually increase for some hundreds of feet. The effect of this partial retardation of the aerial current on the spherical wave-fronts of sound, is to press forward their higher portions more than the lower portions—*in the direction in which the wind is moving*—and reversely to press back the upper portions of the wave-fronts more than their lower portions—*in the opposite direction*. It thus results that sound-rays moving *with* the wind, tend to curve downward toward the earth; and sound-rays moving *against* the wind, tend to rise upward, and at the distance of a mile or so, to leave the observer in an acoustic "shadow"—the sounds passing at some distance above his head. This has been verified by climbing to eminences, where a lost sound is completely recovered. Sound probably travels *as far* against the wind as with it, but it is refracted upward beyond the ears of the listener. (See the Smithsonian Report for 1875, page 210.)

This subject was well discussed by the late Prof. Henry—a copy of whose "Researches in Sound" is herewith mailed to your address. You will find special reference to the abnormal effects observed during cannonading in battles, at pages 492, 493. See also pages 512, 513.

Under certain circumstances, an intervening obstable—as a hill—tends to deflect sound-rays upward to some distance over the adjacent valley; so as to render them quite audible at a considerable distance, while wholly inaudible through the middle distance.

Yours very respectfully,
SPENCER F. BAIRD,
Mr. J. HOKE, *Secretary.*
Chambersburg, Pa.

The reference made in the foregeing to Professor Henry's *Researches in Sound* rne as follows:

"The science of acoustics in regard to the phenomena of sound as exhibited in limited spaces, has been developed with signal success. The laws of its production, propagation, reflection and refraction have been determined with much precision, so that we are enabled in most cases to explain, predict, and control the phenomena exhibited under given conditions. But in cases of loud sounds and those which are propagated to a great distance, such as are to be employed as fog-signals, considerable obscurity still exists. As an illustration of this I may mention the frequent occurrence of apparently abnormal phenomena. General Warren informs me that at the battle of Seven Pines, in June, 1862, near Richmond—General Johnston, of the Confederate army, was within three miles of the scene of action with a force intended to attack the flank of the Northern forces, and although listening attentively for the sound of the commencement of the engagement, the battle, which was a severe one, and lasting about three hours, ended without his having heard a single gun. (See Johnson's report.) Another case of a similar kind occurred to General McClellan, at the battle of Gaines' Mills, June 27, 1862, also near Richmond. Although a sharp engagement was progessing within three or four miles for four or five hours, the General and his staff were unaware of its occurrence, and when their attention was called to some feeble sound they had no idea that it was anything more than a skirmish of little importance. (See Report of the Committee on the Conduct of the War.) A third and perhaps still more remarkable instance is given in a skirmish between a part of the Second Corps under General Warren and a force of the enemy. In this case the sound of the firing was heard more distinctly at General Meade's headquarters than it was at the headquarters of the Second Corps itself, although the latter was about midway between the former and the point of conflict. Indeed, the sound appeared so near General Meade's camp that the impression was made that the enemy had gotten between it and General Warren's command. In fact so many instances occurred of wrong impressions as to direction and distance derived from the sound of guns that little reliance came to be placed on these indications."

By direction of Professor Baird the subject was also referred to Mr. A. B. Johnson, Chief Clerk of the Light House Board, who kindly favored me with the following:

WASHINGTON, Sept. 10, 1884.

Dear Sir: I have the honor to acknowledge the receipt of your letter of Sept., '84, which came to hand by due course of mail.

You state that during the battle of Gettysburg, Rev. C. Cort and others distinctly heard the sound of the cannonading in Westmoreland Co., Western Pennsylvania, in an air line 140 miles almost west from the field of conflict, while during that battle, at Chambersburg, but 24 miles west from Gettysburg, the sound of the guns was not heard, except indistinctly on the outskirts of the town.

You also state that Rev. Dr. Lane says that the sound of the cannonading at Gettysburg was heard in the southern part of Wyoming County, Pa., a distance of over 120 miles northeast, in an air line.

And you also say that at the instance of Professor Baird, of the Smithsonian Institution, you ask my opinion as to the cause of this phenomenon.

In reply, I beg leave to say that this phenomenon has received the attention of scientists for many years.

Dr. Derham, of England, writing in Latin to the British Philosophical Society in 1708, seemed to consider it as caused by variations in temperature, moisture and the direction of the wind. Baron von Humboldt, and after him Dr. Dove, Sir John Herschel and Dr. Robinson, held that aerial flocculence caused this phenomenon, a theory which was adopted and amplified by Prof. Tyndall. Prof. Joseph Henry, long the Director of the Smithsonian Institute, has, however, presented a more satisfactory theory and has worked it out with great care by many experiments. He accepted as a good working hypothesis, the suggestions made by Professor Stokes, of Cambridge, England, founded upon those remarkable observations of the French Academician, De la Roche, which, roughly stated, is this: The several strata into which a current of air may be divided, do not move with the same velocity. The lowest stratum is retarded by friction against the earth; the one immediately above, by friction against the lower; hence the velocity increases from the ground upward, and when the direction of the sound is perpendicular to the sound wave, as when projected against the wind, it will be thrown upward ahead of the observer, and when it is projected with the wind it will be thrown downward toward the earth.

Professor Henry tested this theory by careful and often repeated experiment and announced the results of five different phenomena, with his idea of their cause. One of these formula describes the case you cite in these words:

"*The audibility of sound at a distance and its inaudibility nearer the source of sound.*" The cause of this aberration in audibility, he formulates thus: "*Sound moving with the wind is refracted down toward the earth; while moving against the wind it is refracted upward and passes over the head of the observer.*"

You will see from my several pamphlets on this general subject, which I send you, that I have given this matter some attention, that I agree with Henry rather than Tyndall and that I have cited a number of instances which have occurred under my own observation similar to those which you relate, though on a smaller scale—but that in each of these cases, the wind is blowing against, rather than with the sound.

You ask me for a short statement of the reason of the phenomena you have related. In reply I beg to say that I am of the opinion that the aberration in the audibility of the sound of the guns at Gettysburg was caused by the wind; that is the wind blowing against the sound waves tilted them up so that they first touched the earth near Chambersburg and then passed over it describing one or more curves from there to the hearers in Westmoreland county.

It is not improbable that the length of the cord of the arc described by the sound wave was about the distance from Gettysburg to Chambersburg, and that the sound was heard at intervals of twenty-five or thirty miles from thence to the hearers in Westmoreland county and maybe beyond. It would be interesting to know if this was the case.

An instance of this kind, though on a much smaller scale, is given on page 731 of my pamphlet—Anomalies in the Sound of Fog Signals—and the curve of the sound wave showing the area of inaudibility in the observations made near the White Head Light Station, Maine, is indicated in a rude wood cut on the next page.

The battle of Gettysburg lasted about three days, if I remember it correctly; it is possible that the wind during that time changed, so that the same reasons which would have caused the sound of the guns to be heard in Westmoreland county in one day, might cause them to be heard in Wyoming county on another.

Guns were frequently heard at a great distance from battle fields during the War of the Rebellion, while they were not heard by persons comparatively near, but in the same direction. In one instance those near by did not hear the noise of the guns when they could see their flash. This is the first time I have had to consider this phenomenon when extending over twenty-five miles. Within that distance, it seems to me, to be accounted for. When, as in this instance, the distance is five or six times greater, I speak with less confidence. But I do not see that the question of the distance changes the principle.

Yours very truly,
ARNOLD B. JOHNSON,
Mr. J. HOKE,   C. C.
Chambersburg, Pa.

In the publications accompanying the foregoing letter, Mr. Johnson has specially called attention to several places which he has marked as bearing directly upon the phenomena under consideration. These I annex. The first quotation states Professor Henry's five phenomena of sound, as referred to by Mr. Johnson:

Professor Henry, in considering the results of General Duane's experiments, and his own, some of which were made in company with Sir Frederick Arron and Capt. Webb, H. B. M. Navy, both of the British Light House Establishment, who were sent here to study and report on our fog signal system, formulated these abnormal phenomena. He said they consisted of:

1. The audibility of a sound at a distance and its inaudibility nearer the source of sound.

2. The inaudibility of a sound at a given distance in one direction, while a lesser sound is heard at the same distance in another direction.

3. The audibility at one time at a distance of several miles, while at another the sound cannot be heard at more than a fifth of the same distance.

4. While the sound is generally heard

further with the wind than against it, in some instances the reverse is the case.

5. The sudden loss of a sound in passing from one locality to another in the same vicinity, the distance from the source of the sound being the same.

In illustration of the foregoing the following is cited:

There are six steam fog whistles on the coast of Maine: these have been frequently heard at a distance of twenty miles, and as frequently cannot be heard at the distance of two miles, and this with no perceptible difference in the state of the atmosphere.

The signal is often heard at a great distance in one direction, while in another it will be scarcely audible at the distance of a mile. This is not the effect of wind, as the signal is frequently heard much farther against the wind than with it; for example, the whistle on Cape Elizabeth can always be distinctly heard in Portland, a distance of nine miles, during a heavy northeast snow storm, the wind blowing a gale directly from Portland toward the whistle.

Aberrations of Audibility, or Fog Signals. A parper read before the Philosophical Society of Washington, Oct. 22, 1881, by Arnold B. Johnson, Chief Clerk of the Light House Board.

In illustration of his sound-wave theory, Professor Henry states the following. I copy it from "Anomalies in the sound of Fog Whistles," by A. B. Johnson.

It frequently happens on a vessel leaving a station that the sound (of the fog whistle) is suddenly lost at a point in its course, and, after remaining inaudible some time, is heard again at a greater distance, and then is gradually lost as the distance is further increased. This is attributed to the upward refraction of the sound-wave, which passes over the head of the observer, and continues an upward course until it nearly reaches the upper surface of the current wind, when the refraction will be reversed, and the sound sent downward to the earth. Or the effect may be considered as due to a sound-shadow produced by refraction, which is gradually closed in at a distance by the lateral spread of the sound-wave near the earth on either side, in a direction which is not affected by the upper refraction. Another explanation may be found in the probable circumstance of the lower sheet of sound beams being actually refracted into a serpentine or undulating course.

Upon this sound-wave theory, Mr. Johnson, in a paper read before the Philosophical Society of Washington, said as follows:

Mr. Johnson stated that this ricochetting of sound, these intervals of audibility, ought to be recognized by the mariner, who should now understand that in sailing toward or from a fog signal in full blast, he might lose and pick up its sound several times though no apparent object might intervene. And the mariner now needed that science should deduce the law of this variation in audibility and bring

out some instrument which should be to the ears what the mariner's compass is to the eyes, and also that variations of this instrument yet to be invented, be provided for and corrected as now are the variations of the mariner's compass. The speaker referred to the benefit the mariner had derived from the promulgation of Professor Henry's theory of the tilting of the sound-wave up or down by adverse or favorable winds, and said that by this the sailor had been led to go aloft in the one case and to get as near as possible to the surface of the water in the other, when trying to pick up the sound of a fog signal.

Desiring to make the chapter on the burning of Chambersburg as complete as possible, I addressed letters to several Confederate officers who participated in that event, inviting them, if they desired to place upon record any statement relating thereto, to favor me with the same, and have been favored with the following. These statements have been written expressly for these reminiscences, and have never before been seen by the public. The first is from General J. A. Early who ordered the ransom or burning of our town:

YELLOW SULPHUR SPRINGS, VIRGINIA, }
September 4th, 1884. }

J. HOKE, Esq., Sir:—Having been from home since the 5th of August, your letter of the 6th of that month did not reach me until a very few days ago, when it was forwarded to me from Lynchburg with a number of others. As you desire my statement in regard to the burning of Chambersburg, Pennsylvania, under my orders in July, 1864, I send you a copy of my "Memoirs of the last year of the war," in which you will find, on pages 66 to 70, my account of that affair. All I have to add is that, on my march from Lynchburg in pursuit of Hunter, and down the valley on the expedition against Washington, I had seen the evidences of the destruction wantonly committed by his troops under his orders, including the burning of a number of private houses without provocation, among them being the family residence, at Lexington, of ex-Governor Letcher: also the Virginia Military Institue at the same place, and a part of the town of Newtown, in Frederick county; and in addition there had been a wholesale destruction of private property, including even the wearing apparel of ladies and bed clothing, the beds in many cases being cut to pieces and the feathers scattered to the winds. In addition, there had been the destruction of several towns in the South by Federal troops, among them being the town of Darien, in Georgia, in the year 1863. When, therefore, on my return from the expedition threatening Washington, I found that Hunter, who had reached the lower valley on the Baltimore and Ohio railroad, after his flight to the Kanawa Valley, had been engaged in his accustomed work, and had burned the valuable residences of several citizens of Jefferson county, I determined to demand compensation therefor from some town in Pennsylvania, and in the event of failure to comply with my demand to retaliate by burning said town. The town of

Chambersburg was selected because it was the only one of any consequence accessible to my troops, and for no other reason. The houses mentioned with their contents, all of which were destroyed, were fully worth at least $100,000 in gold, and I required $500,000 in United States currency in the alternative, for the reason that the said currency was rapidly depreciating, being then nearly three to one in gold, and I desired to secure the full equivalent of $100,000 in gold. I will add that according to the laws of retaliation in war, I would have been fully justified in burning Chambersburg without giving the town a chance of redemption.

Compare the expedition of Hunter into Virginia in June, 1864, the campaign of Sherman in Georgia and South Carolina, of Banks in the trans-Mississippi, and Sheridan in the Valley of Virginia, with that of General Lee in Pennsylvania, leaving out of consideration Beast Butler's performances in New Orleans, and then say whether the denunciations of those who applaud the destroyer of Atlanta, Georgia, and Columbia, South Carolina, and him who boasted that, besides burning the town of Dayton, he had so desolated the valley as that a crow flying over it would have to carry its rations, should have any terror for me?

Respectfully,
J. A. EARLY.

Accompanying the foregoing letter was a pamphlet of 136 pages entitled "*A Memoir of the Last year of the War for Independence in the Confederate States of America, containing an account of the operations of his commands in the years 1864 and 1865, by Lieutenant-General Jubal A. Early of the Provisional Army of the Confederate States,*" from which I copy entire the General's own account of the "*Expedition into Maryland and Pennsylvania and the Burning of Chambersburg:*"

On the 26th (July) we moved to Martinsburg, the cavalry going to the Potomac. The 27th and 28th were employed in destroying the railroad, it having been repaired since we passed over it at the beginning of the month. While at Martinsburg, it was ascertained, beyond all doubt, that Hunter had been again indulging in his favorite mode of warfare and that, after his return to the valley, while we were near Washington, among other outrages, the private residences of Mr. Andrew Hunter, a member of the Virginia Senate, Mr. Alexander R. Boteler, an ex-member of the Confederate Congress, as well as of the United States Congress, and Edmund I. Lee, a distant relative of General Lee, all in Jefferson county, with their contents, had been burned by his orders, only time enough being given for the ladies to get out of the houses. A number of towns in the South, as well as private country houses, had been burned by the Federal troops and the accounts had been heralded forth in some of the Northern papers in terms of exultation, and gloated over by their readers, while they were received with apathy by others. I now come to the conclusion that we had stood this mode of warfare long enough, and that it was time to open the eyes of the people of the North to its enormity by an example in the way of retaliation. I did not select the cases mentioned, as having more merit or greater claims for retaliation than others, but because they had occurred within the limits of the country covered by my command, and were brought more immediately to my attention. The town of Chambersburg, in Pennsylvania, was selected as the one on which retaliation should be made, and McCausland was ordered to proceed with his brigade and that of Johnson and a battery of artillery to that place, and demand of the municipal authorities the sum of $100,000 in gold or $500,000 in United States currency, as a compensation for the destruction of houses named and their contents; and, in default of payment, to lay the town in ashes, in retaliation for the burning of those houses and others in Virginia, as well as for the towns which had been burned in other Southern States. A written demand to that effect was sent to the municipal authorities, and they were informed what would be the result of a failure or refusal to comply with it. I desired to give the people of Chambersburg an opportunity of saving their town by making compensation for part of the injury done, and hoped that the payment of such a sum would have the desired effect, and open the eyes of the people of other towns at the North to the necessity of urging upon their government the adoption of a different policy. McCausland was also directed to proceed from Chambersburg towards Cumberland in Maryland, and levy contributions in money upon that and other towns able to bear them, and if possible destroy the machinery at the coal pits near Cumberland, and the machine shops, depots and bridges on the Baltimore and Ohio railroad as far as practicable.

On the 29th McCausland crossed the Potomac near Clear Spring, above Williamsport, and I moved with Rodes' and Ramseur's divisions and Vaughan's cavalry to the latter place, while Imboden demonstrated with his and Jackson's cavalry towards Harper's Ferry in order to withdraw attention from McCausland. Breckinridge remained at Martinsburg and continued the destruction of the railroad. Vaughan drove a force of cavalry from Williamsport, and went into Hagerstown, where he captured and destroyed a train of cars loaded with supplies. One of Rodes' brigades was crossed over at Williamsport and subsequently withdrawn. On the 30th, McCausland being well under way, I moved back to Martinsburg, and on the 31st the whole infantry force was moved back to Bunker Hill, where we remained on the 1st, 2nd and 3d of August.

On the 4th, in order to enable McCausland to retire from Pennsylvania and Maryland, and to keep Hunter, who had been reinforced by the 6th and 19th corps, and had been oscillating between Harper's Ferry and Monocacy Junction, in a state of uncertainty, I again moved to the Potomac with the infantry and Vaughan's and Jackson's cavalry, while Imboden demonstrated towards Harper's Ferry. On the 5th Rodes' and Ramseur's divisions crossed at Williamsport and took position near St. James' College, and Vaughan's cavalry went into Hagerstown. Breckinridge, with his command, and Jackson's cavalry crossed at Shepherdstown, and took position at Sharpsburg. This position is in full view from Maryland Heights, and a cavalry force was sent by the enemy to reconnoitre which, after skirmishing with Jackson's cavalry, was driven off by the sharpshooters of Gordon's division. On the 6th, the whole force re-crossed the Potomac at Williamsport, and moved towards Martinsburg; and on the 7th he returned to Bunker Hill.

On the 30th of July McCausland reached Chambersburg, and made the demand as directed, reading to such of the authorities as presented themselves, the paper sent by me. The demand was not complied with, the people stating that they were not afraid of having their town burned, and that a Federal force was approaching. The policy pursued by our army on former occasions had been so lenient, that they did not suppose the threat was in earnest this time, and they hoped for speedy relief. McCausland, however, proceeded to carry out his orders, and the greater part of the town was laid in ashes. He then moved in the direction of Cumberland, but on approaching that town, he found it defended by a force under Kelly too strong for him to attack, and he withdrew towards Hampshire county in Virginia, and crossed the Potomac near the mouth of the South Branch, capturing the garrison at that place and partially destroying the railroad bridge. He then invested the post on the railroad at New Creek, but finding it too strongly fortified to take by assault, he moved to Moorefield, in Hardy county, near which place he halted to rest and recruit his men and horses as the command was now considered safe from pursuit. Averill, however, had been pursuing from Chambersburg with a body of cavalry, and Johnson's brigade was surprised in camp, before day, on the morning of the 7th of August, and routed by Averill's force. This resulted also in the rout of McCausland's brigade, and the loss of artillery (4 pieces) and about three hundred prisoners from the whole command. The balance of the command made its way to Mount Jackson in great disorder and much weakened. This affair had a very damaging effect upon my cavalry for the rest of the campaign.

In order to give General Early the whole benefit of his own account of the outrages alleged to have been wantonly committed by the command under General Hunter, I quote also several foot notes in his pamphlet detailing scenes witnessed in his pursuit of that force, and on his march down the valley towards the Potomac.

Hunter's delay in advancing from Staunton had been most remarkable, and can be accounted for only by the fact, that indulgence in petty acts of malignity and outrage upon private citizens was more congenial to his nature than bold operations in the field. He had defeated Jones' small force at Piedmont about ten miles from Staunton, on the 5th, and united with Crook on the 8th, yet he did not arrive in front of Lynchburg until near night on the 17th. The route from Staunton to Lynchburg by which he moved, which was by Lexington, Buchanan, the Peaks of Otter, and Liberty, is about one hundred miles in distance. It is true McCausland had delayed his progress by keeping constantly in his front, and an energetic advance would have brushed away McCausland's small force, and Lynchburg, with all its manufacturing establishments and stores, would have fallen before assistance arrived. A subsequent passage over the greater part of the same route showed how Hunter had been employed. (Pages 43, 44.)

The scenes on Hunter's route from Lynchburg had been truly heartrending. Houses had been burned, and helpless women and children left without shelter. The country had been stripped of provisions, and many families left without a morsel to eat. Furniture and bedding had been cut to pieces, and old men and women and children, robbed of all the clothing they had except that on their backs. Ladies' trunks had been rifled and their dresses torn to pieces in mere wantonness. Even the negro girls had lost their little finery. We had renewed evidence of the outrages committed by Hunter's orders in burning and plundering private houses. We saw the ruins of a number of houses to which the torch had been applied by his orders. At Lexington he had burned the Military Institute, with all its contents, including its library and scientific apparatus; and Washington College had been plundered and the statue of Washington stolen. The residence of ex-Governor Letcher at that place had been burned by orders, and but a few minutes given Mrs. Letcher and her family to leave the house. In the same county a most excellent Christian gentleman, a Mr. Creigh, had been hung because, on a former occasion he had killed a straggling and marauding Federal soldier in the act of insulting and outraging the ladies of the family. These are but some of the outrages committed by Hunter or his orders, and I will not insult the memory of the ancient barbarians of the North by calling them "acts of Vandalism." If these old barbarians were savage and cruel, they at least had the manliness and daring of rude soldiers, with occasional traits of magnanimity. Hunter's deeds were those of a malignant and cowardly fanatic, who was better qualified to make war upon helpless women and children than upon armed soldiers. The time consumed in the perpetration of those deeds, was the salvation of Lynchburg, with its stores, foundries and factories, which were so necessary to the army at Richmond. (Page 48.)

Again General Early says, on page 50:

On this day (July 2d) we passed through Newtown where several houses, including that of a Methodist minister, had been burned by Hunter's orders, because as a part of Mosby's command had attacked a train of supplies for Sigel's force at this place. The original order was to burn the whole town, but the officer sent to execute it had revolted at the cruel mandate of his superior, and another had been sent who but partially executed it, after having forced the people to take an oath of allegiance to the United States to save their houses. Mosby's battalion, though called "guerillas" by the enemy, was a regular organization in the Confederate army, and was merely serving on detached duty under General Lee's orders. The attack on the train was an act of legitimate warfare, and the order to burn Newtown, and the burning of the houses mentioned, were most wanton, cruel, unjustifiable and cowardly.

In a foot note on page 72 General Early disclaims all responsibility for the burning of the house of Postmaster General Blair, in the neighborhood of Washington while on his raid to that place. He says that he had nothing to do with that act, and is yet in ignorance as to how the burning occurred, and if done by any of his men it was not by any orders, but in retaliation for some wrong done them in the Valley of Virginia.

On page 67 he further says: "I had often seen delicate ladies who had been plundered, insulted and rendered desolate by the acts of our most atrocious enemies, and while they did not call for it, yet in the anguished expressions of their features while narrating their misfortunes, there was a mute appeal to every manly sentiment of my bosom for retribution which I could no longer withstand."

In a foot note to his account of the burning of Chambersburg, on page 70, already given, General Early assumes the entire responsibility for the destruction of our town in the following words:

For this act I alone am responsible, as the officers engaged in it were simply executing my orders, and had no discretion left them. Notwithstanding the lapse of time which has occurred, and the results of the war, I am perfectly satisfied with my conduct on this occasion, and see no reason to regret it.

From General Early's statements the following facts are established:

1. That by General Hunter's orders or permission, great devastation of private property was wrought in the Valley of Virginia. His account is substantially the same as General Imboden's in *Annals of the War*, although not so extensive and full. General Imboden's account covers fifteen pages of that book.

2. The opinion held by some that one of the reasons, if not the principal one, why Chambersburg was destroyed, was because John Brown had made it his headquarters prior to his raid upon Harper's Ferry, is entirely disproved. General Early declares emphatically that Chambersburg was selected for retaliation because it was "the only town of any consequence accessible to my (his) troops, and *for no other reason.*"

3. The question as to what Confederate force drove Cole's Maryland Cavalry from Williamsport to Hagerstown on Friday, July 29th, and subsequently on the same day entered that place, dispersing those men and burning the cars loaded with government stores, is solved. It was a force of cavalry under General Vaughan.

4. The occasion of the fright of our people on Black Friday, August 5th, as previously stated, when it was reported that the Confederates were again returning to complete the destruction of our town, was the approach of Vaughan's cavalry, which on that day recrossed the Potomac and entered Hagerstown. It will thus be seen that the fears of our people were not entirely groundless.

5. In the presence of Rodes' and Ramseur's divisions of infantry at Williamsport, Vaughan's cavalry in Hagerstown, and Imboden and Jackson threatening to cross the Potomac at Harper's Ferry, on Friday, July 29th, and all threatening Averill from the South, the reason for his moving eastwardly from Greencastle to Greenwood before turning his column towards this place on the morning of the 30th, when our town was burned, will appear. He was evidently afraid of being caught between those forces and McCausland's.

6. The demoralization of McCausland's cavalry and their almost utter worthlessness for the balance of the war, after their defeat and rout at Moorfield on August 7th, as admitted by General Early, is another evidence of the demoralizing effect of permitting soldiers to pillage and plunder while in the enemy's country. The condition of General Hunter's command, after its plundering and burning expedition up the Valley of Virginia is another illustration of the same fact.

7. General Early states the whole loss in prisoners from McCausland's command by the affair at Moorfield Valley, *as three hundred*. Another Confederate, who participated in the affair, and whose account will follow, says: "*About five hundred of our brigade were captured.*" The brigade referred to was General Bradley T. Johnson's, and no reference is made to the loss sustained by McCausland's own brigade. Mr. Slingluff—whose statement is to follow—may mean that the whole loss in prisoners in the entire command was five hundred. At all events the difference in the two statements shows that General Early errs in this case, and if wrong in this instance, is it not fair to suppose that he is also wrong in other statements touching the number of his forces. In no other way can we account for some of the statements given in his pamphlet; notably his estimate of the force he led in his raid through Maryland to the National Capital, which he gives as only about eight thousand.

For the following paper relating to the burning of Chambersburg, I am indebted to Mr. Ephraim Hiteshew, of this place, who, at my solicitation, prevailed upon the gentleman, whose name it bears, to furnish it for these reminiscences. It was written by F. A. Slingluff, Esq., an Attorney residing in the city of Baltimore. Mr. Slingluff was present at the destruction of our town, and took some part in that event, and now presents an account thereof from the standpoint of a Confederate soldier. His statement will be read with interest by our people:

BALTIMORE, AUGUST 1ST, 1881.

EPHRAIM HITESHEW, ESQ., CHAMBERSBURG, PA., *My Dear Sir:*—I have received the papers, sent me by you, containing Mr. Hoke's reminiscences of the burning of Chambersburg, and have carefully read them. At your request I will give you my recollection of the events which immediately preceded and followed that occurrence.

I write from the standpoint of the private soldier, having had no knowledge of the reasons which dictated official orders at the time, nor had my associates. We simply obeyed orders.

I do not pretend to give dates, distances, names of places, of persons, or localities, with precision. Twenty years is a long span in a man's life, and as I passed through many stirring events during the war, this one did not make as great an impression upon me as it did upon those who immediately suffered from it.

I believe though, that that twenty years has so curbed and tempered the excitement of early manhood, and mollified the passions and resentments of war, that I can write calmly and without bias on the subject. At least such will be my endeavor. At the same time I shall not hesitate to speak frankly and freely from my standpoint. To do less would render valueless for the purposes of impartial history, anything which I might say.

Mr. Hoke's articles are as temperate as possible from one whose house was burned by an enemy, and as he thinks without justification. It is true he calls us villains occasionally, and says we seemed accustomed to the business from the expert way in which we proceeded to the task. I will not quarrel with him for this, but I think it proper to take a look at these villains to see who they were then, and what they are now. I was a young man not yet arrived at maturity. I had just left college, when I joined the confederate army. When I marched for Chambersburg I belonged to the 1st Maryland cavalry. This regiment was composed of the very first young men of our State. If they were not guided by the strongest instincts of principle in going into the southern army, and staying there, they were certainly a very peculiar set of young men, for there was anything but pleasure and comfort in our lives. We were generally hungry, slept often, winter and summer, in the open air on the ground, got no pay that we could buy anything with, were scantily clad, and were apt to be killed, sooner or later, in battle. I believe the unbiased man must say this was patriotism, although he can if he wishes, reconcile his conscience by calling it "misguided patriotism." And you may be surprised to know that these young "villains" have generally developed into good citizens, and successful men. Go where you choose through our State, and you will find them respected and at the head of the communities in which they live. In business I can name you a dozen of the leading houses in this city whose members were with Johnson and McCausland, when your city was burned. The bar throughout the State is full of them, and they are in many cases among the leaders of their circuits. They are doctors in good standing in their profession and many of the most thrifty farmers in this State, whose fine farms attest their devotion to duty and to home, especially in such counties as Howard and Montgomery, were also present on that occasion.

In addition to our regiment, there were five or six others in the brigade, most of them from southwest Virginia, and the valley of Virginia. The men who composed these regiments were the substantial citizens of their respective counties, and would compare favorably with the like number of men selected from any agricultural community in our country.

Now you would like to know if the men whom I have described justified the burning of your town, in their individual capacity, irrespective of the orders from headquarters, under which they acted. I must say to you frankly that they did, and I never heard one dissenting voice. And why did we justify so harsh a measure? Simply because we had long come to the conclusion that it was time for us to burn something in the enemy's country. For the campaign of the preceding year, when our whole army had passed through your richest section of country, where the peaceful homes and fruitful fields only made the contrast with what he had left the more significant, many a man, whose home was in ruins, chafed under the orders from General Lee, which forbade him to touch them, but the orders were obeyed and we left the homes and fields as we found them, the ordinary wear and tear of an army of occupation alone excepted. We had so often before our eyes the reverse of this wherever your army swept through Virginia, that we were thoroughly convinced of the justice of a stern retaliation.

It is no pleasure to me to have to recall the scenes of those days, nor do I do so in any spirit of vindictiveness, but I simply tell the truth in justification of an act which Mr. Hoke claims was without justification. We had followed Kilpatrick (I think it was) in his raid through Madison, Greene and other counties, and had seen the cattle shot, or hamstrung in the barnyards, the agricultural implements burned, the feather beds and clothing of the women and children cut in shreds in mere wantonness; farm house after farm house stripped of every particle of provisions, private carriages cut and broken up, and women in tears lamenting all this. I do not put down here anything that I did not see myself. We had seen a thousand ruined homes in Clark, Jefferson and Frederick counties—barns and houses burned and private property destroyed—but we had no knowledge that this was done by "official orders." At last when the official order came openly from General Hunter, and the burning was done thereunder, and when our orders of retaliation came, they met with the approbation, as I have said, of every man who crossed the Potomac to execute them.

Of course we had nothing personal against your pretty little town. It just so happened that it was the nearest and most accessible place of importance for us to get to. It was the unfortunate victim of circumstances. Had it been further off and some other town nearer, that other town would have gone, and Chambersburg would have been saved.

And now having given you the feelings and motives which actuated us, permit me to give my views of how your people felt about the affair. I must be frank enough to say that I think the reason the tribute demanded of you was not paid, was because your people had no idea that the rebels would carry out their threat to burn; nor was this confidence shaken until the smoke and flames began to ascend. I know that this is directly in the teeth of Hoke's tribute to the patriotism of his fellow-townsmen, that sooner than pay money to the rebels, they saw their homes laid in ashes, but he is himself a little illogical, for he gives greater condemnation to a cruel enemy for burning out a helpless people after they had shown to them that the banks had removed their deposits, and it was impossible for them to get the money demanded. Had your people believed that the town was actually in danger I think they could have raised enough money to have avoided the catastrophe. Why this confidence of security? It grew out of the position taken by your people during the war, that we were rebels, soon to be conquered, and that whatever cruelties were inflicted upon the homes of these rebels were in the nature of penalties for rebellious conduct and that such like acts would never dare to be attempted against loyal men. It was further strengthened by the fact, that when the whole rebel army was in your State, no atrocities were committed. I saw this confidence, almost amounting to contempt, on our march to your town, and in the town itself, when the negotiations, preliminary to the fire, were in progress. I happened with a comrade or two, to get behind the command on the march to the town, and in passing through a village of some size (I think it was Mercersburg), the knots of men on the corners poked fun at our appearance, and jeered us, and never seemed to consider that the men upon whom they expended their fun had pistols and sabres in their belts, and might use them. The strange part of the matter to us was too see able-bodied young men out of the service—a sight never seen in the South during the war. In Chambersburg itself, it seemed impossible to convince your people that we were in earnest. They treated it as a joke, or thought it was a mere threat to get money, and showed their sense of security and and incredulity in every act. When the two brigades of Confederate cavalry marched into your town, the order came for certain regiments and portion of regiments to enter and burn it. Our regiment, as a whole, according to the best of my recollection, was not sent in but there were several detachments from it, on different kinds of duty sent there, and I was with one of them. It was afterward a source of congratulation to our men that they had not been detailed for the purpose, for although they regarded it as a proper measure of retaliation, they did not seek the unpleasant task. The men who actually applied the torch may be classed in three divisions: First, those whose own homes had been ravaged, or destroyed, or whose relations had suffered in that way. These men were anxious for the work to begin, and the spirit of revenge which actuated them made them apparently merciless. There were many such in the brigade. Second, the far larger portion who simply obeyed orders, as soldiers, and who saved what they could, and to whose humanity and liberal construction of the orders given them, no doubt you must be thankful for the portion of the city that was saved. Thirdly, the men to be found in all armies who looked upon the occasion as an opportuity to plunder and who rejoiced in wanton destruction. This last element was, I am glad to say, small, but I have no doubt to those who unfortunately came in contact with them, they were but types of the whole command.

As I had never seen the town before, and did not know the names of your streets, I can give you no detailed account of the burning. After it began it was *quickly* done. Men plead to have their own houses saved, but the women acted in a much calmer manner, after they understood the thing was inevitable, and in some cases excited our admiration by their courage and defiance. I saw a number of houses fired, but I saw no abuse of the citizens. Through the scenes of terror which your people passed I have read Mr. Hoke's annals in vain to find mention of an unarmed citizen injured, or a women insulted. Some of the men became inflamed with liquor, but I believe they were few. The most usual method of burning was to break the furniture into splinters; pile in the middle of the floor and then fire it. This was done in the beginning but as the fire became general, it was not necessary, as one house set fire to the other. Most of the houses were vacant when fired, the occupants having fled. When the command was given to retire it was quickly done. One little incident which happened after we left the town will illustrate all I have said about the feeling which actuated many of our soldiers. I think it was two or three miles from the town (it may have been more, or less) some of us halted for a few minutes to get a drink and perhaps something to eat. A brick farm house, with a porch, was located on the road, with a pump to the side of it. Not far off was what we called a Pennsylvania "Dutch barn," larger than the house. It was full of the recently gathered harvest, and bore all the evidences of a plentiful yield to a good farmer. I hitched my horse to the lightning rod on the side of the barn next to the house, and was just returning to get him when some one cried "fire." In an instant the barn was in flames. I had hardly time to unhitch my horse. Some of our party demanded in angry tones of two troopers who came from the barn, and mounted their horses, what they meant by such uncalled for vandalism. The reply was, "Why, damn it, they burnt our barn," and on they rode.

But I am making this letter longer than necessary, and must hurry on.

. One word about what happened after

our retreat. Mr. Hoke seems to think that the fear of Averill was uppermost in our minds. This is a mistake. Whatever may have been the motives that actuated the commanding officers, the men did not fear him at all. They had perfect confidence that they could whip him whenever he thought proper to give us the opportunity, and any soldier will tell you that a feeling like that means victory. At one little town we stopped to feed our horses and rest. His columns were in sight but no attack was made. As we passed through Hancock, his advance fired into our rear guard and made a little dash at us. I saw in this little fight, Harry Gilmor, who was the last man to leave the town, struck, and severely stung by a spent ball, which made him whistle with pain. We also heard on the retreat that some of our men had been left in Chambersburg drunk, and had been thrown in the flames by the citizens, and burned to death. This was camp gossip with us, but I never heard it verified. We crossed the Potomac with some little opposition from an iron clad car in our front on the track of the B. & O. R. R., which was struck by a ball, fired by the Baltimore Light Infantry and immediately left. We also had quite a severe little fight in the Blue Ridge mountains, near Cold Spring, on the advance, in which several from our regiment were killed and wounded, and in which a body of your cavalry showed great spirit and determination, but aside from this we had no fighting at all. I dislike again to destroy a thrilling episode in Mr. Hoke's very cleverly written annals, but the truth compels me to do so. He says when Averill came up to us in the Moorefield Valley, and captured and scattered our command, that they charged us with the cry of "Remember Chambersburg," and cut us down without mercy. The fact is we were down when he charged us. I will give you the plain, prosaic facts, of which I was the unfortunate witness and victim. After we recrossed the Potomac, we marched to the Moorefield Valley to rest and recuperate, after a severe campaign. There is no lovelier spot in all Virginia than this little mountain-locked valley, and as it had escaped the desolation of war it was the very spot for rest. Our regiment was camped nearest the river, and the company to which I belonged was nearest the river of all. My messmate and myself had crossed the fence from the field in which the regiment was camped, in our bed in a soft green fence corner, so that I believe we were the nearest of the whole brigade to the enemy. We had been camped quietly for a day or two, when in the middle of the night the order came to "saddle up." We soon were ready for a reported advance of the enemy, but after waiting an hour or two with no further orders, the men gradually got under their blankets, and went to sleep. Just at the break of day I felt a rude shock, which I supposed came from the careless tread of a comrade, and I made an angry remonstrance. This was followed by a kick, which I thought came from a horse. I furiously threw the blanket from over my head and found a couple of Averill's men, with cocked pistols at my head, one of whom said: "Get up you d——d Chambersburg burning s——n of a b——." I got up at once, and at this moment had Mr. Hoke been there he would have been delighted, for I mildly intimated that I had nothing to do with the burning of Chambersburg and considered it altogether wicked and unjustifiable. As soon as I collected my thoughts I took in the situation at a glance. I saw the blue black column of Averill, winding down the road and breaking off into the fields where our men slept. I saw them to my utter humiliation and disgust dashing in among our men and waking them up from their sleep. Some of our command, who had heard the rush of the charge, succeeded in mounting their horses and escaping. With such, some shots were exchanged, but the greater part of our regiment was caught asleep and captured without firing a shot. A complete answer to the statement adopted by Mr. Hoke, is, that not one of my regiment (to the best of my recollection) was killed or wounded, and as I have already stated, they were the nearest to the enemy, and received the first shock of the charge. Further on down the road, where the shouts of combat had aroused the other portions of the brigade, and they had time to rally to some extent, there was fighting, and some of our men were killed, and I saw some of Averill's wounded brought to the rear, but our rout was complete and irretrievable, and the rallies, as I afterwards heard, were without vigor on our part. As soon as the comrade with whom I was sleeping (a cousin of mine, now in business in this city) and myself had given up our arms, the usual and almost invariable compliments passed on such occasions, took place. "I want them boots," said trooper No. 1. I had just got them in Hancock a day or so before, and as they were regular cavalry boots, and worth with us at least $150 to $200 in Confederate money, it nearly broke my heart to part with them. But the occasion was pressing and they were soon exchanged for a very sorry looking pair. My hat, which was also a recent Maryland acquisition, with a martial black plume, was appropriated by trooper No. 2. The object with which he replaced it was a much greater insult to my dignity than the loss of my boots. My pockets were carefully investigated, but that part of the raid was a complete failure. I was not at all surprised at their attentions, for, as I have said above, the custom was a general; one, and I had myself paid the same compliment to my guests when the situation was reversed. And how was it that the burners of Chambersburg were thus ignominiously routed, scattered and captured by a foe whom I have said, they despised. The answer is a simple one. It was through the carelessness of our commanding officer, and was inexcusable. It happened in this way, and I am again in a position to give the exact facts. When we camped in the little valley, a detail was called on for picket duty. That duty fell to the lot of Lieut. J. G. Bonn, of my company. No truer man or more charming gentleman ever wore a sabre in our cavalry, than he. After the war he settled in Macon, Georgia, became a prosperous merchant, and died some years ago. He went out on the picket post with about ten men, some two or three miles from our camp. This was the only guard between Averill and our sleeping men, and it must be remembered that when this little band went on the outpost they were worn out with the fatigues of the nearly incessant marching for the four or five previous days and nights. So wearied were the men that after their first night's duty Lieut. Bonn sent word back to camp and begged to be relieved, stating that his men were absolutely unfit for duty. I take it for granted this message was sent to headquarters, but whether it was or not it was an unjustifiable piece of cruelty to keep those wearied men on duty. His appeal was unheeded. He told me after the surprise was over, that the men on the outpost actually went to sleep upon their horses, and that in addition to all this no provision was made for their rations. While in this condition, just before the dawn of day, they heard the welcome sound of what they supposed was the relief picket coming from our camp, and soon they welcomed twenty or thirty troopers in gray in their midst. Their rejoicing was short-lived for, as their supposed friends surrounded them they quickly drew their revolvers and in an instant our men were prisoners. To run down the outpost of two men was the work of a moment, and then there was nothing between Averill and the men who burned Chambersburg but a few moments of darkness and a couple of miles of dusty road. These men in gray were what, in those days were known as "Jesse Scouts." They were familiar with the country—knew the little mountain roads and had clothed themselves in the Confederate gray and had managed to slip in between our main body and the picket post and then played the part of the "relief."

As we were captured we were gathered together in a circle, and soon poor Bonn with his pickets were brought in looking unhappy and dejected. He felt keenly the responsibility of his position, but after his story was told no one ever attached any blame to him. About five hundred of our brigade were captured and taken to Camp Chase, Ohio, where for eight long miserable, weary months we bewailed the day that Chambersburg was founded, builded and burned. One more little episode, in which I am happy to say, I agree with Mr. Hoke's statement, and I am done. When we arrived at Hancock, tribute was also laid on that little town, and it was soon rumored in our regiment that, in default thereof, McCausland had determined to burn it. The spirit of indignation aroused by this report was intense, and had the threat been carried out there would have been a fight right then and there without the participation of the boys in blue. And now with thanks for your patience, I can only say in conclusion what I have said in the beginning, that this is not intended as anything but what an individual Confederate observed and said, and that it has been written in the same spirit in which you asked for it, and that is the spirit of kindness and good will.

I am, very truly yours,

FIELDER C. SLINGLUFF.

As the responsibility for the destruction of Chambersburg is placed upon General Hunter, because of his alleged destructive policy in the Valley of Virginia, justice to him as well as to the high Confederate authority by whom these charges are made, demands a fair and impartial consideration of the same. That by his authority and permission considerable destruction of private property was wrought, is not denied. The facts related by General Early, and referred to by Mr. Slingluff, and more lengthily and minutely set forth by General J. D. Imboden, in an article contributed by him to *Annals of the War*, pages 169—183, under the caption, "*Fire, Sword and the Halter*," have been in part confirmed by Federal soldiers, who served under General Hunter and others who were cognizant of them. But while the fact of his retributive policy is not denied, it is claimed that a sufficient justification for the same was furnished in the following considerations: In no part of the South, perhaps, was the hostility to the Union so bitter and malignant as in the Valley of Virginia. With but few exceptions the entire male population, capable of bearing arms, were either in the Confederate army, or the secret emissaries of such as were thus engaged. The entire Valley was infested with guerrillas and bushwhackers who, during the day, assumed to be farmers and tradesmen, and at night carried on the nefarious work of waylaying struggling Federal soldiers and unprotected trains. Familiar with every foot of ground in the Valley, as well as with every mountain fastness, they stole upon their victims and then, under the cover of night, fled to places of safety. As one of the evidences of the facts stated I cite the following account of the massacre of six Federal soldiers by guerrillas, published in one of the papers of Martinsburg, West Virginia, in its issue of July 23d, 1864, under the caption of "*A Fiendish Act*," "Six Union soldiers were found strapped to a fence in the vicinity of Charlestown, having their throats cut from ear to ear. The fiendish act is supposed to have been the work of resident rebels, who are farmers and tradesmen during the day and guerrillas at night. Virginia swarms with men of this class, who have, ever since the commencement of the war, pursued a course of this kind, and who have committed deeds so fiendish in their character as to put to blush the darkest and bloodiest deeds of our Indian savages. It is said that General Hunter is as mad as —— about this barbarous deed, and has arrested some sixty residents of the neighborhood in which these unfortunate men were found, and are now held in order, if possible, to ferret out the guilty parties and bring them to justice."

It is also said that in addition to finding the form of a hand-bill in a printing establishment in Lexington, Virginia, urging the bushwhacking of Federal soldiers, and bearing Governor Letcher's signature, clearly proving him to be the author of it, the house of this man was occupied by a squad of rebel sharpshooters, who fired from it and killed a number of General Hunter's men. It is the boast of our Southern friends that Gen. Lee conducted his campaign in Pennsylvania upon humane principles, and that no wanton destruction of property was made by his men. This is admitted ; but, on the other hand, there was no bushwhacking his men, nor no depredations committed upon his trains. Suppose he had found six of his soldiers massacred so inhumanly by citizens as were the six men of General Hunter's command near Charlestown, or the houses of our people used for sharpshooters, before whose concealed aim numbers of his men had fallen, as was Governor Letcher's, would he not have pursued a different policy, and would not the laws of war and the sentiment of the civilized world have justified him in so doing? That a retributive policy would have been adopted and severe retaliation visited upon our people, is clear from a paragraph in General Order No. 49, found upon page 51 of these reminiscences, and issued by Lieut. General Ewell, while in Chambersburg. That paragraph is as follows : "Citizens of the county through which the army may pass, who are not in the military service, are admonished to abstain from all acts of hostility, *upon a penalty of being dealt with in a summary manner.*" The contrast then is not between the conduct of the army of General Lee in Pennsylvania and that of General Hunter in the Valley of Virginia, but between the conduct of the people in Pennsylvania and their treatment of the Confederate army, and the conduct of the people in the Valley and their treatment of the Federal army.

The policy of the commanders of the Union armies operating in the Shenandoah Valley, had been humane and lenient, notwithstanding the bitterness and bushwhacking propensities of the people, but when General Hunter succeeded, he found the condition as stated, and adopted a different policy. From the time he assumed command in that department he gave evidence that he had decided convictions as to how to deal with such inveterate haters of the Union. He was convinced that the mild and lenient course pursued by his predecessors had only increased their bitterness, and emboldened them in their unwarranted methods of bushwhacking and murder; and he adopted the retaliatory policy which caused them to howl at and denounce him. In this, whether right or wrong, the circumstances surrounding him must decide. He was, as in some other things, somewhat in advance of public sentiment and the sentiment and conduct of other commanders, not only in his own, but in other departments, for at a later period Sheridan adopted a similar policy in the same locality, and Sherman in his march from Atlanta to the sea and subsequently through South Carolina.

Admitting the fact that General Hunter did order or permit the destruction of large amounts of private property in the Shenandoah Valley, the question as to the right to retaliate upon the town of Chambersburg depends entirely upon whether or not he had sufficient and justifiable reasons therefor. If he had sufficient reason, then the destruction of Chambersburg was extra-judicial and wholly unjustifiable; if he had not a sufficient reason, then truth requires that the destruction of our town was justifiable by the laws of war. In the absence of more precise and reliable information, I shall not attempt to decide the question.

The three following papers should have come in sooner in this appendix, but as they were received too late to be placed in their approprite places, and the subjects are of such importance that it is desirable that they be preserved, I give them place here. The first is from Lieut. James Pott, of Fulton county, and is as follows :

McCONNELLSBURG, FULTON CO., PA., }
October 7, 1884. }

MR. JACOB HOKE:—I have read with much interest your "Reminiscence of the War," as published in PUBLIC OPINION.

In your chapter (No 36) in the OPINION of 4th instant, you advert to a second instance of "armed resistance to marauding parties of rebels during the invasion," and you are evidently under the impression that the affairs at Strasburg Pass and Keefer's Gap are the only instances, but I can give you another that occurred in this vicinity not, perhaps, *quite* of the same character, because it was not done *directly* in defence of hidden stock, but squarely against a full brigade of Lee's invading army under Gen. Stuart, composed of cavalry, infantry and artillery, as it crossed the Cove mountain from Mercersburg to McConnellsburg. I have lost the date of this occurrence, but it was a few days before Capt. Jones' brilliant little fight and victory, but little more than a mile from the place where about forty of us attacked Stuart's whole brigade—a foolhardy undertaking as everybody pronounced it.

The case, as briefly stated as possible, is this : There were at the time in this vicinity, a full regiment of Emergency men under Col. Zinn, if my memory is not at fault : the 12th Pennsylvania cavalry under Col. Moss, and an independent "Emergency" company from Huntingdon, under Captain Wallace.

Captain Wallace had left more than half his men for duty at Fort Lyttleton and Burnt Cabins and these, while scouting across the mountain toward Fannettsburg, encountered a squad of marauding rebels and had a brush with them, one of the Union soldiers getting wounded. Captain Wallace with about 20 or 25 of his men was at McConnellsburg at the time of the fracas I am relating.

Col. Zinn's regiment was encamped on top of the Cove mountain on both the Chambersburg and Mercersburg pikes, with a very strong natural position. Col. Moss, with the 12th Pennsylvania cavalry, strong, and of good material, was encamped in the valley, east of McConnellsburg.

This was the situation when a scout brought the word that Gen. Stuart, with his rebel brigade, was advancing by the Mercersburg pike. At once all was excitement. Captain Wallace prepared at once to go with his handfull of men to join Col. Zinn on the top of the mountain, and I hurriedly gathered about 20 men, armed with muskets from the armory of the old antebellum volunteer company, and with these I joined Capt. Wallace and we started for the top of the mountain.

We supposed, of course, Col. Moss would take his fine regiment out to help dispute the passage with the rebels, but he looked up the mountain and then, amid the imprecations and curses of many of his men, he headed them to the west and got out of harms way as fast as possible. One of his men, however, Lieut. McDonald, swore he was not going to run away, and did remain.

When Captain Wallace and myself, with our company, reached the foot of the mountain we met Col. Zinn with his full regiment, bag and baggage, coming pell-mell down the mountain. Captain Wallace hailed the Colonel and begged him to turn back and resist the passage of the enemy. Col. Zinn refused and ordered his regiment onward on the retreat, amid many lusty curses from many of his men, although none of them cared to join Captain Wallace, who said he was determined to go and meet the enemy, and so on we hastened, with Lieut. McDonald acting as scout to inform us of the whereabouts of the rebels.

When our scout first saw the enemy he was well down on the east side of the mountain, so that Col. Zinn had plenty of time to have posted his men strongly, and if Col. Moss had come to his support, that Rebel Brigade would not have crossed that mountain that day, and not likely any subsequent day.

After pressing on up the mountain, Captain Wallace selected a place and posted his two score of men to resist 2,500 well organized, well disciplined troops. Lieut. McDonald kept us informed of the approach. At the proper time Captain Wallace was to give the signal by firing his pistol. Some impetuous fellow prematurely discharged his musket and partly spoiled our plan, and revealed our presence a little too soon. However, we gave them several rounds and did some execution.

Immediately on the discharge of that premature gun, the Johnnies threw out flankers which came very near entrapping all of us, but we all escaped and not one of us was hurt, although volley after volley was rained in among us, but mostly over our heads.

This attack delayed the invading column about three hours; and if our forty or fifty men could check and retard twenty-five hundred for that space, what might not the two regiments, that ran away, have done if they had made a determined stand in so naturally a strong position as the summit of the Cove (North) mountain? If they had done so, there would be a page in the history of the late war recording the battle of *North Mountain*, among Lee's invasions, as a twin to the battle of South Mountain. The foregoing then is the *third* instance of armed resistance made by *citizens* to the invading forces—for half of these men with Captain Wallace were citizens.

In my escape from that "scrimmage," my course was *away* from my home, as the enemy had interposed himself in my path, and that night I laid on top of the mountain. Next day in my efforts to get to McConnellsburg, I was "caught up" by a cavalry picket guard on top of the mountain, on the Chambersburg pike, and was held a prisoner. The squad was of the 1st Maryland, rebel regiment, and I must say, in candor, that they were gentlemen and treated me courteously. They never suspected me being one of the *bushwhackers* of the day before, else the treatment would have been otherwise. Although my enforced sojourn with my new-found friends (!) was not wholly enjoyable, yet while sitting with them on the mountain top, looking down on the rebel brigade in and around McConnellsburg on the one hand, and into the Cumberland Valley, occupied by Lee's army on the other, we twitted each other on the prospect around us, and I was compelled to admit that I had viewed that scene often before under more auspicious circumstances, and when I said that in two weeks time I would do so again, it raised a shout of derisive laughter from twenty-five rebel throats around me. My prediction was correct, and I had full faith in it when I made it. I could relate many interesting incidents of my one day's captivity, but space will not permit, nor is it pertinent to this article.

Respectfully yours,
JAMES POTT.

The following interesting statement of the capture of some of the citizens of Fayetteville has been furnished by Rev. Mr. Detrich:

HEADQUARTERS N. W. BRIGADE,
In the field, Adams Co., Pa.,
July 3d, 1863.

Pickets and Guards will pass Rev. W. R. H. Detrich, J. Foreman, Samuel Disert, Casper Black, J. R. Bixler, J. N. Baxter, J. C. Brown, Henry Dorne, G. W. Harmon, William Rupert, Isaac Millhorn, P. Martin, William Daniels, Cyrus Bachman, John Crawford and James Maloy, to their homes in Fayetteville, Pa.

W. J. HULL,
A. D. C. Off. of the Day.

The above is a true copy of a *Pass* which I have in my possession as a souvenir of the late war. I have it pasted on the inside of the right lid of my "Biblia Polyglotta," because of the sacred associations which cluster in and around it. What anxious hours, what watchings by the light of the silvery moon, what rackings of the brain, what hopes deferred, and fears intensified, are called up by this paper, written twenty-one years ago, on the Battlefield of Gettysburg, I need not refer to in this pen sketch. I prefer to write of the humorous side now that the gates of Janus are closed, and "age-dimmed eyes are made dimmer by the gathering of tears."

The main portion of the Confederate army, under General R. E. Lee, had passed Fayetteville on the way to Gettysburg. On the morning of July the 1st, General Imboden with his cavalry and mounted infantry passed through and encamped at Greenwood, near the base of the South Mountain. About noon of the same day a lone Confederate soldier rode into Fayetteville and was passing through in the direction of Chambersburg, when he was halted by a citizen, and compelled to surrender, which he did by handing over a small pouch of letters. The courage of the citizen then failed him, and he allowed the soldier to return to his camp, near Greenwood. The capture of the letters was reported, and in a brief time a detachment of cavalry under command of Capt. McNeil, of Virginia, rode into Fayetteville, arresting every man on the street. This is how we came to be arrested for "robbing the Confederate dispatches." We were picked up and hurried away *piece-meal.* I was arrested at my residence, at the extreme end of Fayetteville, and marched on foot through the whole length of the town—"a town of magnificent distances"—between two cavalrymen, who rode fiery steeds. From an upper window Miss Lottie Greenawalt, now Mrs. Renfrew, called to me: "I will go and remain with Mrs. D. till you return." Those were happy words, and even now I can hear her speak them. At Greenwool we prisoners faced each other. We were placed under the *Grand Guard*, commanded by Lieut. A. D. Woodly, of Augusta, Va., and taken to the school house, in Greenwood, for safe keeping. It was while in the school house that the wife of James Black, Esq., prepared us a nice supper, but which the hungry guard ate. We tendered her a vote of thanks, and, to this day, have not forgotten her kindness. The army of General Imboden was made up of cavalry and mounted infantry, with the exception of one company, which composed what was called by the soldiers, the "Grand Guard."

As night approached there was an order to "rest on the guns." The cannon pointed towards Chambersburg. Fear took possession of the prisoners—none of us had ever seen a battle. We resolved to remain together, and, if need be, to die together. One prisoner whispered in my ear: "Pray for me." Another one said: "I would give $500 if I were home. Do you think the battle will be before midnight?" Besides ourselves there were seven of General Milroy's men, six negroes and two Confederate soldiers under the Grand Guard. At ten o'clock there was an order to advance to the front. We were ordered from the school house and put in line of march. To me this was new business. Through the "narrows" we had to march single file in order to make room for the cavalry and artillery. We would kick each other on the heels. It is said that many years ago a Major in the Regular Army was employed to drill a company of militia for an approaching "Battalion Parade." He had trouble in getting the men to understand the command: "Right foot, Left foot." On this command he could not enlighten them, when a new idea occurred to his mind. He fastened *hay* on the right foot and *straw* on the left, and then gave the command: "*Hay foot, Straw foot.*" So I thought it should have been with us, on that memorable night, when we marched through the "narrows." We marched from Greenwood to "Corwell's Tavern," near Cashtown, in Adams county, only resting once. Many, indeed, were the humorous incidents that took place on the march, and in the field. Time would fail me in even referring to them. We were cut off from all the world, except the great battle going on in our midst, and of this we knew but little. Through ignorance of what was going on, whether good or bad, our life was greatly perplexed, and we caught ourself repeating: "My kingdom for a daily newspaper." For sixty hours we had nothing to eat, and yet we hungered more for *news* than for *bread.* One thought had taken hold upon our minds—we had "Libby on the brain." A *defeat,* a *retreat,* and "*Libby,*" "only this and nothing more." I was chosen out of the party to call on General Imboden and urge upon him a speedy release or a trial. The Lieutenant of the Guard accompanied me to his headquarters, which was under a chestnut tree, on the battle field. His reception was not marked by any degree of cordiality—it was unflattering and the outlook unpromising. He thought *hanging* the best thing for me. I thought not, as I was too heavy to hang, weighing at the time *225 pounds.* It is not safe for a man of that weight to hang, and when I so intimated he had to smile. This inspired in me a desire for another interview, which resulted differently. I was received with great cordiality, and offered an immediate release. This I politely refused to accept, unless the other prisoners be treated in like manner. I finally succeeded. The prisoners were watching for my return at the headquarters of the Grand Guard, and when they saw my lit up countenance they caught the spirit of *freedom* and tears flowed from eyes unused to weep. Up to this moment all had been vain conjecture and desperate uncertainty, and Piozzi has well said: "Uncertainty is miserable slavery." I wish to record, at this point, that Lieut. A. D. Woodly acted towards us the part of a good soldier and a perfect gentleman. He was as brave as the steel which hung at his side.

When I related to my companions the success I met with, and that in a few hours we should be on our homeward way, I was made to realize that joy never feasts so high as when the first course is of misery. Happier men I never saw, and—I was the happiest of them all. In returning home we got a little mixed with Lee's retreating army—we had cannon to the right of us, and we had cannon to the left of us—we had cannon preceding us, and we had cannon following us, nevertheless,

Boldly we walked, and well.

We could not keep up with the old men of our party. Every man is a book, if you know how to read him—no one could read the *fathers* that afternoon, and no one pretended to read them. It is a beautiful sight to see old men, as I saw them, cheerful, kind and sunshiny—childhood itself is scarcely more lovely. They ran, they danced, they sang, they did the funniest things, and tired not. Foreman was ahead, never minding the rheumatism of yesterday. Black was never so erect as he walked along with a firm and elastic step. Martin was never so funny as he "walked the mountain up." Maloy, who had followed us to Greenwood to protest our innocence, *knew* we would not be taken to "Libby"—he had a revelation we would reach home that day. Crawford's joy was pensive. Baxter's solemn mein was relaxed, and he clapped his hands for joy. Rupert's pain in his back was clean gone, but he was hungry and this annoyed him. Bixler had just left the feet of Hahnemann, where he had completed his studies in *Materia Medica*. He was a handsome *blonde* with a delicate mustache, twisted out to points. When a "reb" charged him with having two mice in his mouth he mildly denied the charge. The "reb" said: "You can't deny it, I see their tails." The "rebs" enjoyed the sight of my *stove-pipe hat*. They knew I was a clergyman, but they were no *respecter* of persons. They fancied I was not delicate enough to be a parson. More than once they called out: "Hat, where are you taking that man." Others said: "Yank, come down out o' that hat—you needn't say I ain't in it, I see your feet hanging out." In this way I might go on consuming time and paper. But suffice it to say that after a long and weary fast we reached "Graefenberg Springs," kept at that time by ex-Sheriff Benjamin Shriver, of Adams county, who took us into a private apartment of his well ordered house and gave us *apple-buttered bread and dry beef*. Hunger is a good cook, and no sumptuous meal ever tasted half so well.

Of the battle I need not write. This has been done by other and abler pens, but to have been there and witnessed it was to have witnessed the grandest, the most sublime sight ever afforded to mortal man. General Humphreys in his address, at the Meade Memorial Meeting, in Philadelphia, among other things, said: "The sights and sounds of a great battle arouse a feeling of exultation, compared to which tame indeed is the sense of the sublime excited by all other great works, either of God or man. No grander sight was seen throughout the war than the great Battle of Gettysburg, between two brave, well-disciplined and ably commanded armies."

On our safe arrival in Fayetteville, on the afternoon of the 3d day of July, the citizens turned out *en masse* and gave us a public reception. The memory of past favors is like the rainbow, bright, vivid, beautiful; but unlike the rainbow memory does not fade away. Here I lay down my pen, but my thoughts run on.

Yours Fraternally,
        WM. R. H. DEATRICH,
To J. HOKE, Esq.,   Newport, Pa.
Chambersburg, Pa.

In the following paper Dr. H. R. Fetterhoff throws light upon the disputed question as to Gen. Averill's whereabouts during the night previous to the burning of Chambersburg. The doctor was resident telegraph operator at Greencastle at the time, and knows whereof he speaks.

BALTIMORE, MD., Oct. 17th, 1884.

JACOB HOKE, ESQ., *Dear Sir:*—Your communication of the 15th inst. is to hand enclosing statements of Messrs. T. R. Bard and W. A. Reid in regard to Gen. Averill's whereabouts and condition on the night previous to the burning of Chambersburg and on the morning of the ensuing day, July 30th, 1864. You ask what information I can give as to the correctness of the two seemingly conflicting statements. In reply I would say that Mr. Bard's statement is very nearly correct in every particular, a few items only differing somewhat as they occurred to me.

At the time these events transpired I was telegraph operator at Greencastle and had the means of knowing what was going on generally. In the evening of Friday, July 29th, 1864, about 8 o'clock, General Averill's command passed through Greencastle on their way from Hagerstown towards Chambersburg and bivouacked a short distance north of the town along the road leading to the latter place. If my memory serves me right Gen. Averill reported his arrival to Gen. Couch at Chambersburg. At least I so reported it to Mr. W. B. Gilmore, operator at that place. The General sent three or four orderlies to my office and informed me of his whereabouts. Mr. D. C. Aughinbaugh, operator at Hagerstown, Mr. T. R. Bard, and I think several other persons from that place, were at the office in the evening and at intervals during the night. The scouts reported that the rebels had built camp-fires in the neighborhood of State Line, four miles South of Greencastle, and it was supposed that they had encamped there for the night. About midnight, or perhaps a little later, Mr. Gilmore informed me that the telegraph lines west of Chambersburg on the Pittsburg turnpike had been cut, showing that the rebels after building the camp-fires at the State Line as a blind had moved in the direction of Upton and Bridgeport on General Averill's right flank. I immediately informed General Averill of this fact when he sent me a message thanking me for the information, and requesting me to keep him posted in regard to any information I might obtain. About 1 o'clock, A. M., July 30th, General Couch sent an order to General Averill directing him to *"Move on to Chambersburg at once."* I immediately sent this message with an orderly, but never heard from him again. In about a half hour General Couch repeated the message in the same words, and I sent another orderly with the message, but still no answer. The same order was repeated about every half hour until my orderlies were all gone and I had no one to carry the last message, when Mr. Bard came to the office and volunteered to deliver it. After searching for General Averill and finding him he delivered the message. I then learned that when I had sent General Averill the information that the rebels were in his rear or on his flank, he moved his headquarters from the rear of his line, where it had been, up into the line without informing the orderlies, or any one else, consequently no one knew where to find him, and the messages had not been delivered and only reached him near 4 o'clock, when Mr. Bard delivered them.

The rebels entered Chambersburg about this time and Mr. Gilmore bid me "good bye," and left the office. Telegraphic communications having been cut off, and not wishing to be captured, General Averill's command took up their march for Chambersburg by way of Greenwood and Fayetteville. Messrs. Bard and A. F. Schafhirt and myself—two in a buggy and one on horseback, interchangeably, started with a squad of cavalry—not belonging to Averill's command—with Lieut. Jones in command, and went by Quincy and Funkstown to Greenwood, where we came in sight of General Averill's troops moving from that place towards Fayetteville and Chambersburg. But before we reached Greenwood, we discovered the smoke ascending from the burning town. Not wishing to run into danger we left the cavalry escort at Greenwood and went to Graeffenburg Springs Hotel, and not being able to obtain any information we went on to Gettysburg in the afternoon, reaching that place in the evening, and there learned that Chambersburg had been burned. On the following morning, Sunday, we made an early start for home and found the smouldering ruins of the town. Mr. Schafhirt and I went on to Greencastle that evening, and Mr. Bard, I think, remained in Chambersburg.

General Averill's troops were very much fatigued when they reached Greencastle, but after some hours rest would have been fully able to have gone on to Chambersburg as ordered by General Couch and saved the town had he informed us where to find him when he moved his headquarters.

Yours truly,
H. K. FETTERHOFF, M. D.

Dr. Fetterhoff's account suggests the following :

1. The statements of Mr. Bard and Mr. Reid are in the main both sustained by the fact supplied by the doctor, that General Averill *moved his headquarters sometime that night without letting either his staff, his orderlies or any one else know where to find him.* Why the General was guilty of this grave oversight under such critical circumstances, remains yet to be explained. Chambersburg owes its destruction, in all probability, to this oversight.

2. General McCausland's command came direct through Clearspring, Mercersburg, Bridgeport and St. Thomas to this place. It must have been a detachment from General Vaughan's command at Hagerstown which lit their camp-fires at State Line and not from McCausland's as the Doctor supposed.

3. The squad of cavalry with which the Doctor, Mr. Bard and Mr. Schafhirt passed on to Quincy, Funkstown and Greenwood on Saturday morning, were no doubt some of the stragglers from Cole's Maryland Regiment, who were scattered from Hagerstown by Vaughan's force on Friday afternoon.

With this number my Reminiscences close. I began these researches under the impression that I would be able to tell the reader all I knew, and could ascertain concerning the war, in ten or twelve articles. They have extended to forty-one. And instead of confining myself to a narration of incidents in and about Chambersburg, as the title indicates, I have given, in the main, a history of the War upon the whole Southern border, and rescued from oblivion an immense amount of historic matter, which may be of interest to the generations yet to come.

CONTENTS.

	Page.
INTRODUCTION, by A. K. McClure, Esq.,	3
CHAPTER I.—Commencement of the War, and Marching of Troops from Chambersburg	7
CHAPTER II.—The Roll of Honor; or the Names of those who first flew to the Rescue' of their Imperilled Country from Franklin County	10
CHAPTER III.—Camp Slifer	12
CHAPTER IV.—General Patterson's Campaign	15
CHAPTER V.—Organization of the 126th Regiment; Fugitives from Slavery	18
CHAPTER VI.—Chambersburg under Martial Law; Visit to the Battle Field of South Mountain; Battle of Antietam	22
CHAPTER VII.—Stuart's Raid	28
CHAPTER VIII.—Jenkins' Raid	33
CHAPTER IX.—The Invasion of Pennsylvania	41
CHAPTER X.—The Great Train of Wounded from Gettysburg	84
CHAPTER XI.—Scouting service	92
CHAPTER XII.—After the Battle of Gettysburg; Early's Raid into Maryland	99
CHAPTER XIII.—The Burning of Chambersburg	104
CHAPTER XIV.—Responsibility for the Burning of Chambersburg	131
CHAPTER XV.—List of Buildings Destroyed	137
CHAPTER XVI.—Caught within the Confederate lines, and what came of it	140
CHAPTER XVII.—Angels of Mercy in the Hospitals	166
CHAPTER XVIII.—The Nation's Shrine, or Three Visits to Gettysburg	171
APPENDIX	177

www.ingramcontent.com/pod-product-compliance
Lightning Source LLC
Chambersburg PA
CBHW031816220426
43662CB00007B/680